Pierre Broué

Revolutionary Historian

Revolutionary History, Volume 9, no 4
Socialist Platform Ltd
Merlin Press

Revolutionary History

Founding Editor: Al Richardson (1941-2003)

Edition Editor: John McIlroy

Editorial Coordinating Team: Ted Crawford, Paul Flewers, Esther Leslie and John Plant

Continental Contributing Editor: Fritz Keller

USA Contributing Editor: David Walters

Reviews Editor: John Plant

Business Manager: Barry Buitekant

Production and Design Manager: Jim Ring

Editorial Board: Toby Abse, Ian Birchall, Tony Borton, Clarence Chrysostom, Paul Flewers, Pete Glatter, Chris Gray, Mike Jones, Stuart King, George Leslie, Sheila Leslie, John McIlroy, David Renton, Alejandra Rios, Bruno Simon, Martin Sullivan, Andreja Živković

ISBN 978-0-8503658-8-7

Copyright © 2007 Socialist Platform Ltd

Web site: www.revolutionary-history.co.uk

E-mail: tcrawford@revhist.datanet.co.uk (editorial)
Barry.Buitekant@tesco.net (business)
trusscott.foundation@virgin.net (production)
jimjepps@hotmail.com (website)

Socialist Platform Ltd, BCM 7646, London WC1N 3XX

Porcupine Press, 10 Woburn Walk, London WC1H 0JL

Typeset by voluntary labour

Printed in Britain by Intype Ltd, London

Contents

Editorial	1
Pierre Broué	5
Remarks on the History of the Bolshevik Party	93
Spartacism, Bolshevism and Ultra-Leftism in Face of the Problems of the Proletarian Revolution in Germany (1918-1923)	105
Five Years On	117
The "Bloc" of the Oppositions against Stalin in the USSR in 1932	159
The Bolshevik-Leninist Faction	135
The Socialist Youth in Spain (1934-1936)	191
Kurt Landau	227
In Germany for the International	235
Van Heijenoort	259
Obituaries	275
Work in Progress	309
Reviews	329
Charles Wesley Ervin, *Tomorrow is Ours: The Trotskyist Movement in India and Ceylon, 1935-48* (Chris Gray)	329
Jean-René Chauvin, *Un Trotskiste dans l'enfer nazi* (Ian Birchall)	331
Guy Debord, *Panegyric* (JJ Plant)	334
Sobhanlal Datta Gupta, *Comintern and the Destiny of Communism in India 1919-1943* (Mike Jones)	337
Julien Papp, *La Hongrie libérée; Etat, pouvoir et société*	

après la défaite du nazisme (Septembre 1944 — Septembre 1947) (Balazs Nagy)   340

Rick Kuhn, *Henryk Grossman and the Recovery of Marxism* (David Renton)   346

Alter Litvin and John Keep, *Stalinism: Russian and Western Views at the Turn of the Millenium* (Ian D Thatcher)   348

Jean-François Fayet, *Karl Radek (1885-1939)* (Reiner Tosstorff)   350

Eros Francescangeli, *L'incudine e il Martello. Aspetti pubblici e privati del trockismo italiano tra antifascismo e antistalinismo, 1929-1939* (Tom Behan)   356

Harry Ratner

A Socialist at War

With the Pioneer Corps

The latest publication from Socialist Platform Ltd; £8.00 including p+p (UK only, elsewhere details on request).

Socialist Platform Ltd, BCM 7646, London WC1N 3XX

e-mail — Barry.Buitekant@tesco.net

Editorial[1]

THIS issue of "Revolutionary History" is devoted to the life and writings of Pierre Broué (1926-2005), who was first of all a revolutionary militant growing up in France during the Second World War and who later became an outstanding historian of the Communist and Trotskyist movements.

Readers of this journal will not be surprised to learn that Broué's historical writings are better known in the continental part of Europe than on our predominantly Anglophone offshore islands. This situation has begun to change. In 2006 Merlin Press published "The German Revolution 1917-1923", a translation of the original "La Révolution en Allemagne", which originally appeared in 1971. This present volume aims to further the process by presenting a series of texts not previously available in English.

By way of introduction to the whole, we begin with a biographical essay on Pierre Broué written by Vincent Présumey, who knew him personally and worked together with him politically for a period. This inevitably has its own political bias, but we believe that it is of considerable value, as it gives the reader some insight into what it felt like to be a Trotskyist in France in World War Two and down to the close of the 20th Century, and that it sheds some light on the recurrent contradiction between scientific inquiry and political orthodoxy, between competing needs, the need for clear vision and that for organisational effectiveness, between the human relations striving to be born that should, as far as possible, prefigure the future communist society and the bureaucratic tendencies that inevitably arise under conditions of unremitting struggle in the dog-eat-dog world of capitalism. [See p.70]

Présumey's contribution also has relevance in regard to the real balance of forces existing between the Stalin-led bureaucracy and its opponents in the Soviet Union in the 1930s [see p. 50] and the subsequent fate of the American Trotskyist movement, a not insignificant part of the Fourth International, which was host to the International Secretariat during World War Two, before handing that baton back to comrades in Europe, only to abandon the FI for a Cuban-style version of Stalinism in the early 1980s (pp. 50-4). In this connection the biographical essay includes some interesting observations on the importance of the "Goldman-Morrow" tendency in the SWP (middle 1940s) dealing with its assessment of the European political situation at that time. Moving forward to the UK in 2007, the call by the OCI leadership to build sections of a workers' party has obvious relevance to current

---

1. Notes marked [RH] throughout this issue have been added by *Revolutionary History*, mainly on the basis of Broué's biographical index.

debates about the desirablity or otherwise of a "Marxist Party" or, alternatively, a "halfway house" between reformism and revolutionary socialism/communism (Marxism). Présumey also includes a criticism of Broué's politics at the point when he finally formed an oppositional tendency within the OCI; by contrast, what he alleges about the reaction in the OCI to Broué's biography of Trotsky when it came out in 1988, published by Fayard, if true, tells us something about the politics of the OCI leadership at that point.

Our first translation is a piece on the history of the Bolshevik Party. Refusing to believe that the CPSU under Stalin was inevitably pre-ordained in the lineaments of Lenin's party, Broué focuses on the uniqueness of the Bolsheviks lying, as he sees it, in being able to take power without abandoning their essential principles, whereas any number of working class parties have given up on their principles without seizing power in any decisive overall sense. He reminds us that this party came to include not only "professional revolutionaries" but "revolutionary working-class militants"; those who wished to confine the party to professional conspirators **opposed** Lenin on this question (examples are given). Broué argues that the working class militants won out thanks to the 1905 revolution — at least as far as 1907. The same process occurred on a much greater scale in 1917 involving workers, soldiers and peasants. Broué gives some interesting instances of working class democracy in action in the discussion and voting on various policies advocated by the Bolsheviks. There is evidence, he shows, that the party was tending to become fully fused with the soviets in the early part of the "heroic period" of the revolution (i.e. in the first two years of 1917-21). As is well known, this trend eventually went into reverse: the final part of the piece attempts to explain why.

There follows Broué's defence of his doctoral thesis on the German revolution, which formed the basis of his later book on the subject. There is no point in furnishing any commentary on this here: the reader is referred to the text.

In the chapter we reproduce from *L'histoire de l'Internationale Communiste* Broué emphasises the double damage inflicted on the International by the loss of a number of tried and tested leaders (including Lenin) on the one hand and by the "developing crisis of the revolution" in the USSR on the other. He stresses the constraints placed on Trotsky in terms of the development of his thought. Short notes on various "second rank" leaders follow — John Maclean, John Reed, Raymond Lefebvre, Christian Rakovsky, Paul Levi, Serrati, Bordiga, Brandler, and others. The focus then shifts to the men who were actually running the International and the USSR in 1924 — Zinoviev, Kamenev and ... Stalin, who was beginning to explore international waters for the first time, so to speak. This leads naturally to the question of the calibre of the International's apparatus personnel in the context of "Soviet" dominance. The result is that we get a credible picture of life at the International's headquarters from 1919 to 1924, a view from **inside the centre**. We also get to understand how Stalin as CPSU General Secretary was able to extend his grip on the CI simply by virtue of the rule whereby all foreign communists working in the USSR (even temporary congress delegates) became automatically members of the CPSU and subject to its discipline. But Broué points out also that the International's headquarters staff were never properly held to account as to their competence either centrally or by the

International's constituent parties. There follows a short consideration of Lenin's advocacy of the United Front tactic, which Stalin effectively jettisoned both in the "Third Period" (c1928-33) and in the subsequent "Popular Front" era (1935-43). Broué was breaking new ground here. Earlier Trotskyist accounts of the Comintern, while establishing the facts against the distortions of both Stalinists and anti-Communists, tended to be defensive in character, regarding everything done in the "first five years" as positive. Broué gives an account which, while in basic solidarity with the aims of the Comintern's founders, is rigorously critical of the defects and weaknesses which afflicted the Comintern from its inception

With "The Bolshevik-Leninist Faction" (Chapter 35 of *Trotsky*) we move to the fortunes of the Left Opposition in Russia following the expulsion of Trotsky's followers from the CPSU. It is refreshing to have an account of what the Opposition actually did, as we have here, as opposed to a rehearsal of its ideas. Nevertheless, Broué also includes (quite unavoidably) a narrative of the disagreements provoked by Stalin's "left turn" (1928) and Trotsky's dignified stand against the bureaucracy's attempts to silence him.

As the introduction to the next (companion) piece, the "Bloc of Oppositions against Stalin in the USSR in 1932", makes clear, the existence of widespread contacts between the various anti-Stalinist communist oppositions then is important, but these contacts are missing from the third part of the standard biography of Trotsky in English, Isaac Deutscher's *The Prophet Outcast*. Broué sees them as an ultimate political reason for the subsequent Stalinist terror of (roughly) 1934-39. Two other groups were involved apart from the LO — the so-called "Riutin Group" and a group of "liberal bureaucrats" whose "standard-bearer" was Sergei Kirov, famously assassinated in 1934. (Ordhonikidze was a member). As we know, the outcome was an unhappy one, and it included capitulation by some prominent followers of Trotsky, of whom Rakovsky is the best known. Broué points out how much Stalin benefited internally from Hitler's triumph in Germany in 1933, which was a severe blow to the hopes of the oppositionists; but he also indicates a certain fragility in Stalin's position which must have existed for himself and Molotov to come out at one point with a circular against what they called a "saturnalia of arrests" — see also the list of strikes, sit-ins, demonstrations and pro-oppositional activity among the working class mentioned — and he explains the discrepancy between the archival evidence uncovered by his team of researchers in the US relating to Trotsky's initiatives in respect of the "bloc" in 1932 and Leon Sedov's pamphlet *Le livre rouge sur le procès de Moscou*, written following the first Moscow Trial in 1936.

The piece on the Socialist Youth in Spain 1934-36 affords an insight into the political evolution of the Spanish Socialist leader Largo Caballero and documentation of demands by various Spanish Socialist Party leaders in the 1930s for a break with the bourgeoisie and the adoption of a plan for a seizure of power by the working class (led by the Socialist Party). These demands, and Largo Caballero's bid for the leadership of the party, were backed by the Socialist Youth. Broué's analysis reveals that Caballero and Prieto were agreed on this course of action, with detailed plans drawn up and implemented to the movement's best ability — even if in the event the uprising was effectively confined to the Asturias province. (See Manuel Grossi, *The*

Asturian Uprising: Fifteen Days of Socialist Revolution, Socialist Platform Ltd., 2000). There was also the complicating factor of the plight of the agricultural workers forced into strike action by the landowners' union-busting offensive. The consequences of this are vividly illustrated (and analysed with characteristic flair) to explain why Trotsky seized on the PSOE youth organisation's trajectory in order to influence the course of the ongoing Spanish revolution. The Spanish Trotskyists, however, chose to orient to another organisation, the POUM; for the results see "The Spanish Civil War: the View from the Left", in *Revolutionary History* Vol. 4, nos. 1/2, Winter 1991-92, Socialist Platform Ltd. 1992).

Finally there are three contrasting biographical pieces. Kurt Landau (1903-1937), who enjoys a somewhat shadowy existence in Trotsky's writings of the 1930s as follower and then critic, clearly possessed sufficient charisma to consider himself as a potential international leader (to Leon Sedov's chagrin); he and his partner were both swept up in the Stalinist purge of the POUM in 1937; she survived, but he did not.

Jan Van Heijenoort [1912-1985] was a very different figure. Clearly he and Broué had a lot in common. The central part of Broué's sketch begins with the Manifesto of the Fourth International on the Fall of France in 1940, which Van Heijenoort drafted and the International issued from New York, followed by articles (mostly signed "Marc Loris") on the war situation in Europe. All this material is of considerable interest, as Van Heijenoort identified the situation's revolutionary potential (later confirmed by events in France, Italy and the Balkans), a potential dependent on the ability of those leading the mass movements to implement a strategy that would ensure true national liberation on the basis of the socialist transformation of society on a European scale. That such a strategy could not be implemented in no way detracts from the insights into the unfolding course of events that Van Heijenoort provided.

The intervening extract from Broué's biography of Leon Sedov, Trotsky's second son and close collaborator, scarcely needs an introduction, except to say that the focus here on the human side of revolutionary socialist activity — in the inevitable political context — is all too rare even among the movement's historians. We ignore such concerns at our peril.

We should like to thank all those who assisted the Board in making this issue possible. Vincent Présumey not only gave us permission to translate his biographical study of Broué, but also provided us with some texts not easily available elsewhere. Richard Kirkwood and Gareth Jenkins assisted with the labour of translation.

A fairly full bibliography of Broué' works can be found at http://www.trotskyana.net/Trotskyists/Pierre_Broue/pierre_broue.html.

Editorial Board

Pierre Broué[1]

(1926-2005)

Translator's Introduction

VINCENT Presumey's article casts an interesting and critical light not only on Pierre Broué, but equally on the political tendency of which he was a member, indeed at times a leader, from 1944/5 until his de facto expulsion in 1989, the PCI/OCI/PT – generally known as the "Lambertistes".

It is fascinating as a description of the tensions between an individual's personal views and his loyalty to an organisation. It is fascinating too as a critical description of the evolution of a political tendency. Many former members of Trotskyist and other Left groups will recognise some of the descriptions as ones that they may feel similar to their own experiences.

But it is, in many senses, an "insider's" view of an organisation which has had little influence on Trotskyist politics in Britain. It is an "insider's" view in a broader sense, too, in that Presumey writes from within certain traditions on the French Left.

As an "insider" there are aspects of both traditions that Presumey takes for granted and which may require a brief explanation for those unfamiliar with the French labour movement, with post-war French history or with the tradition from which Presumey comes. This is the task of this Introduction.

I shall not enter into great detail on any of these aspects, particularly on the history of the "Lambert tendency". Much of the latter is referred to in the article and, for those who can read French, there are easily available good sources.

One tradition that Presumey assumes as a base for some of his arguments is one shared, in different ways, and to different degrees by a wide range of people and organisations on the French Left and Centre-Left – from "left radicals", through Socialists to Communists, Trotskyists and Syndicalists. This is the aspiration to a "République démocratique, sociale et laïque" [a *secular*, democratic and social republic]. I emphasise the word "secular" because this is a particularly important issue among teachers in the state sector (where Broué and the Lambert group were active in the trades union) and explains much of the debate in France over the "Muslim headscarf" issue over recent years. Although

---

1. Translator Richard Kirkwood, 13th. July 2007. The notes, unless stated otherwise, are by the translator.

the secular republican tradition can claim a heritage going back to 1792, its particular origins lie in the debates of the late19th. and early 20th. centuries when state education was made secular and Church schools were pushed into the private sector. This tradition was further reinforced (particularly among Stalinists and Social Democrats) by the confrontations of the 1930s with a Far Right which was not so much Fascist in the German or Italian senses but was anti-democratic, often Catholic and, sometimes, monarchist. This attitude was, in turn, reinforced by the active participation of many of these elements in the Vichy and collaborationist regimes during the Nazi occupation of France (and in the Front Nationale today). This thus relates directly to Presumey's discussion of Broué's views on Trotsky's preliminary debates (cut short by his murder) on the "Proletarian Military Policy".

I turn now to the French trades union movement. As most readers are probably aware French trades unions are (in general) divided into various Confederations along semi-ideological lines. Membership density, with some exceptions, is low and unions operate as activist networks and electoral machines within the corporatist structures created after WW2. The key players in the period of Broué's main involvement were the CGT and FO. The remaining unions were mainly scab, local, organisations; except for the mainly Catholic CFDC whose leadership dropped the Christian reference in the late 1960s to become the CFDT (for a time a "left socialist" union but now a key ally of the wholly reformist PS), still in the 60s/70s mistrusted by more traditional trades unionists – see Presumey's cynical refence to one faction in the teachers' union recruiting from the "CGEN-CFDT".

The CGT after WW2 was dominated by the PCF, becoming increasingly Stalinist. FO, to be more precise CGT-FO, was a minority breakaway encouraged (if not actually created) by the French State and the CIA (which was heavily involved in splitting CP-led or influenced unions and parties in the early years of the Cold War). Its main influences were a mixture of Right Social-Democrats, "Left" Social Democrats and old-fashioned French Syndicalists, some still seeing themselves as "Revolutionary Syndicalists", even Anarchists. Many of the leading figures in all of these political tendencies had become bureaucrats by the late 1950s. FO's main bases were in the state sector. Trotskyists and other leftists held two rather different views about FO. For some, particularly the "Lambertistes" and some old-fashioned Syndicalists, it was the union of choice. For others the CGT, as the biggest union, was where one would want to be, but often the Stalinist leadership made this impossible, so FO was a second-best.

The FEN (Fédération de l'Education Nationale – a telling name, Nationale meaning State, thefore secular) was an exception. It had, for complicated reasons, managed to remain united at the time of the CGT/FO split. Rather like British trades unions, but with the particularly French way of allowing "formal" "tendencies", it was a battleground for differing political and strategic conceptions. Most of the "hard left" belonged, as Presumey mentions, until the splits of the late60s/70s to the Ecole Emancipée grouping which saw itself as inheriting the "old" French Syndicalist tradition. The PCF had its "Unité et Action" grouping. The FEN was divided "vertically" into sectors – SNI represesenting elementary school (up to 14) teachers, SNES/SNET representing high school and technical college teachers, SNESup representing University lecturers. Effectively these were independent unions on Industrial Relations and detailed Educational issues, coming together only on big national questions (incidentally this structure was the inspiration, particularly in the former NATFHE, for those seeking to create a unified teachers' union in Britain).

Because the "Lambertistes" prioritised work in FO it is important to say something about this union. For many others on the left it was a sell-out organisation which, as I say above, they only joined because of Stalinist repression in the CGT , or because it was locally strong. In particular it lined up with French Social Democracy (the SFIO) in supporting, or at least not opposing, De Gaulle's "peaceful coup" in 1958. It was run, until the early 1980s, by corporatist Right Social Democrats (notably Bergeron) but had a sizeable "left social democrat/syndicalist" wing. Sadly, many of those in this "left" were full-time officials and local bureaucrats who were reluctant to take on the leadership in anything other than a purely formal way. At various points Presumey refers to this, and to the "Lambertistes" conniving with it, but never follows the analyis through to any clear critical conclusion . It was from its allies in this "FO Left" that the Lambertistes gathered the rest of the membership of the PT (Parti des Travailleurs – Workers' Party) when it formed it in the 1990s.

Presumey summarises much of the history of the Lambertist tendency but does so very much from the "inside" and thus reflects what other groups saw as a trend after the 1952 split from the "Pabloite" "4th. International" for this group to see themselves and their particular strategies as the sole representatives of genuine Trotskyism and as the essential core of any "restructured" 4th. International in a way that separated them from others. They rarely worked in campaigns initiated by other groupings. Where they did involve themselves in broad campaigns these were generally ones where they could control both the agenda and the allies with whom they worked.

Thus both the famous "desertion" on the May 68 "night of the barricades" (see Presumey pp36/37) and the relations between Lambertists and the FO Left tended to be seen by other groups as "typical" of a style seen as bureaucratic, "rightist" and sectarian. This view was reinforced by the physical conflicts (presented, rightly or wrongly, by Presumey as mainly a case of self-defence) in which they became involved in the late 60s and early 70s. These were seen by other groups as attempts to take control of a movement in which they had failed to be fully involved at its height. On the other hand their associates in FO had, in fact, played an important role (e.g. at Sud-Aviation in Nantes) in the strikes and factory occupations which made May 68 so much more than student romp.

Presumey says little to situate the developments within the Lambert tendency within a wider Left context, except where this relates directly to internal debates or to attempts to "rebuild the 4th. International". To explore all the relevant points needed to explain this tendency is beyond the scope of this Introduction.

7

Those who wish to follow this up and can read French could consult Benjamin Stora, *La dernière génération d'octobre*, Paris: Stock, 2003.
Richard Kirkwood

> *We must acquire a taste for the truth. It is through it that science is created. It is through it that the revolution will forge its victory.* Marceau PIVERT

THE death of Pierre Broué constitutes a significant loss both for liberatory, working-class and revolutionary struggles and for the science of history. These two are indissolubly linked as the significance of this great historian derives precisely from the fact that, for him, writing history was an act of political militancy, something that in no way detracts from the necessity to seek the truth, indeed quite the opposite.

This same necessity for truth is thus the first requirement in relation to Broué himself, now he is dead as much as when he was alive.

I myself was very close to Broué politically and was personally quite fond of him in the period 1982-1985. But I managed this without ever becoming part of the circle of his "disciples", for disciples there certainly were or at least there seemed to be. Looking back I am proud of this. During this period we had a sort of complicity based on our common origins in the Ardèche and on previous relationships of family or friendship, all things that were to become, for him, part of a paranoid episode, something to which he had, in fact, been prone for a long time.

During one of our first real political discussions Pierre Broué said to me "Look out for one thing: don't mix the emotional and the political".

What an ambiguous sentence. It is the private and the political that shouldn't be mixed:

respect for individuals should be both an end and a means for revolutionary militants, the loss of this respect is one of the things that, in a general sense, characterises the Stalinists and their clones. That, sometimes, political struggle both demands and produces an emotional involvement obviously means neither denying this nor combating it but rather recognising it so as to manage it. It is, too, a necessity, precisely in relation to that respect for individuals which is indispensable. For without "emotion" politics becomes unprincipled cynicism. A revolutionary is involved in politics through love and for that reason must respect the separation of the private and the political and respect individuals.

Pierre Broué was hardly dead when the AFP put out a dispatch, hastily put together after a phone call to the HQ of the LCR or somewhere similar, which told us that he had met Trotsky "three times". As a result this tale turned up in various articles in French, English and Spanish. Then followed the "spiritual children", the "he was my master, I was his disciple", or even more the "he was one of us", "no-one can possibly challenge the fact that he had joined our current" and so on. And let us not forget the "he was a great Resistance fighter in '44 in the Ardèche", a rumour that might, at a pinch, spread in northern Dauphiné fifty years later — but never in Ardèche.

As we all know, the dead, for a little while, have all the desirable qualities. But after the flowers and the wreaths the negative revisions and stories start turning up — along with the venom of those who kept quiet, with varying degrees of shame, during the official period of mourning. So, during the months that followed his death, we can note plenty of reactionary historians, along with the unrepentant or unrefined Stalinists whom he loved to taunt, observing just such a silence. And let us not forget the central apparatus of his former party the OCI, now transformed into the apparatus of the PT which affected to be unaware that, after the death in 1997 of Stéphane Just and before that of Pierre Lambert, the organisation had lost one of the key individuals who had helped build it (in this respect the obituary in *Informations Ouvrières* dated 4 to 10 August 2005 and signed by Jean-Jacques Marie is a little monument to things "not said", a veritable non-obituary).

True respect must involve the truth. While I have no more or no less a right to talk about Pierre Broué than any other of his former comrades, it is a matter of duty not of rights to tell the truth, to say what one knows, or at least what one thinks one knows or has come to understand. I say this not only as an individual militant but because the "*Lettre des Liasons*" as a small, but genuine, political "pole" is in part the heir of a struggle in the OCI based on some of Pierre Broué's ideas as well as coming out of the battles of the Filoche current (which has a shared history with Pierre Broué) in the LCR.

This, then, is the reason for this article. A great historian is dead and, to put it simply, if we are to understand his work we must understand his place in history.

While, naturally, I cannot assert the absolute accuracy of everything I write here, I can at least assert that I write what I consider to be accurate. The sources for this text are, in the first place, Pierre Broué's own accounts, told to me generally between 11pm and 3am when I dropped in to see him in his tower in Grenoble to recover my sanity after heavy meetings of the Isère department committee of the OCI. I have then used a range of writings that are readily available to anyone who wishes to avail themselves of them, as well as my own analysis and, above all on his beginnings, accounts by Ardèchois family and friends.

It is a methodological principle for anyone striving to reconstruct the facts to not take at face value the evidence of one of the actors involved, especially when the facts in question are those of the life of that witness. One could therefore quite rightly make the following criticism: in this text much of what I say derives from Pierre Broué's own accounts, even though I do regularly question these accounts. Indeed I have precisely managed to note the contradictions between what I "picked up" from Pierre Broué at any particular moment and what he said, or implied, later on. I have not based myself in this piece on a crude adherence to the statements of this actor but on a critical comparison of his successive statements. I would dare to claim that this is precisely how one develops historical thinking, going beyond crude adherence to a source but also beyond being always doubtful of it.

Conversations with some of those close to Pierre Broué since the first version of this piece was distributed on the internet in August 2005 have led to further clarifications which have tended to reinforce rather than to invalidate most of the interpretations in it.

Since the publication of that first version it has become even clearer to me that the duty to tell the truth is urgently necessary following the publication in a friendly magazine, *La Commune*, the journal of a French trotskyist group, of what was presented as a future biographical entry about Pierre Broué in the *Maîtron* (the biographical dictionary of the workers' movement) which is rightly regarded as an authoritative historical resource.

This journal states that the entry was drafted by Jean-Guillaume Lanuque based on an interview with Pierre Broué in 2000. It proved, if there was any more need to do so, that the work of an historian does not consist in repeating the "evidence" of an historical actor just as it came and that "memory" is not the same as history.

In it are many errors of a personal or private type. These regrettable errors are not in themselves historically or politically significant but demonstrate that it was inappropriate to include all these details without verifying them, or, in other words, demonstrates that the work of a biographer, a collector of pieces of evidence, a historian should not consist of being satisfied to let it be put about by one's subject that he was (for instance) top of his class and to reproduce this tale just like that!

In addition, the article is shot through with contradictions about the period of the war and the occupation which I discuss below. Worse, to judge from the relative length of the different parts of the article, the *Maîtron* will present Pierre Broué as a militant whose core activity took place before the end of the 1940s!

But beyond the issue of the 1940s there is a general lack of serious research. We learn, for example that *"from the 1960's he had spent several periods in Eastern Europe"* followed by the "example" of an academic and political trip to Yugoslavia which we are supposed to see as one specific case among the "Eastern European countries". The article continues by saying that these "journeys" *"enabled him to make contacts in Poland and Czechoslovakia as well as in Yugoslavia itself"*. But in any Eastern European country other than Yugoslavia someone like Pierre Broué could only have travelled in secret, if he travelled at all. If such clandestine trips to Poland and Czechoslovakia had actually taken place a historian should have undertaken some serious research on them rather than leaving us with this sort of confused and convoluted allusions. Be that as it may, the only serious position to take is that this supposed biography for the *Maîtron* will simply serve to create a legend — pure balderdash.

On the other hand readers will find no mention of key names such as Varga or Mélusine, references to whom might have been troublesome, and might well want to know exactly why Pierre Broué was excluded from the leadership of the Grenoble OCI or on what issue he had a *"major conflict"* with Stéphane Just in 1967 — although answers to these questions were available years before 2000 (and can, indeed, be found in this piece) if one had taken the trouble to search for them.

* * * * *

It would be a waste of time to expect to find in this sort of "work" even the shadow of an outline of an analysis of Pierre Broué's political positions or of his disagreements with the organisation — the PCI / *Verité* group/OCI — to which he belonged from 1944 to 1989.

In the course of the article Louis-Paul Letonturier becomes Louis-Paul Tonturier and Jean-Francois Godchau becomes Godechau — the sorts of errors that are a real insult to Pierre Broué the academic. And this sort of stuff is destined, with the best intentions in the world, for the prestigious "Biographical Dictionary of the Workers' Movement". Stop here; we are engaged in secular history, not The Lives of The Saints. Hagiography belongs in the realm of religious freedom and this latter should belong in the private sphere.

* * * * *

My subject is not someone's private life but it is a person, and persons cannot be neatly dissected; furthermore, "private" aspects will necessarily emerge to explain or clarify this or that moment in life. Indeed I have already done this when, because one must call a spade a spade, I earlier used the word "paranoia". But this word goes hand in hand with earlier ones — a militant in the struggles for liberation and a great historian. History and truth form a single unit. We must take them as they are, arming ourselves with reason, or put them aside in favour of "memory" or suppression of facts.

To begin at the beginning

Pierre Broué was born on 8 May 1926 at Privas in the Ardèche, one of two children of the head teacher of the Collège Moderne at Privas (the girls secondary school, formerly the École Primaire Supérieure), she was also a musician and choir leader. His father was a civil servant in the tax office. The family held republican views, no more, no less (neither Syndicalism nor any known involvement with the "left").

But growing up where he did he was close to an important source of inspiration. That source the young Pierre Broué had the good fortune to meet outside but alongside, indeed physically very close to the political world of his own milieu. He was Élie Reynier, retired teacher from the École Normale (he returned there in 1945) historian and militant, a great figure known for his rectitude and erudition who despite (or because of) the clarity of his political, trades union and ethical choices was universally admired in the world of secular education in the Ardèche.

There can be no doubt that the adolescent saw in him an intellectual model, moreover Élie Reynier was the only person whom Pierre Broué was subsequently to refer to as a model, to sometimes claim as an inspiration. However Pierre Broué was far from always emphasising this connection. Thus in that piece supposedly destined for the *Maitron*, Pierre Broué passes rather rapidly over Élie Reynier and, in fact, pushes the start of his political commitment back to his early childhood.

It is of course possible that Pierre Broué fell prey, very precociously, to the appeal of speaking or writing to audiences hanging on every word of a speaker or every sentence of a writer. This was a man who, according to one of his anecdotes about his childhood, started his memoirs at the age of 7 with the words "*I look back on that immense past which is mine*", or something like that. It is possible that the climate of the 1930s (the Spanish war, the 1936 strikes, and, too, the battles between secular and religious education) caught the mind of a precocious child, perhaps over-gifted and very concerned to assert himself.

The more we know about Élie Reynier, both as a militant and as an historian, the more obviously he appears as the decisive figure for Pierre Broué on the threshold of his politically-conscious life. It is not rash to assert that Pierre Broué took from Élie Reynier his own double vocation as both historian and militant. The revolutionary will and the will to talk of struggles, hopes and suffering, to "do history" and to make history are here all of one piece. Anyone who has really read Pierre Broué will agree with this. But it was precisely Élie Reynier who was both the first militant and the first historian to inspire and to educate Pierre Broué.

*   *   *   *   *

So we must say a few words about him here. He came out of the world of Ardèchois schoolteachers, himself the son of teachers — his parents were protestant private-school teachers.

Élie Reynier was a pre-1914 syndicalist. In 1912 he had written a monograph on the Ardèche for Pierre Monatte's *Vie Ouvrière* (the distant, though very different, ancestor, of the CGT journal). Monatte liked to recall that this work was the model of a monograph on a local working class and that it came close to Alphonse Merrheim's "sectoral" monograph on the metallurgical industry. Syndicalist militants would have recognised here, in the very concept of historically and geographically specific work, the double structure of the French working-class movement after 1902; the bringing together of the sectoral federations and the local Bourses de travail in the confederation.

Élie Reynier, local scholar and first among Ardèchois local scholars in a milieu where priests and protestant pastors worked alongside teachers, was, when the young Pierre Broué saw a lot of him, working on his *History of Privas*. But we must careful that the term "local scholar" does not sound belittling. The sort of history that Élie Reynier sought to write was really a total history, a history of the land, of the countryside, of work and of workers. He was of the school, if we can talk here of a "school", of Maurice Dommanget and of Albert Mathiez, the historian of the French Revolution who died in 1932. He was very familiar with the new academic historical school of the journal *Annales* and he opened his library to Pierre Broué, lending him books by Marc Bloch and Lucien Febvre as well as by Georges Lefebvre. But he himself wanted to tell history as it is, as that of struggles conducted by individuals who lived and thought, suffered and acted. This aim was later to become well and truly the programme of Pierre Broué as historian.

Politically, Élie Reynier defined himself as a revolutionary syndicalist and a pacifist. At the same time this individual, in his own way a genuine local worthy, possessed all the traits of a socialist at the turn of the 20th century. He was President of the Ardèche League of the Rights of Man and was one of those few who were to rescue the honour of that organisation when its leaders prostituted themselves in their support for the Moscow Trials. During the war he was interned in the Chabanet camp.

As a respected teacher he made a major contribution to the construction in Ardèche of the United Education Federation. He was closely linked, both by friendship and by common purpose, to Gilbert Serret who was a national leader of this federation and who died in mysterious circumstances during the Occupation. Gilbert Serret and his partner France (who, unlike Élie Reynier, were not among those people that Pierre Broué or his family knew at the time,) saw themselves not as syndicalists following the Amiens Charter, but rather as Leninists. While they were not Trotskyists, they had met Trotsky in 1935. Gilbert Serret was in close contact with the wider left-communist milieu. He also served to deepen Reynier's passion for local monographs from the angle of the role of revolutionary teachers in organising the peasantry.

Reynier and Serret represented two generations, two approaches, different positions — Serret belonged to the tendency of the federation Majority along with Bouet, Dommanget etc., which was an anti-Stalinist communist tendency, Reynier was part of Monatte's Syndicalist League. But between them there was a close understanding and respect. This mutual respect was an expression of the moral essence of the women and men of the old United Education Federation; it had in it plenty of purified Protestantism, of Kantian moralism, but the rigidity that could come from this background, which did indeed come from it, needed to be rounded off, quite simply, by the warmth of friendship.

In Ardèche, after the union re-unification of 1935, the local section of the SNI (the National Teachers' Union) was in fact a continuation of the old Federation, whereas elsewhere this had put an end to it. During the war the clandestine union section continued to operate through the activities of militants such as Yvonne Issartel (who also died in 2005). At the same time the young Pierre Broué was regularly visiting the old Reynier.

This then was the background that Pierre Broué made out, detected behind Élie Reynier's bookshelves among which he had, in 1940, been given permission to ferret about: books are living things!

And there was in this library a book which Élie Reynier lent him, when, in 1940, it was "midnight in the century" and when its author was murdered. A book which he saw as a model of a history book which tells a tale and which, through the stories of events carried through by the actions of people who think, struggle and act and are thus responsible for their actions, rather than by some "deep forces" or other types of *deus ex machina* has the wondrous effect of making us feel just what the real deep forces are — those of classes in struggle made up of living individuals. This book, written by a man who had "done history" because he had *made* history, was Leon Trotsky's *History of the Russian Revolution*.

The War — Memory and Reality

At the time he was devouring old Reynier's library Pierre Broué sympathised with the generally widespread hostility to the petty tyrants and the few Pétainist teachers at the school which was the general mood at the Collège de Privas, he also took part in Scout hikes with his friend, the future psychiatrist Jean Ayme.

It was with all this in his mind that Pierre Broué, after passing his Baccalauréat at the Collège Moderne de Privas (which served as a lycée, even though it wasn't a lycée) entered the hypokhâgne course[2] at the Lycée Thiers in Marseille, where he went to stay with some cousins. It seems evident that this period — his adolescence — greatly shaped him, and, if we want to write history scrupulously rather than hagiography, we must note that it is difficult after the event to distinguish between actions linked to the sorts of ragging, often in dubious taste, which was typical of the "khâgneux" and those linked with a first active militant involvement with the Resistance to the occupation. Here we must be very prudent — we must avoid the sort of story which appeared in a québécois paper according to which Pierre Broué was in the maquis in the Ardèche in 1941. In 1941 there was no maquis, but, that aside, it is not necessary to fabricate after the event a "Pierre Broué, maquisard with gun and bandolier" because the real story is enough in itself and is actually much more interesting.

The story that Pierre Broué in fact told in the early 1980s was simply this: he joined the MUR in 1943, participated in a training course for the maquis which was also a sort of political discussion camp and in autumn 1943, by now in Paris, joined the Communist Party (PCF) and the Union of Communist Students (UEC).

In the preparatory article for the *Maîtron* biography, published by the journal *La Commune* he says that he got in contact with a school supervisor Paul Cousseran who was himself in contact with the Pericles network — one of the resistance networks that were part of the MUR (United Resistance Movements,

---

2. The hypokhâgne (1st year) and khâgne (2nd year) are lycée classes preparing for the Ecole Normale Supérieure. The ENS trained university teachers and senior lycée teachers at a time when there were far fewer lycées than today it was so a far more elite course than British. "teacher training" [Note by RH editors]

bringing together Gaullists and Socialists). With no detail or supporting evidence, the article talks here of collecting intelligence, getting parcels to prisoners and transporting arms and explosives. Who was being spied on, what was to be blown up? Pierre Broué never said anything about this [to me] and it was much later (I come back to this below) that he began to increasingly call up this period. The article continues by asserting that *"Paul Cousseran was approached by the Pericles network and, following this, Pierre was put in charge of setting up a leadership school for maquis officers"*.

Here we begin to tip over into mythomania and it is surprising that so few precautions were taken in drafting a biography. Our lycéen who had never set foot in a maquis became from one day to the next responsible for setting up a training school for "maquis officers" pompously entitled a "leadership school for officers". Even though we know that many young fighters rose rapidly through the ranks of the Resistance an instantaneous promotion like this is not credible.

In fact Cousseran organised resistance activities in Marseille, recruiting from the Scouts at the Lycée Thiers (Pierre Broué doesn't seem to have been involved in this but he may have known about it) and then, recruited by his own father, became a member, indeed a significant member, of another network, the Alibi network, which was directly linked to the British secret services and was particularly targeted at spying on German telephone lines. This was in July 1943 (see: Sylvaine Baehrel: *Alibi 1940-1944. Histoire d'un réseau de renseignement pendant la seconde guerre mondiale:* editions de l'Amicale du réseau Alibi). These activities of Paul Cousseran, which Pierre Broué did not know about, exclude any possibility that he would have been involved in other activities such as propaganda or "actions" and thus mean that he could not have involved Pierre Broué in such actions after July 1943. He could thus only have involved Pierre Broué in the Pericles network in June 1943 at the latest, after observing him over the preceding months.

* * * * *

This training course in the summer of 1943 must therefore have followed after Paul Cousseran's recruitment of Pierre Broué. It took place, according to the interview with J. G. Lanuque, at Theys in the Isère. There certainly was a "maquis school" there, which, in 1944, became a true maquis and took part in the liberation of Grenoble. Pierre Broué's presence at Theys in the summer of 1943 would assume that he travelled from Marseille to the Isère via the Ardèche and La Côte-Saint-André, where his mother had set up home, during the 1943 school holidays. This would not have been a clandestine journey, though one for a clandestine purpose. In a very late article in *Cahiers Leon Trotsky* in April 2002 Pierre Broué nevertheless says nothing about the Theys school and, contradicting what came before, claims to have joined Combat in November 1942 — now the Pericles network was quite distinct from Combat, but had links with it through the MUR — but above all he writes that he had "*discovered the class struggle in the maquis through Captain Durandal's contempt for the workers and the communists and through the courage of the communist worker Prévot who was under a death sentence — both are pseudonyms*". All this information is very confused.

It is impossible to work out what "maquis" we are talking about here; it is fairly certainly the training course of summer 1943. On top of this, we shouldn't confuse Theys with Thueyts in the Ardèche, sometimes referred to by Pierre Broué as another "maquis" area. This would not be possible in the context of his movements in summer 1943. We should further note that in an article by two Italian militants, Paolo Brini and Francesco Giliani of the Committee for a Marxist International written at the end of August 2005 (*Pierre, friend, revolutionary, marxist*: in English on the site: *In Defense of Marxism*) which repeats, with no critical distance, various of Pierre Broué's comments and allusions, there is a further reference to this communist worker Prévot, said to come from Chalons-sur-Saône.

In short to have a clear picture of Pierre Broué in summer 1943 we oscillate between two opposed versions. On one side, the one which he allowed to be understood towards the end of his life: of a summer of "yomping" with a geographical mobility worthy of a Jean Moulin[3]. On the other, in reaction to the suspicions that the first version inspires, we can accept that there was at least one underground training course with a network that was still being built and was looking to select young graduates or future graduates to form a leadership cadre of the MUR, a sort of underground summer school — as the "yomping" corresponded precisely with the school summer break.

Moreover we need to know: did Pierre Broué discover the class struggle through the "communist worker" Prévot, of whom he said nothing else, or in June 1936 at the age of 10 in Privas? Let me dare to resolve the issue: let us render unto Élie Reynier that which is Élie Reynier's.

*   *   *   *   *

In fact his participation in the MUR can be seen as Pierre Broué's first independent political position, as Élie Reynier himself was a resolute pacifist. Indeed Pierre Broué was to remain extremely grateful to him for not giving him a heavy lesson on this issue and for having instead listened to him in a questioning and understanding manner. The move of the MUR over to the CP can be explained by the growing influence of the party over the whole of the youth Resistance and by the way it positioned itself as the most determined force in that fight. In Pierre Broué's case it is possible that it followed heated debates with the "bourgeois", purely nationalist leaders, not so much of his "maquis" but of the network to which he belonged, but it is difficult to be sure. In any case his decision to join the CP corresponds almost precisely with his entry, as a boarder doing the khâgne, in September 1943 to the Lycée Henri IV

---

3. Jean Moulin, a Resistance hero. See Jean Moulin, 1899-1943: the French Resistance and the Republic, Alan Clinton. 2002

in Paris. This was, paradoxically, made easier by the "reunification" of France carried out following the occupation at the end of 1942 of the whole country.

In October 1943 he joined a student communist cell at Henri IV under the patriotic pseudonym of Michel Wattignies (an allusion to a battle during the French Revolution). He took up this pseudonym again for his articles in *Marxisme Aujourd'hui* — this patriotic complexion may have been added by his comrades as Attignies, without a *w* is the name of a character of Malraux's and Pierre Broué was a keen reader of Malraux — the latter, along with Theodore Pliever who wrote the story of Stalingrad, was one of his few "authors".

According the article in *Cahiers Leon Trotsky* cited above, Pierre Broué claimed to have been part, in the spring of 1944, of the "leadership triangle" (*"one of the three leaders"*) of the UEC in the Latin Quarter, along with Vincent Labeyrie (known as Dosseaux) and Jean Poperen (known as Linières). This assertion comes back to claiming that he was one of the three principal underground leaders of the PCF Paris youth in the spring of 1944. With no other source to back this up it is quite simply implausible and doesn't fit with his subsequent activity as a militant. In the interview carried out to prepare for the *Maîtron* piece this "leadership triangle" is not of the whole of the Latin Quarter but rather of the Lycée Henri IV. This too needs to be verified if possible. What we can say for certain is that Pierre Broué had become an active militant involved in comradely relationships which had led him to know many other militants, more, indeed, than he would have been allowed to under the strict security rules based on the "triangle" system which decreed that one should only know one's higher contact and one other. By the spring of 1944 a desire to breathe more freely was on the rise, along with the general sense of tension.

His first serious conflict with the "Party apparatus" occurred quite rapidly. It concerned the first significant action undertaken by the PCF students in the spring 1944 Paris context — a public demonstration, almost with flags raised, in April in the Latin Quarter. Pierre Broué participated in it but expressed disquiet in meetings as to the adventurist nature of the action.

Although he didn't know about it, or at least doesn't mention it, his was not the only such intervention as, according to the biography of Jean Poperen, at the time the effective communist leader in the Latin Quarter — and himself a khâgneux at the Lycée Louis-le-Grand — the latter also criticised individualist and adventurist actions, which bears witness to debates among leaders (see Emmanuel Manuel, *Jean Poperen, une vie a gauche*: Bruno Leprince editions). Jean Poperen in fact found himself on the opposite side to his friend Jean Maspero (killed a little after this) on the matter.

The second point of contention between the young Pierre Broué and the PCF apparatus focussed on anti-German patriotism; Pierre Broué claimed to have argued in his cell that he did not wish to kill ordinary German soldiers but rather SS men.

There is nothing to show that this went further than a sharp debate in the cell although it was always possible that it might have gone further, for example deciding to force the young militant to undertake a mission involving murdering soldiers.

According to his own accounts Pierre Broué thus got himself expelled for "Trotskyism" — Jean Poperen, the future leader of the left wing of the PSU and then of the PS, was supposedly the "expeller" — this would undoubtedly have been in May 1944 just before educational institutions were closed due to the imminent allied landing.

* * * * *

In fact he explains in the interview theoretically destined for the *Maîtron* that he already had a Trotskyist "contact", this being the khâgneux Donald Simon a member of the Communist Internationalist Committees (CCI) which was just about to reunify with the other current laying claim to the 4th. International, the Internationalist Workers' Party (POI) to form what, under the names PCI, OCI or *La Verité* group (also called Lambert group), was to be Pierre Broué's party for 45 years.

To get oneself expelled from the PCF at the end of May 1944 would have been risky, especially if this were for "Trotskyism". Claims, in the interview destined for the *Maîtron*, that his physical liquidation was a real possibility would thus be credible. But it is therefore astonishing that under these conditions he returned to the same place with the same fellow-students and the same roommates when courses resumed in September 1944, and that he claims to have *"resumed contact"* with the PCF though, of course, this was only to *"record the split"*. We can thus surmise that, in fact, the process of distancing himself and finally breaking away was spread over the spring, summer and early autumn of 1944. This puts in doubt the core of the hagiographic version which holds that the young communist had challenged the chauvinism of the leaders and thus discovered "Trotskyism"....

The theme of a future Trotskyist leader expelled in his youth from the CP for "Trotskyism", though he had never heard of this sickness, and then, as a result, informing himself about it and becoming a genuine Trotskyist is in fact a familiar biographical story about Trotskyist militants of the Thirties and Forties and anyway is often true (as in the cases of Pierre Lambert and André Essel). But Pierre Broué's case is different: his reading and conversations at Élie Reynier's had already equipped him to have a much clearer idea of what he was getting into with "Trotskyism". This was "book-learning" but was significant and to it he could add the combined experience of his determination to fight the occupiers including in armed struggle (such as in the FTP) while at the same time remaining an internationalist (like Élie Reynier). Perhaps it was the search for such a synthesis that led Pierre Broué to join the Trotskyist ranks.

In any case, even if Donald Simon had made contact with him in Spring 1944, his activity in the PCI couldn't have become effective until the autumn when he returned to Paris and the Lycée Henri IV. In the interval, which coincided both with the "holidays" of that special summer and with the allied landing, Pierre Broué went back to stay near his mother at La Côte-Saint-André in the Isère. He was deeply affected by the scenes he saw and experienced on his journeys there and back — distressed young German soldiers in the stations, mobs of crass petit-bourgeois who, after making a packet under the occupation, now sought to "get themselves some boches", or, if they couldn't do this, to shave the heads of women accused of having slept with the boches.

According to his recollections in the piece I have already referred to in *Cahiers Léon Trotsky* this was thus the time (the only one in fact) when, as he wrote, he *"found himself in the patriotic militias with a big Colt"* which he used, according to his article in the July 1994 edition of *Démocratie et Révolution* to dissuade a bunch of jingoists from bashing in the heads of young German soldiers with shovels.

* * * * *

I've attached some importance here to clarifying the events of these years and this clarification has ended up, above all, with some uncertainties and with a severe critique of some of the texts I refer to. There is a reason for this: in the last 15 years of his life Pierre Broué said, or, in essence, allowed those who wished to do so to believe — for instance in *Dauphiné libéré* (the Grenoble, but not the Privas edition) — that he had been active in the Resistance at a high level, including involvement in armed struggles. It is astonishing to find the historian that he was giving us no convincing evidence as to facts, places or dates about any of this. Let us be clear: we find ourselves here in mythomania territory and respect must exclude credulity. Confronting the accounts Pierre Broué put about or published in the last years of his life with their multiple contradictions clearly demonstrates this. Let me remind you of the documents which, in addition to "oral memory", I have used here. They are: the biographical note drafted by Jean-Guillaume Lanuque to go in the *Maîtron* the first part of which was published in November 2005 in *La Commune*; Pierre Broué's accounts in nos. 16 and 17, June and July 1994, of *Démocratie et Révolution* (now *Démocratie et Socialisme*); and his article on *La politique du PC pendant la guerre* in: *Cahiers Léon Trotsky* no. 77, April 2002.

For all this, our duty to the truth does not consist in minimising the real commitment of a young man which has no need of hagiography to be recognised as of great human and political interest, but on the contrary of restoring it to its true worth. The encounter with Élie Reynier, his journey through the ranks of the MUR, then the PCF, his distancing himself from the latter and his entry into the PCI at the time it was being constituted — this itinerary is captivating in itself.

In terms of courage the gilded legend of armed struggle is not necessary. When an aide de camp of Marshall Pétain visited the prefecture of Privas some respectable bourgeois shouted "au balcon"[4] so Pierre Broué, Jean Ayme, Pierre

---

4. "To the balcony" — meaning "let's have a speech".

Marijon and some other teenagers set up a shout of "A bas le con" ["down with the cunt"]. This was in itself an act of resistance without a capital R, similar to the actions of thousands of young people — defacing STO posters, imprudently hiding a cross of Lorraine in a sock or a bicycle bell — which led them towards insurrection — social as well as national.

So let's not demand that Pierre Broué should have led a maquis group in the mountains above Privas. Shouldn't it be enough in itself to have been an active underground communist and to have got himself expelled from — or even, perhaps, quite simply to have walked out of — the PCF because of his internationalist position.

* * * * *

From some of his rare subsequent hints, we can conjecture that Pierre Broué didn't necessarily find himself comfortable in his new party the PCI, in which he effectively became a militant at the end of 1944. He had thought it possible to be involved in armed struggle against the occupiers while still remaining internationalist. Now he found himself in a "party" that at the time had about 700 members; which had genuinely remained internationalist and had paid for this in the blood of some of its members; which expressed mistrust of armed struggle and of any zealous actions which might be tainted with nationalism; a party which explained that it had corrected the "nationalist deviation" of its leader Marcel Hic, the first organiser of the underground European Secretariat of the 4th. International (Marcel Hic was no longer there to defend himself as he had died in a concentration camp). This was a party which believed that "bourgeois democracy" would not survive after the war and that civil war, with the PCI playing the role of the Bolsheviks, was on its way at high speed.

This party was born from the fusion of the POI and the CCI, organised by Michel Raptis (known as Michael Pablo) who had taken over from Marcel Hic, fallen in the struggle. The former CCI militants were fewer in number in the fusion but possessed a strong esprit de corps and fought against the nationalism and the "petit-bourgeois" behaviour of the former POI members — between themselves they called the latter the "petits pois". Pierre Broué observed, without fully understanding, the sectarian behaviour of the former supporters of Raymond Molinier, widely regarded as an "adventurer", who had "disappeared" in 1940. The latter were themselves divided by bitterness arising from old faction fights during the dangers of underground life. Among them were both Pierre Frank and Pierre Lambert, the latter, though a bearer of the same political culture, had been banished from the CCI just before they all found themselves back together in the new united party.

Perhaps it is from this period that Pierre Broué's ambiguous relationship with the "Molinier culture", that is to say in more general terms with the rather "naughty boy" and ultra-activist political style affected by these young men, began to take shape. He was to take a critical stance towards them but at the same time wanted to be one of them, indeed to play a major part. In his memoirs the militants who came out of the CCI are often tiresome sectarians but it was they who had initially recruited him, while those from the POI seem, right from 1944, to have come across to him as unreliable bohemians. And he fell under the spell of a pure product of this "Molinier culture" in the person of Claude Bernard, known as Raoul, a boastful "good-looker" who talked up his female conquests — he was later to claim the actress Rita Hayworth among them, a claim repeated by Pierre Broué in the issue of *Cahiers Leon Trotsky* that Broué devoted to Bernard. For Broué, Claude Bernard *was* activism, an activism, by the way that he found brave, intelligent and full of laughs. Part of this was the extraordinary organising work in the Vietnamese workers' camps in France, where Pierre Broué claimed to have been brought in by Claude Bernard for a meeting to build cadres with a view to their return to their own country (see *Cahiers Leon Trotsky* no.56, p41).

Francesco Gilliani and Paolo Brini (see article referred to above) are keen to push to the limit Pierre Broué's oppositional attitudes towards the leadership of the PCI and visibly want to push these back as early as possible. Thus they present, echoing Pierre Broué's statements, made many decades after the facts presented there, what, according to them, would be among the first of his "oppositional" stances: at the end of 1944 Pierre Broué is said to have demanded that the PCI send an enquiry team to the Haute Loire to investigate the murder in the maquis by the Stalinists of several Trotskyist leaders, among them founding member of the Italian CP Pietro Tresso, known as Blasco, but the leadership of the PCI, already casting longing eyes on the PCF, "the great party of the working-class", is said to have refused to do so. This story has too neat a taste of a reconstruction carried out long after the event to be credible. This argument is borne out by one thing: the total absence of the story in the book co-written by Pierre Broué and Raymond Vacheron, published in 1997, *Meutre au maquis*. This book devotes considerable attention to the efforts of Trotskyist militants and of the partners and friends of those who "disappeared" to cast light back to 1944. Their quite justified insistence on demonstrating the lack of enthusiasm by the leadership of the PCI to take up this "business" would have required them to refer to Pierre Broué's positions of the time if these had existed, and one would think that he was in a good position to know about them!

The only kernel of truth in this is that Pierre Broué had a position on the armed struggle and the maquis that was "non-orthodox" — and closer to reality — compared with that of the PCI leadership, and no doubt held this position to a considerable degree at the time. But for decades he stifled this position and gave up, for the time being, arguing about it in the little party.

In this party he was one of the organisers of the youth sector, specifically the student youth. They operated through links forged in the Front National des Lettres, an organisation that existed for a while around the "Liberation" and was linked to the communist students. These student militants, however, tended to be kept out of things because of workerist and sectarian attitudes which led to clashes with the "youth leader" of the time Marc Paillet (later a well-known essayist and novelist). According to Pierre Broué's accounts in the articles in *Démocratie et Révolution* and in the piece supposed to be destined for the *Maitron* he recruited the equivalent of three whole student cells. These responsibilities could have lead to him being brought into the party leadership from this period. He was not far from this in 1948 when he had a friendly relationship with Daniel Renard who (along with Pierre Bois of the UCI, ancestor of LO) set off the 1947 Renault strike (though there is no indication that he organised Renard's *"protection"* as the article destined for the Maitron claims), and spent a brief period on the Central Committee, undoubtedly in early 1948.

But in reality the youth organisation, the JCI (Jeunesse Communiste Internationaliste) rapidly became a mere shell and Pierre Broué, after his last year of teacher training, lived half in Paris and half in Privas. After leaving Henri IV he became a penniless history student, first in Paris, then, in 1947-8, in Lyons, at the same time doing casual teaching in Privas where he was based most of the time.

Though many well-known militants of the organisation in the Paris area came out of the collective recruitment while trying to build a youth organisation (Robert Berné, known as Garrive, Robert Chéramy and Louis-Paul Letonturier) it was in his native Ardèche that Pierre Broué based his political activity.

*   *   *   *   *

Thus the fact is that in following his journey though all the years of the war and the "Liberation" we come back to our starting point, Privas, the town of Élie Reynier. We will thus have passed from the great "yompings" through hill and vale of the Resistance, the lofty spheres of the Latin Quarter, then the PCI, to the organisation of a circle of teacher trainees and sixth-formers in a provincial département near his mother and, in fact, under her grudging protection (the meetings took place in the Collège Moderne).

This apparent shift in dimension, this return to the fold, suggests in my view that, in reality, the adventures and dreams of the war years constituted perhaps a parenthesis, perhaps a censored moment (one to which he was to go back to later in a distorted and exaggerated way in his memoirs, a true political reversion of the repressed). In fact, the whole story of Pierre Broué, historian and militant up to 1989 could well be written with its starting point as the little JCI circle of the École Normal and the Collège Moderne at Privas in the years just after the Liberation, to which the hypothetical yomping in the summer of 1943, the experiences of the Lycée Thiers and of the Lycée Henri IV, and the alleged escapades with Raoul and with Daniel Renard add precisely nothing. I could myself have easily written this while cutting out both the real and the doubtful facts of this period and avoiding putting in doubt a great part of their reality. This would have been a mistake: it is Pierre Broué himself who wrote......in 1989, that the Second World War was the *skeleton in the cupboard* of the 4th. International.

* * *

Michel Broué, Pierre Broué's first son, was born at the end of 1946, his mother Simone Charras, Pierre Broué's partner since 1942, is the daughter of the Director of supplementary education in Privas.

The rise of a militant in difficult times

He gained 5 or 6 members at the École Normal, undoubtedly around ten if we include the sixth forms. In order to recruit, influence and debate Pierre Broué forced himself to join the Youth Hostel organisation that these young people had built, there he had to do the cleaning etc. and sing in the choir. This politically active milieu was equally influenced by the revolutionary syndicalism prevalent among the teachers, with Yvonne Issartel the leader at the time of the SNI in the Ardèche: to a certain degree the "young trades unionists" tended to identify themselves with the young Trotskyists, at least for some years. Here, then, is the real starting-point.

A very small number of lasting militants have remained from this period in the Ardèche, some in the OCI, others who followed the "Pabloite" current then that of Michèle Mestre and Mathias Corvin. Among these was Jean Coulomb who, doing the Stalinist (for we can thus summarise the orientation of this current: one had to "do the Stalinist" because, allegedly, there was nothing else one could do), contributed to swinging over [to the Stalinist led tendency in the teachers' union] the orientation of the departmental union and to a break with, indeed a blanking-out of, this union's splendid past. But we mustn't be misled by the small number who continued to be active in the currents that came out of Trotskyism: all the others still retained something profound from this experience.

The PCI at this time had tried to "broaden" its youth organisation, the JCI into an MRJ (Revolutionary Youth Movement). It turns out that this movement only really developed in the Ardèche and the Hérault departments. In fact the decline of the little party, despite its role in the 1947 strikes, had already begun. It was marked by three splits, one large and two small. The large one was that of the "rightists" (Yvan Craipeau, Paul Parisot, Albert Demazière, Jean-René Chauvin.......) who, in Spring 1948, tried to set up a new political grouping with a part of the former Young Socialists from the SFIO. The first of the small ones was that of the "*Socialisme ou Barbarie*" group (Cornelius Castoriades, Claude Lefort) which considered that the USSR and its satellites should not be called "Workers' States" and saw in them exploitative societies of a new type; Donald Simon [see above] was part of this group which today is one of the great legends of the French intelligentsia. A third group including the teachers Marcel Pennetier and Jaques Galliene saw the USSR as "State Capitalist". There is no indication that Pierre Broué sympathised even to the smallest degree with these currents that left the PCI.

At the start of the 1948 academic year he took up a position as an assistant teacher in the collège [secondary school] of Nyons in the Drôme.

In the summer of 1950 he was part of the big trip by militants of the PCI and other European sections of the 4th. International to Yugoslavia where they worked in the volunteer work-camps and travelled round the country while the leaders were hoping for "contact" with the leadership of the Yugoslav Communist Party whom Stalin had recently excommunicated and indeed had called for their murder.

From the start of the academic year in the Autumn of 1950 he became supervisor of the boarders at the École Nationale Professionnelle at Voiron in the Isère, then, from 1st. Jan. 1951 at the college technique Vaucanson at Grenoble. If this wasn't what he would have hoped for, it provided the professional stability that enabled him to engage in long-term trades union activity, as representative of the boarders' supervisors section of the SNET (National Union of Technical Education, affiliated to the National Education Federation), a milieu in which there was plenty of work to do.

In 1950-1951 he did his Diplome d'Études Superieures [roughly an M.Phil] devoted to an historian of the French Revolution from the Ardèche, Paul Mathieu Laurent, known as "de l'Ardèche", and entitled *Un Saint-Simonien dans l' arène -politique: Laurent de l'Ardèche, 1848-1852*. From 1828 Laurent of the Ardèche took on the task of refuting the lies and the monarchist and priestly distortions about the Revolution.

Then came the "Pabloite" crisis in the 4th. International. This was a confusing and demoralising crisis for the militants, caused, by a divergence between what they [the "Pabloites"] thought was a "bolchevik-type" representation of the post-war and the real world of the "thirty glorious years" which was just beginning and of the Cold War which they then believed could soon heat up. Pierre Broué was part of the [French] majority including Marcel Bleibtreu, Pierre Lambert and Daniel Renard, who were opposed to Pablo — who wanted to force them to bury their positions and their history to launch "sui generis" entrism to the PCF — and which got itself expelled in a bureaucratic manner from the 4th. International in 1952. It was probably because of his union activities as a representative of the boarding supervisors that Pablo put him on the first list, though in the last place, of 16 militants supposed to ask for membership of the PCF and to make every concession necessary to be let in. But Pierre Broué was far from Paris and his memories of this important moment in Trotskyist history stressed above all the confusion of the situation.

During the summer of 1953 he returned to Privas and, with the support of the ageing Élie Reynier intervened in a rally of Guy Mollet's. A few weeks later, Élie Reynier, angered by the sacking of FO post-office militants following that summer's big strike, launched a campaign of demonstrations and petitions across the whole town. A few months later Élie Reynier died.

In the Autumn of 1953 Pierre Broué, thanks to the intervention of the SNES, avoided being sent as a boarding supervisor to North Africa and returned for a year to the Collège of Nyons as an assistant teacher. At this time he wrote his first political leaflet, devoted to the revolution in Bolivia, for the PCI under the pseudonym of Pierre Scali — after, yet again, a Malraux character, from the novel *L'Espoir* — Scali was to be his main pseudonym. The take-off had happened, the start had been made: that is to say the take-off of a Trotskyist militant in the difficult times after the "Pabloite crisis".

In 1954 Pierre Broué obtained a post as assistant teacher at the Collège of Beaune in the Côte d'Or where he settled with his second wife, Simone Pleynet, herself an active militant.

From 1956 he taught in the Paris area, half as a union full-timer and member of joint union-management committees, first at the lycée Concordet in Paris, then from Autumn 1957 at the lycée Montaigne and then for several years at Montereau and became a more and more well-known trades unionist in the SNES "classical and modern".

*   *   *   *   *

This period thus corresponds with the beginning of the crossing of the desert by the French Trotskyists of the PCI expelled by Pablo whose numbers steadily dwindled to about 50, some of whom were demoralised, by the end of the 1950s. This dwindling was made still worse by the expulsion of some notable militants such as Jaques Danos and Marcel Gibelin in 1953, Marcel Bleibtreu, Michel Lequenne and some others in 1955. The party was by now a "group" and began to be known as the "Lambert group", united around a person who was neither a theoretician, nor a man for the masses but, as Claude Bernard called him, a "Contact Man", skilful and pragmatic with links to Messali Hadj, to the leaders of FO and to the expelled PCF leader André Marty, and who could play on these links.

Later, after his expulsion from the OCI, Pierre Broué was to emphasise the oppositional analyses made at the time — in private but well-known to all the comrades in the organisation — by Claude Bernard who was very critical but was also a supporter of loyalty in the ranks and let it be understood that he himself, along with François de Massot (known as François Forgues and to his friends as "Mamasse") had been influenced by these commentaries, personal analyses, the boasting and the "regroupment" projects (see Pierre Broué's *Cahier Leon Trotsky* on Raoul — no. 56 July 1995). Claude Bernard had, moreover remained on friendly terms with the *Socialisme ou Barbarie* group and had already criticised the, at the time unconditional, alignment of Lambert and the group with the Algerian national leader Messali Hadj.

Apart from this former friendship with Claude Bernard, reclaimed 25 or 30 years later, nothing leads us to a hypothesis that would wish us to see in Pierre Broué, from that time onwards, an "opponent of Lambert". He described the group to me personally as a very united circle where *"we debated massively and passionately"* and considered that things became spoiled when there were more people in it, in the 1960s, with the arrival of "intermediary organisers", not always very shrewd and with a tendency to pass on distorted versions of the centre's orders to the militants. This was a version that was fairly close to the way that the OCI itself right up to the 1980s presented the politico-organisational problems of its own development: the difficulty of *"moving from a group to an organisation"* and the need to create *"political units"* (Regions and Federations) in place of simple *"networks"*.

The simplest and most plausible view is to accept that Pierre Broué obviously had, as is normal, some mental reservations about this or that development of his organisation but that at the time he was not at all an "oppositionist" and didn't want to be one and that he was also politically in solidarity with the group, which also means that he freely took on responsibility, whatever he may have thought of them, for the first expulsions which were subsequently to be labelled "Lambertist".

*   *   *   *   *

In 1955, Robert Berné, who had been recruited during the student work after the War and who led the "youth" sector died accidentally of drowning while on a bathing party with Lambert, Stéphane Just and their partners (many years later the worst sort of rumours began to circulate about this drowning but in the absence of any evidence one must retain good sense).

In 1956 Pierre Broué and Cl;aude Bernard worked passionately to decipher the press dispatches of the British Communist Party on the Hungarian workers' council Revolution. The originator of these dispatches was a great CP journalist Peter Fryer. Peter Fryer had watched the working-class population of the small town of Magyarovar lynch the head of the political police who had commanded the murder of 11 demonstrators. Thus he sent this dispatch *"This was no counter-revolution organised by fascists and reactionaries. It was the upsurge of a whole people, in which rank-and-file Communists took part, against a police dictatorship dressed up as a Socialist society — a police dictatorship backed up by Soviet armed might."* (Fryer, *Hungarian Tragedy*, 1956 quoted by P. Broué in the review *Arguments* no.4). This dispatch was censored by the CP. Peter Fryer broke with the party and published a book that began with an account of the struggle in Magyarovar. He joined the OCI's sister organisation in Britain, Gerry Healy's future Socialist Labour League, then fled it at top speed calling it a paranoid sect.

Based on this "live time" work by Pierre Broué on the press dispatches and various other publications his organisation published his pamphlet *La revolution hongroise des conseils ouvriers,,* written under the pseudonym François Manuel.

Through this work of political and theoretical analysis and of solidarity with refugee militants he came into contact with Balàzs Nagy, one of the organisers of the Petofi Circle, the student circle that had been at the origin of the '56 movement. For many years Pierre Broué claimed that in 1960-61 he had recruited Nagy under the pseudonym Eugène Varga, along with a group of emigrés, to Trotskyism and to the organisation. Later he said rather that the "recruitment", certainly prepared by him had suddenly been announced by Lambert who, in short, had "robbed" him of his Nagy. This version of events is contradicted by the choice he made in 1963 to dedicate his *The Bolshevik Party* to Nagy. This was doubtless in part a reconstruction after the event to try to come to terms with his own role in the "Varga affair" which we will come to later. In any event Nagy-Varga became an important figure in the organisation, because he represented the "East" with all that this implied politically and symbolically.

Following this, in 1960, Pierre Broué undertook for the organisation a correspondence with the old Polish militant Kazimieriz Badowski, a Trotskyist who had survived under the Stalinist dictatorship in his country and who organised a small circle in which two future important figures in Polish history, Jacek Kuron and Adam Michnik were participants.

Also in 1956 Pierre Broué collaborated, episodically, with a small left review of great merit *Arguments,* created by intellectuals, notably Edgar Morin, who had recently been expelled from the PCF or had left it.

His main contribution to *Arguments* was for issue no. 4, June-September 1957, devoted to the workers' councils in Hungary (and, worthy of note, also contained the debate between the *Socialisme ou Barbarie* group and Edgar Morin) Under the title *Témognages et Etudes sur la révolution hongroise* he presented an overview of the books and articles on the subject and concluded by posing a number of questions. These included the question of the relationship between the Hungarian workers' councils and a constituent assembly; he stated that "*all*" the workers' councils had demanded the latter but that he himself, as a good "orthodox Trotskyist", or assuming himself to be one, thought that this should be ruled out in a future Hungarian Council Republic as likely to lead to the restoration of capitalism. He also raised the question of party pluralism in the Hungarian workers' councils where he stated that the councils had restricted this solely to parties recognising common property in the means of production.

The Hungarian socialist François Fejtö responded in the same issue of *Arguments*, emphasising the national and democratic dimensions of the revolution and the fact that the Stalinists had deprived Hungary of a "bourgeois revolution" which it had perhaps needed to make for itself. The dissident communist Jean Duvignaud, though still in the grip of a very ideological view of Stalinism as simply authoritarian dogmatism, noted that Pierre Broué failed to grasp the significance of a figure such as F. Fejtö for his moral and "*existential*" worth due to a "*too traditionally historical and political*" analysis.

This fascinating debate had, as such, no follow-up (at least not in public). It did however pose questions about the relationship between revolution and democracy.

* * * * *

All that we have just referred to had turned Pierre Broué into a kingpin in the policy of the creation of broader regroupments that, under the impetus of Pierre Lambert, the group was pursuing at the time. This took the form of the "Liason and Action Committee for Workers' Democracy" (CLADO) and its paper *La Commune*, a regroupment formed, on the basis indicated by its name, to defend militants supporting Algerian independence as well as anti-Stalinist Hungarian fighters. Pierre Broué housed and transported leaders of various tendencies of the centralised Algerian nationalist party, the Movement for the Triumph of Democratic Liberties, and then, after it broke up into FLN and MNA, of Messali Hadj's MNA. He was the editor in chief of CLADO's paper which published 6 issues until February 1958 and which involved the old Marceau Pivert, the young Michel Rocard of the Socialist Students and intellectuals who had broken with Stalinism: Edgar Morin and Jean Duvgnaud. It constituted a space for free opinions and in it Edgar Morin presented his self-portrait, of what he was at that time — a militant who had broken with Stalinism — and expressed his astonishment at the divisions among Trotskyists (no. 3, June 1957).

Pierre Broué's historical work which was now beginning was a ferment of collaborations with historic militants from various currents. He exchanged views on Spain with Marceau Pivert an important figure on the socialist left and in the early sixties was to go for a short stay with the Rosmers, Alfred and Marguerite, friends of Trotsky and figures of militant honesty after the fashion of Élie Reynier. It was during this period that a petition in defence of Algerian militants was brought out including the signatures of Lambert and of the Abbé Pierre (1955).

* * * * *

The Gaullist coup d'état of 1958, the advent of the 5th. Republic and Messali Hadj going over to De Gaulle put an end to this period which is the one in which Pierre Broué undoubtedly joined the central committee and the political bureau of the little organisation in a long-term way. The uncontested leader was Pierre Lambert but Pierre Broué's role as a trades unionist, in his international contacts with the Hungarian refugees and in the regroupment round *La Commune* was significant. This role was to expand even further in the even more difficult period that began with that defeat of the working-class and of democracy which the coup d'état of 1958 constituted.

The most important aspect of this period, and that which will remain as its resulting monument, is naturally his historical works, but we must first say some words about his trades union activities as he was at the centre of the policies of the PCI/Lambert group/OCI in secondary education between 1956 (and particularly 1960) and the end of the sixties.

Before his arrival this policy was represented by two noteworthy militants; Robert Chéramy and Louis-Paul Letonturier (known to his friends as "Tontu") who were both leaders of the Paris academic section of the SNES "classical and modern", as it was called at the time (the National Union of Second-Level Teachers affiliated to the FEN). From 1953 the group no longer intervened under the label École Émancipée inherited from the old unified Federation but integrated itself into the federal majority known as "autonomous", that is, to use "revolutionary" jargon, into the reformist union apparatus. It was in this context that Pierre Broué appeared among the leading names on the majority's list for the 1956 SNES internal elections and was later to sit on its national bodies (his role was thus far greater than that summarised as *"representative of assistant teachers in the Paris section of the SNES-FEN"* — as Jean-Jacques Marie's non-obituary in *Information Ouvrières* implies).

The FEN was the most powerful federation of the French workers' movement, the fortress of secularism, the only national union federation to unify the different historic tendencies in the workers' movement and to recognise their rights to organise within the union, the only one to have fought against both the repression in Hungary and the Suez intervention and the pillar of the struggle for trades union unity and of a reunification in a big CGT. It was to be the only one really to resist the establishment of the 5th. Republic, first on the streets and then in the voting-booths. In First-Level education (the SNI) the revolutionaries, including the Trotskyists, agitated for and within the École Émancipée (EE) tendency. In Second-Level (the SNES) the EE was weak and the Trotskyists were integrated into the "autonomist" majority, which itself had a certain internal diversity. When one is in a union one has to play one's role in a union, but it serves nothing to inappropriately paint this in red. A militant writing in Pierre Monatte's magazine said of this *"I have known, in the FEN and elsewhere, revolutionaries from Marxist, anarchist or even straightforwardly syndicalist backgrounds who held official positions. We didn't just talk the talk, when confronted by the realities they acted like reformists or they didn't do their job. I await a riposte."* (Charles Cordier, *Révolution Prolétarienne*, January 1967).

I believe that Pierre Broué was well aware of this point on which he was in agreement with Lambert, providing that it was well understood that playing one's role in a union did not mean backing any old policy in order to become integrated in the leadership.

Now it was in fact in 1959 that Lambert and Hébert for the first time voted to endorse FO's *"rapport moral"* (Annual Report). This in 1959, when the Bothereau leadership had a pitiful record in relation to Gaullism, quite different to that of the FEN and to the latter's advantage. The FEN, along with the CGT, had appealed for a "No" vote on the Gaullist constitution but FO had not. This vote on the Report constitutes a significant moment which is ignored by the various "historiographies" of "Lambertism". Its adversaries have a cosmic hostility to Lambert which leads them to lay as many charges as possible against him and to push these back to the most distant times (see Michel Lequenne in *Le trotsysme, un histoire sans fards)*, while hagiographies written by those who were themselves involved accord historical worth to the Lambert's vote for the *rapport moral* in.........1969 which they falsely present as being the first such vote (see for example the book *Itinéraires* by Daniel Glückstein and Pierre Lambert).

It is obviously more "acceptable" from a "revolutionary" point of view to link [the group] going over to the leadership of Force Ouvrière with the No vote in the Gaullist referendum of 1969 which constituted a working-class and democratic victory rather than with the endorsement of the refusal to vote No…..in 1958. But facts are facts and we gain from knowing them: they are borne out by the union archives and by the surprised, indeed shocked, articles in *Révolution Prolétarienne* and by anarchist and revolutionary syndicalist currents. Alexandre Hébert, Secretary of the Loire-Atlantique Union Départmentale for many decades, was not a member of the OCI or the group but was nevertheless associated with its leadership from this period on. Let me take advantage [of raising this issue] by noting in passing that the call by FO for a No vote in 1969, which was a genuinely significant point in the victory over De Gaulle, emerged from a bureaucratic deal between Lambert, Hébert and Bergeron according to which the Union would have participated in the "corporatist Senate" in the case, which they thought probable, of a Yes victory!

In *Cahier Leon Trotsky* no 78, November 2002, in his obituary of Robert Chéramy, Pierre Broué wrote these lines about this period at the end of the fifties and the beginning of the sixties:

> This period constituted a golden age for the trades union work of the PCI. Chéramy gave to Lambert his immense human qualities, to the profit of the group. We were all well aware of this.

This trades union work can be summarised as that of the Lambert and Hébert current in FO and the rising position of Pierre Broué in the SNES and the FEN along with the intervention of Paul Duthel among the primary-school teachers in EE. All the leaders in secondary teaching except Pierre Broué (Robert Chéramy, Louis-Paul Letonturier, Charles Cordier) were to be lost to the group. These militants, with the agreement of Lambert had joined the PSA (Autonomous Socialist Party) which had been created by socialists who supported the No to De Gaulle. But when in 1960, after a fusion, the PSA became the PSU (Unified Socialist Party) under the aegis of an important bourgeois politician, Pierre Mendès-France, the group considered that they must leave it as the future PSU would not be a potential context for regrouping militants who broke from social-democracy or Stalinism but was rather a deception covering up manoeuvres to fabricate "democratic" bourgeois parties against De Gaulle — here we already find, this time over the PSU, the debate that was to be reproduced over the nature of the PS founded 11 years later at Epinay and led by Mitterand.

These militants like Chéramy who had come to be quite happy in the PSA refused to lead the struggle against "Mendès". Pierre Broué was even sent in to the PSA for a time to recapture Chéramy. There were many to-ings and fro-ings at this time: Claude Bernard who was practising his particular entrism in the UGS (Union of the Socialist Left) was to really try to carry out a struggle against the fusion with "Mendès" and founded the ephemeral Union For Socialism before officially returning to the *La Verité* group ("Lambert group"). Among the youth won by the Trotskyist organisation from this little group was Jean Ribes. Among the youth won from the PSA was the last spiritual son of Marceau Pivert, Jean-Jacques Marie.

Chéramy was thus expelled from the group. At the same time he joined the national Bureau of the SNES and became a genuine reformist union leader, in the end he was to be a presidential advisor on education questions from 1981-1984. In the obituary that I quoted above, the Pierre Broué of years later claimed him with vehemence as *"My friend, my comrade"* and presented this expulsion as follows:

> Lambert writes in IO [this refers to the obituary of Chéramy in *Informations Ouvrières* at the time of his death in 2002] that Chéramy was not expelled for allowing himself to be won over by the PSA (the first version of the PSU), which he had been sent into as a "faction", as Lambert listened to his heart and betrayed his memory: he drafted an expulsion motion which he was to support and one against which he was to entrust to me. I have forgotten the rest of what happened except that all this nauseated me.

It is clear that Pierre Broué wanted to imply the opposite of what he wrote: on the one had he had forgotten nothing of what happened and had taken an active part in it. On the other hand he is like Lambert, or would like Lambert to be like himself: to have "listened to his heart and betrayed his memory". But the memory remains, repressed though it be, and the heart suffers for it. This, too, is what he says here to Lambert......

* * * * *

From 1960 Pierre Broué was to write more regularly in *École Émancipée*. In 1962 and again in 1964 he headed the EE list in the SNES "classical and modern" (4% to 5.5% of the vote). The return at this point to the tactic of belonging to the union tendency that called itself revolutionary set him against the position of Chéramy and Letonturier. It allowed Pierre Broué to intervene in École Émancipée as a whole which he did on a pragmatic basis — supporting a "binomial salary" for teachers, a compromise between the theoretical and historical position of the revolutionary syndicalists in favour of a single salary-scale and the demands for an hierarchical revaluation of salaries proposed by the SNES section at Montereau.

Trades unionism in French secondary education in the 1960's was an ever-shifting field of activity. Various sub-tendencies had left the autonomous majority: some supporting the privileges of classical teachers against the weight of the primary-school teachers in the SNI, others on the other hand wanted to move closer to the SNI, the latter included people close to RP and to FO (e.g. Paul Ruff). The numbers in the profession were growing, the union was expanding but teaching conditions were declining and the "actions" launched particularly under pressure from the "Unity and Action" (U&A) tendency linked to the PCF, such as banning overtime or boycotting administration, led to defeats. The U&A tendency, which was far from a mechanical reflection of all the PCF's positions, advanced strongly. The fusion of the SNES "classical and modern" with the SNET (technical teachers) gave birth in 1966 to the SNES and the leadership was taken over by U&A the following year.

There is no doubt that Pierre Broué had demonstrated flexibility and powers of adaptation in this changing union. Without having to research in detail just what he did in the union there are two indices which are enough to understand it: his relationship with Louis Astre and his influence on the student supervisors in the U&A tendency.

Louis Astre had been the General Secretary of the SNET and became the joint General Secretary of the new SNES just before losing the internal elections to André Drubay, an U&A leader. He was, in short, the leader at the secondary level of the majority tendency in the FEN known as UID ("Unity, Independence & Democracy") at the moment when it lost its leadership position. This pure and sincere reformist socialist, today and since its creation in the FSU — a fact not without significance — spoke before Pierre Broué's cremation: only a trades unionist, even a reformist, and no-one among the Trotskyist or socialist clubs and groups which laid greater or lesser claims to a share of Pierre Broué, could have done it as he did.

The secretaryship of the MI-SE (supervisors), a bastion of U&A, was held in 1963-4 by the former UEC leader Philippe Robrieux who got to know Pierre Broué in this period: he never became a Trotskyist but was to be the true historian of the PCF, which no doubt, and by his own testimony, would not have been possible without this crucial encounter. Through this "youth" section of the union, in these pre-68 years when he was himself envisaging "passing on" to the University, Pierre Broué came into contact with students. Let it be said in passing that this shows that it was not only the Ligue and the Maoists who fed off the crisis in the UEC. Pierre Broué recruited to the organisation the leader of the Dijon UEC, Pierre Roy, today the historian of the heritage of pacifist and anticlerical war memorials and a PT militant.

* * * * *

If we align Pierre Broué's trades union work, his emergence as an historian (which we will discuss below), his role in the regroupments around the Trotskyist group and in the formation of Balàzs Nagy's Hungarian group and consider that, during the years 1958-62 the organisation had lost the Chéramy and Letonturier team, that Stéphane Just stopped being active for several years and was not to play a significant role in the orientation of the organisation until 1965, that Daniel Renard was tired and that new generation of militants; Jean-Jacques Marie, Charles Berg, Jean Ribes, François Chesnais, Pierre Roy, Claude Chisserey etc. were either completely new or had not yet joined, then it appears clear that for some years, with, but behind Lambert, Pierre Broué was without doubt a central figure in what was to become the OCI at precisely the moment when that organisation had started recruiting and was beginning to create a small structural apparatus of organisers and full-timers. At the very beginning of the

1960s the other key personalities in the organisation, Nagy/Varga and Boris Fraenkel were in effect in a much more marginal situation as was Gérard Bloch to whom, rightly or wrongly (probably both) was attributed a sort of "Professor Nimbus" image[5].

We have already come across Balàzs Nagy, as to Boris Fraenkel, he had been recruited directly by Lambert eight years earlier as education organiser for the organisation. But in 1967 Boris Fraenkel was expelled in great haste along with some of his young comrades like Jean-Marie Brohm (but one of them was a coward: Lionel Jospin) for having had printed on the presses of the organisation a pamphlet of translated texts by Wilhelm Reich. He was soon to be accused of putting the sexual struggle in the place of the class struggle and we read in *Quelques enseignements de notre histoire [Some lessons from our history]* that he had created a "*sexual-sectarian clique*" — no more details are given!

It is worth noting, and the "leftists" of the time would not have missed the chance to note it, that the OCI was an organisation from which one could be expelled for propaganda in favour of sexual liberation. But it just as worth noting that it was precisely this organisation which, for eight years had "sheltered", as its organiser of youth education, the person who promoted the ideas of Reich and of Marcuse in France. The real characterisation of the organisation is not to be found in the first of these facts but in both of them and in the contradiction between them. We can note that in his little book of memoirs (*Profession — Révolutionnaire,* Le Bord de l'Eau, 2004) B. Fraenkel says that at the time Pierre Broué had "*howled with the wolves*".

*

From 1966 Pierre Broué was based in Grenoble. It seems probable that, during this period, as his stature as an historian was growing, his role in the leadership of the organisation was, relatively, diminishing. In 1967, following a meeting in Lyons on the fiftieth anniversary of the October Revolution which was attacked by the Stalinists, he considered that Charles Berg, a youth organiser who had been present, had put out a false report about this meeting and, at the OCI congress, opposed his election to the Central Committee, this cost him an aggressive intervention by Stéphane Just in defence of the "youth" — and Charles Berg was duly elected. It is this incident which is evoked, but not explained in the article which was announced as due to appear in the *Maîtron* as a "serious conflict" with S. Just in 1967. It is not certain if it had considerable significance at that point although it undoubtedly marks a certain distancing from and weakening of Pierre Broué's personal position in the organisation at a national level. Later on the latter was to consider this as one of the founding events in relation to the conflicts in which he was to oppose first Charles Berg and then Stéphane Just.

5. Professor Nimbus, a character in the "Tin-tin" comic books.

* * * * *

Thus Pierre Broué "passed on" to the University sector in 1965-6, first as an assistant and later as a Professor of Contemporary History in the IEP (Institute of Political Studies) at Grenoble. His first officially "academic" work consisted of republishing, prefacing and annotating the *Histoire de la Fédération unitaire de l'enseignement des origines à l'unification de 1935* written by the core of the old Federation (Bernard, Bouet, Dommanget, Serret) which was the key work of reference on this subject until the recent publication of Loïc Le Bars' *La Fédération Unitaire de l'Enseignement (1919-1935). Aux origines du syndicalisme enseignant* (Syllepse, 2005).

Pierre Broué the university teacher, still held a seat on the national body of the SNESup, during the May 1968 period. But in terms of the OCI's union work, and undoubtedly of Pierre Broué himself, there is a break at this point. With new horizons opening towards his students he probably underestimated it even though he played a major role in it; we are talking of the death, through its 1969 split, of the old École Émancipée. In expressing myself thus I have no doubt that I shall excite the fury of thus who claim historical continuity, that Holy Grail which must be held by someone to prevent the demons from controlling the cosmos, but people like this are no less fetishist among "revolutionary syndicalists" than among "Trotskyists".

The facts, in outline, are as follows: to the extent that École Émancipée had a clear orientation in the years 1964-68, this came from the Trotskyists of the OCI. The tendency condemned the Gaullist projects aiming at integrating the unions with the State and their concrete form as "administrative reform" — that sea serpent now called "reform of the State". For this story continues along with the 5th. Republic and will do so to a "bastard and uncompleted" end as the OCI used to say. In EE's name, its primary teachers' representatives, led by Paul Duthel of the OCI, had, at Lille in 1964, resigned from the national bodies of the SNI. This "act of Lille" was denounced, by those militants whom we can describe (to further simplify things) as of more "libertarian" tendencies, as having been imposed as a fait accompli. A sickness set in. It turned into an abscess when, in May 1968, EE said what amounted to very little and OCI militants led an invasion of the FEN's offices at the time when the latter was trying to organise a return to work. The EE disavowed this action while at the same time deploring the sanctions that followed it within the union.

From then on matters speeded up, for the OCI's Political Bureau saw EE as an obstacle in the struggle for the workers' united front, an obstacle to be destroyed while at the same time claiming its historical heritage: according to Pierre Broué, who wrote this much later, in passing, (*Cahier Leon Trotsky* no.62, May 1998), the CAOTE (Committees for a Workers' Alliance of Education Workers) had been created to this end and had, moreover, ceased to exist after the split. At the end of 1968, Marcel Valière, the last secretary, in 1935, of the old Federation had taken the lead and pushed through a motion declaring membership of the CAOTE incompatible with membership of EE; this was a split.

Without falling into the mythological characteristics that this episode has acquired over time in the real or fictitious memories of EE militants of a later period (Lambertist hordes are said to have taken meetings by storm, taken over the platform, rigged votes etc.) and thus not taking their side on the matter (a desire to expel the Trotskyists was clearly recognisable), one cannot help being struck by horrified feeling, among the "old guard" of the tendency, that they were dealing with an attack on free thinking and trades union independence. The majority of this "old guard" came together in a common declaration in September 1969 where they compared the OCI offensive with the one waged by the Stalinists against the old Federation in the late 1920's. Even Yvonne Issartel signed this declaration, though she was later to join the PT she certainly never changed her views on this point. In Marseille in 1930 the young Stalinists had abused the old Federation. Valière believed that he found himself in the same situation at the meeting of the EE assembly on 23 December 1968 where the young people in the audience, members of the OCI and the CAOTE, harassed and interrupted the platform: a troika of leaders, Broué, Duthel and Neny organised these manoeuvres.

Of the two EEs which were born in 1969 one straightforwardly the EE, called EE-SR (meaning revolutionary syndicalist) by the OCI was soon to be filled by the whole extreme left of the period, including the Mao-Stalinists, and to recruit non-union members and members of the SGEN-CFDT, which was not exactly what Valière had hoped for in 1969. The other, EE-FUO (Workers' United Front), was to become simply the union appendage of the OCI which swung between becoming a union tendency and trying to fit in, when this was possible, with the union apparatus of any given time, trying to make the latter "play its proper role" — this was, moreover, what Pierre Broué seems to have done in the SNESup.

Today, four tendencies in the FSU come out of EE: the "official" EE in reality is part of the leadership of the FSU: the *Emancipation* tendency tries, quite sincerely, to reclaim what it sees as the "old" revolutionary syndicalism; the PRSI tendency is an extension of the PT, and thus of the FO leadership: the United Front tendency corresponds with the supporters of Stéphane Just, who was expelled from the PCI in 1984. None of them carries on the "old" EE and even less the "old" Federation, which, moreover, one cannot purely and simply regard as revolutionary syndicalist. One can certainly think that this disappearance of an historic current in the French working-class movement was inevitable, but it remains the case that this was not a natural death: the assassination well and truly took place in 1969.

A great historian asserts himself

Pierre Broué's association with the people from *Arguments*, particularly Edgard Morin, opened up doors to publication for him, through Éditions de Minuit.

He had been working on the Revolution and war in Spain since 1948 and had nourished the idea of writing this history as an adolescent, at Élie Reynier's, at a time when the memory of the refugees of 1939 was still fresh.

From this, thus came *Revolution and Civil War in Spain* of which he wrote the first part which goes up to the point where the revolution was crushed in Republican Spain. Émile Téminé, later to be the historian of migration in Marseille, wrote the second part in which there is no longer a revolution but only war, which was thus lost, against Francoist barbarism. The tome came out in Éditions de Minuit in 1961. With it began a series of major books to which we must also add republications and prefaces such as Bukharin & Preobazhensky's *ABC of Communism* from Maspéro (from before1968, republished in the "petite collection Maspéro"), Oscar Anweiller's *Soviets in Russia* from NRF in 1972, the dossier on *The Moscow Trials* from Juillard in 1964, *The Chinese Question in the Communist International* from EDI in 1965 and the start of publishing all the texts of the latter's congresses (two volumes from EDI, in 1969 and 1970).

* * * * *

Revolution and Civil War in Spain is a great book for it succeeds in creating that same synthesis that Trotsky achieves in his *History of the Russian Revolution*; to tell history as it effectively is, a succession of events, of gestures, of acts and from that itself forming movements of social classes and political forces in struggle. This poignant book tells how a revolution, initially victorious against Franco's putsch, was to be destroyed from the inside, firstly through the hesitations and uncertainties of its leaders and then deliberately by the Stalinists organised from top to bottom as a policing power and who, for the first time, were to develop in Spain as a cancer on the body of the revolution. They aimed, through the Popular Front, to create a republican, rather than a revolutionary, Spain; they thus assured the defeat of the Republic and the terrible victory of Franco, therefore, reversing Lenin's formula, transforming a civil war into an imperialist war and opening the door to the Second World War.

This book was to play an active role. It is without doubt the one of his books that engaged Pierre Broué the most, for it became a bible, a source of rejuvenation and reflection among the sixties and seventies generation of anti-Francoists and anti-Stalinists. Smuggled into Spain it became the base for contacts and debates. These discussions between the OCI, the POUM and the anarchists in exile, notably during the memorable study days organised by the Circle for Marxist Studies in Paris at which the main protagonists were Wilberto Solano of the POUM and Pierre Broué, are enthralling despite the fact (and, perhaps, enthralling for that in itself?) they never led to common organisational initiatives.

It was frequently read by anarchists, socialists in the Caballerist tradition and even by young trades unionists and young CP militants.

Paradoxically — but this is the paradox of post-Franco Spain — it was to be a less effective weapon when it was published in Spain after Franco and debated on the spot. This "transition" had as its base the claim that this past had been buried. This amounts to saying that this book will return and that its republication is particularly necessary, as today, especially since the Spring of 2004 the shock-wave of the past is again rocking Spain.

*   *   *   *   *

In 1963 *The Bolshevik Party* came out in the same collection. This is the most read of Pierre Broué's books, although it is much less innovative than others. But it lent itself the most to being used, incidentally in the Ligue as much as in the OCI, in a "training school" type of way. To put it another way, although it is a good book it is by no means the best of them. It consists of a synthesis of the historical facts as they were known at the time on Bolshevik and then Stalinist Russia and explained for the first time in a systematic manner the stages of the factional struggles (between Stalinists, Trotskyists, Zinovievists, Bukharinists) in the Communist Party of the USSR between 1923 and 1929.

It was dedicated to *"my master"* Élie Reynier and *"my friend"* Balàzs Nagy — a double dedication which has been missed out of the recent electronic edition of the work on the *Marxist Internet Archive* website.

Contrary to the symptomatic error in Jean Birnbaum's sympathetic obituary in *Le Monde*, it does not deal with *"how the party of Lenin finished, under Stalinism, by wiping out the totality of the October generation"*, rather it explains how the Stalinist bureaucracy wiped out the party of Lenin and the October generation, which is obviously not at all the same thing.

However, an ambiguity inherent in his treatment of the subject facilitates this sort of misinterpretation. The structure of the book appears to deal with one single party that transforms itself over time, while at the same time Pierre Broué presents the party which emerged from the purges as a different party, a counter-revolutionary party in power, from the revolutionary Bolshevik party.

We cannot blame the author for this ambiguity, which may even have been imposed without his knowledge. It is at the heart of the problem, of that *continuity/discontinuity* between October and Stalinism through which passes the whole calamity of the century. If Stalinism had only presented itself like Versailles massacring the Commune everything would be altogether more simple.

In this ambiguity resides the question of the relationship between democracy and revolution. Pierre Broué situates the roots of Stalinism entirely in the conditions facing the Russian Revolution and, most decisively, in the isolation of the revolution caused by the defeat of the European, and notably the German, revolution; the Russian tragedy thus comes back to the key issue of Germany, as we shall see later. This did not prevent him thinking and writing — not so much in the book itself but in an aside, that is to say in his article *Remarks on the history of the Bolshevik Party* in *Arguments* no. 25/26 (the penultimate issue 1st. and 2nd. Quarters 1962) — that the *apparatchiki, komitechiki* and other "old Bolsheviks", with whom Lenin often clashed, in the most radical way in 1917 to assure the victory of the revolution, did have a tendency to operate as bureaucrats. But essentially, on the fundamental issues Pierre Broué — and let me add we too — agreed with Rosa Luxemburg when she spoke thus of the October Revolution:

> In the present period, when we face decisive final struggles in all the world, the most important problem of socialism was and is the burning question of our time. It is not a matter of this or that secondary question of tactics, but of the capacity of action of the proletariat, the strength to act, the will to power of socialism as such. In this, Lenin and Trotsky were the **first**, those who went ahead as an example to the proletariat of the world; they are still the **only ones** up to now who can cry with Hutten "I have dared".
>
> This is the essential and **enduring** in Bolshevik policy. [........] In Russia the problem could only be posed. [........] And in **this** sense the future everywhere belongs to "bolshevism." (Rosa Luxemburg The Russian Revolution).

*

In 1967 his *The Communist Movement in France* came out (again published by Minuit). This was a selection of articles by Leon Trotsky on France with a significant critical apparatus and introductions by Pierre Broué. With this book he began to make himself the editor of Trotsky. The cutting remarks that he let fly in passing in the notes at Pierre Frank and the Molinier current would not have pleased those to whom they were addressed but, leaving aside the legend according to which Molinier (who was soon to reappear in the Ligue) had become a circus director in Latin America, they were not let fly at random — and they do pose the problem of "methods" and of mutual respect in the revolutionary movement.

*   *   *   *   *

In 1969 Minuit published the French translation of the first volume of *The Russian Revolution* by Edward Hallet Carr, a great democratic figure, former Foreign Office official, gripped by passion and sympathy for his subject but whose career as an historian was to be brought down in full flight because he had been deceived by a fake document.

This work has to be counted as part of the series of fundamental and indispensable ones along with Pierre Broué's other tomes published by Minuit. On the one hand this is because in it we can find a part of his own inspiration, a way of writing close to his own, as well, incidentally, as an irreplaceable account *in all their detail* of the early years of Bolshevik power and an account of the internal debates in Russian revolutionary social democracy which is far more detailed than the overview in *The Bolshevik Party*.

It must, on the other hand, also be taken into account because this first volume was translated into French by Andrée Broué, head of the language laboratory at Grenoble IUT, Pierre Broué's third wife and mother of his four other children — Françoise, Catherine, Martine and Jean-Pierre, with whom he had gone to live in Grenoble. Two other volumes, covering the economic and foreign policy of the "soviets" up to 1921, appeared in 1974.

*   *   *   *   *

1972: this is his greatest work, and the one that Pierre Broué's adulators know least well, this is his *The German Revolution (1917-1923)*, the book that, of all Pierre Broué's works was, for him, the hardest struggle to write.

This book was a struggle as a piece of work, a huge piece of work which had, in reality, been started in 1957 and which had forced its author to learn to read German as he went along (he learned it to write the book, then forgot it!), to research the archives, to have the doors of those who, at the time, were on "the East" closed to him and which, above all, was to be his weapon for confronting the University and becoming "Professor", as it was his Thesis. Obtaining this title became a matter of political confrontation, Pierre Broué was obliged to assert himself as a worker by force upon a jury of academic superstars, in their majority dubious on the political level (apart from Pierre Naville, and even then…) and with a fundamentally hostile president of the jury: the former Stalinist harpy Annie Kriegel who had led the attacks on syndicalist and Trotskyist pro-Yugoslav meetings in 1949 and who had by then, faithful to herself, become a harpy of the Right. The thesis was accepted — not to have done so would have created a massive academic, political and intellectual scandal — and thus allowed its author to become himself an officially recognised "big shot", indeed a superstar, something of which he was entirely aware and satisfied. While, let us note, his son Michel was, in exactly the same period, to become a significant mathematician.

This book was above all a political struggle, in the first place against the main objection which, though wrapped up in praises, was made at the time of the viva on the thesis by the historian Jacques Droz. Pierre Broué, in the little report that he typed up of this greatest moment of his life as an historian and a militant, summarised it like this:

> JACQUES DROZ: stated that he was fascinated by this work […] M. Droz, for his part, thought that at no point had there existed in Germany a real revolutionary situation and **that the idea of revolutionising Germany was a dream.** Social Democracy had its reasons for gaining the maximum political and social advantage, could doing so be considered a betrayal? [my emphasis — VP]

Pierre Broué recounted as follows his response, in the form required to play the bull in this courteously bloody arena where it is claimed that careers can be created and destroyed:

[in response] to Droz, I acknowledged his general critiques and recognised that I should have expanded on the balance of forces, given that it was the communists in this period that I was studying. [...] Finally I said to him that **if revolutionising Germany was a dream, then struggling against barbarism was one too, and I refused to believe that.**" [my emphasis — VP].

In demonstrating — through facts, accounts, biographies and equally the photographs at the end of the book — the reality of a revolutionary confrontation, not among Ukrainian or Andalucian peasants, nor metalworkers from Petrograd or Barcelona but in the industrial heart of Europe, facing an extremely sophisticated state bureaucracy in a country with extremely dense cultural traditions Pierre Broué had been very naughty: the revolution could not, truly could not, be treated as exotic and the concrete problems encountered by the German revolutionary communists between 1918 and 1923, while they had the bloodstained dimension of a revolution at stake, also appeared to be of much the same nature as the concrete problems encountered here and now by Western European militants.

In particular this concerned the question of the Workers' United Front, the fetishised formula in all the recent crises in the École Émancipée. In *The German Revolution* Pierre Broué shows us its origins: the formulation of the need for *"transitional slogans"* by the leadership of the working-class bastion of Chemnitz in 1919; the proposal by reformist union leaders of a *"workers government"* to defend the [Weimar] republic against the military putchists of 1920; the *Open Letter* from trades unionists and those close to Paul Lévi in the VKPD (Unified German Communist Party) proposing united action around the most urgent demands and the disarmament of the pre-nazi paramilitaries; and finally the discussion and eventual adoption of the United Front policy by the Communist International in 1921-1922.

As an historian Pierre Broué takes sides, without moreover needing to say so, but this emerges from the very exposition of the facts and of the arguments: he not only situates himself, obviously, in the camp of the revolution and the German Communists, but also, within this camp, he is with the most "rightists" — that is to say those who developed the Workers' United Front policy against the "leftists" and who, he thought, had thereby created a possible route to victory.

Taking this position might annoy those currents who took inspiration from the left communism of the period, represented by the KAPD and the trade union groups such as the AAUD. In truth Pierre Broué accorded them very little significance, including at those points where he talked of "leftism". This early "leftism", associated with the refusal to join unions or take part in elections, was in a majority among the first great wave of German communists and contributed to sending them into futile battles. But it later emerged in the form of leaders, full-timers with authoritarian mind-sets who wanted to force the pace of things. The leftism with which Pierre Broué crossed swords was not

— one could say, to their great annoyance, *was not even* — that of the KAPD, of Goerter and Pannekoek; it was that of the emissaries of Moscow, of Bela Kun and Rakosi, passed on into the VKPD by the current led by Ruth Fisher and Arkadi Maslow. This is a leftism whose features are far more authoritarian than libertarian and which does not seem as "juvenile" as the other one, the one targeted by Lenin in his *Infantile Disorder*. But take care: for Pierre Broué there are two, complementary, perceptions of this leftism. On the one hand there is a leftism which is already bureaucratic in its methods, which comes to ally itself with Zinoviev in Moscow. On the other hand there is a mass *"working-class leftism"* which the first type builds on and which runs through the entire history of German communism from 1918 to 1923.

Pierre Broué thought that leftism could get on perfectly well with bureaucratism and that the methods of directives from above were its characteristic feature. In March 1921 these methods were to engage the German party in a catastrophe, a sort of equivalent of the 1917 July Days in Russia, but which were to be badly led by the party; thus we even saw, in industrial Germany, guerrillas attacking banks and police stations. Paul Lévi publicly attacked the "March Action": so he had to be expelled. Lenin and Trotsky, themselves in difficulties in relation to their own "leftist bureaucrats" or "bureaucratised leftists" — officials of the revolution, little bosses sending the rank-and-file into battle — had to agree to the expulsion and denunciation of the "traitor" Lévi. Pierre Broué liked this woman's man, a refined intellectual and the spiritual son of Rosa Luxemberg (this too is a detail that the spontaneists who claim this title for themselves find disagreeable).

There is thus a debate about Paul Lévi (dealt with at the end of the book in the chapter *Paul Lévi était-il communiste?*) to whom Pierre Broué has restored his true stature. But this debate is but the antechamber to the main debate — that on 1923. For official history 1923, the German October does not exist and ought not to exist. For Stalinism there can be no question of a German October because — from…1924 — it is a matter of building so-called socialism "in one country". And even for the left communist currents (left of Trotskyism: Bordiga, KAPD, Pannekoek etc.) the story stops at the latest in 1921 and we must not go as far as 1923. Well?

Well, in Pierre Broué's account, in 1923 the Workers' United Front made the victory of the revolution possible in Germany and the insurrection was minutely prepared. United Front governments were formed in some *Länder*, in Saxony and Thuringia (Karl Korsch, who was later to become an ultra-left theoretician, was then a minister in Thuringia!). But the left social-democrats hesitated and the emissaries of Moscow agreed with the VKPD leaders to call off the insurrection. The counter-order reached Hamburg too late, leading to carnage and defeat. The final catastrophic retreats can be explained by the long wait that had preceded them, by the hesitations impelled from the top, right back to Moscow, to a party that, despite the great progress it had made, was still immature, for it had been beheaded at its birth by the murders of Rosa Luxemburg and Karl Liebknecht, but also because the expulsion of Lévi and the weight in it of the "bureaucratic leftists" — soon to become "Zinovievists", foot-soldiers of Stalinism — had, since 1921, truncated the party's development.

This precise factual account and the analyses made by the actors themselves were rounded off in the 1990s by the publication of the wonderful reportage of Victor Serge and, in *Cahiers Leon Trotsky*, by speeches from Trotsky, Zinoviev and Radek from the period as well as what Paul Lévi himself thought (he was totally sceptical — on this Pierre Broué was thus no longer "with him") all put together by Pierre Broué. All this, we must fully understand, bears on the major turning-point of the 20th. Century: the German revolution, and thus the European revolution, would not take place, there would be Stalin and Hitler, the second world war followed by the division of the world and the cold war, in short the conditions that led to minority struggles and the distancing of perspectives, through to the fall of the Berlin Wall.

Pierre Broué himself, in a quite striking fashion, returned little to his major work, which had left him both worn out and satisfied. He spoke about the German revolution and Rosa Luxemburg often with reticence, he who was so talkative, even "gossipy", about every subject. This was partly for a bad reason — he wanted to be, first and above all, the "historian of Trotsky" — and partly for a good one — he felt that the "knot" of the common drama was to be found there and thus that the threads of the individual tragedies were tied up with it. As an event, and more than that as a *non-event* whose absence was to be decisive, the German October, which for academic historians is not even discussed — for it should not have had even the shadow of a beginning of an existence — is at the heart of the thinking of a Marxist historian of the 20th. Century and of the understanding by militants of the past that has forged their present.

The German Revolution is thus Pierre Broué's most significant book and the one whose republication would be politically the most useful both for the culture of militants and for those who really want to cultivate their minds. Studying it, if done seriously, would in fact constitute the most certain antidote for sparing young, and not so young, theoreticians from talking nonsense on the "United Front". One such theoretician will explain to you that the united front is worth nothing today as there are no longer any workers' parties, nor even workers' unions, while another such will explain to you that Pierre Broué's works on Germany show that Lenin was wrong to found the 3rd. International, a surprising conclusion to say the least. All these theoreticians are in need of some rereading — and therefore of its republication. Though I talk here about "theoreticians", rank-and-file worker militants for their part know that workers have an organic need to unite together in full independence in their unions, their strikes, their mass meetings, their struggles with all their organisations. But republication would be even more useful for them, as they would learn how a great struggle had been brought, once and once only, right to the threshold of a victorious revolution in a major, modern, European country.

* * *

The great collection of "tomes" published by Minuit finished in 1975 with a new collection of texts by Trotsky chosen, presented and commentated by Pierre Broué, *La Revolution Espagnole (1930-1940)* — he had begun with Spain, now he signed off with it. This last book added some significant details to *Revolution and Civil War in Spain* notably through documents published as appendices. Pierre Broué had been put on the track of some of these by the old left communist militant Gaston Davoust. These documents tended to relativise, contextualise and explain the conflict between Trotsky and the POUM which had been the subject of a great debate that had begun in the 1960s following the publication of the first book and which Wilbaldo Solano, leader of the POUM youth in Barcelona in 1936 and Pierre Broué's main interlocutor on this topic, was still pursuing in depth — in my opinion pretty effectively in favour of the POUM — in his book *Le POUM: Révolution dans la guerre d'Espagne* .

Let us note that by his manner of seeming to wish to reconcile the great revolutionaries Trotsky and Nin, over and above their shared murder by the same Stalinist police, as well as his open sympathy for Paul Lévi in the German revolution, Pierre Broué ranked himself, in relation to the orthodox activists that the OCI and the AJS were starting to mass produce and in relation to their cousins in the Ligue, enthusiasts for guerrilla struggles in the Sierras, or by default in the salons and the Latin Quarter, as an arrant "rightist" — with them as "Zinovievists"? But all this, in 1975 and for some length of time thereafter, was to be reserved to the initiates, and Pierre Broué had no intention of widening this circle.

In *La Revolution Espagnole*, and here too mainly for the initiates — to the extent that one must admit that taking the trouble to read everything in a book is something for an initiate to do — Pierre Broué settles his accounts with the accusation of neglecting the "underlying forces" in history. Marxist history is *factual* for it revolves around class issues whose resolution depends on the attitudes and choices made by *responsible* human beings. He added the following note to a passage by Trotsky. It worth quoting as Pierre Broué wrote little explicitly on his conception of the historian's work. Yet here was truly his subject, though we will observe that this work is wholly envisaged as needing to be that of a revolutionary militant:

> we can, moreover, note the current vogue in intellectual milieux for that interpretation of history, presented as "Marxist" which looks exclusively in the infrastructure — relations of production, relations between classes etc. — for *a posteriori* explanations of the history of class struggles and revolutions. Historians who seek explanations at the level of the policies carried out by human beings, parties and organisations stand accused of carrying out "factual" history and of neglecting the "true" explanations, which would involve looking, according to these critiques, solely at the level of "deep structures". If such an interpretation were correct this

would only signify that the defeat of the socialist revolution in all the countries where it has been defeated since October 1917 was engraved in the "reality" of social relations. It would be honest for the defenders of this sort of interpretation of Marxism to present themselves not as Marxists or "marxisants" but as the resolute conservatives that they really are, seeking to show that the revolution had only ever been defeated because it was not possible and that all the rest — in particular the revolutionary organisation — is but gesture and chit-chat.

This note was a comment on the following passage of Léon Trotsky's article *Class, Party and Leadership* which takes up, so to speak, a defence of the revolutionary capacities of the masses against the leaderships:

> The historical falsification consists in this, that the responsibility for the defeat of the Spanish masses is unloaded on the working masses and not those parties that paralysed or simply crushed the revolutionary movement of the masses. The attorneys of the POUM simply deny the responsibility of the leaders, in order thus to escape shouldering their own responsibility. This impotent philosophy, which seeks to reconcile defeats as a necessary link in the chain of cosmic developments, is completely incapable of posing and refuses to pose the question of such concrete factors as programmes, parties and personalities that were the organisers of defeat. This philosophy of fatalism and prostration is diametrically opposed to Marxism as the theory of revolutionary action.

Apogee and Turning-Point

The years 1968-1975 were years of great activity, in fact of hyperactivity, for Pierre Broué. He completed and defended his thesis and finished the publication by Éditions de Minuit of his series of great tomes, he had a family and, above all, he was building the OCI in Grenoble and the region around it.

Let us note that Michel Broué independently joined the OCI in 1970 after being "trained" in the GER (Revolutionary Study Groups) by Lionel Jospin who had been attached to Pierre Broué's cell some years earlier and who was at the time a militant with a special status (not intervening publicly) in Stéphane Just's cell. In particular Michel Broué organised the Committee of Mathematicians at the end of the 1970s and the beginning of the 1980s. This had obtained the liberation from the Stalinist bureaucracy of the Ukrainian Leonid Pliouchtch (on this see: Laurent Schwartz, *Un mathématicien aux prises avec le siècle*, Odile Jacob, 1997).

* * *

The list of militants recruited at this time as a result, directly or indirectly, of the effervescence coming out of Political Sciences (the Grenoble IEP) in the climate of the years 1968 and 1970 is a significant one. Most, but not all, were students: René Revol, Martine Verlhac, Jean-Paul Joubert, the Québécois Roch Denis, the Venezuelan Armando Gaviria, André Tiran, Jean-Pierre Doujon, Marceau Rochette, Michel Barbe, Dan Moutot, Danielle Moutot, Fabien Gallet, Gérard Roche, Jean-Jacques Ayme, Antoine Thivel, Paule Gauthier, Bruno Flasher,. This list is eclectic in terms of their evolutions and is incomplete.

One of them, Jean-Pierre Juy, has given this testimony on the atmosphere of Pierre Broué's lectures in this posthumous tribute:

> An amazing teacher. He did not turn up to read us what he had written earlier. He took his place before us for a moment of intellectual creation. For me, Broué's lectures were living thought in action. Through all that he explained there was a person engaged with what he expressed in his strong, deep voice. That deep voice, at times tinged with the accent of his native Ardèche, resonated like no other. He would half-pause for an instant, look questioningly at his audience and then carry on. For me the best lectures were those on the Russian Revolution. There, his evocative powers were literally captivating: he recounted the seizure of the Winter Palace as if he had taken part in it. We had before our eyes not only Broué but also Eisenstein's images and Mayakovsky's inspiration! It was as if the revolution shook the lecture theatre which, through this, became the theatre of history!

These words of Jean-Pierre Juy well recall the enthusiasm aroused by Broué's lectures: they were truly lectures, without inverted commas, magisterial lectures in the highest sense of that term. His voice counted for a lot, a voice spontaneously or deliberately (undoubtedly both) honed over decades, including in his lycée teaching, though at the lycée the mood of the students and the constraints of the syllabus gave less freedom that that which Pierre Broué was to enjoy hereafter. Jean-Pierre Juy goes on:

> The students came as much to listen to him as to learn. Seated behind the wide desk that filled the entire platform, he spread out before him a few sheets of folded paper and a watch with a gilt metallic strap. These were his navigation instruments. On these half-sheets of paper he had written out his line of argument in close writing, it was the route map for rolling out his thinking. He glanced at it from time to time, no doubt to maintain the course of his speech, but it was his brain that created the words at any given instant. (He was) like certain great conductors who can lead the orchestra without reading the score. He went on for two hours, the lecture theatre full, hanging on his every word, with no mike, and, at the break, groups of students congregated around him
>
> Like all young people we were insatiable, we always wanted to know more. So, with the most politically advanced students, he set up the Grenoble Marxist Study Circle. We decided together what questions to

debate, we prepared talks. The meetings took place in the back room of a café, all the people concerned with the subject of the day were invited. Who came? The majority were students but there were also young workers. It was Wednesday evening, the room was quickly packed out. The discussion there was completely free and fraternal.

Naturally, however much time, shorter or longer, was spent in a "study circle", and even though Jean-Pierre Juy doesn't say so directly, it was the OCI, the Internationalist Communist Organisation, which was being built this way, it was to this that the students were recruited, integrated into cells, attending more and more meetings, distributing leaflets for the liberation of this or that Bolivian or Polish militant or just selling *Informations Ouvrières*, with a short speech, every day, be it at the University canteen, at factory gates or at markets.

This time of construction, which was the time of May 68, was, there is no doubt, an exhilarating time. May 68 in Grenoble was its summit. [There were] daily meetings of the SNESup, whose local leadership had just been taken away from the Stalinists and mass demonstrations of students and youth at which Pierre Broué spoke regularly. It is probable that the intervention of Trotskyist militants and the study circle around them had, at that time, a greater local influence than at national level: indeed it was after De Gaulle's radio intervention of 30 May, which, across the country, marked the beginning of the great retreat, of the counter-attack by the regime and of the break-up of the general strike that a central and united demonstration with 30,000 participating was again called in Grenoble by the CGT departmental union, the SNESup and the UNEF. The police went crazy over rumours — totally fantasist ones — of an anticipated appearance of Cohn-Bendit at this demonstration....

However, on the national level the CGT had appealed for its supporters not to support the demonstration called for 1 June by the UNEF. The capacity to pull the UD CGT into such as demonstration was to have no follow-up. Nationally the OCI had been very shaken-up by the general strike, even though the wave of factory occupations had been set off by their militants, starting 14 May with the FO section in the Sud-Aviation factory at Nantes. On the one hand the absence of slogans at the level of taking power — such as demanding a PCF/PS government — and the subsequent absence of self-criticism and on the other hand the decision to not participate in the "night of the barricades" in the Latin Quarter as well as the police repression, had placed the organisation on a paradoxical defensive vis-à-vis the "leftist" wave for the rest of 1968 and the years that followed.

* * * * *

At what rate did this atmosphere of relative downturn, of a citadel under siege, gain ground in the "Grenoble federation" of the OCI? Certainly not straight away. The exhilaration could still be fully sensed, although it is on a tragic subject, in the pamphlet *Le Printemps des peoples commence à Prague* written by Pierre

Broué with a lyrical pen and published by the organisation under his own name. With his help, a refugee Czech comrade, Karel Kostal, settled in Grenoble.

As a political educator Pierre Broué at the same time appealed to the intelligence of his audience and played on seduction and fascination. At the end of one political meeting he announced to the young people present that now we would "play a Stalinist meeting": in this, falsely impromptu, happening he played the role of Jacques Duclos and those present had to try to throw him by taking on this or that role. His imitation was gripping, with the cheeky humour and the treachery of the old "GPUist"; Pierre Broué dominated all his theatrical interlocutors except, partially, Bob Lacondemine, teacher and former militant, who took the role of a "progressive Christian" who had come to seize the hand held out by the "stal". All this was full of humour and intelligence and showed to the young militants to what point the Prof was capable of being a Stalinist if he decided to act as one…

* * * * *

But the group of young people insatiable for "free and fraternal" discussion carried on its shoulders the consciousness of being responsible for the reconstruction of the 4th. International and thus of the future of humanity and, for that, in the immediate period, to battle against participation in the management committees of the university (which, incidentally, Pierre Broué practiced in his SNESup capacity) by preserving the union, UNEF, as a tool, against leftists and Stalinists. Soon a coalition of these two emerged against the "AJS-SS", "AJS-iron bars" and utilising to the maximum the confused order issued by Stéphane Just on the evening of the night of the barricades in Paris in May: to march away as a procession because a mass meeting had been planned and it could not be cancelled as this would "liquidate" the building of the party, thus to march away leaving thousands of young people fighting the police and the state.

It so happens that this fight was at its most bitter in Grenoble. A loose grouping calling itself anarchist specialised in the "anti-AJS struggle". At the end of 1969/beginning of 1970 the Grenoble university campus became infected by a group specialising in anti-Trotskyist struggle. This was held together, from a base in the Berlioz university residence, by a person known as "Max" who came in some sense or other out of the Mao-spontaneous group "Revolution" and who was manipulated by the police. It escalated from the spectacular — a young woman exposed her buttocks on which she had had tattooed "AJS-SS" — to the violent: the militant André Tatin was hit and hospitalised. The OCI and the AJS locally and nationally, Pierre Broué, Stéphane Just, Pierre Lambert, and the growing team of stewards led by Lionel Malapa, stood up in total solidarity to "Max's gang" and returned blow for blow, and sometimes more. The OCI, the AJS and the UNEF (Unité Syndicale) asserted their right to exist. It had to be done, but this came at the price of developing an esprit de corps at the highest level of sectarianism and authoritarianism.

In Pierre Broué's view the Grenoble OCI, and himself personally, became, at this time, entitled to a sort of special treatment, which it might not be going to far to think had been plotted in the top levels of the state apparatus, and which served the function, objectively at least, of aligning the Grenoble OCI with the relatively sectarian style and form of the organisation at the national level.

Gestures, habits, life-styles became "identikit", assuming that they were not so to some extent already. And, because one was from the OCI, in short from the Bolshevik Party, bearer of an "historical continuity", from the "last generation of October" — understood as those who would *make* October in France and in Europe, who would *take power* — so one was not a leftist, sprouting after the last rains, or a studentish 68er like the "Pabloites" of the LCR. One cultivated the appropriate, nay distinguished, look; one was scholarly but virile, one was not a feminist pain in the neck...(to be accurate: the macho aspect of militant student culture in this period, sometimes accentuated in the AJS-OCI to the point of homophobia, had without doubt appeared less in Grenoble before 1975 due, according to a comrade who knew this period, to the presence of a number of female militants with leadership positions, but the militant "style" was globally the same for the rest).

But we must not therefore imagine that this "culture" did not exist in the time of the OCI Isère Federation and its student section led by Pierre Broué; that these were at that time just splendid intellectuals, valiant students and remarkable historians who were suddenly followed, after Pierre Broué, by the gang who were "identikit", super-activist, did little academic work, at once a bit lumpen and a bit bureaucratic on the edges. This was how they appeared (to others!), when, with 80 militants on the campus already, I was one of them myself.

On the international level it was during these years that the OCI broke with Healy's Socialist Labour League (SLL) in Britain and at the same time found itself new allies, incidentally infinitely less respectable, the Bolivians of Guillermo Lora's POR (Workers' Revolutionary Party) who are the heart and soul of the working-class movement, of miners' unionism, in their country.

Until General Banzer's putsch in August 1971, Bolivia had been going through a revolutionary upsurge. The POR had played a central role in this. They had pulled the Bolivian CP and national union, the COB, into forming a unified command and then a "People's Assembly", hailed by the OCI, but also by many workers in Latin America, as *"the first Latin American Soviet"*, but had judged it premature to call for a workers' government, only for the coup d'état to intervene. For this they were accused of "Menshevism" by other currents, with the exception of the OCI.

Bolivia had also been the key country for the other big branch of Trotskyism, the Unified Secretariat of which the Ligue Communiste then constituted the French section. Here the Bolivian myth was centred around the figure of Che and the "Lora" POR, linked to the OCI, was held up to public obloquy for having stayed resolutely impervious to the seductions of guerrilla struggle.

In fact, it was once, two years later, the Chilean working-class and the Chilean people had been crushed that, as a result, the partial defeat of the Bolivian revolution became definitive.

Balàzs Nagy-Varga was hostile to the formation, based on the OCI and the POR, of the new Organising Committee for the Reconstruction of the 4th. International (CORQI). In reality, in the new situation arising from 1968, what would have been needed was an open, in depth, debate, taking into account the evolution of all the currents of Trotskyist origin, about the appropriate organisational forms for Trotskyists. The new perspectives were positive, indeed exhilarating; so they should be grasped — and this should not be the dead grasping the living.

This debate was not to take place. Indeed Nagy had not sought it, but, suspected by Lambert and Just of "factional activity" behind their back — indeed of maintaining contacts with Healy — he, and his supporters, were expelled in an extremely violent manner (physical violence took place, genuine and serious beatings-up), all in the name of Stéphane Just's alleged discovery, that Nagy-Varga was *"a KGB and CIA double agent"*. The damning proof of this is supposed to be found in Just's pamphlet *L'itinéraire d'un provacateur*. Anyone of sense who reads the pamphlet will search in vain for the *proof*, in any rational sense of the word, of the accusation set out in it. But the militants were enjoined to acquiesce: "yes, Nagy is a provocateur" — those who did not explicitly acknowledge this could therefore well be ones themselves...

To demand explicit acceptance of the absurd is a procedure characteristic of bureaucracies based on belief. *I believe because it is absurd* said St. Augustine. To accept that something has been demonstrated when, quite explicitly, it has not been is a test of orthodoxy of the type demanded by the Popes of the 17th. Century; that is to say, for example, that the Jansenists had formulated this or that thesis when it was well-known that this was not in the writings in question, but to say it all the same because the leaders demanded it and because what mattered was unconditional allegiance to the absolute collective — to the Party of which these leaders are supposed, by definition, to be the incarnation.

For the "rank-and-file militants" in 1973 Pierre Broué was one of those leaders who demanded and obtained such things. In reality he was mortified. He said in private and continued to repeat that it was crazy rubbish. Or he implied this to a young militant who didn't know what to think, with a mysterious or menacing air and no further word. Moreover, in this matter, Pierre Broué wanted, later on and perhaps at the time, to be basically as distant from Nagy as from Lambert between whom there had developed, at least since the 1966 London "world conference", a battle of leaders, a sort of game of liar poker or of billiards off many cushions, where the third actor was Gerry Healy.

But, however this may be, he ratified the position, he advised obedience even though he didn't actually force people in his own cell to swear to a lie and he broke with the "Varguistes". At the end of a general meeting in Grenoble on the "affair" one militant asked Pierre Broué what one should do if one met "Varguistes" in the street and he replied that this had happened to him recently and they had said hello to each other but that *"now that I know what I know I would spit in their faces"*. The comrade who told me this said that it seemed to him that Lambert was in the room to oversee what he said. If old Reynier had been there he would have, this time, really given Pierre Broué a lesson. A well-deserved one.

* * * * *

I must here return for a moment to the article by Francesco Giliani and Paolo Brini. Pierre Broué had indeed clearly claimed to them that in 1971, at the time of the foundation of the new Socialist Party at Epinay, he had fought for entrism with flags unfurled into this party, which would have avoided a drift like that of Lionel Jospin whose entrism had nothing at all unfurled, which made him into that which everyone knows. They therefore took up this episode in the article and made of it, as well one would, a step in the long march of Pierre Broué away from Lambert and towards Ted Grant.

Assuming that a debate like this took place, this version is, sadly, highly questionable. Charles Berg, then leader of the AJS, the youth organisation parallel to the OCI has also claimed to have, at the time, supported this position — one which indeed merited real examination. Pierre Broué professed a certain degree of hostility in his regard. It is remarkable that both of them should have claimed to argue for this same political position.

At the time of the Epinay Congress it seems that the dominant debate in Lambert's eyes was rather about whether the new PS was still a "bourgeois workers' party" (organising the working-class and coming out of its struggles, even though led by an apparatus tied to the bourgeoisie) or whether, from the fact of it being taken over by the bourgeois adventurer Mitterand it was a replay, worsened and magnified, of the takeover of the PSU at its birth by Mendès-France in 1960, that is to say a party analogous to the American Democratic Party or, as Alexandre Hébert thought, a party contaminated by Christian Democracy. There wasn't really any debate, but if the above was the dilemma for the leadership of the OCI the eventuality of entrism by the AJS youth thus had few chances of being seriously considered. As to the clandestine entrism of Jospin and a few others it was the subject of no discussion at all as it was in a reserved area — "defence secrets" so to speak…

* * *

In the 1960's Stéphane Just had developed his characteristic talent as a self-taught theoretician and pamphleteer. He was fond of fierce attacks, in a rather heavy manner, on Ernest Mandel who on the one hand wrote under his own name in journals of the left intelligentsia and on the other, as a militant who claimed to be a Trotskyist, used his pseudonym Germain, and, according to Just, didn't necessarily say the same thing, or not always in the same way, in each case: Just glossed him as "Janus-Germain-Mandel".

This figure of Janus comes to mind when we follow Pierre Broué's route through this period and it was in the minds of militants, historians and many students who knew or appreciated his works and at the same time observed the organisation in which he was, let us remember, not a marginal figure but the figure best known to the "great public" — more so than Lambert — even though he wasn't "the" leader and doubtless no longer even "a" leader. Janus-Broué-Scali?

We have reached 1975, Broué's last tome from Minuit has just appeared.

"The Historian of Trotsky"

Pierre Broué, rank and file militant? He claimed to have special relationships with the leadership, with Lambert himself and to take on confidential missions. He was soon to be the "Contact Man", or at least he would have liked to be recognised as such, vis-à-vis the Unified Secretariat and the American SWP (Socialist Workers' Party), towards which the OCI and the CORQI had turned after the break with Healy and the "Varga affair" — Pierre Broué had hosted Ligue militants after its dissolution. He was the educator of the young militants that the OCI were in the course of recruiting…inside the LCR (therefore as "moles") around Christian Nemo (Leucate). He also implied that, with Lambert, he followed through the "East" work — but in fact a large part of this work was followed up in an entirely independent way by his son Michel. And, seen from Paris, Pierre Broué had not, already for some years, been considered as an important person in the organisation and was beginning to be perceived by the young militants as an out of touch intellectual.

At the formal level he had not been on the Political Bureau since 1973 and what is more not on the Central Committee since 1975. From the same date he was no longer responsible for the Isère Federation, nor for his main "pillar" the "student sector". The latter was led by Jean-Paul Joubert who successively appeared as the "anti-Broué and then, when the national leadership took away all his local leadership roles from him, became closer to him (the more so as they became colleagues at the IEP). At the beginning of the 1980s the student sector with Yacime Halmechat as leader and the General Association of Students (UNEF Unité Syndicale then UNEF-ID) led by Denis Bailly, were carefully kept apart from Pierre Broué and Jean-Paul Joubert. Pierre Broué was later to renew his contact with students through Damien Durand, then through the author of these lines and later still through two new militants, Patrick Enreille and Alain Dontaine.

*   *   *   *   *

Ever since the "Varga affair" he had considered that the problem of his organisation was that it had endowed itself with an apparatus of bureaucratised intermediate cadres — but he didn't say "bureaucratised", he said "Zinovievist", this was less risky but also gave more to reflect on. He reflected on the question of *methods*, as he was not in disagreement with the general political line developed in *Informations Ouvrières*: achieving PS-PCF unity to kick out Giscard, direct organisation of youth and workers around this objective and the developments of strikes and class-struggles in general. But this general line was distorted in its application: phoney committees were created, the group passed from one petition to another without any sense of follow-up, militants ran from one place to another, the militants got slagged off, militants were incapable of discussion with militants of other tendencies, any old ten-franc piece from a guy who had left his address at a market sale counted as a militant's "phalanx" (a sub-payment)…

Incidentally, the theme of "the OCI's methods" was at the heart of critiques and sometimes ukases hurled against this organisation by the rest of the far left, notably by the LCR. Seen from the outside, Pierre Broué was henceforth to be "the historian", less simplistic and less brutal than the impolite organisation to which he belonged and whose methods he concealed, even though he didn't use them himself. The great storyteller had learned how to manipulate an eloquent silence, the art of implication…of whatever people were willing to have implied.

"People often say to me that I am an honest man in an organisation of crooks. I reply that they are undoubtedly not as crooked, and I am undoubtedly not as honest as they imagine". At this he would let out a big laugh; this time the laugh served to avoid explanation, the laugh was no longer an open one.

* * * * *

Debates on the future of the organisation and thus on revolutionary perspectives never went beyond the leading circles and always took the form of "factional" struggles that were resolved by expulsions and anathemas. In retrospect, it is not difficult to understand how in the second half of the 1970s the question of the building of the OCI could present itself from different angles, more or less complementary with each other but which could well become contradictory with each other.

There was the possibility of building directly on a (relatively) "mass" scale; this was the official line for "an OCI of 10,000 militants" — it had reached 6,000 soon after this, the biggest force calling itself far-left in France, and that by a long way. Including the turnover at least ten times more had passed through it.

There was its identification with a union sector, essentially in FO where the former FO lefts had been absorbed or liquidated to the benefit of the tendency embodied by Pierre Lambert and Alexandre Hébert, the customary left cover for André Bergeron.

There was the battle for "Trotskyist unity", looking to an eventual unification with the Ligue (indeed, in theory, with LO) in a party which would inevitably be made up different tendencies and factions, this would assume a global debate on the history of the IVth. International, that debate which had in reality burst out earlier, after the failure of the Bolivian revolution and for which the violence of the "Varga affair" had been a substitute.

What is more there was the unsaid (to militants), that is to say Jospin and his comrades in the PS — where it was easy to "rise" — "as a faction". Mitterand, incidentally, was well aware of this game and wasn't worried by it in the least.

From 1976, under the pressure of the Portuguese revolution and of the official contacts opened up in 1975 between the OCI and the American SWP, an official discussion had begun between the Unified Secretariat and the CORQI, the latter had been demanding this since 1973. Neither of the leading groups really wanted unification which would have assumed that all the cards would be reshuffled and all the "occupied spaces" called into question. Nonetheless there really and truly was an "objective" pressure for such a discussion.

Undoubtedly Pierre Broué had sincerely hoped this discussion would let in some fresh air. In retrospect — for I am rather sceptical as to whether he thought this so clearly at the time — he told me that in 1962 the OCI ought to have taken part in the re-unification through which Mandel and the SWP had formed the Unified Secretariat, although they should have set out political reservations (this was roughly what Nahual Moreno's Latin American current did when it entered the SU in 1964). To the extent that this or that leader of the OCI identified himself with a particular model of [party] construction his was thus more that of "Trotskyist unity" and stood opposed to that of Stéphane Just and Charles Berg, the adulators of the "party of 10,000", even, indeed, for the latter of the "third workers' party" on top of the PS and the PCF.

His fame as an historian allowed Pierre Broué to organise debates with people from the SU, who were by no means a homogeneous bloc. It was at this time that he gained the respect of and influence over a young leader of the rather turbulent LCR, Gérard Filoche, who then wrote a remarkable book on the revolution in Portugal *Printemps Portugais* which was to be published by editions Acteon in 1984. This fine book owes much, as one can feel in reading it, to Pierre Broué's great narratives of revolutions in the Minuit editions. It could be added to the series; this is one of the greatest compliments one could pay to its author.

* * * * *

But the fact is that there are two sides to this story. Two commissions of enquiry were to mark the Trotskyist landscape in 1976-1977.

One had been demanded by the supporters of Nagy-Varga, although he himself had refused to participate (and had set up his own made up entirely of his own current). Leaving aside the divers twists and turns in the relations between the currents who participated, some less, some more, in this commission (the Ligue, LO, the American SWP, the Spartacist tendency and Alan Thornett's British SWL — a group of worker trades unionists expelled from the Healy group), what obviously emerged from its investigations was that nothing in the accusations formulated against Varga could be proved. Pierre Broué and Jean-Jacques Marie, who had known Varga before he joined the OCI, refused to respond to the commission, although it had nevertheless heard Pierre Lambert, Claude Chissery and Gérard Bloch. This refusal was obviously under orders.

The other commission aimed to defend the honour of two historic leaders of American Trotskyism, Jo Hansen, Trotsky's former bodyguard, and George Novack, who had been accused by Gerry Healy's current and its American group (David North) of having been CIA and GPU (KGB) agents. This bout of paranoia towards another organisation followed on, in the case of the Healyite current, from the crisis in its American organisation where suspicions of CIA infiltration (incidentally quite possible) had appeared and had provoked the expulsion of two leaders, Tim Wolforth and Nancy Fields. The crisis of internal terror, here too, allowed a ban on all debate about the future.

A large number of revolutionary militants from all countries signed the "verdict" defending Hansen, Novack and the SWP against the calumnies. For France, in addition to Margarerite Bonnet and Daniel Guérin, Pierre Frank, Alain Krivine Pierre Rousset and Gérard Vergeat were the signatories for the LCR, Arlette Laguiller and Michel Rodinson for LO, and for the OCI: Pierre Lambert and Pierre Broué.

To put the moral authority of the OCI behind such an affair thus required two signatures in all and for all, and it had to be these two: Lambert and Broué. But the difference in attitude towards these two commissions of enquiry also shows that, to paraphrase Orwell, for these are Orwellian phenomena which we see here, "though all calumnies are equal, some are more equal than others"....

* * * * *

The fortieth anniversary of the proclamation of the 4th. International in 1978 and the study days to which it was to give rise, together with the approach of the opening of the closed section of the Leon Trotsky Archives deposited in the Houghton Library at Harvard, due to the end of the forty year's delay imposed to protect militants, friends and relatives notably in the Soviet Union, mark out this period linked to the debate between the Unified Secretariat and CORQI.

Pierre Broué now really got to know the "old guard" of the American SWP after having, along with George Breitman, defended Jo Hanson, who died in 1978, against calumnies. George Breitman was Trotsky's publisher at Pathfinder Press, the expert on the American workers' movement, the man who had won Malcolm X to Trotskyism just before his assassination by the FBI : he fought politically from the wheelchair to which he was confined by a painful illness. With men like these Pierre Broué rediscovered militants who were his elders towards whom emerged the admiration that he had had in the past for Reynier and, differently for Claude Bernard who had remained a turbulent old mate but invisible to rank-and-file militants, although organiser of the sector of the OCI working with artists and actors, invisible perhaps to Pierre Lambert too, but now no longer.

The story of Pierre Broué's relations with the men coming from the SWP thus begins at the same time as the project of publishing in French the complete works of Trotsky and of creating for that purpose a cadre that would be "ecumenical" in relation to diverse organisations but would at the same time be an cadre of recognised academics and would be controlled by Pierre Broué who would, in any case, be the indispensable worker: this would be the Leon Trotsky Institute.

The Leon Trotsky Institute was founded in 1977, its first president was Marguerite Bonnet and had associated with it academics such as Michel Dreyfus (until 1985) or Jean Risacher and Broué's OCI militant colleague at the IEP, Jean-Paul Joubert. It had the support of the OCI but also of the LCR (a point that Jean-Jacques Marie "forgot" in the non-obituary signed in his name) notably in the form of François Godchau. It set itself the aim of publishing the works of Leon Trotsky and the publication of journals. Pierre Broué had established contact with Sieva Volkoff, Trotsky's grandson. The first volume of the *Works* came out in 1978 and the first *Cahier Leon Trotsky* the following year. The task was to recapture, in French and by introducing, after 1980, the supplementary material from that part of the archives up till then closed, the publishing work carried out by George Breitman and supported in the US by the SWP. This signified a double, wholly justified, choice in the manner of starting the publication of the whole of Trotsky's works: firstly the choice of making known the correspondence and the vast quantity of articles of short or medium length, immensely rich material, full of life, of details, of lessons, which was the least known type of Trotsky's writings; then the choice, by beginning with the year 1933 which is that of the victory of Hitler and consequently, for Trotsky, of the decision to fight for a 4th. International, to focus on questions relating to the 4th. International. This is confirmed, incidentally, by the first number of the *Cahiers* which published the minutes of the 1938 founding conference, held discreetly at the home of Alfred and Marguerite Rosmer.

This editorial orientation conceived around the 4th. International, while judicious in itself, was obviously not unrelated to the immediate Trotskyist context of the end of the 1970s, that of a possible re-unification of the SU and the CORQI or at least of a regroupment that would favour the discussion of issues hidden away for decades — the evolution of capitalism, Stalinism the political experiences and the organisational forms of Trotskyists themselves...

Pierre Broué thus began, so to speak, the second great phase of his work as a militant/historian. His greater free time since 1975 allowed him more than before to travel enormously to conferences and seminars. After the great series of tomes from Minuit, publishing Trotsky together with his academic work made him genuinely the "historian of Trotsky" to which his name will stay attached.

It was in this capacity that he was invited to appear on the TV programme *Les dossiers de l'écran* alongside Krivine, Ellenstein and Sanguinetti where, no doubt feeling cornered or tired, perhaps, too, preoccupied with not getting into any polemics while his publication project was just getting started, he was to intervene above all to state that *"Trotsky had the head of a lion"* and was thus far greater than the actor who portrayed him in the sorry film that went out that evening! The innocent public saw in him a decent bloke with a passion for his hero. For its part the Political Bureau of the OCI turned out a humiliating note on the political capitulation in front of the cameras of the historian.

* * * * *

This misadventure, in itself of no great significance, signalled the end of the political hopes of the second half of the 1970s. There would be neither a reunification of the Trotskyist movement nor a sufficiently profound international debate nor an evolution in the running of the OCI. Worse still, the Trotskyist movement was, with the transformation of the SWP into a Castroist and anti-Trotskyist group, to experience one of the tragedies in its history. Despite all this the opening of the closed section of the Trotsky archives was to nourish the work of Pierre Broué as the historian of Trotsky though it did not therefore continue under the political circumstances in relation to which it had been started.

* * * * *

On the international level the turning took place in 1979. By way of a prologue, the OCI expelled the Bolivian POR and the Argentinian group Politica Obrera. Stéphane Just made himself the prosecutor of these Latin American militants who, placed in the most difficult of conditions, found themselves accused of having, in Argentina and Chile, participated in union structures controlled by the state (when one has no choice, one does what?). This, therefore, avoided a debate in depth around the — quite normal — differences that were emerging notably around the theme of the Constituent Assembly slogan and, rightly, around the way to reconstruct the 4th. International and to discuss with the SU.

But these discussions were to stop short in the second half of the year. There was a revolution in Nicaragua; Nahual Moreno's current had organised a Simon Bolivar Brigade which had intervened to expropriate bosses on plantations on the East side of the country, but the new Sandinista government, with the help of Cuban forces had intervened and arrested these militants, some of whom were mistreated.

As OCI militants we had a tendency to see here the history of the Spanish Revolution repeating itself, with our Trotskyist comrades, though they came from an exotic current of which we knew little, playing the role of revolutionaries repressed by the "republicans" just as in Broué and Téminé's book.

Conversely, a sector of the Unified Secretariat considered that Nicaragua was a second Cuba and the Simon Bolivar Brigade operation was a provocative diversion which the Sandinistas had been right to repress. And this was not any old sector; not the former guerrillistas of the Latin Quarter but the supposed orthodox Trotskyists of the American SWP.

The Morenoist current (the "Bolshevik Faction") and the Trotskyist-Leninist Tendency (TLT, led in France by OCI moles), under the impetus of Moreno, then decided to split from the SU whose leadership could not make up its mind to condemn clearly the SWP's attitude of support for anti-Trotskyist repression in Nicaragua. And very quickly three movements, CORQI, the Bolshevik Faction and the TLT declared a "Joint Committee for the Reorganisation/Reconstruction of the 4th. International".

For Pierre Broué this amounted to giving up the hunt to chase shadows. Indeed one and a half years were to suffice for the official idyll of Lambert and Moreno, the two moustaches, to turn into a split and, as Claude Nougaro was to say "each went back to his own car": at the end of 1981 Moreno accused the OCI of opportunism towards the Mitterand-Mauroy government which had just been formed in France following the 10 May 1981 [election] victory, the dance was over.

* * *

Pierre Broué claimed to have been informed and consulted by Lambert and Just at each stage of the process. Stéphane Just had proudly shown him the many amendments with which he had repackaged the proposals for theses submitted by Moreno, Pierre Broué had grumbled. Nahuel Moreno — a great personality — had insisted, during his French tour, on a trip to Grenoble and in front of a packed hall had paid homage to the "great historian" who was sitting in the body of the hall rather than on the platform. Pierre Broué telephoned Ernest Mandel: he claimed to have declared to him "Basically this suits you well, the Moreno business, we are no longer your interlocutors?", which Mandel had not contradicted. At the root of his thinking was the view that this suited Lambert just as much. I think that he had a small "soft spot" in the joint committee regroupment for the Central American groups which had joined the TLT, whose figurehead was a militant whose history placed him in a difficult position: Fausto Amador, former Sandinista leader had renounced the Sandinista movement under torture then, once free again, had become a Trotskyist. But it was precisely these groups in Nicaragua, Honduras and Panama that had been excluded from the joint committee, as a paragraph in *Correspondence Internationale*, the organ of said committee announced without further explanation. The joint committee was Lambert and Moreno, the TLT being merely the French section, which in the end purely and simply joined the OCI (from which came the provisional name, so to speak, when it then became the "Unified OCI"). There was no question that any other components than those who had signed the central pact existed in any autonomous way, right up to the denunciation of that pact. Adolfo Gilly, the historian of the Mexican Revolution and more of a "Pabloite" said to Pierre Broué "You should say to Lambert, from me, that if he wants to ally himself with Moreno, he'll need to do some politicking but he'll also need to always keep his hand on his wallet". He passed on the good advice. When it came to the break-up Lambert phoned Pierre Broué "And you should say to your mate Gilly that I always kept my hand on my wallet!". No-one would have doubted this.

I've just given here a version of these events which is not an analysis of them but which attempts to restore Pierre Broué's view of them, for this is an issue which we discussed in considerable depth.

We should add some further points, some other clarifications. Seen from the "other side", from the LCR, according to the accounts of militants, all the issues concerning the evolution of the American SWP's evolution towards Castroism after its "turn to the workers" (advocated at the time in the LCR) with its positions on Nicaragua, but equally on Iran, Afghanistan and Poland, had generally escaped the attention of rank-and-file militants. Thus Mandel along with Charles Michaloux and Charles-André Udry seem probably to have sincerely wanted the debate and the reunification and considered this the route to a "party of 10,000 members" in France; but Daniel Bensaid and the majority of the French leadership who came out of the JCR didn't want it, and here there was a real contradiction. This story, rich with virtualities and missed appointments, thus remains largely to be told.

One of these virtualities was that of a regroupment of currents which had drawn the lessons from each other, militants who had come back from leftism and were vaccinated or in the course of being vaccinated against the methods of apparatuses and authoritarianism of infallible mini-leaders. It would have been nice to believe after the event that such regroupments were going on, a ferment of the reunification of world Trotskyism around its principles and its programme and with a democratic debate as we stood on the thresholds of new revolutions in Poland, Nicaragua and Iran and with the birth of the Workers' Party in Brazil. And now come Francesco Giliani and Paolo Brini, in the articles cited earlier with what they think will come as a revelation: Pierre Broué had formed a "secret tendency" with Raoul (Claude Bernard) against the leadership of the OCI. A book published in Italy with a colleague, a professor of history (and not a member of the OCI), Hubert Desvages, was supposed to provide the secret funds for the secret tendency.

There is a certain unintended cruelty in such a "revelation". As, on the one hand neither Pierre Broué's private remarks nor Claude Bernard's boasts were unknown. On the other hand can a secret tendency, so secret that it is only spoken of after the death of its two members, be seen as a great political success? "To pose the question is to answer it", as Lambert would have said.

In the absence of who knows what secret tendency, whose possible existence amounts in reality to its non-existence as a political current carrying on a real struggle, there were in the late 1970s one or more subjective "sympathies" inspired, without he himself having sought them, by Pierre Broué, at once from his books and from the impression [that he carried on] a broader and more intelligent political practice than the major part of the OCI

This started from Grenoble militants, but also spread among the Quebec group, largely built or intellectually influenced by Pierre Broué, who himself had links with Quebec, and undoubtedly among Italian militants where the organiser of the Italian cell of the OCI, Franco Grisolia, who had distanced himself from the OCI at the time of the Varga affair but had been, through various successive regroupments, the originator of a significant Trotskyist current. And a worker trades unionist militant like the English Alan Thornett, kicked out by Healy in 1975, the originator of a small organisation that had participated as an observer in the meetings of the Lambert-Moreno committee and was later to join the SU, would undoubtedly have been close to these "sympathies". But in fact neither Pierre Broué nor Claude Bernard had organised anything which, from near or from far, looked like an international current and if such an "axis" had existed anywhere it was above all in the suspicions nursed by Lambert and Just.

The sequel to this story, rather, shows clearly that this theme, of a "secret tendency" organised against Lambert, in the statements that Pierre Broué may have made to his two Italian listeners is mere bragging which veils his attachment to regrets for battles not fought and, perhaps, something worse still. And whether this was real or imaginary changes nothing about the matter, for if it was real this is even worse for it means this: "in secret" we are valorous battlers for democracy in the organisation; in practice we cover up we apply the policies and we may well add to them. What we have here are habits of mind which are a feature of bureaucracies and their members.

*   *   *   *   *

At the national level in the OCI itself 1979 was to be the year of the "Berg affair". Charles Berg was, for Pierre Broué, the prototype of the young "look at me" leader, authoritarian and "Zinovievist". Bit by bit a personal antagonism had developed between them. At the 22nd. Congress of the OCI a problem that had arisen in the accounting of the "phalanges" brought to light the gap between fiction and reality, between the theoretical number of militants and the real number of comrades effectively operating in the cells of the organisation. The congress very quickly unearthed a guilty party, which was very handy because he denounced himself as corrupt, for having kept a part of the funds collected in his possession. This was Charles Berg. Stéphane Just conducted the trial with as much speed as that with which he had, politically, pushed the "party of 10,000" line, along with Charles Berg, on the Political Bureau.

*   *   *

This political and personal elimination gave satisfaction to Pierre Broué but he knew, if only from his children who had passed periods time in the ranks of the organisation, that Berg was not the only one to profit from the system, that there was an "apparatus" made up of full-timers who would soon have their expense accounts, with variable limits, enabling them to draw on the funds of the organisation to satisfy their needs or to pay for hotels and that they were a long way, a very long way, from the poverty of the few full-timers at the end of the war....

He was therefore to try to drive home the point and to undertake a "sortie" in the internal bulletin. This sortie was to be the only serious attempt that Pierre Broué was to make to modifier the internal regime of the OCI/PCI, and it was a timid one.

In this text *Drawing Our Strengths from Our Weaknesses* he puts forward the idea that the *"authority principle"* is in essence bourgeois and one has to be aware of this when, as is sometimes necessary, one has recourse to it, that methods have a certain autonomy in politics, and if an apparatus is necessary one must beware of it and that the way to do this is to be careful and to cultivate debate and the level of education in it (I say all this from memory as I no longer have it to hand, but I am certain that I have reconstructed the spirit of it).

Basically this was a text that didn't go very far. But the reply from Lambert, though courteous in its form, showed that the message had been both received and challenged one hundred percent. *"Comrade Broué's text lacks any direction for practice"*; this little phrase wasn't addressed to Broué but to the militants to say to them "this is an intellectual with his head in the clouds". Lambert went on to say that as far as bureaucracy was concerned *"all the seats are taken"*; there was the reformist bureaucracy which lived off the emoluments of the bourgeois state and the Stalinist bureaucracy which lived off those of the degenerated workers state and that, all in all, there was nothing left in the till to sustain a third bureaucracy. These arguments show, between the lines, that Lambert understood very well what was at issue: was he a bureaucrat? Was Berg one? Could the OCI apparatus become bureaucratised? The "materialist" response was No. This pseudo-"materialism" reduced the sources of bureaucracy to dosh and thus excluded any autonomous role for power relationships although these are fundamental (and are at the heart of the Marxist analysis of the state). It implied that, in very essence — in a thoroughly metaphysical way! — Lambert couldn't possibly be a bureaucrat. What perfect theoretical protection!

Lambert's "response" was finished off by Stéphane Just in *La Vérité* where he launched a polemic against Pierre Broué without naming him and drove home the point: Berg was just an *"adventurer"*, the OCI was pure and spotless, the problem of "Berg's methods" had been solved, there was no problem of "OCI methods", on the contrary these should be strengthened in the way they were already developing — more centralisation, more of the "objectives — results method" — there had been but one tumour in a healthy body and it had been *"eradicated"* (why had it appeared? A mystery!). So the issue was closed, there was silence in the ranks and silence from Pierre Broué who retired into his shell, so if he shut his mouth others would not take the risk....

*   *   *   *   *

The decade of the 1970s thus drew to an end with the closure of the hopes with which it had begun and in a climate of suspense; Pierre Broué was regarded as a dissident but he had the ear of the leadership. This type of relationship can be found in all bureaucracies, including, above all, the Stalinist bureaucracies — it is that, to call a spade a spade, of "His Majesty's Loyal Opposition", who would be easy to get rid of but who may also be useful in case of need.

Trotsky, the SWP, Van and back to the Second World War

This decade, however, ended on a different note. This was his journey to the United States (Pierre Broué had had to give up a trip to Nicaragua to get his visa for this) [to work on] the greater part of the up to then closed archives of Leon Trotsky. Their discovery, the complementary discoveries of other pockets of archives, such as the Sedov dossiers found by Jean Van Heijenoort at Hoover University among the papers of Menshevik historian Nicolaievsky's widow, the work of perusing this in its entirety (an enormous task that began with six young researchers) as well as getting rid of a Healeyite squad who wanted to get their hands on the heritage, all took place following a significant 2 month visit in January/February 1980.

The main new historical facts that came out of these archives were to be exploited by Pierre Broué and Jean-Paul Joubert who were to establish that Trotsky's contacts in the USSR right up to the middle of the 1930s were more significant that had been thought, that the position of Stalin had been seriously weakened at several points, notably at the time of what Pierre Broué called the "Moscow Spring" of 1932 and again in 1934/1935 and that the trials and purges of 1936-1938 could not be considered only as an hysterical crisis of a paranoid tyrant massacring his real and, even more, his supposed opponents but really as a series of acts of a civil war against real adversaries — that although the broken victims of the Moscow Trials no longer represented what they once had done, they remained a force in the Soviet Union, and a force that might have been capable of uniting the workers against the bureaucracy, even going as far as its physical elimination.

This new conception of the history of the USSR had not (apart from Moshe Lewin's work which was parallel to it but operating on a different plane) been taken into account by official history which had been, willingly, sterilised by the asphyxiating myth of "Bolshevik totalitarianism".

In this context, these archives also allowed Pierre Broué to quite rapidly bring out a small book *'The Assassination of Trotsky"* (editions Complexe) and above all to reconstruct the history of the mass struggles carried out by the Trotskyists in the camps and "isolators" and of their debates as well as those of the decist current (an oppositional Bolshevik current that placed itself to the left of the Trotskyists). In these debates, which he presented without comment, the question of the nature of the Soviet Union was obviously a key issue and one to which the response often did not correspond to the theory of the "degenerated workers' state" that Trotsky had formulated in exile, as they tended generally to no longer consider the USSR as a "workers' state"; thus Rakovsky spoke of a *"bureaucratic class"* holding power.

* * * * *

In travelling and working on both sides of the Atlantic, not only in the Anglo-Saxon United States but also in those heterogeneous United States which are the Brazilian lands (where he was to participate in summer camps and forums of the Workers' Party, then on a rapid rise), Pierre Broué was also confronted as an involved spectator by the tragedy of the American SWP which, from its traditions and its way of operating had been the organisation which most resembled what had been the OCI.

The United States Socialist Workers Party was born in 1938 at the same time as the 4th. International. This, the biggest in the world of the small Trotskyist parties, weakened by the 1940 split with Schachtman and his supporters for whom the USSR was no longer a "workers' state" and after having literally handed over the 4th. International to Pablo after the war, had been the international ally of the OCI (and Healy) from 1953 to 1962. As a pillar of the Unified Secretariat, which had been founded by its reunification with Ernest Mandel's current in 1962 (Pablo, at the time an adviser to Ben Bella in Algeria, had left in 1964) it had set itself in the 1970s to oppose those who, for the OCI, were "Pablo-Mandelites" on the issues of guerilla struggles in Latin America and of the United Front. The prestige of the SWP came not only from its historical and intellectual proximity to Trotsky at the end of his life but also from the fact that it was led by a valiant "old guard" of typically *yankee* worker militants, former leaders of strikes that were quite rightly mythologised, like the Minneapolis truck drivers of 1934.

The "old guard" had traversed the McCarthyite desert of the 1950s and during this period had lost their union positions. In the 1960s it had recruited a youth organisation, the YSA, which had played a leading role around 1970 in the struggle on the campuses against the Vietnam War. After the expulsion of Tim Wolforth who had opposed the over-unconditional support offered to Cuba and Fidel Castro and who was then to sail in Healy's waters, this youth organisation was then to be led with an iron hand by Jack Barnes. At the end of the 1970s the "old ones", Tom Kerry, former Seamen's Union leader and Farrell Dobbs, former leader of the heroic truck drivers' strike, to whom Cannon (who died in 1974) and Hansen (died in 1978) had already passed the baton, passed it in their turn to Jack Barnes.

The Barnes leadership of the SWP then launched itself into a new political orientation (though one could find partial antecedents for it) of unconditional support for the Cuban and Nicaraguan governments, supporting, as we have already seen, the repression against the Simon Bolivar Brigade. Although this political line was seen as a turnaround on the international level, for it was a quite explicit and cynical turnaround — *"You can call me Pablo"* declared Barnes — as the SWP had up to then battled against the Guevarist and guerillerist errors of, for example, the Ligue in France, it was followed in an apparently homogeneous manner by the SWP militants (the first departures involved isolated militants or former leaders with eccentric histories such as Tim Wolforth — who we have already encountered in this tale and who had returned for a brief period to the SWP — and John Keil). The crisis in fact broke out in the SWP in the years 1980-1983, that is just at the time of Pierre Broué's most frequent trips to the United States, who thus witnessed them and drew close to the "old guard" militants, George Breitman to start with, who were entering into opposition.

The oppositions appeared one at a time, as and when Barnes went further down a neo-Stalinist route: unconditional support for the "Iranian Revolution" (interpreted as being the ayatollahs who were its supposed leaders), refusal to support the Polish *Solidarnosc* unions — Pierre Broué for his part had been able to travel to Poland in the summer of 1981 — and finally taking up Stalin's old "theoretical" critiques of Trotsky (the "under-estimation of the peasantry" etc.) and an explicit break with Trotskyism. The major part of the Trotskyists in the SWP, that is the old militants were to become "dissidents". But to do this they had to join together, to create external "islets", as if they were in exile, to contact each other secretly, to dissemble — exactly as under a Stalinist regime.

As these militants began to reflect on the situation the omnipresent question was obviously "how did we get to here?" Their Party, or what they thought was theirs (as Trotsky had considered the USSR as his state) had turned against them, had trapped them and wanted to make them repudiate everything or to impose silence on them. If it had been in power we would have had a one-party regime — this was Barnes' "Cuban" model — and these militants would have been in prison!

The old generation of the SWP who had been thrown out regrouped mainly in two organisations, between which there were many links, the Fourth Internationalist Tendency (FIT) and Socialist Action, linked to the SU, which, however, in fact gave no help to them. Pierre Broué was to be regularly invited to meetings and education schools of these groups who weren't cut off from life but continued, in the hard conditions of the Reagan years to intervene in the class-struggle in the US, supporting strikes and working in the unions.

The conclusions that a majority of them reached are now available on the internet in English (on the Marxists.org site) but these significant texts had not at the time been published outside the US and had been little circulated, but Pierre Broué knew of them. As a general rule, the FIT and Socialist Action militants considered that James Patrick Cannon's old SWP was a model of workers' democracy. Frank Lovell, for example argued that the regime in the organisation — which, according to a 1946 speech by J. P. Cannon, saw itself as the already existing American revolutionary party — had become routinist during McCarthyism, that the leaders Dobbs and Kerry had then allowed a system operated by activist petty apparatchiks to develop among the youth in the 1960s, and there had then emerged an intergenerational break between the working-class old guard and the young intelligentsia. This was something that Tom Kerry in particular had become aware of only on the eve of his death and he had begun to prepare to attack Barnes. Thus the degradation of the regime followed as Cannon bit by bit withdrew [from leadership].

The description of the militants from the Barnes generation, recruited on the campuses, bears a striking resemblance to that of the AJS and OCI militants in the 1970s, in this latter case the "Cambadélis" generation. It is enough here to evoke a "detail": Benjamin Stora in his book of testimony *La dernière generation d'October* recalls that the Francis Ford Copppola film *The Godfather* was a cult movie for him and his mates, and that they felt very clearly who was their godfather (Lambert; it was then to be Mitterand!). Paul Le Blanc in a text on the SWP also raises the point that this film was a reference point for Barnes and "his" militants, Barnes went so far as to argue that the essence of Leninism could be understood through it. This Mafia-type manipulation by enlightened leaders with the militants and the working-class as a mass to be manipulated, theory and history as decorative accessories if needed but which should not be a constraint, here lies a moral universe which is at the antipode to that of a Reynier, which disgusted Pierre Broué too, but he himself had one foot in it and had passed through it.

Finally, the SWP at the end of the 1970's was in good condition. The party had dollars and so there was an extraordinary proportion of full-timers (one in 10 or one in 7), members were controlled in their working lives in the name of "proletarianisation", and this was soon to be extended to their private lives too — whereas this type of thing did not occur systematically in the OCI where French "laique" culture had acted as a shield against this sort of drift. The old generation who got together to restore continuity with Trotskyism and with the American working-class and trades unionist tradition which was joined with it in the SWP were thus a generation of survivors of a shipwreck that they hadn't seen coming.

What the reflections of this old generation seem to have excluded is to go back as far as Cannon to look for the causes that had produced Barnes, and while we are at it why not as far back as Trotsky. Now it is probable that Pierre Broué had posed this question to himself as his historical work had presented him with the components in the form of the stages, fusions and splits that had gone into the building of the SWP in the 1930s and particularly in what might be called its founding, or at least paradigmatic, crisis of 1940.

He discovered that Cannon had a "hard fist" and that Trotsky had often acted to moderate this and had worried about his authoritarian tendencies. He had thus found there that damned "Zinovievism", that brutality of militants, who were not bureaucrats but who became apparatchiks, who built the antechamber for bureaucrats. This resonated with his earlier encounter in the course of his research with the "leftist" emissaries of the Communist International in Germany, with the critique of "Molinier's methods" in the

1930s which was long rejected by Trotsky and then picked up by him with his words about this *"poison of the Comintern"* which is still amongst us (interview between Trotsky and C.L.R. James in *Le mouvement Communiste en France*) and, inevitably, with the living experience of the OCI, what he had seen develop, what he had seen done, what he had done himself...

Pierre Broué was not to go further in this line of thinking at least not in the written traces of it that he has left us. He established that, in the 1939-1940 debate on the nature of the USSR, which was a very concrete debate prompted by the Hitler-Stalin pact and its consequences in Poland and Central Europe, and which ended in the split and the expulsion of Max Schachtman's current from the SWP, Cannon had had a tendency to be more heavy handed than Trotsky who had even written that the existing difference on the nature of the USSR ought to be able to survive in one and the same organisational context, therefore that in itself it justified neither a split nor an expulsion. But Trotsky had also characterised the Shachtman current as a *"petit-bourgeois opposition"* and the Cannon current as a *"proletarian core"* and by this provided a decisive cover for the split and the expulsions. Pierre Broué did not, at least in writing, involve himself in a more extensive investigation of this important moment in the history of Trotskyism which is also the moment that the second world war began. The double barrier — that of Trotsky's own organisation conceptions in 1939-1940 and that of the critique of the theory of the USSR as a "degenerated workers' state" — was not crossed.

This is not some Byzantine issue. These two subjects come back basically to one; that of democracy. Is it conceivable to characterise a totalitarian state denying all democracy and crushing the working-class physically and politically as a "workers' state"? And doesn't characterising oppositions who raise this question as "petit-bourgeois" play the game of that *"poison of the Comintern"* elsewhere denounced by Trotsky? Pierre Broué did not take the step towards this critique, in other words he remained on the terrain of "orthodoxy" as can be confirmed, for example, by re-reading his preface to volume 22 of Trotsky's *Works*, written in 1985, which discuses the SWP crisis of 1939-1940. In this preface he even finds curious the development into discussion of the dialectic that occurred, on Trotsky's initiative, in this debate, seeming not to see the significance of the necessary confrontation between Marxism and American pragmatism (nor of what place that this might have in this debate). This confrontation was precisely aborted, on the philosophical level as well, by the 1940 split.

Nonetheless we could say that he did go back "as far as Cannon" as far as methods were concerned. One of his interlocutors on these questions was the researcher and militant Alan Wald who had been looking into the evolution to the right of the American anti-Stalinist intelligentsia (this work was echoed by Pierre Broué) and who — temporarily — quarrelled with George Breitman because he had argued that Cannon had not, at various points, been a "democrat" or, one might prefer to say, had not respected the principles of workers' democracy. *A contrario*, Breitman had republished texts by Cannon from the 1950s and 60s which showed that the old leader had been more and more preoccupied with questions of democracy. He recalled that, by the testimony of the most zealous of Barnes' apparatchiks themselves, Cannon would have been expelled from the SWP in the 1980s for practising direct "horizontal contacts" with the militants, without passing via the appropriate authorities (the "horizontal" circulation of texts had become a reason for arrest for party members in the USSR in about 1922....). George Breitman died in 1986.

> George was a friend of the ILT, collaborated in the work of Cahiers and wanted to do a special issue on the history of the trotskyist movement in the United States.
>
> George Breitman, many times operated on, amputated, disabled had more than his share of suffering but undoubtedly the greatest would have been his expulsion from the party to which he had given his entire life — he didn't "leave" it, contrary to what The Militant cynically wrote. [...]. This was a precious man for, even on complex questions, he spoke and wrote in a very simple and directly comprehensible way. [P. Broué, obituary, CLT no. 26, June 1986.]

* * * * *

His reflections on and from the experience of the SWP had been important for Pierre Broué, hence, no doubt unexpectedly for certain comrades, the importance that it has here. For these reflections were, through a key encounter, to take him back to his own point of departure, to himself.

This encounter was with Jean Van Heijenoort, formerly Trotsky's secretary, who, after his withdrawal from militant activity in 1948, had become an eminent mathematician and logician. Pierre Broué had known him since the end of the 1960s but their relationship took on considerable importance once he had become involved in his work on the Trotsky archives. Although he took his time Van seems to have chosen Pierre Broué as the person in whom, to use the latter's expression, to "dump his bag". This is a curious expression but well describes the curious process that developed between them:

> Year by year I seemed to notice that he couldn't remember anything at all about episodes which he had personally recounted to me. Once I had verified and re-verified this I cautiously mentioned it and he dumbfounded me with his smiling self-satisfaction. He was, he said a very well perfected machine because, as he got older he solved the problem of his brain overload by only cutting out those things which he was sure had been preserved. [Obituary of Van in the same CLT as that of Breitman.]

Van died in 1986, killed in a domestic quarrel by his lover, he had visited Pierre Broué in Grenoble a few months before on the occasion of Olivia Gall's presentation of her thesis on Trotsky in Mexico. Van had thus "unloaded" a part of himself into Pierre Broué.

Among the many memories and experiences that he brought to him were those of the SWP during the 2nd. World War seen from Van 's perspective.

> He [Van] became frankly angry when he brought up the audiences that James Cannon ,the leader of the American party had accorded him on the theoretical and practical problems of the 4th. International, on the national question in Europe, on the problem of democratic demands and on the necessity for aid to European militants surviving under the heel of Nazism. Aware of the enormous responsibilities which had fallen on him after Trotsky's death, Van had considered returning clandestinely to France. He often asserted to me that, after hours of passionate pleading about the International he got nothing [from Cannon] but inarticulate mutterings and the assurance that "we'll see".

The International Secretariat, put together during Trotsky's lifetime and taken on by Van, was thus paralysed. It was to be the European Secretariat, put together during the War by Marcel Hic and then taken on by Michel Pablo, that would take over the baton after the war.

* * *

Van, a victim of Cannon and Cochrane's "Zinovievism" thus set Pierre Broué on a trail that he was to follow and dig into deeply. The Goldman-Morrow tendency, to which Van was linked, was kicked out of the SWP in 1946, its texts were not published in the Internal Bulletin etc.. Pierre Broué (*CLT* no. 67, October 1999) was then to talk of *"the legend of James P. Cannon, close disciple of Trotsky and invincible class battler"* which *"has remained very much alive in the milieu and the disrepute occasioned by his critiques is solidly rooted among the 'elders'"*. He acknowledged however an ambivalence in Cannon. When the *de facto* expulsion process of the Goldman-Morrow tendency began, Cannon was in prison. He wrote to the leadership of the SWP using phrases such as *"Any appointed leadership is a bureaucracy"* almost expressing the view that "we are a bureaucracy, but we must be aware of it and deal with it". And Cannon stressed that "concessions" should be made to the opposition *" which they only pretended to do* (wrote Pierre Broué) *which thus allowed [Cannon] to maintain his own reservations"*. In fact Cannon also talked about the opposition as *"intellectual boils"*…

And Pierre Broué wondered why the old militants, in their introspection after the death of the SWP as a Trotskyist party, had *"never considered re-opening this dossier even when the events that they were going through might have suggested this to them"*.

As far as Cannon was concerned Pierre Broué was finally to resolve the question, though he only published his point of view after the death of George Breitman: no, Cannon was not a "democrat".

Nevertheless he never saw the parallel, admittedly a caricature, but also real between the two situations: that of 1944 with Cannon in prison and thus advising from the sidelines, a leadership going beyond his "democratic" advice, but doing so based on his own conceptions and that in 1940 of Trotsky "moderating" Cannon against Shachtman while supplying the ammunition for the split. For a full 40 years this was to be the same story repeating itself in a more and more grotesque way right up to the death by asphyxiation of the SWP.

Van hadn't developed his memories of the Goldman-Morrow tendency in a detailed way in discussion with Pierre Broué. So Pierre Broué's investigation of this subject continued in the years that followed Van's death and he found himself in profound agreement with the deep-rooted questions around which the tendency had been built, which were about the European revolution during and after the 2nd. World War: putting forward demands around democracy and national independence; rejecting the view that the advance of the Red Army constituted a step forward for the revolution; then an evaluation of the situation (in Europe) as likely, in the absence of revolutionary parties, to lead to stabilisation, this last justifying a policy of lasting entrism, particularly in the social-democratic parties.

*   *   *   *   *

Simultaneously, the publication of Trotsky's 1939-1940 exile papers gave him a firm conviction, entirely confirmed by the papers from which this came, that Leon Trotsky had begun to conceive revolutionary politics during the Second World War in new terms which he had summarised in the formula of the *"Proletarian Military Policy"*: rejection of any form of pacifism as it would lead to collaboration or equivocation with the bourgeoisie (as with Pétain in France), adapting to the *"militarisation of society"* and preparing armed struggle against the Fascist occupiers without surrendering in the least to chauvinism and retaining the internationalist United Socialist States of Europe perspective which Van, under the pseudonym of Marc Loris, had linked with the struggle for national independence of all the occupied nations. We should add that, in Pierre Broué's view, the crisis in the SWP and refuting Shachtman's theses on the USSR had lost Trotsky time that he thought precious for formulating conceptions that were relatively new but fully in accord with the spirit of Marxism as the theory of revolutionary action. Many of Trotsky's texts which show these (in the first series of the *Works*) remain unfinished interrupted by the blow of the ice-pick.

These reflections on the past and these discoveries nurtured the significant number of the *CLT* on *The Trotskyists in the Second World War* which came out in 1985, followed by two others on the same subject in 1989 and 1990. In this he underlined the gap between Trotsky's nascent conceptions on the eve of his murder and those of most Trotskyists. For the latter, either the "PMP" was a formal adaptation to certain aspects of militarisation which justified demands such as combat training under union control, which was put forward by the American SWP at the end of 1940 — this was purely a formal tribute to Trotsky and didn't grasp the new essence of this policy, or, at worst, it was social chauvinism. It is nevertheless clear that Trotsky's PMP was the implementation of the conception of transforming the imperialist war into a civil war and in no sense involved going over to the camp of the "democracies". But Pierre Broué had few illusions on this point -— if the Trotskyists *had* known Trotsky's point of view they would either have sabotaged it in Cannon's "Zinovievist" way or have rejected it as social-chauvinist.

The result was, historically, of fundamental importance. The foundation of the 4th. International in 1938 was justified, for Trotsky, not by the sterile preservation of cadres and ideas but by the need to have an organisational instrument which could open the road to victory *"in the next ten years"* i.e. through and during the war that was looming. The "really existing" 4th. International paid no attention to these perspectives and had considered that the fact of "having held on" during the war was quite sufficient.

We must pursue this point to its logical conclusion: the fact that these groups and sections "held on" and had, heroically, carried out exemplary internationalist activities such as the clandestine cells in the Wehrmacht certainly confirms the *"right to exist"* of the 4th. International, but *which* 4th. International? That of the struggle for the victory of the world revolution in the real world here and now or that of [an organisation] set up [in a condition of] sectarian waiting and self-proclamation? The 4th. International reconstituted in 1946 by the SWP and the European Secretariat was not Trotsky's 4th. International — it was not, in reality, a 4th. International at all!

Here is the immense *"skeleton in the cupboard"* evoked but not clarified by Pierre Broué which was on the one hand the source of a type of party — the party-fraction-sect — which was not Bolshevik even if it thought it was and which cultivated bureaucratic deformations behind closed doors and on the other hand the source of the splits to come, starting with the Pabloite crisis.

Nonetheless, not all the movement had fallen into this sterilisation. We could remake history: "if" the Trotskyists across Europe had advocated, from 1940 (and therefore before the Stalinists who, let us remember, had at that time signed the pact with Hitler), armed struggle (or at least preparation for it) against the Fascist invader….We can't remake history with an "if", but on the other hand we do know that it was their control of armed formations born of the social and the national liberation struggles that allowed the Stalinists to crush the revolutions….

Pierre Broué tracked down the exceptions, those who had "carried out" the "PMP", for the most part without knowing that they did. These are significant: the great figure of Chen Duxiu, founder of Occidentalism, then of Communism, then of Trotskyism, in China, isolated in his Szechuan mountains is one of them, and he is not the least! There is Arpen Tavtian "the" Trotskyist of the Manouchian group and of the Affiche Rouge. There are those British militants from the RCP who, with Ted Grant, had intervened in the ranks of the British Army through organising "soldiers' parliaments" in North Africa to explain the objectives of the war as being the liberation of the peoples — the Trotskyists intervened there so that there would be true liberation of the peoples and the liquidation of Fascism[6]. The Stalinists denounced them to the Admiralty and the "soldiers' parliament" experiments in Libya and Cyrenaica came to an end. Then, finally, research in depth showed that there were exceptions everywhere, which, everywhere, sought to assert the revolutionary line.

Finally, at the end of it all, Pierre Broué, in these exceptions, went back to his own youth and reminded himself that, while remaining wholly internationalist like old Reynier, he had wanted to engage in armed struggle against the Nazis and the Milice[7] and to follow this through to civil war. This rediscovery was to surface quite brusquely in an article in the second CLT on the Trotskyists in the Second World War (September 1989) — at a time when he had just been expelled from the PCI and his wife Andreé was dying. Replying, which he could well have refrained from doing, to the sectarian, intellectually dishonest and rather stupid critique of the first Cahier on this topic by the "International Spartacist Tendency" (this was precisely all he had to get his teeth into; the silence of all the various Trotskyists on that little "bomb" of the "PMP" is eloquent, is it not?) he wrote:

> "Broué takes up the gun" wrote the Spartacist CEI, thinking himself witty and obviously unaware that I had really "taken up the gun" and that this had led me to Trotskyism, something he will have some trouble understanding from the American Sirius' point of view that he holds.

Whatever may have been the real significance of "the gun" in Pierre Broué's youth — I've discussed this in the first part of this study — it was not the fact of picking up a possible and very fleeting gun that had, in his case, led to Trotskyism but that he had picked up books in Élie Reynier's library. However it may be, Pierre Broué's thinking on the history of the 4th. International is of fundamental importance. But it was not to go further, neither looking back (to the 1940 split and the nature of the USSR) nor looking forward (Pierre Broué was never to write the history of that in which he had himself been implicated — often as a leader).

His Majesty's Oppositionist.

From 1980 the split in Pierre Broué, between on the one hand an historian who went over the Atlantic and reflected on the discoveries about the history of Trotskyism, at the epicentre of the history of the 20th. Century, that he had made

---

6. Grant never served in the army as he failed his medical but his organisation, the Revolutionary Communist Party, did good political work in the forces to mention only 3 members — Charlie van Gelderen, Duncan Hallas and Harry Ratner. [Note by RH editor].
7. Vichy paramilitary forces.

and, on the other hand, the OCI militant "without responsibilities", becomes more and more striking. The truth is revolutionary and does not tolerate legends. The story of the "oppositionist" Broué finally expelled bureaucratically in 1989 is both pitiful and calamitous. With the benefit of hindsight, I had at first a tendency to see this as the story of a man who was unfortunate and racked by contradictions, but that the worst thing for him was that he did not wish to share these and that he wanted to appear as having always had clean hands, which, let us be clear, was not the case. With even more hindsight, it appears to me that he energetically denied these contradictions and that he worked hard to build up a sort of heroic self-portrait and was encouraged, like many other "great leaders", by the fact that a small circle believed in it or made a show of believing in it.

At the beginning of the 1980's the OCI, which renamed itself the PCI in 1982, achieved its highest membership and widest coverage (much more than it has had since, under the name of the PT). But any quantitative progression requires qualitative change at a given moment if it is to be pursued.

Building a revolutionary party in France by way of "Trotskyist unity", whether or not one takes this hypothesis seriously, had been compromised by the 1979-1981 events described above.

The building of the "10,000 member party" required a change of methods. The analysis that was made of the situation created by 10 May 1981 was that it was one basically analogous to that of 1936, with a Popular Front type government, supposedly the last barrier to a revolution — or to a counter-revolution, to fascism. But why, if we use this analogy, didn't we have the equivalent of the 1936 strikes, supposed to open the way to splits in the traditional parties nor the emergence in these parties of left currents (there was only Lionel Jospin who, though we didn't know this, was supposedly in the ideal position to cultivate this and make it bear fruit!)? The contradictory characteristics of this period — which was distinguished by the existence of bureaucratic apparatuses in the PS and the PCF which were much larger than in 1936 with a French working-class that was rather blasé, very different from the young working-class of 1936, and that had begun, particularly since 1978-9 (with the industrial "restructuring", the crisis in the Lorraine steel industry etc.), to suffer defeats which were reshaping its very fabric — were not analysed.

We situated ourselves at the opposite extreme from the PCF's phrases about "society's shift to the right" or the LCR's about "the end of the radicalisation of the 1960s". We always minimised or straightforwardly denied the defeats. Thus the putsch in Poland simply showed the sharpening of the struggle, the collapse of the great British miners' strike simply showed the proletariat's willingness to fight. In short: the fact that there were deaths proved there had been struggle, which is a little thin as an analysis or a perception of reality.

In these conditions the launch by Lambert and Hébert of the idea of forming "sections for a workers' party" aiming to regroup other currents and many rank-and-file workers' with the PCI in a relatively broad and organically developing framework did correspond with a real need, constituted an attempt at a response to the situation and could have permitted some move forward had it been done on the political basis of the United Front continuing that which had already been set in train at the beginning of the decade with the campaign for the PS-PCF majority to "respect the mandate". But, in reality, this policy corresponded with the attempt to develop, or not develop, the party as a left cover for a trades union current, which was soon, in the person of Marc Blondel, to take over the leadership of Force Ouvrière. Furthermore, by implication, it buried all perspectives looking to build the "Trotskyist party of 10,000 militants".

This turn was to force Stéphane Just into opposition. As the author of many and various theoretical and polemical articles, as well as being the chief prosecutor ever since the Varga affair, Stéphane Just was the de facto number two in the organisation. This had not been the case in the 1960s where Pierre Broué's role had been undoubtedly more significant.

His relationship with Pierre Broué was curiously mixed — at least from the point of view of the latter (I am not in a position to pronounce on what it was for Stéphane Just) — much acrimony and a sort of affection. Stéphane Just embodied pure sectarianism with such candour that it made one laugh: when Pierre Broué began his research on the Second World War Stéphane Just claimed that *"my own war"* had consisted of *"screwing"* the German farmer's wife for whom he was working in the STO[8] on the grounds that there was nothing else that revolutionaries could do during the War. Pierre Broué repeated this and several other anecdotes in his obituary of Stéphane Just. This greatly shocked his friends and provoked a truncated polemic with *Carré Rouge*. He could only ever talk about Stéphane Just in this fashion. Indeed the anecdote of the farmer's wife is in fact very revealing, not just about Stéphane Just but about "orthodox Trotskyist" conceptions that see revolutionaries as being on earth to keep programme and organisation in the fridge so that they keep fresh and are well preserved. Pierre Frank's presentation of his 4th. International was much the same...But let's return to our story.

Stéphane Just, far more than Lambert, came across as the one who bawled people out, who shouted, who made adopting a threatening air a matter of principle and who expelled people. But Pierre Broué was well aware, because they had discussed it, that Stéphane Just had many disagreements with Lambert and that the "Lambert and Stéphane" façade which some simplistic or naïve comrades took to be Lenin and Trotsky was completely cracked. Pierre Broué knew that Stéphane Just thought that it was necessary to engage in a political struggle with Lambert. He claimed that he had asked Just if he intended to take up a battle over the question of the methods and functioning of the organisation and to have been told to go and take a running jump as far as this subject was concerned.

---

8. The STO was the organisation that supplied French "volunteers" and forced labourers to work in German factories and farms.

When this battle began — very alarming for rank and file activists (our Lenin and our Trotsky no longer agree with each other: good heavens, what will come of this? Is it the beginning of the end of the world?) — Pierre Broué said to me, and I agreed, that it would be good for the organisation to have different tendencies in it. Liquidating oppositionists seemed to be impossible this time because the opposing tendencies reflected a debate among the leadership. A few weeks before the congress he seemed worried and said *"Lambert is cracking up, there's one of Just's guys who has been clumsy in texts for the Internal Bulletin on the activities of our councillor representing Minguettes on Lyons council and he wants to make an example of him by expelling him."* Then Pierre Broué came to speak at the congress for the first time since 1975. Undoubtedly, this was to make sure that the debate should take place with no concessions on basics but in a respectful way and that the party would come out of it greater than before.....

Even Jean-Jaques Marie found a way of recalling this in the non-obituary published in his name: Pierre Broué was in fact to be the prosecutor for the expulsion of this militant targeted by Lambert. To achieve this he built up a grandiloquent structure of denunciations on the foundations of microscopic or non existent facts about the minutes of a Lyons municipal council, which he seemed to place on the same level as the Moscow Trials. He didn't try the "CIA KGB double agent" line as Just had to Varga: he had the intellectual ability to present the same message — those who employ the methods of falsification are the pupils of Stalinism who.....etc. — but the moral accusation was the same. And following that (as he told me when he came back), what a surprise: Lambert, without warning him in advance declared that anyone who didn't vote for Broué's report against the Lyons militant would be putting themselves outside the party, thus forcing a split of all those who supported Stéphane Just, in practice expelling them while halting the debate in depth which was being sought. Then, as if to both excuse and heighten his role, he nevertheless claimed that when Mélusine left the hall after his expulsion and senior steward Malapa got up to accompany him, he Pierre Broué had got up too and gone with the two of them. Malapa asked him why and he had responded with virile self-confidence: *"If Mélusine were to have fallen down the stairs no one would have believed, unless there was a witness, that you hadn't pushed him."* Things had been done cleanly, with no bloodletting!

Because I was in close relationship with Pierre Broué, I therefore lived through these events myself. It is nevertheless worth asking whether it hadn't been his intention from the first to be Lambert's prosecutor or if he had shifted his position during the congress.

In relation to the little central core of the organisation (at that time this consisted of Lambert and the stewarding group) Pierre Broué assumed the attitude of being one "who knew things", who covered-up and then deplored things in private. I was appalled by this attitude which, for me personally, smashed the image of dignity and political courage that I'd had of Pierre Broué. He knew this but in trying to get himself off the hook actually dug himself in even further by telling me stories to make one's hair stand on end: such as about the couple of comrades that he knew, suspected of having "factional" documents at their home, had their home searched, were pushed up against the wall, half-stripped and assaulted....

This oral account has been published by Pierre Broué himself in a sort of self-interview in his journal *Le Marxisme d'Aujourd'hui* — it is only for this reason that I have allowed myself to repeat it, though we must be clear that we can't take it at face value as he had so great a general tendency to fantasise.

But whatever be the case we were fighting for a free and frank humanity so what was this odious world, a miniature reflection of the order against which we fought? And what, moreover, was this great historian, incapable of speaking publicly or raising a scandal about these sorts of things — in *his* organisation, which he had designed and built, with Lambert and with Stéphane? Was he really incapable? In the last resort, no and this made it worse: he had chosen to cover up and it was this choice that had rendered him incapable. I remain absolutely convinced that Trotskyism and Stalinism are antithetical. But facts are facts and these facts place us on a planet which is that of *L'Aveu*.

* * * * *

At the end of 1984 I began to fear that the launch of the sections for a workers' party, which were to become the "Movement for a Workers' Party", would in the end take us nowhere and considered, rightly or wrongly, that the question of its method of functioning should be raised openly in the party. So I took the initiative of writing an internal text which demanded the election of full-timers at all levels by the militants and made clear that this would involve a small revolution as it should not simply consist of a plebiscite to endorse the full-timers who were already in place. The basic point was to have a party that controlled the full-timers rather than full-timers controlling the party by opening and closing the cells. I was putting into practice one of Pierre Broué's ideas, and, though I never sought his endorsement or support I had kept him informed. But when, at the regional congress my dangerous proposal was refuted, characterised as "outside time and space" by a full-timer famously close to him, he never lifted a finger. Pierre Broué and the militants at that time closest to him defended the firm and their place in the firm, full stop.

Two years later the MPTT was formed around the orientation of Lambert and of Hébert who implied that the working class no longer had any political representation at all and had broken with the PS and the PCF. This was an obvious absurdity whose logic was, later, to be the proclamation in France of the "Parti des Travailleurs" [PT]. After the 1986 legislative elections which, at the same time, saw the victory of the right due to Mitterand's policies and the PS coming to seem like the main pole of resistance, Cambadélis, the student Féderale and the leadership of the UNEF-ID, who had been in regular contact with Mitterand since 1981, split away, taking with them the student union. Pierre Broué considered the student team, Cambadélis, Plantagenêt, Rosenblatt.... to be "remarkable blokes" who he placed above the former youth leadership of the

1970's notably Charles Berg. While he almost regarded the latter as a police agent he saw the former as brilliant intellectuals. The respective histories of these people have shown that one might say the opposite of some of these personalities. He obviously didn't support this split but for him it had great importance as a warning. *"This is that last time that something like this should happen"* he wrote in the Internal Bulletin.

Incidentally the story of the "election of full-timers" was to have an epilogue at the same time. Lambert and Camus, of the Control Commission (Olivier Jospin, brother of Lionel), produced a declaration that bolshevism assumed the election of full-timers! All the existing full-timers who had denounced this dangerous innovation two years earlier were to applaud the circular and they were all proclaimed elected! But it remains true that the need felt by the leadership to take this fake initiative proves that a real battle about the type of party and the type of apparatus that should be built, linked to the policy of defence of the workers' united front, was possible in the 1980s. A democratic debate would have seen a sectarian left and a "democratic" right both confronting the centre. What I had learned at the time from Pierre Broué, or had grasped thanks to him, led me to hope for the formation of an authentic "right wing" — and the sooner the better. The longer the wait, the more one would be compromised. He had specifically forbidden any initiative in this direction, by his general waiting-game, his submission to the laws of the party, rather than to the theoretical statutes of it and his chosen role as prosecutor in the bureaucratic expulsion of Just's sectarian current.

In the end Pierre Broué was to be the originator of a tendency in the PCI, in 1988; the tendency *"pour la Fidelité au Front Unique"* (FFU).But this was not a current fighting for full democracy in the party, for a struggle for an authentic workers' party in France, denouncing the Mitterand-Chirac "cohabitation" and fighting for parties originating in the workers' movement to break with the 5th. Republic.

On the one hand the texts of the FFU concerning the methods, democracy and functioning of the party were not explicit. They were just as ambiguous on this level as had been those of Stéphane Just four years earlier — but these contortions did not protect them from the wrath of the apparatus, for the latter knew what Pierre Broué really thought about this.

On the other hand the FFU had made the choice of putting forward a defence of a traditional policy — that of campaigns addressed to the leaders of the PS and PCF but of refusing, in the style of Just and a certain "orthodoxy", to propose, as a concrete form of a break with the bourgeoisie and as a democratic demand, a break with the 5th. Republic, which was, at the time, one of the strong points of Lambert's and Hébert's speeches. Pierre Broué took the trouble to write to the Internal Bulletin to explain that a slogan such as that for a Constituent Assembly was indeed valid, in conformity with the sacred texts, but in China in the 1930s not in France today. At the same time the FFU comrades came to formulate their proposed slogan as "a PS-PCF government responsible to the National Assembly" (where there was a PS-PCF majority). The tendency was shot through with contradictions, advanced only to the point of retreat and only brought together the comrades already close to Pierre Broué along with a few "Justites".

But he only took this step because he thought that he couldn't be expelled. It is even probable that he thought Lambert was genuinely indebted to him for his nasty role in the 1984 expulsions. The FFU comrades told us that repression would fall on all of them, one after another but *"not on Pierre"* and on the other hand that the appearance of a new tendency, the DLV (after Drut-Langevin-Vania the respective pseudonyms of Michel Panthou, André Lacire known as Langevin, at the time editor-in chief of *Informations Ouvrières*, and Roland Michel) was a leadership manoeuvre to block the expansion of the FFU, returning fire, which was a crude error (the tumbrel behind, in 1991, was to be that of the "DLV").

* * * * *

The last act: in June 1989, in a series of deft manoeuvres, Pierre Broué was put *"outside the party by his own actions"*, not for factional activities, nor for this or that political position ("we don't expel people for political divergences", Lambert had always declared, with that involuntary humour that characterised him!) but for …..having gone to do a promotional meeting for his recently published biography of Trotsky organised by Mr. Renouvin's NAR, Nouvelle Action Royaliste; now there's an idea!...

* * * * *

It was a trap — the political bureau had seen the promotion plan for the book and had chosen to ambush Pierre Broué at the crossroads. He was summoned to explain himself but he counter-attacked in a prose that was incomprehensible to the non-initiated, above all the young militants, where he tried to accuse Lambert of keeping bad company with Roger Sandri, alias Angelo Geddo, an FO leader previously involved with an agency famously linked to the CIA. This was a way of alluding to previous "trials" (Varga), but all of it was covered over by a cartload of things left unsaid. Thus Pierre Broué found himself "outside" without wishing it, nor being able to predict it; what possible interest could he have had in going to see Nouvelle Action Royaliste? It is worth noting, in a point of detail that tells us a lot, that this respectable agency had a journal, *Le Royaliste*, which, for financial reasons, was printed by Abexpress…the printers founded by the OCI.

A brief parenthesis

Broué himself was rather a "rightist", in particular a supporter of the "democratic line" laid down by Lambert to sabotage any revolutionary programme. By participating in the bureaucratic elimination of Just he obviously intended to push forward his own line more easily without having to burden himself with the long detour of a genuine political struggle based on rational discussion

The group that wrote this commentary (the CRI, "Communiste Revolutionaire Internationaliste") offers me a legitimate opportunity to make some political comments of more general relevance on this period, as it commits an error which is symptomatic [of other similar ones].

Pierre Broué's involved himself in the bureaucratic elimination of Just not to promote his own "rightist" line but, on the contrary, because this latter was not sufficiently clearly developed or stated and because he didn't fight for his positions (perhaps using the excuse of the "secret tendency" with Raoul!?)

If his positions had been put into action in 1984 this would have been a genuine action for the workers' united front, for PS-PCF unity and a break with the 5th. Republic as against what Lambert was pretending to do under the title of "Movement for a Workers' Party". It was not because he was a "rightist" that Pierre Broué took an active part in the bureaucratic elimination of Just but because he wasn't a sufficiently consistent one.

The Achilles heel, the key aspect of this inconsistency was his refusal to fight for democracy in the party. But there was a second one, undoubtedly linked to the first: the maintenance of an "orthodox" position according to which revolutionaries don't fight for democratic institutions based on universal suffrage (in short don't fight for a democratic, secular and social Republic) but for "soviets". On this point, I've quoted Pierre Broué above ("and us too", I said) lining himself up with Rosa Luxemburg for taking up Bolshevism, taking up October. But it is in the same text — *The Russian Revolution*, published after Rosa's death by Paul Lévi — and as part of the same movement in thought and struggle that she criticised the rejection in Bolshevik Russia of *"representative bodies based on universal popular election"*. It is thus as part of the same movement, the same way of thinking, the same struggle, that Rosa Luxemburg has, since 1919, invited us to both support and criticise Bolshevism and to support democracy to the very last through and during the revolution.

*   *   *   *   *

In the revolutionary movement it is obviously good form to be "on the left" and when one opposes to do so from the left. It was nevertheless Lenin who was the first Marxist to fight certain left wings (to be accurate he wasn't the first, Marx had preceded him in 1848). The "rightist" Bolshevik tradition that Pierre Broué helps us to rediscover, above all in his book on Germany, is that of the workers' united front and also — though these are points that Pierre Broué didn't develop — of the integration, at the heart of the revolutionary struggle of the proletariat, of democracy, as much direct as indirect, representative as councilist and of national questions. This is, for us "rightists" the road to revolutionary victory…

* * * * *

Obviously it is so easy to mix up the defence of democracy with Lambert's building of apparatuses that "leftist" militants would be wrong to deprive themselves of the chance. But when it comes to bureaucratism the "leftist" tradition, including Stéphane Just who shouted for the expulsions of Varga, of Berg, of Lora, of Altamira... has no need to envy Lambert. Let us move to another level: the leftist Zinovievism, which had howled at Paul Lévi, guilty of speaking against a stupid bloodbath in 1921 (while Zinoviev was never disciplined for publicly speaking against the preparation of October 1917!), was, for all its courage, its devotion, its sacrifice, no less the antechamber to the Stalinist apparatus. Read Pierre Broué the historian...

But a consistent democratic rightist — a Bolshevik for the 21st. Century!! — can but wish for a free confrontation with leftist tendencies in a single party.

The party that we have not had would have had its leftists and its rightists and through their confrontations, through free debate, through dialogue with the workers, through successive approximations it would have gone forward.

Will militants who seriously reflect manage not to forget this for the future....

The End of an Epoch

The end of the 1980s thus marks a turning-point both in the international class-struggle and in the life of Pierre Broué. *"From 1989 Pierre Broué pursued political activities whose examination falls outside the scope of this article"* was the miserable comment in the non-obituary signed by Jean-Jacques Marie in *Informations Ouvrières*. The PT militants must be kept in the dark both about their own history and about the later struggles of Pierre Broué, as much a Trotskyist after 1989 as before.

1989 was also the year that Andreé, his wife and the mother of 4 of his children was to die of cancer. This took place only a few weeks after his expulsion from the PCI. We have reached Autumn 1989: a time when mass demonstrations in the city squares — Pierre Broué was soon to claim they were the biggest in history — shook Central Europe. The Wall, Pink Floyd's *The Wall*, around which Wim Wenders had, a year earlier, filmed *Wings of Desire*, the Berlin wall collapsed after it had been preventatively opened a few hours before the demonstrators would have taken it by storm.

* * * * *

Pierre Broué's new tome, appeared at the end of 1988, this time published by Fayard. It was the first for a long time. Not that he had not been working in the meantime but the great series of books on revolutions was finished and his activity as an historian had been to dive into Léon Trotsky's archives. It was from this work that a new big book emerged, it was called quite simply *Trotsky*. A whole programme in this title.

Is this Pierre Broué's best book as Wilebando Solano wrote in his obituary paper in the name of the Andreu Nin Foundation? Personally I don't think so. But I can understand how one can become profoundly attached to this book which, in the classic form of biography, explores Trotsky's development, rise and years of power and then goes on to explore at length his exile and the political life of the 4th. International that was being formed and above all to explore Trotsky as a person, not as a romantic hero, not as a fascinating biographical subject, not as a personality to be dissected or psychoanalysed but as a *living individual* in Marx's sense. Here are to be found the new elements that Pierre Broué adds to Isaac Deutscher's biography — which itself still remains worth reading. Pierre Broué, the historian *par excellence* of events and "facts", much to the displeasure of the mode of dominant academic (including "Marxist") ideas, was bound to one day be landed with that most "factual" *par excellence* of genres which is *biography*. He had begun to do this in his own promotional reviews of the books published by Minuit and it was logical, not to say inevitable, that he should do it with Trotsky. The link between personal and political life is thus the nub of this work and it is here that it becomes poignant, as for example where he recounts the mutual incomprehension between Trotsky and his daughter Zina who committed suicide in 1933, the year of Hitler's seizure of power.

The book didn't please a lot of Trotskyists, any more than did the fact that the view, which was becoming clearer and clearer to Pierre Broué, that Trotskyists, in general, were not worthy of Trotsky was often, by implication at least, present in the book. In the incredibly funny style of the non-obituary signed by Jean-Jacques Marie we thus read:

> In 1988 he published an enormous (this is a defect?) biography of Trotsky, of which some passages are questionable and which the PCI organised systematically to sell to its militants.

The second assertion in this sentence is untrue. This is but the third reference in this astonishing paper to the money or the sales that the PCI is supposed to have procured for the work of Pierre Broué, whereas it rather the opposite that is true (to say nothing of the indebtedness of the average militant for financing the loan repayments on the former Grenoble headquarters, which was of the size needed for a "party of 10,000"!). As for the beginning it is equally astonishing and merely reflects the reaction of the PCI leadership when the book came out: "there are questionable passages". What the militants were in effect told was "we advise you to buy it but watch out; there are questionable passages". No-one was ever to know which ones.

In fact there is, in passing, one aspect of the book which is questionable. This is Pierre Broué's view that, in proclaiming the 4th. International as such in 1938, the delegates went further than Trotsky had wanted, for him it would have been sufficient to take note of its existence as acting in reality like a 4th. International. Behind this nuance are historical stakes: the worth of the act of formation or proclamation. Here, Pierre Broué leaps to the other side of the fence from many currents, apparatuses and sects who claim that, in the great order of things, their birth as groups of the Elect dates from this point and who number (differently the one from the other) their "world congresses" starting with 1938. Be this as it may, he went too far in attributing to Trotsky a rather voluntarist position of the "as long as it exists" type. This can be shown by a careful study of the texts that he himself had published. Without mentioning Pierre Broué, Roger Prager's foreword to the second edition of Volume 1 of *Congresses of the 4th. International* (editions La Brèche) is devoted to refuting this over-stated position.

* * * * *

Now outside the confines, which had long been shackles, of the PCI, but still a Trotskyist, one might think that Pierre Broué's historical and militant activities would flourish in these new conditions.

This is only true on one level, though, it is true, on a significant one. The possibility of travelling to Russia, to meet the old guard, the survivors, the descendants of militants, to visit archives, to reaffirm the memory of Trotsky or of Rakovsky certainly gave great pleasure to Pierre Broué but did not add any shattering new historical insights, tending rather to confirm the thrust of his earlier work — which is something in itself. The opening up of the soviet archives was partial, dispersed and often financially motivated. Thus it took place in conditions that were far from satisfactory and an assessment of this has yet to be made.

The story Pierre Broué's trip to the Soviet Union in October 1988 was related at his funeral by Louis Astre who organised it. Here are some extracts which will suffice in themselves:

* * * * *

The previous year, 1987, the year of the great launch of Peristoika, I had been part of a strong French delegation of some 200 leading figures from all parts of the political, trades union, community and religious spectrum who were invited by Gorbatchov to meet with him in Moscow to find out about the potentially revolutionary advances of Perestroika, and to discuss it freely with its instigators, in front of the media. This was a major first in the USSR of that time.

The following year 1 was preparing to return with a big delegation from the Paris region when I bumped into Pierre at the Pompidou Centre where had come to present his monumental biography of Trotsky.

This seemed to me to be too good an opportunity for Pierre to miss He must seize it, make the leap and come with us to the Soviet Union. At first he was a little perturbed and he hesitated, but not for long.

The times were changing, the Soviet embassy couldn't refuse me an emergency visa for him.

A few days later there was Pierre, sitting next to me on the plane and carrying under his arm, clearly visible, his voluminous red book with the title in giant letters TROTSKY.

[…] Bernard Guetta, the Le Monde correspondent (…) hurried us by telling us that that same evening there was to take place the second public meeting of the MEMORIAL association that sought to bring to light, to expose the truth about the October Revolution and its instigators.

[…] Guetta told the organisers about Pierre; we were reserved seats at the end of the front row. The hall was packed.

There were a thousand, young and old, some with their children.

The tightly-packed and fervent atmosphere reminded me a bit of May 1968.

There was even a group of opponents who systematically obstructed the meeting.

But the spirit of democracy asserted itself.

[…]

The meeting was chaired by the daughter of Joffé, that very close collaborator and friend of Trotsky who was to commit suicide in 1927.

[…]

But some questions went unanswered. Buried beneath Stalinist obscurantism, history, on these points, stopped emerging.

Then Pierre rose, his red Trotsky in his hand. He presented himself, in a loud voice, as the historian of Trotskyism, offered his book to the Chair and then attempted to bring to the assembled company, now suddenly silent, the answers they sought on the life and the political struggles of David Ivanovitch (Joffé).

[…]

There was silence, then applause.

And, all the time, that sense of fervour.

Pierre turned back to us and sat down, upright, his face running with tears.

None of us could keep back our own.

In the rest of this account, which can't claim to be exhaustive, I shall examine Pierre Broué's political activities, in the strict sense of that term, and dwell at some length on his last great book, his monumental history of the Comintern.

In pursuit of some political activity

Now he was outside the OCI Pierre Broué wanted to create something with the people from the FFU and with others. He created a magazine with a smart cover, into which he was to put his time and money, increasingly writing most of the articles himself under different names. This was *Le Marxisme Aujourd'hui* (*LMA*). The Circles of the same name (or the "Federation of Circles") hardly existed outside their founding conference in January 1990.

For how could one make an assessment of the past while at the same time drawing out concrete lines of intervention in the present-day world? In any case the first condition for doing this was an open discussion with no taboos. This was absolutely not to be the case. Any proposal about a political orientation that was in the least precise or led to carrying out some action was in practice regarded as an attempt to impose a return to a militant activist past that was held in contempt. The analysis of various political orientations, in France and in the wider world, took the form of giving out good and bad points accompanied by mysterious aphorisms and obscure allusions and was reserved for Pierre Broué. In reality there was nothing but his magazine, lacking in any political orientation but containing interesting and sometimes rare international news.

The inability to create an organisational structure worthy of the name does not, we need to understand, mean that Pierre Broué didn't want to fall back into the type of closed-off and authoritarian relationships that had dominated his old party, but firmly the contrary — it was this type of relationship that endured. In this regard the responsibility is far from being his alone. The majority of the "old guard", once expelled or resigning, had continued to function as minelayers of thought in the sense criticised by Immanuel Kant in *Reply to the Question — What is Enlightenment?*. They had no very clear orientation (which is their right) but they wanted nevertheless to exist in the form of some sort of group, taking as a reference point some former leader, preferably a former member of the Political Bureau (this was doubtless unconscious, but it is a factual observation!). When presented with a global analysis of the situation they would cry out in indignation "here's someone else who wants to prevent me thinking, who wants to drag me back into my past!", but operating in the "Pierre has said that…" mode didn't bother them. The type of apparatus that he had built in the PCI had given its shape to the type of thinking and the type of personality of these groups even when they were expelled or had left. There was a continuity of methods.

Thus it was that when the magazine *Democratie!* was set up by the majority of the former DLV tendency (which appeared in 1989 and left the PCI in 1991) the militant that I was became one of the first signatories of their appeal for regroupment. At that particular point (for things varied in a cyclical manner) I didn't possess the odour of sanctity for Pierre Broué, so he demanded of the initiators that my signature disappear, which it did, along with phones put down with no explanation and personal contacts cut off . Anyway, once these same people realised that I had trades union comrades and ones in elected positions who would not accept these procedures it was enough for them to change their behaviour with no further explanation. But does one create militants with these sorts of methods? Has one the right to lecture about methods as alleged victims (though in fact also co-authors!) of "Lambertist methods" when acting in just the same way oneself?

Moreover questions need to be asked about the attitudes of militants (and indeed of non-militants too) named on the Editorial Board list of *Marxisme Aujourd'hui* but who manifestly did not intervene to prevent its real and sole poly-editor from sliding increasingly often into writing notes that were aggressive, incomprehensible to the non-initiated and sometimes simply false and into continuing to publish these right to the end, even to beyond his death. Is this attitude really different from that of those who hit out at "Varga", is it really different from those who, starting from a revolt against an oppressive society, ended up hiding under the skirts and kissing the boots of the "little father of the peoples"? This question must at least be posed. A "friend" of Pierre Broué who fails to pose it is starting on the wrong foot for taking up the task of passing on the best of his work.

There is no desire on my part to engage in a posthumous settling of accounts. On the one hand I had settled these accounts with the person concerned during his lifetime and he knew well, indeed I ask myself whether he did not count on it a little, that one day I would talk about how one could understand him without following him like a disciple. On the other hand if I put in all the details I could end up writing a novel and I have no desire to do that.

* * * * *

But this involves a serious question, the same indeed with which Pierre Broué's conscious life began, if it is true, and it is, that his consciousness was awoken by the moral consciousness of an Élie Reynier: the question of responsibility, of being able to say "I myself think that", of risking getting things wrong, of taking on one's own responsibilities, of exposing oneself to act on others, of weighing up a situation, of trying to transform the world. The authoritarian structure of a party-faction-sect is a structure where militants renounce their own responsibility in favour of that of guides who can in different organisations and at different times be good and fatherly guides or an abominable but ridiculous bogeyman like Healy. Authoritarian relationships are not effective for fighting bourgeois society and it was such relationships that he had denounced in the OCI's IB in 1979, but he himself had produced and reproduced them as much as they were being produced and reproduced around him.

I am not in any sense an anarchist (it is, moreover, obvious that relationships of authority, of substitutionism, of mesmerisation are omnipresent in anarchist currents) but I think that the moments of fusion between historic currents, of organisations with their own intellectual traditions, and the movements of much greater masses, those moments which characterise contemporary revolutions, are the moments when such [authoritarian] relationships break open and are called into question — these are the very situations studied in Pierre Broué's books on revolutions, this is, at its highest point, the situation of October.

* * * * *

In Bolshevism at its highest level, Bolshevism involving that which was strongest and most noble in it, we don't need to call on bourgeois authority relations but rather on discipline in action resulting from sincere confidence and freely given commitment. In his study published in English *Leninism in the US and the Decline of the Socialist Workers' Party*, Paul Le Blanc, one of those American Trotskyists to whom we referred earlier as defenders of the Cannon tradition (which he saw as a democratic tradition) made a penetrating remark. He drew attention to the essential distinction between an *authoritarian personality* and a *revolutionary personality* and quoted the psycho-analyst Erich Fromm (in *The Dogma of Christ and other essays* first published in 1932):

"The most fundamental characteristic of the "revolutionary character" is that he (or she) is **independent** that he (or she) is **free**" in this sense that "the individual thinks, feels and decides for himself and through himself (or herself). More still, that he identifies himself with humanity [as a whole] and transcends the narrow limits of the social order in which he lives" thus establishing, Erich Fromm goes on to say, a relationship to the world, including one to those organisations which he freely chooses to join, based on a "critical mode".

This revolutionary personality is not as rare as one might think, it is aroused by the class struggle, but it is, naturally, repressed and as often as possible, killed. The authoritarian personalities who, in Fromm, are not only the leaders but also those who need leaders and who follow them, or believe that they follow them, play a key role in the struggle — at the service of bourgeois society — by picking out, isolating, asphyxiating and killing revolutionary personalities.

In a well-run party-faction-sect revolutionary personalities are invariably accused of having "a petit-bourgeois temperament" and, by liquidating or absorbing them, the party-faction-sect plays its role as an institution of bourgeois society. As a general rule, authoritarian personalities cannot stand someone maintaining an opinion unless it comes from a "leader" (to be a "leader" is to be awarded [with this title] through some ritual, some visible sign, some perception of deference by others, or by belonging to some institution, present or past — to a group co-opted by leaders: in this case a former member of the Political Bureau).

If one tries to convince these personalities of something they have difficulty understanding that one is no longer trying to manipulate them and they spontaneously look for "where is this from" or "on whose behalf" are those who speak to them acting and thus they never reach the point of examining an opinion for itself. For the "exes" the over-caution which belongs to the authoritarian personality that of which they haven't divested themselves expresses itself, moreover, quite easily in the way they make a fuss against those who, when they talk about their conscience or their thought seem, in their eyes, to be attempting to violate them by wanting to force them to obey "those methods we have known".

A revolutionary personality, for his/her part, never regards him/herself as an "ex".

Pierre Broué outside the PCI was not, in fact, Pierre Broué in the fresh air. He always had problems in this universe. He did not himself have the temperament of those weak authoritarian personalities, but rather that of the strong ones, deep down very weak, who have need of the weak ones, who can never find equals and seem not to want friends, though actually they really miss having them.

* * * * *

Having said that I have, practically, made the main point. Those that get angry about it will be confirming by that very fact that they can feel targeted too. But I have done no more than describe a phenomenon that, in France, on a much larger scale, characterised the militants in the PCF, that big Stalinist party which became the model for its enemies on the Left.

To finish briefly with Pierre Broué's political positions, we can distinguish three phases after 1990.

* * * * *

The first was the hope of creating his own current which got precisely nowhere apart from carrying on — at arms length and with the help of devoted friends (rather than militants convinced that this was indispensable work) — of the magazine *LMA*.

* * * * *

The second phase was that of seeking to insert himself in broader regroupments. Through the magazine *Démocratie!* this led Pierre Broué to interest himself in the beginnings of the Mouvement des Citoyens founded by Jean-Pierre Chevènement (who he had met, and liked, rather by chance during a trip to Mexico a long time earlier) and then to envisage helping to educate new generations of militants in the context of the left currents of the socialist party.

It was it this point that, through Gérard Filoche, *LMA* became associated with the magazine *Démocratie et Révolution,* which was later to call itself *Démocratie et Socialisme* which, for all that, was not "the magazine" of Pierre Broué but a platform that was always open, Pierre Broué was also put in contact with the minor "elephants" of the left of the PS at the time, Julien Dray and Jean-Luc Mélenchon. By a vote which, contrary to what Gérard Filoche stated, was not "unanimous" (there were some circumspect abstentions) *LMA* became considered as a magazine associated with D & S — which, concretely, had no tangible political implications.

Noting a new and rich epoch opening up since the fall of the Berlin Wall and the end of the USSR and feeling that the failure of the little Internationals necessitated a period of the insertion of revolutionary militants into existing organisations led Pierre Broué to an extreme prudence towards any critique of these organisations. This got to the point where in *LMA* he did not present his own positions on them but specialised in articles denouncing those critics and opponents of them judged really or supposedly to be sectarians or ultra-lefts. He acted like this over the Brazilian Workers' Party but also towards the French PS.

During the first years of the Jospin government, when all currents in the PS, including the left wing ones, lined up behind its reactionary policies which began, indeed, to stir up social struggles — notably at the time of the minister Allègre's attacks on state education — Pierre Broué still had a relatively considerable stature which could have allowed him to make a critique that would be listened to — or at the least to deliver a warning shot — aimed at these currents. He refused to do so and only did so in an individual and far from systematic way a little later, when it was too late — and he sent packing, in an insulting way, anyone who suggested that he should do so.

* * * * *

Further to this when he was questioned at this time by journalists in search of the scoop they were hoping for about Lionel Jospin, formerly of the OCI now in the PS, he either denied this or claimed not to know anything about it, thus seeming, on the one hand to be protecting the Prime Minister himself and, on the other, to be avoiding any responsibility to explain the policy and methods of the former OCI. Thus in Chapter 2 of Gérard Leclerc and Florence Muracciole's *Lionel Jospin, l'héritier rebelle* Pierre Broué confirmed that there had been "moles" in the PS and emphasised a meeting with an Elysée advisor after 10 May 1981 — this was probably with Robert Chéramy and the meeting, if it took place, had no great significance at a political level — but it totally "exonerated" Lionel Jospin.

Yet many former OCI militants affirmed that Lionel Jospin had been one of them. Charles Berg and François Chesnais exposed Jospin as a former comrade in *Libération* in early June 1999. This finally speeded up the "outing" of Lionel Jospin. Following this "outing" it was to be Michel Broué who, starting with a first interview in January 2002 followed by a series of programmes produced by Jean Birnbaum on the Trotskyists, recounted on France Culture how Lionel Jospin had been recruited and educated (through his "GER") by the OCI in 1970.

It is thus even more striking that Pierre Broué interviewing himself in one of the last numbers of the magazine LMA justified his silence as follows: *"I am not a squealer"*. The choice, though certainly unconscious, of a mafia expression with macho connotations, seems here to bear witness to a feeling that he belonged, on the one hand with Jospin and on the other with Lambert, to the same *gang* and to a view that those who had "talked" were *squealers*....this is Francis Ford Coppola winning out over old Reynier.

* * * * *

The third and final phase of Pierre Broué's political involvements after 1989 can be dated from the Presidential elections of 2002 when he indignantly denounced the advice to vote Chirac in the second round, in a letter on the net, resonant with energy, and sent to various groups and magazines (including the *Lettre des Liasons*). In an obviously irrational way and contrary to the truth he later accused us in *LMA* of having campaigned for Chirac.

* * * * *

With health worries adding to everything else, his contacts with the militants who found themselves in the French Socialist Party became less frequent. From 2003 he received visits from Greg Oxley and Alan Woods on behalf of the Committee for a Marxist International inspired by the old British Trotskyist, Ted Grant. In his obituary articles Alan Woods wrote that Pierre Broué had become one of them: he hadn't formally joined but talked with them and spoke of "us", carrying out political projects and publications of Trotsky together.

Pierre Broué easily tended to say "us", even when he was, in reality, quite alone and always when he had the feeling that good work in common was possible or, at least, so as to be able to claim that he was not all alone and that he was "followed". I am far from wanting to minimise that he could have recognised the theoretical seriousness of this current who combined long-haul work in mass organisations with Trotskyist education. Be this as it may, the psychological factors in this last rapprochement are unquestionable. Pierre Broué had created the conditions for considerable genuine isolation, though many people had thought about his well-being and had suffered for this. Ted Grant's current had not been a sudden revelation for him in 2003, he had been studying it for a long time at an historical level, for, as I said earlier, Ted Grant had carried out work in the army that he considered exemplary and which was an example of what he would have wished to do as a young man. He had been thinking more and more about this since his researches of the 1980s and his expulsion in 1989. What's more Ted Grant gave the impression of an old guy still in full form, older than Pierre Broué and the only Trotskyist still living who had tried to do what was needed during the second world war. All these reasons make up the starting point for this last attachment.

Pierre Broué thus conducted his last polemics — with astounding ferocity — in defence of this tendency in Bolivia against the critiques of it by the Argentinian PO (Partido Obrera) and therefore at the same time in defence of in-depth work in working-class organisations such as the Bolivian COB. But he also criticised the policy of this same current which was in favour of prioritising work in France in the PCF.

* * * * *

Things had reached this point when Pierre Broué died, only a few days after Vlady Serge (an objective coincidence in André Breton's sense of the term).

The giant conclusion for a giant of an historian: the Comintern

The production of Trotsky's *Works* was not to be continued after 1989. In total this represented 27 volumes covering the years 1933-1940 and three covering the years 1928-1929, to which it is worth adding the correspondence of Leon and Natalia Trotsky (prefaced, translated and edited by Van) and the correspondence in the 1930s between Leon Trotsky and Alfred and Marguerite Rosmer (presented and annotated by Pierre Broué) both in the Temoins/Gallimard collection.

As far as I know, this failure to continue the publication of the *Works*, which left unfinished the intended publication of them at least up to 1933, was for financial reasons. The non-obituary signed by Jean-Jacques Marie in *Informations Ouvrières* heavily emphasises the help of the OCI in selling the *Works*. But it is important to equally heavily emphasise the sabotage of their distribution when their editor became an "enemy". That being said I think that it is true that Pierre Broué thought, following Trotsky, that he had, in the volumes that had already come out, published the most significant work in the latter's life and did not consider publishing the older writings to be a priority.

* * * * *

Pierre Broué had published several small books in the period from1989 to the end of the 1990s: on the one hand, in 1993 on Trotsky's son Leon Sedov, also in 1993 on the role of Stalin in Spain (complementing his earlier work in the light of Russian archives) and a book in 1996 (which was perhaps too hastily written) on Rakovsky, for whom he had a soft spot; on the other, two small works on contemporary events, enriched by observations through his travels. One was on the end of the USSR and is ignored in the majority of bibliographies that are circulating; *Moscou, le putsch du 19 août 1991* was published as a supplement to *LMA* with a preface from the leadership team of the "Filoche current" in the LCR at the time. This is a little book which has the merit, unique in France, of strongly conveying the weight and strength of the Russian working-class. The other was on the mass demonstrations in Brazil in 1994, published by L'Harmattan as *Quand le peuple renverse le president*. One will search in vain through this book for a political analysis but one will find in it rousing descriptions of turbulent demonstrations.

* * * * *

But the major work that was then in gestation was to be published by Fayard in 1997. This was his *Histoire de l'Internationale Communiste; 1919-1943*. This is genuinely speaking a monster of a book, a sort of sum total of stories put together into a coherent whole, which, one could say, pulls everything together. The contributions, that is the detailed points and necessary confirmations, emerging from the opening of the Russian archives are, of course, an integral part of it. Above all, at one and the same time, it can be situated in the centre of Pierre Broué's overall work and as the conclusion to it. This is for two reasons:

❶ the aspect of his historical work which is, in reality, the politically richest, his work on the German Revolution, is recycled and integrated in this work whose true centre, if centre there be, remains or returns to Germany, that is to the European socialist revolution;

❷ after having been the historian of revolutions (Russia, Spain, Germany) and then the biographer of a revolutionary (Trotsky), Pierre Broué then turns himself into the biographer of a collective, that is (and hence what we may call the monster character of the book, it is a eulogy) a simultaneous biography of hundreds of militants, amongst whom one can, moreover, recognise revolutionary and/or authoritarian temperaments, the majority of whom met tragic ends. Thus it is a tragedy of the destiny forged by living men on the scale of the 20th. century itself.

There is thus a sort of compound rhythm that structures the work of Pierre Broué. The series of tomes published by Minuit remain the base without which any discussion of his works would go off the rails — before he was "the historian of Trotsky" he was the storyteller of the European revolutions of the 20th. century. Then followed his intellectual and biographical focus on one individual — Trotsky. But in the third, and last, moment there is the synthesis of the collective story and of individual biographies in a tragic portrait which is this *Histoire de l'Internationale Communiste*, which seems almost to become a person in the feminine: *la Comintern,* as Pierre Broué liked to insist on as the correct usage — backing this up with convincing linguistic and historical arguments.

* * *

This work, the fruit of work that cannot but have exhausted and crushed its own author includes, in its present state, some small defects, gaps here and there — little detail on China in the 1930s for example. But faced with a work like this these defects turn into the inevitable reverse side of the great tragedy. A militant in a hurry who is worried that he will not have the time to read all Pierre Broué's historical works should read this one. Then, if they really wants to "educate himself politically" he should "do" the books on the German Revolution and the Spanish Revolution. This is why the necessary work of republication should first of all concern these two essential books. If our serious militant and honest man then has the luck of getting his hands on his pamphlets he would gain still more from reading those on what the Trotskyists called "political revolutions" against the bureaucracy: the pamphlet on Hungary 1956, that on Czechoslovakia 1968, without forgetting that which he will not find, for it is not published, but which must exist, on Poland 1980.

This intelligent route is not the easy one which emerges from the Pierre Broué bibliographies that appear here and there, favouring the books according to their lightness of weight and "forgetting" (as, obviously, in the non-obituary in the name of Jean-Jacques Marie in *Informations Ouvrières!*) Germany and the Comintern...

To this monument we should add two annexes of worth: *Communistes contre Staline — le massacre d'une generation* (2003) and *Meutre au maquis* written with Raymond Vacheron following Raymond's discovery of survivors and precise details of the political murder by the Stalinists in the maquis of the Haut Velay of a group of Trotskyists who included the founder of Italian Communism, Pietro Tresso (known as Blasco) along with Pierre Salini, Abram Sadek, Jean Reboul and a young Communist, influenced by them but thinking for himself, Paul Maraval. In this book Pierre Broué's regrets about the war period did not lead to a claim to a role in the "maquis" but to a brutal critique of an old militant of the period, Albert Demazière.

* * * * *

This compound rhythm in the work of Pierre Broué — revolutionary pictures in the 1960 to 1975 books; then the focus on one personality, Trotsky; finishing with the attempt to capture in a new way the collective picture through adding-up individual destinies — has something in it of the tragic, for it corresponds too, even in its grandeur, with its author's growing difficulties in making a global analysis of this welter of facts and ideas. We cannot conceal the fact that the books from the 1990s, including the "Comintern" include a growing number of mistakes, slips and repetitions and suffer from a growing difficulty in getting away from crude storytelling just as the articles and notes in *Marxisme Aujourd'hui* suffer from a certain "airport novel" feel to them. His attempt to capture a global sense of a whole generation, fighting and defeated, sometimes pushed to betrayal and then defeated once more, this attempt by Pierre Broué the historian at grasping the horrors of the century ran side by side with a tightening grip on him of obvious psychiatric problems. A more and more dry and hard view of the world, instrumentalising people, and women in particular, like a tide emerging from the unconscious, coincided with the sharpest and most subtle of his work as an historian and began to threaten it.

* * * * *

The dimension of Stalinism as a killing machine and a machine of lies is at the centre of this great work and of its two appendices. Its sentimental (in the theatrical sense of the word) nature does not conceal, but rather reveals the ensemble of political tactics forged by Stalinism in the 1930s, and repeated since in divers modes by diverse political forces, as counter-revolutionary and stained with blood. In this respect Pierre Broué, quite rightly never made any concessions towards the mystique and the embellished memories of the "Popular Front" which is presented for what it was, covered with blood and resulting quite logically in the Hitler-Stalin Pact. This aspect of the book distressed that other great historian of the workers' movement in France (along with Jean Maitron), Madeleine Rebérioux, who was in other respects impressed by the work. But facts are facts and, if one is to defend the truth, myths must not stand in their way.

*   *   *   *   *

It is this view that had guided me in writing this text, which, against my intentions, has taken on the scale of a pamphlet, for what needs saying must be said. Real history is complex because it is concrete and there can be no truth which is not concrete. The easy and thoughtless way in which Pierre Broué could be turned into an angel among demons (the "Lambertists") should be treated with the disdain that he himself had for trashy historians and lazy thinkers. For it is absolutely right to say, as Joelle Lesson wrote:

> for Pierre there could be no real political activity without a common understanding of events and tasks. When a comrade falls we continue the struggle. For Socialism. Sans Dieu ni Maître [No God, No Master].

Sans Dieu ni Maître, that is what our fighters need.
Vincent Présumey, Moulins
First version   14 August 2005
Revised version   January 2006

Remarks on the History of the Bolshevik Party

THE study of the history of the Bolshevik Party is one of the first essentials for a militant who has questions about the problems of the past and present of the working-class movement, and in particular for one who wants to answer the question — as yet unresolved — of the place and role of parties. It is not an easy task. There is a great temptation to accept accomplished fact in a fatalistic manner, to confuse explanation and justification, to replace real life with formulae and to break down history into causes and consequences which are mechanically articulated. So in order to undertake it, there is a necessary condition, the choice of the most fertile hypothesis, that which does not close off any possibility, the refusal to admit the conclusion that would make this study futile, namely the notion that the Stalinist party was entirely "implicit" in the little group of professional revolutionaries of Lenin's day, the refusal of the assumption that history could not have followed any other course from that which it did follow and that it only crowns the victors. Even if one scrupulously enumerated the facts and ideas put forward, one would then be condemned to classify them according to idealist criteria and a belief in final causes, and to carefully distinguish, as does the serious American historian Robert V Daniels,[1] between the "real" Lenin and the "false appearance" of his utterances or his actions. The present article has no other aim than to indicate possible directions for study, to suggest certain illuminating perspectives and finally, to pose problems which, in our opinion, are still posed for the contemporary working-class movement.

* * * * *

What constitutes the originality, some would say the greatness, of the Bolshevik Party is that, alone among working-class parties which have given themselves the goal of taking power, it succeeded in doing so without having abandoned any of its essential principles, and yet it did not refuse to adapt its methods to the circumstances. The fact that this power subsequently gave birth to a society that was very different from the one it had aimed to create often obscures this fact, which is nonetheless fundamental. It is necessary here to recognise the existence of a contradiction which the historian of the Bolshevik Party should not leave unmentioned. However we

---

1. Author of many books on Russia and Communism.

must admit that commentators and historians have tended to turn to the second aspect, and have been more inclined to study the divorce between aims and achievements rather than the achievement of the first objective. Nonetheless an essential tool is missing: no comparison is possible with reference to the "degeneration" of the party in power, whereas there is no shortage of examples of working-class parties having abandoned their aims before coming anywhere near the capture of power.

A conception of the building of a working-class party

Quite rightly most historians refer to Lenin's work *What is to be Done?* in order to find the conception of the party which was to become the first workers' party to be victorious in a revolution. The role of *Iskra*[2] and its organisation, and Lenin's intervention in the *Iskra* team, are however no less significant. It was a question of a new concept, adapted to the Russia of the time, of the building of a workers' party which Lenin perceived as the Russian equivalent of the German Social Democracy. Now not a single line of *What is to be Done?* contradicts this interpretation, which is confirmed by the study of many subsequent texts. Thus in the 1907 preface to a new edition of his works, Lenin reproached the critics of *What is to be Done?* for treating the pamphlet "apart from its connection with the concrete historical situation of a definite, and now long past, period in the development of our Party". He stated in particular that "in the historical conditions that prevailed in Russia in 1900-05, *no organisation other than Iskra could have* created the Social-Democratic Labour Party we now have ... *What is to be Done?* is a *summary* of *Iskra* tactics and *Iskra* organisational policy in 1901 and 1902. Precisely a "*summary*", no more and no less."[3]

A similar orientation is suggested by the study of Lenin's attitude towards the problems of international social democracy, providing that we are willing to accept the man at his word and do not attribute to him, in politics, ulterior motives which are foreign to that sphere. Before the 1914 war, he asserted on several occasions that the Bolshevik current was a purely Russian current, that it did not aspire to be an independent current, but was simply the working-class social democratic current as required by the specific Russian conditions. "When and where," he wrote in *Two Tactics*, "did I ever claim to have created any sort of special trend in International Social-Democracy *not identical* with the trend of Bebel and Kautsky? When and where have there been brought to light differences between me, on the one hand, and Bebel and Kautsky, on the other?"[4] It was only after the capitulation of German Social Democracy that he was to revise his estimate of the Bebel-Kautsky current, and to

2. *Iskra* (Spark) was founded in 1900 by Lenin as the paper of the Russian Social Democratic Labour Party; it was printed in Western Europe and smuggled into Russia; after 1903 taken over by Mensheviks.
3. VI Lenin, *Preface* to the collection *Twelve Years* (1907) at http://www.marxists.org/archive/lenin/works/1907/sep/pref1907.htm.
4. VI Lenin: *Two Tactics of Social-Democracy in the Democratic Revolution*, section 8, footnote 1, at http://www.marxists.org/archive/lenin/works/1905/tactics/ch08.htm#v09zz99h-065.

concede, after the event, that Rosa Luxemburg had been right as against him on this point. We may recall that he believed that the issue of *Vorwärts* which published the patriotic statement by the Social Democratic faction in the Reichstag[5] was a forgery by the German general staff. The same conception appears clearly in 1920 when, speaking of Rosa Luxemburg, whom nobody, at that time or ever, could have identified with Bolshevism, he insisted that she had been an "outstanding representative ... of the revolutionary proletariat and of unfalsified Marxism".[6]

A conception of the workers' party

In April 1917 Lenin was to be the only delegate at the Bolshevik Congress to vote for his proposal to drop the words "social democratic" in the Party's official name. Doubtless this should suffice to stress the fact that he was not afraid to find himself isolated in his own organisation, and that if he hadn't made this proposal earlier, it was because until then it had not seemed necessary to him. In fact, there are three distinct organisations generally referred to by the term "Bolshevik Party":

1. The Russian Social Democratic Labour Party between 1903 and 1911, in which several factions struggled for leadership;
2. The Bolshevik faction within this same party;
3. The Russian Social Democratic Labour Party (Bolshevik), finally founded in 1912, and which was to receive substantial reinforcements, notably from the Petrograd Mezhraiontsy[7] including Trotsky, before becoming the Bolshevik Party which was victorious in October 1917.

Even if we make Lenin responsible for the 1903 split, because of his determination to apply his line in an organisation where his opponents challenged the circumstances which had put him in the "majority" (Bolshevik) faction, it is impossible to consider that it was his deliberate intention. It fact, it appears that he did not even expect it, that he had not foreseen the danger. It was to have a painful impact on him, and he paid for the shock and disappointment with a nervous breakdown and an uncharacteristic demoralisation. If he and his faction organised the 1905 London Congress on an exclusively Bolshevik basis, and if he tried to strengthen his faction by using the title of the Party, he was nonetheless the joint author of a resolution which was kept secret at the time and which committed the Central Committee to work for reunification with the Mensheviks. Nor have we any right to say, as too many historians have done, that Lenin saw the reunification of 1906 "imposed" on him: his demand for the election of leading bodies on the basis of political platforms at least shows the concern to build a serious and lasting united organisation, in which his faction would have some chance of winning support. To go further: at this time he

---

5. The German parliament building where the Social Democrats voted for the war credits in August 1914.
6. VI Lenin, *A Contribution To The History Of The Question Of The Dictatorship* (1920) at http://www.marxists.org/archive/lenin/works/1920/oct/20.htm.
7. Inter-District Organisation.

considered that the Social Democratic Labour Party was a party in which revolutionaries and opportunists should exist side by side. On 7 December 1906 he asserted: "Right up to the social revolution there will inevitably always be an opportunist wing and a revolutionary wing of Social-Democracy."[8] The context shows that he envisaged the disappearance of the "opportunist" wing by the proof of victorious revolution, by persuasion, and not by expulsion or split. Nor have we any right to consider as a mere stratagem the statement by twenty-six of the Bolshevik delegates to the Stockholm Congress, which declared both their hostility to any split and their determination to continue their efforts to convince the whole of the Party and to win it over to their positions. The organisation of the Bolsheviks as a faction, and the establishment, probably from the moment of reunification, of a clandestine Bolshevik Centre in the Social Democratic Labour Party, are in no way contradictory to this statement. In the eyes of the Bolsheviks — and in the eyes of the historian, it must be admitted — this form of organisation was the most effective means of winning over a majority of the militants. Lenin pursued the same line before 1912, when he was reconciled with Plekhanov and formed a "bloc" in the Social Democratic Party with the "pro-Party Mensheviks" against the "liquidators". What was at stake here was the preservation of a clandestine apparatus which the Bolsheviks considered to be necessary and which the liquidators wanted to get rid of. It was on this basis that the Russian Social Democratic Labour Party (Bolshevik) was established, with a "revolutionary" wing and a Menshevik "opportunist" wing...

Clandestine Apparatus and Bureaucrats

Despite hagiography and systematically hostile interpretations, the history of Bolshevik thought is relatively simple to reconstruct. The same is true of the life and conflicts of the émigré groups. The job gets harder when we have to deal with the fundamental tool, the Russian Party, and its structure and functioning. We can even speculate to what extent it will ever be possible, after decades of Stalinist domination; the memoirs of Bolsheviks published in the years after the Revolution, and a part of the Okhrana[9] archives on the question, are a meagre source, which only enable us to sketch an outline. Yet it is on the facts of this period that those who put forward a fatalistic picture essentially base themselves. The *Iskra* emissaries, ten to begin with, thirty at most in 1903, perhaps around a hundred for the Bolsheviks in the following period, form a clandestine "apparatus" whose field of action is constituted by the working-class movement, which selects militants, takes them out of their original working milieu and turns them into "professional revolutionaries". Was the Bolshevik professional revolutionary before 1917 not a direct ancestor of the post-revolutionary Bolshevik leader or bureaucrat? Were the *Komitetchiki* ('Committeemen') not a breeding-ground for "apparatchiks". Serious researchers like Merle Fainsod[10] think

8. VI Lenin: *The Crisis of Menshevism* (1906) at http://www.marxists.org/archive/lenin/works/1906/crimensh/iv.htm#v11pp65-359.
9. The Tsarist secret police.
10. Merle Fainsod (1907-1972): author of many books on Russia and Communism, notably *How Russia is Ruled* (1953).

so: were not 60% of regional secretaries before 1930 "old Bolsheviks" from the era of clandestinity? Was not Stalin the prototype of these "professional revolutionaries" who became bureaucrats? Despite appearances, there is far from being a direct connection between the apparatus of the clandestine party and the apparatus of the party in power, which is not to say there is no connection at all. At the London Congress in 1905 Lenin launched the struggle for the recruitment of workers who were not — and could not be — "professional revolutionaries", but were simply revolutionary working-class militants; this was evidence of a conflict with the committeemen. Krupskaya has described in her memoirs this struggle between Lenin and Rykov, the spokesperson of the clandestine activists[11]: "The *'Komitetchik'* ('Committeeman') was usually a fairly self-assured person ... he generally did not recognise any inner-Party democracy whatever... At the same time they did not like innovations."[12] According to her, Lenin could scarcely contain himself when he had to "listen to them saying that there were no workers suitable to be members of committees".[13] He proposed that it should be compulsory for the committees to contain a majority of workers; the apparatus was already responding as such, and Lenin's proposal was defeated at the Congress. But for all that the apparatus was not victorious: from 1905 and until the Stolypin reaction[14] in 1907, the practices of the Party changed as the gates were opened. From now on the leaders were elected by the rank and file, the bureaucratic spirit was in retreat, new individuals began to establish themselves, orators, agitators and men of action who were not committeemen. However, the sectarian spirit was to keep the Bolsheviks at a distance from the first soviets, where many seemed to fear a rival organisation. Years before Lenin and the Bolsheviks, the isolated Trotsky was able to perceive what the soviets were, the Commune-state, the organisation of the class for the seizure of power. The young Bukharin was also to anticipate, on many points, the analysis made by Lenin in *State and Revolution*. But is it not significant that this analysis, which was to guide action in 1917, was only gradually elaborated, and that it was never really enforced either from within or from without? Inside the united party, it was from the Bolshevik faction that came, repeatedly, the demand for analyses, for theoretical discussions quite alien to the bureaucratic spirit. It was the Mensheviks who accused the Bolsheviks of turning the party into a discussion circle or a "sociology club", and who rejected "theses" in favour of the "practical tasks" or "concrete practical tasks" which every bureaucrat thrives on. The Bolshevik Party was a combat party, but also a party of ideas.

11. AI Rykov (1881-1938): old Bolshevik, spent years in penal servitude; vice-president of the council of People's Commissars under Lenin.
12. N Krupskaya, *Memories of Lenin*, (London, 1970), pp114-15.
13. *Memories of Lenin*, p116.
14. Pyotr Stolypin (1862-1911): Russian Prime Minister from 1906, organised repression after 1905 revolution.

The Bolshevik Party and the Revolution

The party which took power in October 1917 was the continuation of the party founded in 1912 and of the faction which had existed since 1903. Yet it was also quite different. In a few months it had recruited extensively among the younger generation of workers, peasants and soldiers. In January 1917 the clandestine organisation numbered at most 25,000 members whose connection and identification with the Bolsheviks was uncertain. It had 80,000 at the time of the April conference, 200,000 by the time of the Sixth Congress in August: the Old Bolsheviks and *a fortiori* the committeemen formed a minority of little more than one tenth. Not all the new members joined as individuals; they included groups of workers who did not define themselves in relation to the pre-war factions and disputes. The Mezhraiontsy, which had scarcely more than 4000 members in Petrograd, saw three of its members, including Trotsky, elected to the Central Committee. The Bolsheviks welcomed other tendencies who joined their organisation. It is true that they themselves did not form a monolithic bloc : out of fifteen full members of the Central Committee who came directly from the Bolshevik organisation in the strict sense, at least seven had been in open disagreement with Lenin on one subject or another. On this point Robert V Daniels admits that "the new leadership was anything but a collection of disciplined yes-men". Nor did the Bolshevik Party form a network spread out evenly across the whole of Russia. In April, its Petrograd organisation alone numbered 15,000 members, that is 18% of the whole of the Party, and in August 40,000, or 22%. Petrograd and Moscow had half the total membership, and the rest was divided between a few bastions in the other proletarian centres, the Donetz Basin, the Baltic Fleet and Kronstadt. Elsewhere the Bolsheviks were only a minority, sometimes a very small minority, inside the working class which was a minority of society. Certainly the mass character of the party in the industrial centres, and the trust which the vast majority of conscious workers put in it, explain the ultra-democratic atmosphere in its ranks during the months before and immediately after the taking of power. The Bolshevik Party — it must be admitted even if that contradicts the caricature — knew and accepted indiscipline. Zinoviev and Kamenev revealed and disavowed the decision to move towards insurrection: the Central Committee instructed them …not to do it again. But they did do it again and for a some days Kamenev headed a broader opposition to the decision to form a purely Bolshevik government. People's Commissars and members of the Central Committee voted in the Congress of Soviets against the majority positions, against the Party positions. Only after this lapse did the Central Committee take the initiative in replacing Kamenev with Sverdlov as president of the Executive Committee of the Soviets. Lenin's most violent attacks would be against the "deserters", those who resigned. What mattered was not to expel, but to draw the undisciplined comrades back into the Party. The same phenomena recurred at the time of the debate on peace and the Brest-Litovsk negotiations in 1918. The Moscow regional bureau and its newspaper publicly opposed the government position, and Bukharin and his group of "Left Communists" published a daily paper which launched vigorous attacks on the leadership of the Party and the soviets. The Central Committee guaranteed them total freedom of expression within the Party; it expected, without taking any sanctions, that the oppositionists should freely abandon their initiative outside the party, and tried to persuade them.

In reality, during this revolutionary period, Bolshevik policy was every day submitted to the criticism and approval of workers, soldiers and peasants in mass meetings, rallies, trade-union and soviet meetings. The Petrograd workers interrupted Trotsky who was declaiming to them on the necessity of defending themselves against Krasnov,[15] and very roughly shouted at him that he would do better to go to the front instead of preaching to the converted. He complied without taking offence, and it was he himself who recounted the episode. Better than any analysis, the testimonies of contemporaries show how and why the Bolshevik Party was a party where true democracy reigned. John Reed, for example, has left us an unforgettable account of a mass meeting of an armoured car regiment, where the Bolshevik point of view defended by Krylenko was only successful after a long discussion.[16] In the end all the soldiers took up a position for or against, and the overwhelming majority supported the position defended by the Bolshevik speaker. The Menshevik Sukhanov[17] has also left us many accounts of this sort and concludes: "The masses poured life and vigour into the Bolshevik Party, they were entirely in the hands of the party of Lenin and Trotsky".[18] The converse is no less true. Zinoviev and Kamenev appealed to the Party against the decisions of the Central Committee, but from organisations and assemblies of workers throughout the country came the protests which swept away their opposition.

The Birth of the Apparatus

There is a striking contrast between the debates of 1917 and those of 1923, where Stalinist practices and the grip of the apparatus began to assert themselves. Most historians sympathetic to Bolshevism explain this change of character by the necessities imposed by the civil war and the adoption of authoritarian methods which were efficient but undemocratic. This viewpoint is indisputably correct, but how direct was the relationship between the methods of the civil war and the Party regime? This is much more questionable. During the first year of the civil war, the Party seems to have been literally dissolved in the soviets. It had no apparatus and hardly even had any finances of its own. Its secretary, Sverdlov, was at the same time president of the Executive Committee of the Soviets and preferred the latter channel for sending general political directives. The Communists led the soviets according to

15. General PN Krasnov (1869-1947): freed by Bolsheviks when he promised not to take up arms; organised rising of Don Cossacks; later put himself at Hitler's service for a projected Cossack state; handed over to USSR in 1945 and hanged.
16. This is described in Chapter VI ("The Committee for Salvation") of *Ten Days that Shook the World* at http://www.marxists.org/archive/reed/1919/10days/10days/ch6.htm.
17. Nikolai Sukhanov (1882-1939): active revolutionary from youth, took part in 1905 revolution; member of Petrograd soviet 1917, but very critical of Bolsheviks in power; published *The Russian Revolution* 1922; arrested and convicted as Menshevik 1931, shot 1939.
18. NN Sukhanov, *The Russian Revolution 1917* (Princeton, 1984) p490. [This is an abridged translation, and only the first half of the quotation appears in the English text.]

the policy laid down by the Central Committee, but there was no intermediary to transmit orders and directives, no full-time official even on the local level. Sverdlov had around him a staff of just fifteen comrades. Bolsheviks like Preobazhensky[19] could propose the disappearance of the Party as such, without provoking any indignation. In their eyes it seemed useless so long as Communists were inspiring and giving life to the soviets. Others proposed the fusion of the leaderships of the Party and the soviets in order to achieve at the top the unity which already existed on the ground.

A different position prevailed: it was necessary to rise above the local considerations which meant that towns, factories and regions wanted to hang on to their militants. The forces of the Party had to be shared out across the whole country, in order to organise the "mobilisation" of militants to face the most immediate dangers. With respect to these considerations, the Eighth Congress was to attempt to maintain the independence of the soviets from the Party and vice versa. Krestinsky,[20] the new secretary of the Central Committee — Sverdlov had died of typhus — had five "technical assistants", created bureaux and the central administration of the Party: there were eighty full-time staff in 1919. The numbers rose to 150 in 1920, and 600 in March 1921. Only in 1922 had the secretariat got all the members card-indexed, something which was essential for the intended "mobilisation". The apparatus was born at the same time: at this date it had only 15,325 full-timers, of which 5000 were at the level of localities and factories, and as many more at intermediate levels. All were subject to the "Communist maximum", wages which put them on a level with a skilled worker. However, already at this time there were increasing complaints against the "hierarchy of secretaries" which was ever more substituting itself for that of conferences and congresses. It was not yet based on material privileges: a Petrograd leader, Zinoviev's brother-in-law, in this period lost a young child who died of hunger. But it was established by the powers it enjoyed over the assignment of members to positions. Certain bodies, for the most part new ones, concentrated exceptional powers in themselves: regional bureaux, where for the first time in the history of the Party apparatchiks like Kaganovich,[21] Kuibyshev,[22] Rudzutak[23] and Mikoyan[24] appeared prominently. They were under the supervision of the organisation bureau (Orgburo), but especially of the section of the secretariat of the Central Committee for organisation and training, which from 1922 onwards was led by Lazar Kaganovich. By the use of "responsible instructors" and of "plenipotentiaries of the Central Committee", who had the right of veto over the

19. EA Preobrazhensky (1886-1937): Party member from 1903, Party secretary 1920-21; expelled 1927, capitulated 1929; executed without trial.
20. NN Krestinsky (1883-1938): active from 1903; Vice-commissar for Foreign Affairs, then ambassador to Berlin; at least close to the Opposition; executed after third Moscow Trial.
21. Lazar Kaganovich (1893-1991): Bolshevik from 1911; close ally of Stalin in 1930s, known as "iron Lazar"; lost influence after death of Stalin, expelled from Party 1961.
22. VV Kuibyshev (1888-1935): clandestine Bolshevik militant; Red Army commissar; member of Politburo from 1927.
23. JE Rudzutak (1887-1938): Latvian Bolshevik worker in 1906; trade-union leader.
24. Anastas Mikoyan (1895-1978): old Bolshevik, close ally of Stalin; held senior posts under Khrushchev and Brezhnev.

decisions of local organisations, the power of a few men was extended. The nomination bureau moved imperceptibly from the "mass mobilisation" of members to the recommendation, then the appointment pure and simple of leaders at various regional levels, above all within the Party but subsequently outside the Party. The People's Commissariat of Workers' and Peasants' Inspection, conceived by Lenin as a means of controlling the bureaucracy, became in Stalin's hands a tool whereby the bureaucracy controlled the Party. The Central Control Commission, created at the demand of the Workers' Opposition, also became a parallel apparatus. In 1922 the power of the bureaux became embodied in Stalin, who had become secretary general of the Central Committee. Alongside him, Molotov, secretary since 1921, Kaganovich, head of the section for organisation and training, Kuibyshev, head of the Central Control Commission and efficient and devoted regional leaders — Ordjonikidze,[25] Mikoyan, Rudzutak, Zhdanov ... The Stalinist "team" had been formed. In 1923 already it was able to "fix" elections of delegates to conferences and congresses, and to eliminate the opposition in indirect elections. It would be the faithful and originally discreet ally of Zinoviev and Kamenev against Trotsky.

Vanguard and Working Class

How can we explain this stranglehold? The "Party regime" is not a sufficient explanation, since that regime had changed. It is necessary to turn to broader historical explanations, going well beyond the framework of the Party itself, to explain why the same people who in 1917-18 practised the most demanding working-class democracy were capable of submitting themselves, in their great majority, to the emergent authority of the bureaux. First of all, there was no longer a working-class vanguard; the Bolsheviks who formed the general staff of the working-class forces in the great cities of Petrograd and Moscow, at Kronstadt and in the Donetz Basin, were now dispersed. The Kronstadt sailors were all over the place in the most varied positions of responsibility: Dybenko[26] at the head of the Red Army, Roshal[27] in Romania where he would die, Raskolnikov[28] in the East, Markin[29] leading a flotilla on the Volga, Pankratov[30] at the head of a cheka[31] in Transcaucasia. The workers of Petrograd and Moscow had provided the first detachments of red guards, the first armed force of soviet power. They provided the bulk of the commissars whom

---

25. Grigory Ordjonikidze (1886-1937): Old Bolshevik; Central Committee 1921, Politburo 1930; ally of Stalin but distanced himself from some decisions; circumstances of death remain obscure.
26. PE Dybenko (1889-1938): joined Party 1912; 1917 president of Baltic sailors' council; led division against Kronstadt in 1921; shot June 1938.
27. Ensign SG Roshal: one of Bolshevik agitators behind the Baltic fleet mutiny in 1917.
28. Fedor F Raskolnikov (1892-1939): Bolshevik from 1910; commanded Volga fleet, then became ambassador; refused to be recalled.
29. NG Markin (1893-1918): sailor, party organiser at Kronstadt, friend of Trotsky's children; commanded Volga flotilla, killed in action.
30. VF Pankratov: Kronstadt sailor, then member of Cheka; deported 1928.
31. Branch of the All-Russian Extraordinary Commission for Combating Counter-Revolution and Sabotage.

Trotsky demanded to supervise the career officers in the Red Army, as well as the cadres of the soviets in outlying regions or those won back from the Whites. A former Putilov engineering worker, Valek[32], was leading the Omsk soviet. Another, Bodrov,[33] was leading the political staff in Budienny's[34] cavalry. These former vanguard workers were leading chekas, were commissars of regiments, battalions and divisions. It was they who provided leadership for the workers and peasants across the entire territory, depriving the workers in the big centres of its most active and conscious elements.

The working class, deprived of its vanguard which had moved into governmental and administrative functions, bled by the losses of the civil war, was also no longer in its large mass what it had been in 1917-18. While there had been three million industrial workers in 1917, there were only a million and a half in 1920, 1,250,000 in 1921. Moreover the disorganisation of the economy was such was such that one can scarcely speak of real "employment"; "normal" absenteeism was of the order of 50% in the factories, and the difference between a wage and unemployment pay was often purely theoretical. The trade unions estimated that in some factories half the products manufactured were misappropriated and resold by the producers themselves. Famine was a very real threat in 1921 when — supreme irony — there were reports of cases of cannibalism, and all the initiative of the best of those who remained in the factories was devoted to trying to survive, at the price of great demoralisation. Lenin was to say that it was impossible to speak of a "working class" in the sense that Marxists had given to the term.[35] Bukharin would speak of the "disintegration of the proletariat". It was this situation which gave birth to the crisis of 1921, of which Kronstadt was only the most spectacular episode. Whatever historical analogies present themselves to the historian of today after the events of 1956 in Poland and Hungary, should not this historian, while listening carefully to the defenders of the Kronstadt insurgents and the supporters of Makhno, try to grasp the totality of the economic and social conditions, and the ensuing political conditions, which would force the Bolsheviks first of all to accept a political monopoly for their Party — quite contrary to their original objections — and then the stifling of internal democracy? Is not the whole dilemma summed up in Radek's lecture to the Military Academy on the eve of the Kronstadt rising: "The Party is the conscious vanguard of the working class. The time has come when the bulk of the working masses are weary and are reluctant to follow any further a vanguard which continues to lead it along the road of struggle and

32. Anton Valek (1887-1919): revolutionary from age of seventeen; exiled twice and escaped both times; worked at Putilov, then fought on Siberian front; died after being tortured and flogged. There is a short sketch of his life in Victor Serge's *Vie des révolutionnaires* (1930), reproduced in *Mémoires d'un révolutionnaire* (Paris, 2001), p297.
33. Probably Mikhail Bodrov, Moscow metal-worker, later Oppositionist who in 1928 took valuable documents to Sedov in Alma-Ata.
34. SM Budienny (1883-1973): civil war cavalry leader; became Marshal, survived purges and served throughout World War II.
35. See for example his *Summing-Up Speech to the Tenth Congress of the RCP(B)* (March 1921) at http:// www.marxists.org/archive/lenin/works/1921/10thcong/ch02.htm or *The New Economic Policy and the Tasks of the Political Education Departments* (October 1921) at http:// www.marxists.org/archive/lenin/works/1921/oct/17.htm.

sacrifice. Should we yield to workers who have exhausted their physical strength and their patience, and who are less enlightened than we are as to their own general interests? At times their state of mind becomes plainly reactionary. The Party considers that it cannot yield, that it must impose its will to win on the weary workers who are inclined to give way."

* * * * *

The contradictions tearing apart the Bolshevik Party in power are contained in full in this speech by Radek. The future as well as the past; the workers' conscious "vanguard" party as well as the Stalinist party of bureaucrats who substitute themselves for the working masses because they are "more enlightened". It is certainly easy to recall here Trotsky's predictions and his polemic against the Jacobinism of Lenin and the Bolsheviks, his famous phrase about the "dictatorship *of* the proletariat" conceived of as "dictatorship *over* the proletariat".[36] Most commentators have not failed to take this opportunity. Nonetheless this is a simplification which borders on falsification: "Bolshevism", as a form of organisation, certainly ends up, from 1923 onwards, in the dictatorship of the party , that is, of the bureaucracy, over the proletariat. Can it seriously be maintained that the same was true in 1917 and 1918? Can one consider as merely secondary factors material and cultural backwardness, the passivity and ignorance of the peasant masses, the disintegration of the proletariat, the isolation of the Russian Revolution? Can it be claimed that this development was implicit in the circumstances, that the Bolsheviks, by force of circumstances, had to find themselves as the sole advocates of soviet power and were inevitably forced to repress the other working-class tendencies, the Mensheviks and the anarchists? In the judgements made by historians about the degeneration of the Bolshevik Party in power, there is a systematic prejudice to consider the Party as a historical factor which is absolutely independent of the other fundamental factors of human history. To say that the Stalinist counterrevolution was implicit in *State and Revolution*, that the Moscow Trials were implicit in the ban on factions in the Party, means considering as of no significance both the foreign intervention against the young Soviet republic and the alliance of the German Social Democracy with the general staff, not to mention the capitalist system which was itself responsible for the world war. It means denying the intervention in history of the conscious will in the elementary form of organisation, and preaching renunciation and resignation, condemning struggle and even partial victories. In the eyes of the militant, how preferable seems the position of Rosa Luxemburg who, at the end of a pamphlet which was extremely critical with regard to Bolshevik policies, nonetheless wrote:

> In the present period, when we face decisive final struggles in all the world, the most important problem of socialism was and is the burning question of our time. It is not a matter of this or that secondary question of tactics, but of

36. Cf. Leon Trotsky, *Our Political Tasks* (1904) at http:// www.marxists.org/archive/lenin/works/1920/oct/20.htm.

the capacity for action of the proletariat, the strength to act, the will to power of socialism as such. In this, Lenin and Trotsky and their friends were the *first*, those who went ahead as an example to the proletariat of the world; they are still the *only ones* up to now who can cry with Hutten: "I have dared!"

This is the essential and *enduring* in Bolshevik policy. In *this* sense theirs is the immortal historical service of having marched at the head of the international proletariat with the conquest of political power and the practical placing of the problem of the realization of socialism, and of having advanced mightily the settlement of the score between capital and labour in the entire world. In Russia, the problem could only be posed. It could not be solved in Russia. And in *this* sense, the future everywhere belongs to "Bolshevism."[37]

Among others, it is from this point of view that we must set the objectives of a historical study of the Bolshevik Party. The methods used will not be the same if the authors are motivated by an immoderate taste for abstract questions and a desire to prove that nothing can be done to change the world, or alternatively by the quest for historical instruments, of necessity limited, to transform it. It is comforting to observe that it is the latter point of view which leads to real history, faithful to the concreteness of the authentic factors of classes and masses, restoring for us the solidity of living contradictions instead of the aridity of logical diagrams.

---

37. R Luxemburg, *The Russian Revolution* (1918), at http://www.marxists.org/archive/luxemburg/1918/russian-revolution/ch08.htm.

Spartacism, Bolshevism and Ultra-Leftism in Face of the Problems of the Proletarian Revolution in Germany (1918-1923)[1]

THE work which is briefly presented here has been in preparation more or less continuously for nearly fifteen years — this is understandable in the case of a researcher who, throughout this period, has taken on heavy teaching duties, but who has never enjoyed the slightest material aid. It is not the work of a specialist on Germany and is not approached from the point of view of German history, but from that of the history of the international Communist movement, a subject to which the author has devoted a great deal of his time since his adolescence, for reasons that are so obvious that he will be forgiven for not referring to them here.

If we have been attracted by this set of problems, it was because we wanted to find an answer to questions which, in our view, had not hitherto been treated in a satisfactory fashion. We were struck by the place occupied by Germany in the general, global perspectives of the Russian Bolsheviks and the role they assigned to the German Revolution. For them, in fact, the Russian Revolution itself was not, and could not be, anything but the first stage of the world revolution, of which the second decisive stage, in which the whole history of humanity could come to a turning-point, could only be the German Revolution. This belief, whether merely implicit or made explicit, can be seen in all the analyses of the world situation developed by the Bolsheviks until 1923.

In this context, the very fact that the revolution — the world revolution — did not triumph in Germany itself, became a major fact of capital importance, at least in the history of Communism. It certainly cannot be denied that the events frustrated some of the Bolsheviks' expectations, since the German Revolution

---

1. Defence of his doctoral thesis at the University of Paris X.

was not successful. But it is also true that what happened in Germany between 1917 and 1923 did not refute, but rather confirmed, and not only in their own eyes, the Bolsheviks' analysis of the imminence and chances of success of the German Revolution, and of its key role in the history of the unfolding world revolution.

From that point on, the question was raised as to what role had been played in the development of the German Revolution by the Russian experience as it was understood by the Russians, but also as it was understand by the German militants who aimed to emulate them. In other words, in these historical circumstances dominated by the victory in Russia of the first proletarian revolution, by what strategy and tactics did the revolutionaries who called themselves Communists seek to ensure its victory, that of a proletarian revolution? Of course here it was not merely a question of "theses", but of the forms adopted — whether through or against the influence and the pressure of the triumphant Bolsheviks — by the translation of these theses into organisational forms, above all that of a Communist Party which was the German section of the Communist International.

It was this double initial preoccupation which led us to classify the subject under the description of "Spartacism, Bolshevism and ultra-leftism in face of the problems of the proletarian revolution in Germany", which is the correct title of this work, even if unfortunately the book which has been published has a different and less appropriate title.[2]

In fact it is clear that the attempt to create in Germany a Communist Party capable of becoming in that country the "revolutionary leadership" which the Bolshevik Party had been in Russia, to form the organisation which could take the leadership of the mass movement which was natural, necessary and indeed "spontaneous", and which could give a conscious expression to the unconscious process, took on forms which were different to those adopted in Russia during the formation and emergence of the Bolshevik Party. For in Russia, even if the conference of August 1917 revealed the real convergence, through a common attitude to the problems of the revolution, of several organisations or groups, the solid foundation of the revolutionary party was Lenin's Russian Social Democratic Labour Party (Bolshevik), into which flowed the various "streams" of which Radek spoke. In Germany several currents of varying origin, weight and consistency, but in practice of equal importance, really fought and converged simultaneously in the long birth of the Communist Party.

It is *Spartacism* which is generally identified with German Communism in its first years. Doubtless there is an optical illusion here. In fact Spartacism was merely the colour taken on by the prehistory of German Communism, a pure product of social democracy, even if it was conceived and constructed in reaction against it, and even if it appears to be profoundly marked by a World

---

2. The book was originally published in Paris in 1971 under the title *La révolution en Allemagne 1917-1923*. The English translation is *The German Revolution 1917-1923*, (Leiden, 2005).

War which the main body of social democracy did not experience in the same way — not by a long chalk.

At first sight *Bolshevism* seems external, if not alien, to the German movement. After all, was it not conceived and defined by Lenin himself as the means of building *in Russia* the social democratic workers' party, the "revolutionary party" which, in his view, already existed elsewhere? There were no German Bolsheviks, or scarcely any, merely German militants who, as individuals, adopted during the war the international positions of the Bolsheviks. Nonetheless it is impossible to treat Bolshevism as though it were a purely Russian current: in its very conception, its essential features — and all the Bolsheviks stress this — show that it was, all in all and making all necessary adaptations, the reproduction in Tsarist Russia of the German "model" of social democracy. This is what Zinoviev stressed, after the Halle Congress,[3] when he was celebrating the triumph of the "old school". But in historical terms, it did not weigh with its full weight in Germany, by a sort of rebound, or if you prefer by a dialectical turning back of history on itself, until after October 1917 and its victory in Russia.

Ultra-leftism — for there was a genuine current in Germany, and there were to be ultra-left organisations — appears in a substantially different manner. It presents itself as a concrete and correct interpretation of the two other currents, and at the same time runs through them and impregnates them. It also takes on contradictory characteristics. Without any doubt we can find its origin in the tenuous but real current which periodically shakes the grassroots organisations of pre-war social democracy and on occasion is expressed in the press, in unofficial strikes and even in congresses. But it will assert itself in the explosive rejection, in many respects circumstantial, by a whole generation of soldiers of the social democracy's attitude to the war, and eventually by rallying after October 1917 to the Russian model of revolution with which it was to identify itself for a long time.

These three currents came together during the years 1917 to 1923, and were mingled in varying proportions both within the KPD (Spartacus),[4] which was affiliated to the Communist International, and also in the even broader layers of German workers who were organised until the end of 1920 in the Independent Social Democratic Party,[5] where "Spartacism" was despised and "Bolshevism" was celebrated... It is this convergence, its rhythm, its shape and the true extent of the merger, and the relative survival and even the resurgence of the three currents within the KPD, that we have attempted to study, in terms of its forms

---

3. The Special Congress of the Independent Social Democratic Party at Halle in October 1920 voted to affiliate to the Communist International, following which the majority fused with the German Communist Party. See Broué, *The German Revolution*, pp439-43.
4. In December 1918 the Spartacus League split from the Independent Social Democratic Party and formed the Communist Party of Germany (KPD). See *The German Revolution*, pp198-225.
5. Formed at Easter 1917 when the anti-war opposition split from the Social Democratic Party. See *The German Revolution*, pp73-87.

and of its consequences. At the very heart of this subject is the study of the people who organised so that the proletarian revolution should be victorious.

The object of our research was therefore not the German Revolution in itself, and even less Germany during this period, but rather, in a sense, the German Communists in their organised form, in the framework of their party and their International, a framework which at the same time they were striving to build in order to be able to overcome and to bring to victory. Their procedure interested us not as an ideology taken in itself, but as a historical phenomenon. These militants undertook this task with their own baggage of ideas and experiences, with their own past, that of social democracy, its traditions being still more alive and powerful within them than they were conscious of, and which imposed themselves on them both in the form of their theoretical tools and in the form of experience, which was not always direct. They also took on the task on the morrow of the Russian Revolution which they had not lived through, but only imagined from a distance, an experience which had been transmitted to them and which they had perceived in a distorted fashion, and which they were far from having always assimilated in all its aspects, but which they had translated for their own use in the form of theses and revisions, in short of theoretical and practical acquisitions, centred for the majority of them on the notion of armed insurrection.

We were and still are aware that such a subject was perhaps too ambitious, above all with regard to the substantial material obstacles we have encountered in the field of documentation. When we embarked on our research, conditions seemed very favourable to us: abundant source publications, archive materials, leaflets, posters, considerable and apparently accessible resources in several European libraries. But soon difficulties began to build up: the closure till further notice of the archives of the Feltrinelli Institute which we thought we had moved closer to when we came to Grenoble (and the virtually clandestine reopening which we only learned of when it was too late to call everything into question), documents from outside the Communist movement, like the Potsdam police archives, which remained closed to us despite various approaches and interventions, internal documents, for example the archives of the Central Committee, which were likewise inaccessible, in the Institutes of Marxism-Leninism in Berlin and Moscow, although at one point we thought we might finally get access to the documents in the latter. We wondered whether we should carry on or not, whether "politics" pure and simple did not make such research impossible, especially for a researcher who made no secret of his opinions and his activity as a militant. There was great temptation to give up. But for various reasons we thought we should not do so.

First of all contemporary polemics on the one hand, and on the other the opening of the Paul Levi[6] archives in the Buttinger Library in New York, made

6. Paul Levi (1883-1930): lawyer, close to Luxemburg, President of German CP in 1920, but expelled 1921 for public opposition to March Action; later returned to Social Democratic Party.

available documents which either replaced the inaccessible originals or else allowed us to cross-check with a high degree of probability. And also because in the last ten years, researchers in the GDR such as Mr Reisberg[7] have begun to publish documents which prove that the opening of the archives is no longer directly subordinated to immediate political concerns, and because other foreign researchers, who were not victims of the same prejudices as myself, were publishing extracts, summaries and conclusions of documents which could prevent us going too far: in particular this was the case of the works in Serbo-Croat by the Yugoslav historian Vera Mujbegović.[8] Finally, and above all, because giving up would have meant giving in, surrendering without a fight in a struggle for history, when we were firmly convinced that the continuation of our work, its academic defence and publication were one of the most effective means of inciting or even compelling the publication of, or at least improved access to, sources which have hitherto been kept hidden for reasons which could not be acknowledged. And that is why we did not give up.

Numerous difficulties remained. We shall merely mention the distance between the locations of archives and the high cost of travel and microfilms when we never received any subsidy, the extraordinary volume of press material, the time and the expense of analysing them for a provincial researcher, the difficulties of a "political" nature, the sudden ending of a subscription service, the refusal of a meeting, the refusal to guarantee a story which had just been told to us, not to mention the unpleasant surprises such as the discovery of an unpublished document followed by its publication in thousand of copies, or the fact that after spending weeks and months tracking down an extremely rare document, it suddenly appeared as a reprint. In the most recent period, a flood of studies and publications bearing witness to a growing and encouraging interest in our subject eventually threatened at any moment to make our manuscript into Penelope's tapestry.[9]

Despite these difficulties and the undoubted inadequacies which are at least indirectly the consequences of them, even if they cannot all be attributed to "objective" conditions, we have nonetheless arrived at some essential conclusions which we are presenting here in outline.

* * * * *

The first concerns the heterogeneous nature of currents which were originally distinct. It is clear that Spartacism had many faces, that despite their shared tragic fate, Liebknecht and Rosa Luxemburg were not identical, and that there were moreover profound divergences between the two of them and the rest of the nucleus gathered around them, the Spartacus League in which existed side

---

7. Arnold Reisberg (1904-1980): Austrian-born historian of Communist movement.
8. Author of a study of the German Communist Party 1918-23 (Belgrade 1968).
9. Penelope, wife of Odysseus, kept her suitors at bay during his long absence by saying she would not remarry until her tapestry was complete; but each night she unravelled what she had woven during the day.

by side men like Paul Levi — a right-wing Communist — and Otto Rühle[10] — a typical ultra-left. It is also apparent that between the various spokespersons of "Bolshevism" there were more than mere shades of difference, that there were contrasts and even contradictions; and this was not the case merely in the sphere of application, of practice, but in such fundamental theoretical questions as that of the conception of the party: on this point Lenin did not think the same as Zinoviev, and this was not merely a temporary difference... Finally the ultraleft current seemed to us to take on a character which, if not permanent, was certainly chronic, for the organisations or groups which it inspired rapidly disintegrated and were born again almost immediately in a different form in a different organisation: it was a deep current, with roots in the revolt against the social structure and rigidity of social democratic practice, but also a current produced by specific circumstances, linked to the context of Germany after defeat, born of the anger of broad social layers and being reignited at the slightest shift in the conjuncture.

Not only did German Communism aspire to be a synthesis of these three currents, themselves heterogeneous, but it also aimed, basing itself on its Russian model, to achieve this synthesis on a higher level, that of the German working-class movement in its totality, becoming reunited on the road to victory and by the very fact of this potential victory.

Our second conclusion deals with the causes of the failure of this enterprise, and we believe, in the course in the thousand pages to which our study runs, that we have added enough nuances so that we can sum up this judgement here in a way that can only seem to be very brief. The failure of the German Communists in their enterprise of split and reunification was only partly due to factors that were external — in time and space — to the framework of our subject, for the role of "German factors" is considerable and generally underestimated, both in the policy carried out by the Communist International until 1923 and in the history of the Bolshevik Party itself before and after 1923.

It is true — and many historians have already pointed it out — that the influence of the Russian Revolution, then that of the Soviet state, weighed very heavily on Germany, on its working-class movement, and on the very course of the class struggle which unfolded there: the role played in 1921 by Bela Kun[11] in launching the March adventure[12] is obviously a clear illustration and a classic example. But it is less often understood that there is another side to the coin. The perspective of the German Revolution, the second stage of the world

10. Otto Rühle (1874-1943): Social Democratic deputy, backed Liebknecht 1915; spokesman at KPD Founding Conference for ultra-left majority; joined KAPD and later expelled by it; returned to SPD in 1923; emigrated to Mexico, helped organise Dewey Commission on Moscow Trials.
11. Bela Kun (1885-1937): Founder of Hungarian Communist Party, briefly in power 1919; sent to Germany at time of March Action 1921, played important role in Comintern, opposed Stalin's German policy 1932, and later opposed Popular Front, for which arrested, tortured and executed.
12. The March Action, a premature and unprepared general strike launched by the German CP in March 1921. See *The German Revolution*, pp491-503.

revolution, imminent, within reach, was not only valid from 1917 to 1919 — where it was the background to the dispute between Lenin and Bukharin about Brest-Litovsk[13] — but also in 1920, 1921 and even more in 1923, when it formed the axis of the international perspective on the basis of which the Bolsheviks worked out their policy. It is moreover obvious that Germany in these years formed an experimental laboratory in Bolshevik eyes, a measuring device which they believed enabled them to test and verify their policy, to refine and adjust it. There they sought and thought they had found the theoretical expression and the immediate slogans which would enable them to translate into a foreign language the political line and the practice of the Bolsheviks, in other words to transpose Bolshevism into Western Europe. Thus the notorious Twenty-One Conditions[14] devised by the Bolsheviks on the basis of their general analysis of the world situation and elaborated on the basis of their analysis and characterisation of the Independent Social Democratic Party seemed to them to have been tested and verified in the strong sense of the term by the vote of the majority of the latter at Halle, in favour of affiliation to the Communist International. It was the debates opened up in Germany, after the successful response of the working class to the Kapp Putsch,[15] by the proposal of the trade-union leader Legien[16] to form a "socialist government", and which was followed up with the "declaration of loyal opposition"[17] of the KPD to such a government which formed the crucible in which was developed the slogan, soon taken up by the whole International, of the "workers' government", then the "workers' and peasants' government". It was the initiative of the Communist engineering workers in Stuttgart in late 1920, an opportunity seized on by Radek, and developed by him and Paul Levi in the *Open Letter* of January 1921,[18] which formed the basis on which the Communist International was to develop the strategy of the workers' united front from December of the same year.[19] Finally, the so-called "Bolshevisation" — coming after the failure of a genuine Bolshevisation which would have been achieved by the transposition attempted previously — certainly came from Moscow, when it was imposed on the KPD in 1924, but it was also, to a large extent, the translation into Russian and the

13. Peace treaty, signed on 3 March 1918 between Russia and the German Empire, Austria-Hungary, Bulgaria and Ottoman Empire, marking Russia's final withdrawal from World War I; Bukharin opposed this, advocating revolutionary war against Germany. See *The German Revolution*, pp101-2, 117, 123.
14. Conditions for admission agreed at the Second Congress of the Communist International in 1920. See *The German Revolution*, pp423-32.
15. Attempted right-wing coup in March 1920, defeated by workers' action. See *The German Revolution*, pp349-80.
16. Karl Legien (1861-1920), German trade union leader, right-wing Social Democrat, member of the Reichstag from 1893, President of the German Trade Unions; supported war in 1914, but called for general strike against Kapp Putsch. See *The German Revolution*, pp353-71.
17. See *The German Revolution*, pp361-71.
18. See *The German Revolution*, pp468-73.
19. See *The German Revolution*, pp585-98.

response to what had happened and above all to what had not happened in Germany up to this time …

Finally, the genesis of the KPD, and its construction between 1918 and 1923 remained a unfinished process, which was not only interrupted by external factors, since it was precisely the fact that it was incomplete which was the main reason for the free play of other factors, whether it was the solidarity of foreign capitalists in "saving" Germany from disaster or the brutal interruption of the perspective of the German Revolution in the eyes of the Russians. In fact it confirmed the isolation of the Russian Revolution on the basis of which would develop in Russia both the bureaucratic layer and, as a result, the theory of "socialism in one country". Well before this period, the deference of the German Communist leaders towards the Russians could already be explained by the awareness they had, or the anticipation they felt, of their own failure, at least as much as by the confidence and authority of the Russians.

From this point of view, the history of the struggles of the German revolutionaries, among themselves and against the old world, did not seem to us to be comprehensible except by a rejection of any rigorous determinism. Nothing was really laid down in advance, and undoubtedly it was rare for human beings to have within their reach the achievement of their ambition, which was to change the world. We do not mean by this that the story of the first years of Communism in Germany can be reduced to a tale of missed opportunities, but the study, to take a single example, of the "Levi affair", shows without any possible doubt that many other developments were possible for the history of Germany and of the world starting from these "crossroads". If the World War launched in 1939 appears implicitly more than once during these pages devoted to working-class struggles, it is not only because, less than ten years later, Adolf Hitler was to come to power. There was a real choice dependent on the action of Marx's disciples in the Germany of the 1920s, between "socialism" and "barbarism", and the question we face, which is doubtless a long way from being satisfactorily answered, is why they missed the opportunity when so much was at stake.

This is the question we have attempted to reply to, and it would not be possible to sum up all the points made in a few lines or even in a few pages. In the minds of its founders the KPD was certainly a privileged historical tool, aiming to solve in terms of revolutionary leadership the crisis of humanity which had been revealed so blatantly during four years of world war. It was nonetheless the object of history, a social organism subject to its environment, to the past, to external social forces and to the internal divisions of the class on which it claimed to base itself; it went through phases of growth and of disease, of progress and retreat, not always grasping in time the changes of conjuncture on which it needed to base its own formation in the course of class struggles which it did not and could not control.

Thus the KPD during the period being studied presents numerous contradictory features: in fact it brings together the German past, the "old school" of social democracy and the emergent tradition of Communism on its

Bolshevik foundation, in a sense which is actually very different from that which Zinoviev gave it, but which Lenin's remarks to Clara Zetkin[20] show him to have understood quite differently.[21] Just like the German Social Democracy, the KPD, already a "mass party", was in 1922 showing all the signs that a real "counter-society" was beginning to appear, although, for all that, unlike the pre-war social democracy, it did not show any signs in its theory and practice of a tendency towards social integration in this complementary form.

On the basis of this observation it is possible, without putting forward what would be a mere banality, to conclude that the KPD during the period being studied, and taking into account the general and national context, was a formation whose margin for development was relatively slender, and which would very rapidly win a total victory — reunifying the German movement on new bases — or, on the other hand, degenerate, and that therefore, in any case, it was only a transitory formation. This observation would provide a useful working hypothesis for another piece of research: in any case it is far removed from the notion that there is some sort of ahistorical "essence" of Communism, and, of course, is quite opposed to all points of view which identify Bolshevism and Communism and especially Bolshevism and Stalinism.

The political character of the problems posed, the impression left on historiography by "everyday" politics, the monuments of falsification, distortion and evasion which we have had to clear aside in order to draw out the lines of development of the overall process presented us with special requirements, notably that of reconstructing in detail, in certain given circumstances, a context and a development which some would perhaps describe as factual history: there is no history, in general and even more so in a case like this, which can, without such a way of proceeding, offer its readers the guarantee that the work is based on a very careful examination of the texture of a development which was not laid down in advance, and not based on an *a priori* ideology, even if it is hidden behind a so-called scientific vocabulary...

It must be clear that above all we wanted to give an account of what we have decided to call the "conscious part" of the "unconscious process" which was unfolding in the depths of the German working class during this period, that is, the visible part of the iceberg, the efforts of the militants to organise, master and qualitatively transform a class movement which they did not control. We shall not deny that it would have been just as interesting — perhaps more — to deepen our knowledge of the unconscious process, to try to dismantle the mechanisms of a "spontaneous" movement which formed the basis of the intervention of the militants whom we have applied ourselves to studying. Is it really necessary to say that in order to carry out such a task in our day we should have needed not only different political conditions, but a whole different

20. Clara Zetkin (1857-1933): Veteran German Social Democrat, organised Socialist women, close to Rosa Luxemburg; joined German Communist Party shortly after its formation and remained on its right wing, supporting Paul Levi.
21. A reference to Lenin's discussions with Zetkin during the Third Comintern Congress. See *The German Revolution*, pp549-51.

political development behind us? We did not have at our disposal, and in all likelihood no-one will ever have at their disposal with regard to the German Revolution, those materials which enabled Trotsky, in his *History of the Russian Revolution*, to give an account of those hidden but decisive phenomena which form the framework for all the political initiatives, for the ground in which thought and militant practice were rooted. We have had to be satisfied — and in the end it is at least something — with recording this movement through the reflection and awareness of the people who strive to make history consciously.

From this point of view, it would be unfair to criticise us for having written a history simply on the level of the party leaderships, which would first of all imply that there were "several" leaderships, and then that we constantly remained on the level of political bureaux and central committees, whereas the scope of our work includes a party with hundreds of thousands of members, without counting its periphery, the revolutionary "milieu" in which it operated. It is true that the problems we are confronting are indeed problems of "leadership", if what is meant by that is the attempts of human beings to make their own history. But then we should expect to be told, without lapsing into the crudest and most unscientific determinism, how human history — and indeed "History" — can be achieved through a functional analysis of structures, which would obviously be the perspective to contrast to our own, and which we for our part consider to be totally sterile outside of artificially demarcated and narrowly limited circumstances, that is, taking no account of the movement of history itself. Such a method could only be used for circumstantial partisan purposes, not for the understanding and ultimately the control of human history.

However, we must indicate that we should never, throughout the length of our work, lose sight of the presence and interaction of factors which we have neither forgotten nor underestimated, but on which we did not insist because they were not our subject, and that for obvious reasons in view of the extent of the material used and dealt with: economic and social power; intelligence, that is the political experience of the German bourgeoisie which was able to assimilate to its own advantage the Russian experience at a time when the working class perceived it only in its most schematic form and sometimes even as a caricature; its scientific practice of class struggle, its capacity for foreseeing the future, for taking the initiative, whether by reforms, promises or provocation; and finally international factors, other than the Russian Revolution in the strict sense, above all the hatred of the world revolution which had just appeared in Russia, the Holy Alliance of the privileged in their "Great Fear".

It remains that our study — at least we think so — has brought to light some "terrifying seeds of reality" which ideologists of various shades will find it hard to assimilate. We have no doubt that, in such cases, they will not blame their own fixed ideas or their own cult of the accomplished fact — the most unhistorical approach possible — but rather what they will call our "ideology", whether or not they consider it to be "coherent". We can simply offer them our apologies: it is not our fault if the Russian Revolution preceded the German Revolution chronologically, if the Communist militants who thought they should adapt the lessons of the Russian Revolution to their own country played a more determining role than the supporters of anti-authoritarian philosophies, if the role of Lenin and even of Radek was far more important than that of the very likeable Otto Rühle, whose part was not completely insignificant. It is also not our fault if the people who were the subject of our study were not able to take advantage of the recent development of social sciences which is said to prove irrefutably, according to some people, that their "project" — the cause for which a number of them sacrificed their lives — was in fact only a second-rate utopia! Let our critics refrain from criticising us for not having written the book they would like to have written! For our part, in the framework of this historical study, we have tried to give an account of the German Communist militants, and of their thought and action.

The other questions, despite the inevitable interactions — whether accidental or malevolent — belong to a different framework in which we shall always be ready to continue or to begin a public discussion of.

Five Years On[1]

IN the early months of 1924 the executive set about using 'bolshevisation' as a pretext for purging the Communist International and cleansing it of any independent-minded spirits. Yet only five years earlier, in a small room in the Smolny, a handful of militants had proclaimed its birth. Communist parties, both big and little, now existed in every corner of the world. Every Communist believed that these parties would grow and grow, both in number and in size, and that within a reasonable space of time (a matter of years) the revolution would end in triumph across the whole planet.

Crisis or uneasiness?

Many of those roused to political consciousness and action by the Russian Revolution had unreservedly immersed themselves in revolutionary struggle but were now affected painfully, to a greater or lesser degree, by what had happened and was happening in Russia. They were conscious of incomprehensible developments, of unacceptable oppositions and of unimaginable accusations.

In the first months of 1924 they knew that there existed a serious conflict at the top of the International. But as the case of Boris Souvarine[2] shows (despite his lucidity, he tried but failed to comprehend), not even the best and most intellectually gifted among them ultimately had any grasp of what was developing in the capital of their revolution, at the head of the first country to witness a victorious revolution.

Severe losses

Of course, soldiers, and sometimes even generals, die in war. Of course, as peddlers in 'politically correct' commonplaces repeat *ad nauseam*, the revolution devours its children. But even so, what an appetite! The history of the International started, as we have seen, with the disappearance — three murders and one unhappy death — of four of its founding fathers: Rosa Luxemburg, Karl Liebknecht, Leo Jogiches[3] and Franz Mehring.[4] Five years later, it lost

---

1. Chapter XVII of "L'histoire de l'Internationale Communiste" Tr. Gareth Jenkins. All biographical and historical notes are added by RH editors.
2. Boris Souvarine (Lifschitz) (1895-1984): Founder member of French Communist Party and leading figure in early years; expelled 1924 for supporting Trotsky; did not follow Trotsky, but became writer on Comintern without militant activity.
3. Leo Jogiches (1867-1919): Polish socialist and close collaborator with Rosa Luxemburg; leading organiser of Spartacus League in Germany; murdered in prison while investigating Luxemburg's death.

Lenin who had been the most constant, lucid and determined fighter for the founding and construction of the International. Can we grasp what this meant? The International had been decapitated — literally. To measure the extent of this mutilation, let us imagine that Karl Marx and Friedrich Engels had disappeared a few years after the publication of *The Communist Manifesto*. What would have become of that 'Marxist' body of thought which left such a deep imprint on the political and social ideas of the nineteenth century? Who in their wake would have ensured its development and growth? We are talking here of an entire front rank being destroyed.

How is it possible not to recognise what is, after all, undeniable? The disappearance of these tried and tested Marxists, these indisputably theoretical 'brains', had an inescapable significance for the crisis in Marxist thought that was exploding in tandem with the developing crisis in the revolution. Our intention is not to underestimate the importance and striking character of Trotsky's thought (he was the unchallengeable giant of political thought in the century). But is it not clear that the deaths of Rosa Luxemburg and Lenin in a way clipped his wings? Was he not, to some degree, forced to mount a conservative defence of the revolutionary thought of those who had disappeared? At the very moment when, undeniably, his creative faculties were most needed, we see the eagle Trotsky confining himself — and what else could he have done? — to proving that he was the most 'Bolshevik' and 'Leninist' of them all. He was thereby condemned to play, in the strict sense of the term, a conservative role (that of preserving the threatened body of theory). He was condemned to exalt the old, venerable, yet worn-out tools, instead of perfecting or forging new ones from them.

Lost leaders

Behind the pioneers who had disappeared stood a second rank, the men who doubtless would have been summoned to succeed them and become the first rank. Not all the rich potential of their intelligence and consciousness had yet developed. Nevertheless these men had already, at different times, embodied a stage in the socialist awareness of workers, of human consciousness. They too were missing at this point at the beginning of 1924, even if they were not dead or rather not yet all been killed off.

John Maclean,[5] the schoolmaster and Marxist teacher, had organised the Clydeside shipyard workers in the middle of the war and been a friend to the oppressed Irish people. He had just died in solitude, impoverished and in a minority, having never made the journey to Moscow or belonged to the International. Exhausted by prison and repeated hunger strikes, he had been

---

4. Franz Mehring (1846-1919): German historian, won over to Marxism; founding member of German Communist Party, died shortly after Luxemburg.
5. John Maclean (1879-1922): Scottish teacher, opponent of World War I; health damaged by imprisonment, died prematurely.

powerless to persuade his comrades in England and in the Communist International that a Communist party was needed in Scotland.

John Reed,[6] 'Jack', was much more than the romantic revolutionary that is the usual image of him. He was, quite simply, a revolutionary — a man of immense intelligence and unfailing courage, whose lucidity was respected by all. Typhus, or, to put it another way, the exhaustion and wretchedness that the blockade inflicted on the human body, had killed him in a matter of weeks.

Raymond Lefebvre,[7] as we have seen, had bewitched all those who had known him. This writer, thinker and orator had drowned — that is, he too had been killed by the blockade of the supposedly 'democratic' Allies. 'Tomorrow's leader' would never lead — and without a doubt was irreplaceable.

Of Lev Davidovich Trotsky's future we have spoken. But what a past this young man had already had! He had been chairman of the St Petersburg's workers' soviet in 1905 and his defence at his trial had been an historic indictment of a backward and autocratic regime. He had led the October insurrection in Petrograd, created the Red Army from scratch and been its victorious commander. He was now diagnosing the crisis of the revolution and the evil from which the fatherland of the oppressed was suffering. He was engaged in a struggle against the apparatus.

Christian Georgievich Rakovsky[8] was another of these soaring individuals. A leading intellectual of the European workers' movement, who had become a member of the bureau of the Second International, he had revived international relations in the middle of the war and laid the foundations of the Communist International before embarking on and winning the most terrible of the civil wars as head of the Ukrainian Soviet government. He had taken up the struggle against the apparatus with Lenin, even before Trotsky had done (reckless as ever, according to the latter). Though neither Lenin nor Rakovsky were dead (at least not yet), they had been sidelined. Rakovsky was in exile, together with Bredis and Andreychin,[9] and could no longer participate in the leadership of the International, above whose leaders both he and Trotsky towered head and shoulders.

Others too were sidelined, for example, Paul Levi,[10] Rosa's disciple and also her

6. John Reed (1887-1920): American journalist, author of *Ten Days that Shook the World*; leader of Communist Labor Party of America, and member of Comintern Executive; died of typhus after Baku Congress 1920.
7. Raymond Lefebvre (1891-1920): French lawyer and journalist; after two years of military service became opponent of war; attended Second Congress of Comintern and was lost at sea in the Arctic Ocean on his way home.
8. Khristian Rakovsky (1873-1941): Bulgarian revolutionary, friend of Trotsky, organiser of Zimmerwald conference; send abroad as diplomat by Stalin because of oppositional views; later deported; "repented" in 1934, imprisoned, later executed.
9. Giorgi Andreychin (1894-1952): Born in Macedonia, militant in Bulgaria, then emigrated to USA; became miner and IWW activist; in Moscow 1920, oppositionist 1923, exiled 1928, released 1945; returned to Bulgaria and worked in Foreign Ministry; liquidated.
10. Paul Levi (1883-1930): lawyer, close to Rosa Luxemburg; followed her as leader of German CP, brutally expelled "ultra-lefts", but excluded from CP for indiscipline after March Action; returned to Social Democrats.

talented successor, who had shielded the infant party against Noske's[11] killers and its own hotheads — he, at least, had 'a head', a rare thing, as Lenin recognised. Also about to be sidelined was Heinrich Brandler,[12] the imperturbable, calm and cautious building worker. So too would the jovial Serrati,[13] leader of a mass party that had melted like snow in the sun, and the eloquent Bordiga.[14] So too would Pierre Monatte[15] and Alfred Rosmer,[16] those respected symbols of French syndicalism whom the Communist movement had won to its side, the better to lose them. So too would Willy Münzenberg,[17] that leader of men who had taken up business. So too had Louis Fraina,[18] kept out of touch in Mexico by the International. So too had the Poles Marchlewski,[19] Warski[20] and Kostrzewa,[21] who brought up the debate about the post-October politics of the Bolsheviks that Rosa Luxemburg had intended to open and that never took place. Shunted to one side, in other words, was the German-Polish 'KPD-KPP political axis', attributed by Felix Tych to Rosa Luxemburg, which Levi had never believed in and which after Levi's departure Clara Zetkin would not champion.

11. Gustav Noske (1868-1946): Right-wing German Social Democrat, became War Minister in 1918; the *Freikorps* whom he protected massacred Berlin workers, killing Liebknecht and Luxemburg; career ended with Kapp putsch when military leaders betrayed him.
12. Heinrich Brandler (1881-1967): Founder member of German CP, and member of Comintern presidium; involved in preparing 1923 rising in Germany, made scapegoat for failure and expelled in 1929; then formed KPO, close to Bukharinite tendency.
13. Giacinto Serrati (1874-1926): Leader of maximalist wing of Italian Socialist Party, opposed 21 Conditions and only admitted to Italian Communist Party in 1924.
14. Amadeo Bordiga (1899-1970): Leader of "Communist abstentionist" current in Italian Socialist Party; became leader of Italian Communist Party, but removed 1926 by Gramsci and Togliatti; secretly expelled from CP for "Trotskyism" and "factionalism".
15. Pierre Monatte (1881-1960): Revolutionary syndicalist, friend of Trotsky and Rosmer, joined French CP but expelled 1924; returned to revolutionary syndicalism.
16. Alfred Rosmer (1877-1964): Revolutionary syndicalist, opposed World War I, became friend of Trotsky; in 1920 went to Moscow for seventeen months, active in Comintern and Red International of Labour Unions; expelled from French CP 1924 for opposition to Bolshevisation; 1929-31 organiser of Left Opposition, but broke with Trotsky; see *Revolutionary History* Volume 7, No. 4.
17. Willi Münzenberg (1887-1940): Leading Swiss Socialist, secretary of Communist Youth International till 1921; organised International Workers' Aid, then built influential campaigning "Münzenberg Empire" (newspapers, films, publishing-houses); later opposed Comintern line and condemned Hitler-Stalin Pact; interned in France where he was murdered.
18. Louis Fraina (Lewis Corey) (1894-1952): Member of American Socialist Labor Party, international secretary of American CP, sent to Mexico by Comintern, withdrew discreetly; well-known writer under name of Corey.
19. Julian Marchlewski (1866-1925): Veteran Polish socialist, represented his party in Moscow in 1920.
20. Adolf Warski (1868-1937): Veteran Polish socialist, internationalist during World War I, founder of Polish CP, twice removed from its leadership by Comintern; as refugee in Russia arrested and executed in 1937.
21. Vera Kostrzewa (1876-1938); Veteran Polish Socialist; on Central Committee of newly founded CP and was part of leadership twice removed by Stalin; in Russia from 1930, arrested and executed in prison.

The new leaders

Who then was now leading this International? What kind of men had they been when, in the dark night at the beginning of the world war, revolutionaries had been searching each other out, lantern in hand? The leaders of the Communist International were the leaders of the Russian Communist Party, the *troika*, as it was called in Moscow, Zinoviev, Kamenev and Stalin. Of the three, Kamenev[22] had never had much to do with the International; Stalin had only just begun to interfere; and Zinoviev had been its chairman since its foundation. Their personalities, role and importance should not be minimised. They were unquestionably out of the ordinary. But they are far from being comparable with their predecessors.

Zinoviev had been Lenin's devoted lieutenant in exile, the talented vulgariser of his thought. He had also carried out Lenin's dirty work in factional struggles, a role that had won him numerous enemies. He was a passable writer, though with a somewhat overblown style. On the other hand, he was an orator with exceptional powers of conviction, a man, moreover, who was passionately fond of convincing and persuading. But on several occasions he had collapsed in moments of danger or when major decisions needed taking — and there were those who had not forgotten some of his big panics, as when General Yudenich had launched his offensive against Petrograd in 1919. He had become the chairman of the International because he had lived for a long time in the West, where he knew many people, and because he spoke German fluently. But he was also available in that March of 1919, it must be said, because his terrible lapse — the public denunciation of the insurrection being prepared in October 1917 — had meant he had been passed over for all the key posts in the first year of soviet power. He had certainly pulled off a feat of oratory at the Halle congress of 1920 and brought great political success. All the same, that was insufficient to make of him the undisputed leader of the International that he wanted to be and thought he was — or to have his authoritarianism and summary methods forgotten.

Up till then, his accomplice Joseph Vissarionovich Djugashvili, or Stalin, had shone in the International above all by virtue of his unobtrusiveness. A delegate from the Russian party at its founding congress, he had not spoken. There were dark areas in his political past before 1917. Lenin valued him as a solid worker. But he was a party man, who had only lived abroad for a short while, knew no Western language and few foreign militants. Having become the all-powerful General Secretary of the party in 1922, he had rationalised the apparatus, of which he was the organiser, and rigorously centralised, homogenised and subjugated it. Those who knew him said he was surly, vindictive and brutal. What was not yet known — the Russian people would have to wait nearly forty years to find out — was that before his death Lenin had broken off all personal

---

22. Lev Kamenev (1883-1936): Closely linked to Zinoviev; part of coalition against Trotsky, then of troika against Stalin; never involved in Comintern; shot after first Moscow Trial.

relations with him after condemning his brutality and 'cop' mentality. Nor was it known that the postscript to Lenin's testament had recommended Stalin's removal from the Secretariat, where he had concentrated 'excessive power' in his hands. In 1924 Stalin took his first cautious steps on the terrain of the International, which he was now getting to know.

We shall only speak of the others in passing.

The problem of formal leadership

The difficulties with providing the Communist International with an appropriate structure were immense. For some considerable time the parties were not keen on sending what they considered their leaders to Moscow. On occasions they even seized on the need to have a representative in Moscow as a pretext for getting rid of someone they saw as an embarrassment or simply a malcontent. There too things developed in a very ad hoc manner. The first executive remained a fiction, the real work of leadership being consigned to a handful of Russian leaders.

From the Second Congress onwards, some rules were adopted but what emerged from the executive was a tight leadership, the real one — the 'small bureau' that would become the Presidium. The institution of 'enlarged executives' — with several hundred people present — allowed party representation to be reconciled with a permanent leadership arising from the International Congress and not from the parties as such. Above all, the central apparatus was reinforced by reforming the statutes at the Third Congress. The political leadership would henceforth depend on a truly bureaucratic apparatus.

It was the secretariat, limited in number, together with a certain number of departments that guaranteed the power of the apparatus in the main. The most important of these departments was the organisational one, the *orgburo*, led by a member of the executive whose business it was to regulate the organisational problems raised by the sections. The agit-prop department, also led by a member of the executive, was responsible notably for running and controlling the world press of the Communist parties. In addition there was a department for the Far East, to carry out work in Asia and 'colonial' work in general; a department for information and statistics; the very important trade union department; and the international women's department. Preparation was underway to create an international control commission. Any Communist living on soviet territory was, according to rule, a member of the soviet party. So too were political refugees and even temporary delegates. They all had to submit to its discipline and therefore to the authority of the all-powerful General Secretary.

The strength of the Stalinist bureaucrats

What gave the people who led the International after five years' existence their authority? It was not genius. It was not their gifts as theoreticians or leaders of men, nor their role in the revolution and the survival of the victorious workers' state. Quite simply, it was a system — the bureaucratic system of degeneration that had infected the Russian party after those terrible years of isolation and unspeakable suffering caused by the blockade and the civil war following foreign intervention. The system worked well. It was one in which someone like Stalin would see off someone like Trotsky and in which a revolutionary worker like Ivan Nikich Smirnov,[23] whom Lenin called 'the conscience of the party', would give way to wooden-arsed Molotov, the man who, in his own words, lacked genius but not perseverance.

With its triumph in the Russian party and its domination reaffirmed in the battle over the New Course at the end of 1923, this system began to infiltrate the International via the apparatus. It was constructed on the same pattern, often using the same men, whose only distinction consisted in the defeats that the working class in their countries had suffered under their leadership and that had forced them into exile. These were men with the temperament of subordinates — hard men, underlings and enforcers, the Guralskys[24] and Rákosis[25] educated in the school of what Lenin called 'kuneries'. [26]And it was the self-same Bela Kun[27] we saw in 1919 and in 1921, who returned from his exile in the Urals at that very moment, following Lenin's death.

It was not, however, because they appeared as what they were — defenders of the new bureaucratic order — that these men now had authority. It was because of what they said they were — professional revolutionaries who represented the Russian Revolution and the party that had led it to victory. For these Communist leaders who had turned into bureaucrats were still in some sense Communists who truly wished for the victory of the revolution — provided, of course, that it did not overly disturb them! Their followers, however, took matters on trust without always understanding or approving them.

Historians of the Communist parties have shed some light on this problem. Speaking of the French Communist Party line in 1924, Philippe Robrieux[28] points out how the 'war chest' accumulated the previous year for the German Revolution was put to use by the new leadership and how a series of young

23. Ivan Smirnov (1881-1936): Old Bolshevik from 1903, member of Left Opposition, capitulated 1929, but subsequently built opposition group, imprisoned and executed after first Moscow Trial where he "confessed".
24. August Guralsky (1890-1960): Joined Bolsheviks 1919, worked with Zinoviev in Comintern, sent to Germany at time of March Action; sidelined after fall of Zinoviev and sent to Latin America; imprisoned during purges but survived and died in Moscow.
25. Matyas Rákosi (1892-1971): People's Commissar in Hungarian revolution of 1919, then worked for Comintern; imprisoned in Hungary 1925, exchanged and returned to Russia 1940; Stalinist dictator in Hungary after World War II, but after 1956 exiled to Central Asia.
26. An untranslatable pun meaning 'stupidities of Bela Kun'.
27. Bela Kun (1885-1937): Founder of Hungarian Communist Party, briefly in power 1919; sent to Germany at time of March Action 1921, played important role in Comintern, opposed Stalin's German policy 1932, and later opposed Popular Front, for which arrested, tortured and executed.
28. Author of the *Histoire intérieure du parti communiste*, 4 vols, Paris, 1980-84.

militants, many of whom, from Jacques Duclos[29] to Benoît Frachon[30] and François Billoux,[31] would become leaders in the Stalinist epoch, were 'professionalised'. He describes French militants coping with the pressure from those they felt were the 'giants of October':

> How could one stand firm when torn or trapped in a vice of contradictory feelings and ideas? On the one hand, there was devoted admiration for the towering figure of Trotsky and attachment to the International; on the other, there was a professional feeling that keeping one's mind on meetings, people, the International took precedence over critical examination of political issues and being able to weigh them up [...] How conceivably could one be right against these men and what they represented? How could one resolve to give up the position of professional militant to return to the factory? It would not have been easy to swap the heady atmosphere of meetings and rallies for the depressing surroundings of the workshop, with its never-ending, tedious round of activity. At the end of the day, to resign oneself to anonymity was extremely difficult to accept.[32]

More broadly, it dawned on everyone sooner or later that capitalism had stabilised, that the Dawes plan had put an end to the German crisis and that the revolution was now, as Trotsky put it at the Third Congress, 'a matter of years'. For all that revolution had not slipped off the agenda. The German workers were still there — so were the Austrian workers, with their workers' militias, and the Italian workers, who in the aftermath of Matteotti's[33] assassination would soon seem to be within a hair's breadth of overthrowing a shaken Mussolini. And there were the Spanish who in a dozen years would bring about a revolution comparable in depth to that in Russia — an even deeper one, according to Andrés Nin,[34] who experienced both. Trotsky himself believed up till 1933 in the probable revival of what he called the 'working class kernel of the Bolshevik Party'. Furthermore at stake was not only Europe. Other perspectives opened up, quite unexpectedly sometimes, which might have reversed matters.

29. Jacques Duclos (1896-1975): Joined French CP shortly after foundation, on Central Committee 1926, Executive of Comintern 1935; lived clandestinely in occupied France, returned to Party leadership at Liberation.
30. Benoît Frachon (1893-1975): Founder-member of French CP; after World War II leader of CGT.
31. François Billoux (1903-1978): Leader of French Communist Youth in 1920s, Comintern agent in Spanish civil war; imprisoned under German occupation, minister under de Gaulle at Liberation.
32. P. Robrieux, *Histoire intérieure du parti communiste*, Vol. I, pp210-211.
33. Giacomo Matteotti (1885-1924): Italian Socialist deputy, murdered by Mussolini's Blackshirts.
34. Andrés Nin (1892-1937): Member of Spanish Communist Party, in Russia in 1920s as secretary of Red International of Labour Unions; supporter of Left Opposition; returned to Spain 1931, formed Communist Left, which became one of components of POUM; entered Catalan government, leading to break with Trotsky; kidnapped, tortured and murdered on Russian orders.

Joffe,[35] as we have seen, negotiated with Sun Zhongshan [Sun Yat-sen][36] and Borodin[37] arrived in China — the advance guard of numerous diplomats, military advisers and other Communist advisers.

The dark crossroads

However, this particular moment, what Victor Serge[38] called 'the dark crossroads' marked the start of a quite different story. The Communist International, the Comintern, was no longer what it had been — and would never again be. From the International of Lenin's time we slide darkly towards that of Stalin's. We could call it the Komintern if we wished to. It hardly matters from now on, even if the Cominternians (to coin a horrible neologism) were becoming Kominternians (to coin an even worse one) and would later receive a bullet to the head in the Lubyanka (something, incidentally, which never happened in Lenin's time and which even the blindest of historians might recognise as signalling a change of direction).

A history of ideas, requiring decades of team-work, might allow us to uncover the mechanisms and stages of a transformation that had barely surfaced in 1923. In reality there had been a transition from the idea of the party as an indispensable mount for the history-making mass movement to ride on, to the idea of the party-state (characterised by the bureaucratic regime) as having to be established by the insurrection as its pre-ordained object.

. One whole school of thought, including Victor Serge, dates the beginning of this metamorphosis to 1920. In our opinion, that is to confuse the beginning of an accumulation of features that around 1923 would transform quantity into quality.

International centralisation

The International centre, in the shape of its leading bodies, was, like the Russian party, a highly centralised organisation, an apparatus of rigorously trained professionals. But it was no less the product of a political will that had grown over the years than it was the product of day-to-day empirical politics. It is difficult to accept Karel Svátek's argument that the Zimmerwald left was the ancestor of the institutions of the International. It was the ancestor of the International, without doubt, but not of its apparatus. For the left had only drawn leaders together.

35. Adolf Joffe (1883-1927): Old friend of Trotsky, Soviet diplomat in Berlin and China, committed suicide when gravely ill, making death a political protest against Stalin.
36. Sun Yat-sen (1866-1925): Father of Chinese nationalism and founder of Kuomintang.
37. Mikhail Borodin (1884-1951): Old Bolshevik, emigrated to USA, returned to Russia 1918; travelled widely as Comintern official, but removed from all Comintern activity in 1927.
38. Victor Serge (Kibalchich) (1890-1947): Writer, born in Belgium of Russian origin, anarchist, became Bolshevik in post-revolutionary Russia, worked for Comintern press, expelled for oppositional activities but returned to West where he did much to publicise repression in Russia.

As we have seen, the top men of the Comintern came from the foreign bureau for revolutionary propaganda abroad, which was appointed to the commissariat for foreign affairs. The Russian federation of Communist groups, highly centralised in the image of the party, was answerable to this office and existed formally up till 1920.

The men of this apparatus were first and foremost Russians, Poles or Latvians, familiar with life abroad, having worked and lived in exile. Initially they had acted as semi-diplomats and returned to that role from 1920-1921 onwards (we have in mind here three of the first secretaries of the Comintern, V V Voroski,[39] Jan Berzine[40] and Mikhail Kobetsky).[41] Abramovich,[42] Bratman,[43] Bronski[44] and Karakhan[45] reappeared in embassies or consulates. One exception was Walecki,[46] who remained within the apparatus of the Comintern: he was one of the few needed for negotiations.

Amongst those who remained or kept their positions there were only a few Russians — and these, moreover, had jobs reserved for them requiring confidentiality or specialist techniques: for example, Zinoviev's two young secretaries, Richard Pikel[47] and A Tivel,[48] an orientalist who had played an important role in Turkestan. Alongside the Russian Piatnitsky,[49] the all-powerful boss of the OMS,[50] which acted to liaise and to control finances, were two deputies, also Russian, the former railway worker, Peter Wompe,[51] who was in charge of liaison, and Aleksandr Abramov,[52]

39. Václav Vorovski (1871-1923): Polish professional revolutionary, diplomat after Russian Revolution, murdered at Lausanne by a reactionary.
40. Jan Berzine (1881-1938): Organised Bolshevik faction in Latvian Social Democratic party; secretary of Comintern Executive, later diplomat; arrested as "nationalist" in 1937.
41. Mikhail Kobetsky (1881-1937): Active in Russia and Denmark, then from 1929-1934 in Comintern apparatus, subsequently as diplomat; arrested and executed.
42. Aleksandr Abramovich (1888-??): Bolshevik from 1908, emigrated to Switzerland, returned to Russia with Lenin; worked in Comintern apparatus till 1931; apparently arrested in 1930s but survived purges.
43. Stefan Bratman (1880-1937): Pole, emigrated to Switzerland; worked on Comintern Executive, then as diplomat; arrested and executed.
44. Mieczyslaw Bronski (1882-1937): Represented Poles at Zimmerwald; returned to Moscow with Lenin, and took part in several missions abroad, but not subsequently active in Comintern; disappeared during purges.
45. Lev Karakhan (1889-1937): Old Armenian Bolshevik, member of Mezhraiontsy, worked for Comintern, then as diplomat; shot.
46. Maximilian Walecki (1877-1938): Polish socialist, took part in Zimmerwald, leader of Polish CP, worked extensively for Comintern, arrested 1937, executed.
47. Richard Pikel (1896-1936 or 1937): Joined Bolshevik Party from Mezhraiontsy in 1917; political commissar in civil war; arrested as "Trotskyist counterrevolutionary" in 1936 and executed in prison.
48. Alexander Tivel (1899-1937); Originally anarchist; MN Roy's secretary and interpreter in Tashkent; leading official in Comintern; arrested in 1936 and executed.
49. Ossip Piatnitsky (1882-1939): Bolshevik from 1903, member of Comintern Executive from 1921; Central Committee of Party from 1934; imprisoned, denounced as spy and executed for voting against Stalin on CC on question of Bukharin.
50. The Comintern's international liaison department.
51. Peter Wompe (1891-1925): Menshevik, joined Bolsheviks 1917, Piatnitsky's deputy in Comintern; played important role in preparing for German October in 1923.
52. Aleksandr Abramov (1895-1937): Russian, active in organising Comintern's international liaison department in Central Europe; arrested and shot, accused of establishing contacts between Bela Kun and Trotsky.

who controlled the movement of funds. Watching over all these people was the Chekist Meyer Trilisser (Moskvin).[53]

The remainder were émigrés — revolutionaries who had had to flee their countries after the defeat of the revolution and who had been transformed into pilgrims or into international controllers who carried out directives or checked their application. There were Balts — Zigmas Alexas,[54] a Lithuanian, and Jan Anvelt,[55] who was Zinoviev's man. There were Finnish Communists. To start with, there was Otto Kuusinen,[56] one of the four first secretaries of the CI after 1922, of whom Lenin wrote that he could think, a rare thing in revolutionaries. Mauno Heimo[57] was an outstanding operator of the apparatus, in some sense its administrative secretary. Tuure Lehén[58] was in charge of training officers, of military teaching for the cadres — in short, he was the Comintern's specialist in military matters. There were Hungarians: Rudnyánszký,[59] who disappeared with a large sum of money in 1921, but who, despite that, was to reappear; Béla Szántó,[60] former war commissioner in his country, and of course Béla Kun, who made no public appearances; Matyas Rákosi, who was also one of the secretaries; and Jozef Pogány[61], who, under the name of Pepper, was distinguished for his stupidities. There was also Ilona Duczynska,[62] who lasted no longer than Levi, whose analyses she shared. The Bulgarian Kolarov[63] came and went,

53. Meer Trelisser (1883-1941): Russian party member from 1901, one of first Chekists, held leading positions in GPU; 1935 GPU man in Comintern presidium; organiser of 1937 purge, arrested 1938, sentenced to death.
54. Zigmas Alexas, known as Angaretis (1882-1940): Lithuanian Socialist, member of provisional government 1919; took refuge in Moscow and from 1924 member of Comintern Executive; active purger in 1936, executed in 1940 for "Lithuanian nationalism".
55. Jan Anvelt (1884-1937): Estonian Social Democrat, supported Bolsheviks in 1917, became head of Estonian government 1918; close ally of Zinoviev, played important role in Reval insurrection of 1924; removed from Comintern Executive 1936, accused of "Estonian nationalist deviation" and killed during interrogation.
56. Otto Kuusinen, (1881-1964): People's Commissar for Education 1918, founder of Finnish CP; leading figure in Comintern, and kept his position till dissolution in 1943.
57. Mauno Heimo (1896-1937): Finnish student, joined Communist Party at time of Revolution; said to have sympathised with Trotsky in 1923; leading figure in Comintern central apparatus till his arrest and liquidation.
58. Tuure Lehén (1893-1976): Finnish student, commander in Red Guard, responsible for military training in Comintern, sent on mission to Spain at start of civil war, returned to Finland in 1946.
59. Endre Rudnyánszký (1885-1943): Hungarian revolutionary, elected to Comintern Executive in 1920; sent to Vienna 1921 and fled to Romania with large sum of money; returned to Russia five years later, spent fifteen years in jail, and remained in Russia till death.
60. Béla Szántó (1881-1951): Hungarian socialist journalist, People's Commissar in 1919 revolution; exiled in Moscow, worked in Comintern apparatus, survived purges of which he was one of main organisers among Hungarian émigrés.
61. Jozef Pogány (1886-1937): President of Budapest Soldiers' Council 1918, held various posts in Hungarian revolutionary government; took refuge in Moscow, worked in Comintern apparatus, was in Germany March 1921; dismissed 1929, arrested and executed 1937.
62. Ilona Duczynska ((1897-1978): Supporter of Zimmerwald, member of Hungarian CP, she went to Moscow 1920, worked in Comintern apparatus; expelled as supporter of Paul Levi; joined Austrian Socialist Party, later with oppositional group in Austrian CP; emigrated to Britain in 1937, pilot with RAF in 1940.
63. Vassil Kolarov (1877-1950): Bulgarian Narrow Socialist, founder-member of Bulgarian CP,

while remaining in the apparatus with a number of his less important compatriots. Kabakchiev[64] paid for his defence of the policy of the Bulgarian CP in 1923 with a major demotion.

One myth upheld jointly in the 1930s by the Stalinists and the hacks writing for the most anti-Communist ruling classes cast Georgi Dimitrov[65] in a key role as a giant of the revolutionary struggle. In reality, however, he was no more than an embarrassing exile, always being offered different jobs because he drank too much and took liberties with the secretaries...

It is astounding (and certainly many at the time were astounded) to see these men, whose main achievement as revolutionaries was not knowing how to win and whose 'international' responsibilities led (as Lenin put it) to one 'kunerie' [Bela Kun stupidity] after another, retaining their positions and not being submitted to any obvious form of control, either by their international bodies or the parties they came from.

The International that emerged after the period of revolutions was incapable of making its leading militants read and think, despite Lenin's advice. Its structural transformation into an apparatus with an executive role, which from now on would settle everything from the outside and from above, did the rest. Henceforth there was no point in being intelligent and well-informed or in having experience of workers' struggles in order to become a Communist cadre. The one thing needed was discipline. The misuse of the 'military' comparison led to an excessive multiplying of the number of warrant officers who lacked vision and of empty-headed, second-class soldiers.

Was everything still possible?

In theory, however, everything still remained possible after the great German defeat of 1923. Of course, detailed discussion, comprehensive questioning, allowing lesser mortals and rank and file militants to speak would have been the pre-condition. Instead, the diktat method of the Russian movement won out over the use of debate. The defeats had been terrible; the future defeat was still more so.

False moves led to a fall — a collapse into the incapacity to tolerate contradiction and criticism, the incapacity to grasp what was novel about a situation. It led to thought as catechism, to ordering people about as the only way to mobilise. How many young men and women would burn themselves out in the years to come? How many would turn away from the Comintern, having devoted body and soul to it? And how many would come to believe that the servility demanded by Moscow was the

leading figure in Comintern; after World War II succeeded Dimitrov at head of Bulgarian government.
64. Khristo Kabakchiev (1878-1940): Bulgarian Narrow Socialist; secretary of Bulgarian CP, imprisoned after 1923 rising.
65. Georgi Dimitrov (1882-1949):Bulgarian Narrow Socialist, then Communist; left Bulgaria after 1923 insurrection; leading figure in Comintern; tried by Nazis for Reichstag fire, and acquitted, which launched his career in Comintern, of which he was General Secretary from 1935; after World War II head of Bulgarian government.

price to be paid for getting rid of 'fascism', which every human being worthy of the name henceforth knew to be the leprous plague of modern times?

When we look back over these six years, we cannot help being drawn to Antonio Gramsci — to repeating, on behalf of *all* the workers studied in this period, his commentary and the words of respect and admiration he uttered on the occasion of the last of the Fiat workers' strikes in April 1921. Gwyn Williams's introduction puts it in terms one would have liked to have written oneself:

> There is another equally important, patrimony to inherit. It was not 'history' which created the council movement. It is men who do all this [...] ordinary workers and working women — who were extraordinary men and women, trying to live Communist in a hard time. Their conduct is part of the memory of the working-class movement which needs all the memories it can get. It needs memory to defeat death.

Gramsci wrote:

> The workers of Fiat have gone back to work. Betrayal? Denial of the revolutionary ideal? The workers of Fiat are men of flesh and blood.
> They held out for a month.
> They knew that they fought and resisted not only for themselves, not only for the rest of the Turin working class, but for the whole working class of Italy.
> They held out for a month.
> They were physically exhausted because for many weeks, many months, their wages had been reduced and were no longer sufficient to keep their families alive.
> Yet they held out for a month.
> They were completely isolated from a nation sunk in weariness, indifference, hostility.
> Yet they held out for a month.
> They knew that they could not hope for help from outside. They knew that for the Italian working class the tendons had been cut. They knew they were doomed to defeat.
> Yet they held out for a month...
> The Italian working class is flattened under the roller of capitalist reaction. For how long? Nothing has been lost if consciousness and faith remain intact, if bodies surrender but not souls. The workers of Fiat have struggled hard for years and years. They have bathed the streets in their blood. They have suffered hunger and cold. They remain, with their glorious past, the vanguard of the Italian proletariat. They remain faithful and devoted soldiers of the revolution. They have done as much as it is possible for men of flesh and blood to do.

We take off our hats before their humiliation, because to sincere and honest men, there is something of greatness in it.[66]

In that gesture there is also greatness. No leader of the Communist Party was to imitate Gramsci in that gesture.

How could another revolution be made?

Not everything we have just looked at (dare one say, the human side of things — but isn't that the very foundation of revolutionary struggle?) disappeared. Quite the contrary. One can point to the birth of a truly coherent revolutionary tradition in countries where at the beginning of our period it had been no more than a coming together of different upsurges and individual initiatives. The challenge of late 1923 that Communists had to face, even if it was a challenge they had yet to put to themselves, was a terrible one because it cast doubt on their very identity, their choice of life and death, their *raison d'être* and their reason for being a Communist (which for them was the same thing).

Everyone recognised that what had first given birth to the Russian Revolution had been a gigantic mutiny, mass desertions and the refusal of a generation bled dry to be massacred. More than anything else 1917 had been the revolt against the war, the Great War, the World War, as it was called. War (at least the Great War) was no more. The last clashes to follow it were directed against its illegal continuation. After the peace, soldiers and sailors were sent (to the Black Sea, for example) and put paid to the policy of intervention against the revolution in central and eastern Europe. The Allies became fearful that their initiatives were stirring up the very blaze they hoped to extinguish, with the risk of new revolutionary explosions. They therefore cut their losses, withdrew their troops and, after the blockade, made do with a temporary cordon sanitaire and economic offensive.

After 1923 it is fair to say that the exactions of the occupying troops and the execution of 'terrorists' and 'saboteurs' only caused outrage in the world of their victims and among a handful of Communists and libertarians in the aggressor countries. The condemnations that began to rain down on colonial exploitation, then on the unequal and ferocious repression of colonial people in revolt, fell flat. The French working masses would not rise up on the morrow in the factories and worksites of France to defend the inhabitants of the Rif or the Druzes, with whom no French soldiers were 'fraternising' (and the majority of Communist cadres wondered whether the slogans put forward by their party were too daring...) Everywhere the electoral results confirmed that the Communists had real, if patchy and limited influence. However, this was far from being the 'majority of the working class' that everyone agreed was the precondition for taking power.

As we have seen, this change in the situation, an end to the revolutionary period opened up by the victory of October 1917, was what Trotsky announced at the Third

---

66. G Williams, *Proletarian Order*, London, 1975, pp 308-9, and A Gramsci, *L'Ordine Nuovo*, 8 May, 1921.

Congress when he said that revolution was no longer a matter of days or weeks but 'of years'. The victory perceived as straight ahead had once again disappeared into the distance. And the price to be paid began to dawn on militants. Naturally, the ready-made answer that came to Communist lips was: 'We must build the party,' 'We need a party like the Russian party.' Did that require two decades? Could a mass revolutionary party be built independently of gigantic class battles? Worse still. These battles — in March 1921, for example — did not always favour building the party; some even strongly contributed to destroying the forces mobilised to that end. In 1923, the KPD had barely begun to rebuild itself when it was forced to cancel the minutely prepared insurrection and retreat without a fight.

Working class unity, power and revolution

These were the questions put by the German and Russian parties to the Comintern and its sections, then to its executive. They arose following the catastrophic 'March Action' of 1921 and ended with the adoption of the United Front line in December 1922. By then these bodies had given their answers; at stake was how to put into practice a policy that had been the fruit of a wide-ranging debate, without doubt unprecedented on such a scale, the policy of a united working class front and that of a workers' (or workers' and peasants') government. If we are to understand what motivated the shift in ideas, we need to recall the context of the split in the workers' movement as seen through the eyes of the Bolsheviks, a split Lenin had wanted, even though the decisive impulse had come, more often than not, from their social-democratic and reformist enemies.

In the short-term perspective of world revolution then held by the Bolsheviks, the prime objective had been to expel opportunist and potentially treacherous leaders from the workers' party before the decisive moment of the struggle for power. Once victory had gathered all the forces behind its flag this split would rapidly disappear of its own accord. The same assumption could be found forming the background to the discussion of the united workers' front: the proletariat would rid itself of its right wing leaders (the 'Mensheviks'), bring victory and in the process reunify itself. Even though not fully worked out, this appears to us to have been Lenin's line of thought on these crucial problems.

Lenin did not see the split in the workers' movement as needing to last longer than a few years (certainly not half a century). To his way of thinking, the united workers' front, which would be the route to victory in the advanced countries, was also the thread leading to the mobilisation of working class forces that would make this victory possible.

As we have seen, the German defeat of 1920, then of 1921, demanded a fresh elaboration of the slogans concerning a transition to the dictatorship of the proletariat, particularly the slogan of the 'workers' government'. No opportunity arose to carry it out, with the whole business derailed at the worst moment and ending in a retreat without a fight. The death of Lenin and the crisis in the revolution prevented any real debate.

Everything took place as if for his successors Lenin's daring and theoretical innovations rested on a faulty appraisal of the situation — Stalin would still be saying so in 1943 — and that this was to blame for the defeat of the revolution. Zinoviev's resulting theorisations to preserve his authority and power fully coincided with Stalin's conservatism and with that of apparatchiks like Molotov[67] and Rákosi. They feared revolution, which they had glimpsed anew in Germany in the summer of 1923, with party 'big wigs' howled down in stormy mass meetings, and international complications on the horizon.

In a word, the men who with Stalin seized power in the USSR threw overboard not only Lenin's conclusions about the apparatus and the bureaucracy, the national question and Russification, but also his reflections on the workers' unity aimed at in the united workers' front — the first step on the modern road to revolution in an advanced country.

As we have already noted, Trotsky, who understood the gigantic enterprise of falsification that was getting under way, would make himself the guardian of the temple and defender of Lenin's ideas, in opposition to these people. He took care not to go further than Lenin. That way he protected his flank against fresh accusations and avoided giving the impression that he was using Lenin's thought in self-defence. Further than that he would not go. Instead, he made do with a wealth of analysis about the new phenomena of Stalinism and fascism.

The Comintern in a dead end?

In 1921 some had thought that acts of provocation, such as bombs and kidnappings, might serve as the engine of warfare and atrocities to anger workers and help reconstruct the framework in which revolution could put down roots at a time when below there was no longer any desire for it. But this was no more than a derisory and dangerous expedient, which in any case could not have been easily revived. Henceforward, the Comintern would no longer call for insurrection in an advanced country. In addition, rejection of the united front proved magically capable of being put to multiple uses. The social democratic parties, who wanted none of it either, would benefit enormously from the politics of the Communist parties, with its denunciation of the leaders and its attempt to 'lure the troops away'. They benefited from the systematic attacks on them, which they used to justify their passivity in the face of power.

Better still, the Communists' fiery denunciation of the social democrats allowed the latter to divert the aspiration for unity to their own advantage and point the finger at the Communists as 'splitters'. These, however, were only minor gains and losses. There were other, more serious, ones.

The Communist leadership's rejection of the united front, the refusal even to meet socialist leaders, tipped the scales definitively in favour of the status quo, with ups and downs in the rivalry between the parties but within a reality that made the

---

67. Viacheslav Molotov (1890-1986): old Bolshevik, became Stalin's main lieutenant, head of Comintern between Bukharin and Dimitrov.

advance towards decisive change an impossibility for as long as there subsisted two workers' parties that were opposed to, and even enemies of each other.

This split in the working class ensured the protection of capitalism. It led to fresh conflicts between workers' parties, to militants becoming disheartened, to loss of confidence, to passivity. And it also meant, if only as a dream, constantly attempting to take power through an alliance with a bourgeois coalition. In the years from 1923 to 1933, for all the Comintern talk of 'revolution', the perspective remained one of retreat. The class enemy, as well as the social democrats, talked of revolution as obsolete, surpassed, outdated — a bloody utopia whose cost outweighed the sufferings from which it claimed to deliver humanity. And the Soviets would reply with fairy stories or insults.

How could one be a revolutionary without a revolution? In the final analysis, the class enemy appeared to be still very fearful of the revolution it strongly believed would occur. So we return to the problem, the terms of which Miloš Hájek[68] put to Lenin in 1921: the revolution might yet be triggered by a counter-revolutionary coup aimed at forestalling it. Perhaps this is why the point of Hitler's preventative struggle was to ensure state power before unleashing the forces of civil war on the working class and its parties. In this instance, whatever the truth of the idea, the counter-revolution did not provoke a revolution — Stalinism thus came before the tribunal of history, alongside social democracy, for having allowed Hitler's gangs to seize the state without a struggle.

'Socialism in one country'

Following the abortive German revolution of 1923 Stalin came up with a theoretical justification that was to become necessary for his politics. This was the theory that it was possible to 'construct socialism in one country' and that ultimately it was necessary to do so. He first touched on the question in the preface to his writings of 1917, entitled: 'The October Revolution and the Tactics of Russian Communists'. Here he blamed the German defeat on the proletariat's lack of support from the peasantry, which differed from what had happened in Russia. He wanted to show that Trotsky's perspective of world revolution could only offer the Russian people the perspective 'to vegetate in its own contradictions and rot away while waiting for the world revolution'.[69] He backed this up with a quotation from Lenin which he had to manipulate to make it useable: 'The victory of socialism in a single country is altogether possible and probable, even if that country is less developed from the capitalist point of view and even if capitalism continues to exist in more developed countries from the capitalist point of view.'[70] The American historian R V Daniels has

---

68. Author of *Storia dell'Internazionale Comunista 1921-1935*, Rome, 1972.
69. http://www.marxists.org/reference/archive/stalin/works/1924/12.htm
70. The above sentence is translated from Broué's French. The quotation from Lenin used by Stalin in the above article is 'the victory of socialism is possible first in several or even in one capitalist country taken separately'. Lenin, *On the Slogan for a United States of Europe*, (1915), http://www.marxists.org/archive/lenin/works/1915/aug/23.htm [Note added by *Revolutionary History*]

commented: 'It marked the beginning of a pervasive process of reinterpretation and reconstruction, the effect of which has been to bring what is represented as Marxism-Leninism into accordance with the actual evolution of the Soviet state.'[71]

It is clear who benefited from this operation. Christened 'socialism' and later 'communism', the Stalinist bureaucratic regime would retrospectively become the goal of past workers' struggles — the one to be defended then and in the future. No longer was it a question of some hypothetical and far off world revolution but of the socialism being constructed in the here and now, of the Russia which exemplified this process and was the concern of all. As a result, the Russians and their party were assured of hegemony in the Comintern and the subordination of the latter to Stalin's foreign policy and 'socialism'. Trotsky, Zinoviev, Kamenev and the other oppositionists were not mistaken. In their political struggle against Stalin they showed that this pseudo-theory was no more than the rationalisation of indifference to, and a preparation for struggle against world revolution. The fight they began in 1924 went on in different ways till 1933, the date on which the German revolution, namely, the revolutionary cause at the heart of proletarian Germany, was defeated without a fight. It had, nevertheless, been a long, hard struggle and had produced many more victims.

---

71. RV Daniels, *The Conscience of the Revolution*, Cambridge, Mass., 1960, p252.

The Bolshevik-Leninist Faction[1]
Chapter XXXV of Broué's *Trotsky*[2]

IN the period immediately after their expulsion from the party, Trotsky's supporters in the United Opposition, which had just broken up, always insisted that, no matter what might happen to them, they still considered themselves to be members of the party, and that they were organised, of necessity secretly, in the Bolshevik-Leninist faction.

In their ranks, three groupings could be distinguished, although they were in contact — reluctantly and in one direction only, it is true. Firstly there were those whom LS Sosnovsky[3] called "the new colonists of the third generation": that is those exiled, or deported, who could be found in some hundred "colonies" in urban centres and even villages scattered throughout Siberia and Central Asia, where they were required to live. And there were those on "the other side", or "on the outside", as the exiles said, those who remained, men and women not yet arrested, "free", from now on active in clandestinity. Finally there were those who had been sent to prison, either after being sentenced, or on remand, the Bolsheviks-Leninists in those prisons called "isolators" and whose numbers were continually growing with additions from the first two categories.

We know very little about the prisons in 1928, and about the fate of the arrested oppositionists in them. A whole group of militants, among them SV Mrachkovsky,[4] YA Kievlenko[5] and others, had been accused of a "military plot"

---

1. The first systematic study done on the correspondence of Trotsky to Sedov at Alma-Ata was that by Isabelle Longuet in her *maîtrise* thesis, *The Crisis of the Left Opposition 1928-29*, Department of Slavonic Studies, Paris VIII. But in the context of the party and government, the well documented book of Michal Reiman, *Die Geburt des Stalinismus* [The Birth of Stalinism] Frankfurt am Main, 1979, should be consulted.
2. Translated by Ted Crawford and Ian Birchall.
3. [RH] LS Sosnovsky (1886-1937): Bolshevik from 1904, journalist on *Pravda*; expelled 1927, capitulated 1934, arrested 1936.
4. [RH] Mrachkovsky to Trotsky, 14 April 1928, Trotsky Archive at Harvard [hereafter *AH*], T 1310.
   SV Mrachkovsky (1888-1936): born in jail, party member from 1905; member of Left

and were imprisoned for almost two months; they complained particularly about the overcrowded cells. They had been released because there were no confessions, prosecution witnesses or evidence. They were immediately deported. Several soldiers were also arrested, accused of having plotted an attack on the official poet Demyan Bedny.[6] They were Arkady Heller,[7] Bulatov,[8] Lado Enukidze[9] — the nephew of Avel,[10] who had been secretary of the Executive Committee of the Soviets.[11] They were eventually released and deported like the others. Those who were in prison were concentrated in the isolators,[12] in Verkhne-Uralsk, Cheliabinsk and Tobolsk, and were held there together with common criminals, and subjected to harsh conditions.

We know much more about the clandestine organisation, that of the people "on the outside" as the deportees said. The reports sent to Trotsky, the clandestine bulletins preserved in his archives and the information taken by the authorities after certain hauls[13] enable us to reconstruct its broad outlines.

First Moscow, where the "centre" was apparently very active, publishing several issues of a substantial bulletin, leaflets, statements and proclamations. It was this centre which succeeded in maintaining, for most of 1928, contact with Trotsky and Alma-Ata. Its leader signed his reports "Otets" (Dad) or "Starichok" (little old man): it was the old Bolshevik Boris Mikhailovich Eltsin,[14] father of Victor Borisovich,[15] a man exhausted by life, probably suffering from Pott's disease, a fact which initially enabled him to escape arrest.

Among his collaborators we have some names, sometimes just the silhouette of men little or not at all known: MJ Blumenfeld,[16] formerly one of the leaders

    Opposition, then of Smirnov group in 1932; sentenced to death in August 1936 trial.
5. [RH] Kievlenko to Sedov, 14 March 1928, *AH*, T 1211.
    YA Kievlenko: oppositionist; accused of plotting, then deported.
6. [RH] EA Pridvorov, known as Demyan Bedny (1883-1945): Russian poet, party member from 1912, after 1925 a sort of official poet.
7. [RH] Arkady Heller: student of the military academy; expelled 1927 and deported.
8. [RH] Bulatov: soldier, member of the Left Opposition.
9. [RH] Lado Enukidze (?-1938: nephew of Avel Enukidze; member of Left Opposition and member of military academy, from which expelled in 1928 before being deported; shot at Vorkuta in 1938.
10. [RH] Avel Enukidze (1877-1937): railway worker, party member from 1899, organised clandestine printshop under Tsarism; secretary of the Executive Committee of the Soviets 1918-35; expelled 1935, sentenced to death 1937.
11. Trotskyists in Moscow to Trotsky, *AH*, T 1175.
12. The "isolator" was a prison formed of isolated cells where in theory the prisoner was alone. But the great number of prisoners made isolation impossible and there were several prisoners in each of the overcrowded cells of these prisons which were "isolators" in name only.
13. Hoover Archives, Nikolaievsky Collection.
14. [RH] BM Eltsin (1879-1937): party member from 1899; member of nucleus of opposition from 1923; imprisoned at Suzdal and deported to Orenburg.
15. [RH] VB Eltsin: party member from 1917, divisional commissar in Red Army, then student at Institute of Red Professors and secretary to Trotsky; deported 1928, no trace of what happened to him after 1936.
16. [RH] MJ Blumenfeld: leader of Young Communists; member of Moscow Centre in 1928, capitulated 1929, but almost immediately sentenced to ten years jail in connection with

of the Communist Youth, and Sokrat Gevorkian,[17] a young economics lecturer at the University of Moscow, were men of the generation of 1917. A little older, Khanaan Markovich Pevzner,[18] a former member of the Cheka, a badly disabled veteran of the civil war, who had responsibility for the editing of the publications, and Grigori Yakovlevich Yakovin,[19] a historian of Germany, and a militant from Leningrad. The last-named of these is known to us by two testimonies, that of Victor Serge[20] and that of Rosa Léviné-Meyer.[21] Others are only names which are found in documents from the archives, often militants whose role was important, like V Yanuchevsky[22] or B Volotnikov,[23] but of whom we know nothing more.

There were other "centres", in other cities, as can be deduced from the news of arrests or the source of information being circulated. This was the case in Moscow, Leningrad, Kiev and Kharkov, Baku and Tiflis, in Odessa, Dniepropetrovsk, Nikolaev, Saratov, Ivanovo-Voznesensk, Krasnoyarsk, Ekaterinoslav, Kremenchug, Rostov, Tula, Kostroma, Briansk, Nizhni Novgorod, Tver, Zaporozhe, etc

Thus we have relatively plentiful information on the activity of the Left Opposition. Its militants inspired actions and gave accounts of them: some record has been preserved in the Harvard and Hoover archives.

There was a working-class mobilisation, for example, in June 1928, in Kremenchug, in the railway workshops, against a reform of the payment system. The workers of the tram repair shops of Dniepropetrovsk threatened to go on strike following the decision to remove their right to free transport won in .... 1905.

Many of these actions related to votes or hostile attitudes to the party leadership in workers' organisations: in the Vek factory at Kharkov, in Spartak at Kazan, in a factory at Kiev,[24] workers assembled in a mass meeting denounced the "opportunist" decisions of the July plenum. Numerous discussions also took place about the campaign for "self-criticism", where it was remembered that sometimes those who made criticisms were deported, and where it was thought

Blumkin affair.
17. [RH] Sokrat Gevorkian (1900-1938): Bolshevik in 1917; lecturer in economic theory; member of opposition from 1923; member of Vorkuta strike committee, shot.
18. [RH] KM Pevsner: Red Army officer, seriously wounded; joined party 1920, expelled 1927, deported and disappeared.
19. [RH] GI Yakovin (1896-1938): Bolshevik, fought in civil war, studied history at Institute of Red Professors, leader of Opposition in Leningrad, then Moscow; in 1938 member of strike committee in Vorkuta and first to be shot.
20. Victor Serge, *Memoirs of a Revolutionary*, Oxford, 1967, pp207-8.
21. Rosa Léviné-Meyer, "Yakovin and Pankratova", in *Inside German Communism*, London, 1977, pp209-213.
22. [RH] V Yanuchevsky: Moscow Communist, arrested 1930, disappeared in GPU prison.
23. [RH] B Volotnikov: one of Trotsky's best informed correspondents in 1928; arrested same year.
24. Letter from Moscow, September 1928, *AH*, T 2439.

that such would be the fate of new critics.[25] In the course of a meeting of women textile workers at Ivanovo-Voznesensk, a worker quoted the example of her own daughter, sacked for having made criticisms. At the beginning of September, there was a strike at the Kolomensky factory, then one by 5,000 workers at the Khalturinskaya textile factory.[26] In various places free elections and a rise in wages were demanded.

From July 1928, the oppositionists started to express themselves freely in open meetings. They asked for an end to repression, sometimes obtaining a significant number of votes: at the end of July, in the Ilyich factory in the Zamoskvorechye district of Moscow, 19 against 270 voted to readmit those expelled.[27] In the Krasnaia Oborona factory, the oppositionist Nefel[28] obtained 72 votes — out of 256 voting — for a resolution describing the policy of the Moscow Soviet as "anti-working-class.[29] After speaking, oppositionists were elected to committees, trade-union posts and factory committees at Pervy May, a tea factory at Tilmensi and at the tannery at Bogorodsk.[30]

The Opposition also drew up news bulletins of several pages — three can be found at Harvard — as well as leaflets, circulated during power cuts, flyposted or sometimes distributed with the assistance of sympathisers. Certain leaflets were immediate responses to repressive measures: on 20 October in Kiev, to protest against arrests, at the same time, at a factory in Moscow to protest at the dismissal of GM Novikov,[31] an well-known oppositionist who had formerly organised the partisans against Kolchak.[32] On the eleventh anniversary of the October revolution, 10,000 copies of a leaflet were distributed by the Left Opposition in Moscow.[33]

There were at least of two actions organised against repression that year. In Tiflis, on 3 May, at the time of the arrest and deportation of the oppositionist leaders in Georgia,[34] and in Kiev on 27 October after the arrest of several oppositionists known in their factories.[35]

The reports addressed to Trotsky and Sedov[36] give the impression that the Left Opposition was growing in the country, in particular among workers:

25. Letter from Moscow, 13 September 1928, *AH*, T 2560.
26. Letter from Moscow, 7 September 1928, *AH*, T 2502.
27. Letter from Moscow, end of July 1928, *AH*, T 2001.
28. Nefel: oppositionist worker.
29. Letter from Moscow, 1 November 1928, *AH*, T 2854.
30. Letter from Moscow, September 1928, *AH*, T 2533.
31. [RH] GM Novikov: Moscow worker, Bolshevik in 1917; organised partisan struggle against Kolchak; returned to factory at end of civil war; joined Left Opposition.
32. [RH] Letter from Moscow, 13 September, *AH*, T 2560.
    AV Kolchak (1874-1920): Vice-Admiral who tried to unite White armies; defeated in Siberia, captured and shot.
33. Letter from Moscow, mid-November, *AH*, T 2875.
34. Tsintsadze to Trotsky, 17 May 1928, *AH*, T 1476.
35. Letter from Kiev, November 1928, *AH*, T 2849.
36. [RH] Leon Sedov (1906-1937): elder son of Trotsky and Natalia Sedova; active in Left Opposition in USSR; exiled with father in 1929; in Berlin 1931, Paris 1933; probably murdered.

moreover, in the correspondence more and more references can be found to militants who took their distance in 1927 and who had become active again. New elements also joined the Opposition.

Under these conditions, repression struck hard and repeatedly. The Georgians were arrested later than their comrades in Russia or Ukraine. A few days after, a letter from one of the most brilliant products of the younger generation of "red professors", BS Lifshitz,[37] reported the development of what he called, not without a sense of humour, "the St Bartholomew's Day Massacre", namely 150 arrests in Moscow alone.[38] A bulletin from Moscow dated 22 November 1928 gave an estimate of the recent arrests. There were said to have been, between late October and early November, more than 300 known arrests: 80 oppositionists were arrested in Leningrad, 51 in Kharkov, 47 in Kiev — among them several old Bolsheviks and Korfman,[39] a real working-class leader — 28 in Odessa, 16 in Tiflis and 15 in Saratov.[40] Among the 150 arrests carried out in Moscow we find names familiar to the reader of the Trotsky archives: B Volotnikov, GY Yakovin, and an "Eltsin" who might be the old Boris Mikhailovich.[41] But they were replaced, for the "centre" continued, as the very fact of the publication of the bulletin showed.

How many oppositionists were arrested, deported or imprisoned? Trotsky and his supporters, on the basis of official figures and private information, arrived at a total of 8,000 for the one year 1928: it seems that the underground sector of the Opposition continued growing with a surge of new recruits, but that all the same it lost both old and new members under the blows of repression. The ratio between oppositionist deportees and those arrested also appears variable, as a number of deportees were arrested.

It was the cadres of the Opposition, between 1,000 and 2,000 militants considered as "diehards" who, shortly after the capitulation of Zinoviev and Kamenev, were deported, that is, required to reside in a distant locality as from January 1928. But this was not all of them. Like the Zinovievites, some escaped deportation by a precipitate capitulation, often predictable, but which produced an effect when they were well-known people. This was the case with Piatakov,[42] who for a long time had been known to be demoralised, but whose confession was a blow; it was also the case with Antonov-Ovseenko[43] and NV Krestinsky.[44]

37. Boris Lifshitz (1896-1949): Bolshevik in 1917, political commissar in civil war; Left Opposition from 1923, capitulated in 1930; arrested 1932 with Smirnov group, but subsequently released; war correspondent 1941-45.
38. Lifshitz to Trotsky, 28 May 1928, *AH*, T 1552.
39. [RH] Korfman: Bolshevik from 1903; worker at Kiev and member of Left Opposition.
40. Letter from Moscow, 22 November 1928, *AH*, T 2898.
41. *Pravda*, 29 February 1928. Piatakov, "Statement".
42. [RH] GL Piatakov (1890-1937): anarchist, then party member from 1910; Left Communist in 1918, head of Ukraine government; member of Left Opposition, capitulated 1928; sentenced to death 1937 after public "confessions".
43. [RH] A Antonov-Ovseenko (1884-1938): career officer, Menshevik, knew Trotsky in emigration; member of Left Opposition, capitulated 1928; worked for Stalin notably in Spain; shot.

A quite large group of ex-Zinovievites, coming from the Youth, who had not followed their leaders in December 1927, were included in the first wave of arrests and deportations: they were referred to as the "leaderless". Their front-rank leaders were however GI Safarov[45] and the Yugoslav Voya Vuyovich[46] — a former active militant with the Young Communists in France. The group made a public statement in April 1928,[47] which meant the return of its members from exile though not without difficulty.

At the beginning of 1928 all the other militants of the opposition who were at all well-known were expelled and deported, with only a few exceptions: Victor Serge, Andrés Nin, Aleksandra L'vovna Sokolovskaya[48] and BM Eltsin. Christian Rakovsky[49] was in Astrakhan, where letters from Moscow took six days and newspapers three. Serebriakov[50] was in Semipalatinsk, Smilga[51] in Kolpashevo, Preobrazhensky[52] in Uralsk, Radek in Tobolsk, Muralov[53] in Tara, Sosnovsky in Barnaul, IN Smirnov[54] in Novo Bajazet, Beloborodov[55] in Ust'-Kulom, Mrachkovsky in Voronezh. Only a few were near a railway line. It was decided

---

44. [RH] Antonov-Ovseenko, "Statement", *Pravda*, 4 April 1928.
    NN Krestinsky (1883-1938): lawyer, active militant from 1903; Vice-Commissar for foreign affairs, then ambassador to Berlin; at least close to opposition; executed after third Moscow trial.
45. [RH] GI Safarov (1891-1942): responsible for "Eastern" questions in the Comintern; with the Bloc of Oppositions in 1932, but denounced it 1935.
46. [RH] Voya Vuyovic (1895-?): student in France, active in Communist Youth; secretary-general of International Communist Youth 1924-26; member of Left Opposition, deported and capitulated; arrested again in 1935 and disappeared during purges.
47. *Pravda*, 31 May 1928.
48. [RH] AL Bronstein Sokolovskaya (1872-193?): recruited Trotsky to Marxism, married him in prison; mother of his two daughters; was raising her grandchildren when arrested in 1935.
49. [RH] CG Rakovsky (1873-1941): revolutionary involved in socialist movement in several European countries; member of Central Committee of Russian party, then leader of Left Opposition; died in prison.
50. [RH] LP Serebriakov (1890-1937): metal-worker, Bolshevik from 1905; secretary of Central Committee in 1919-20; expelled as member of opposition, and sentenced at second Moscow trial.
51. [RH] IT Smilga (1892-1938): active in 1905; party member from 1908 after execution of father; president of Baltic Council in 1917 and assisted Lenin in preparing insurrection; in United Opposition, then probably in Smirnov group; executed in jail without trial.
52. [RH] EA Preobrazhensky (1886-1937): party member from 1903; party secretary 1920-21; supported Trotsky in trade-union debate, participated in economic debate with Bukharin; expelled 1927, deported 1928, capitulated 1929; leading member of Smirnov group, capitulated again, executed without trial.
53. [RH] NI Muralov (1877-1937): party member from 1903; led Moscow insurrections in 1905 and 1917; one of main leaders of Red Army; Left Opposition from 1923; deported, did not capitulate, but broken in prison, "confessed" at second Moscow trial and shot.
54. [RH] IN Smirnov (1881-1936): factory worker, party member from 1899, frequently arrested; nicknamed "the conscience of the party"; member of Left Opposition, capitulated 1928; then formed own group, met Sedov in Berlin in 1931 and formed Bloc of Oppositions in 1932; arrested 1933, sentenced to death and executed.
55. [RH] AG Beloborodov (1891-1938): electrician, Bolshevik from 1907; People's Commissar after revolution; expelled 1927, capitulated 1928, but shot 1938.

to put them in remote places. The small towns and the villages where the authorities put the oppositionists did not often allow them the possibility of benefiting from elementary comforts or the advantages of culture. For the others, the obscure and the rank and file or at least the NCOs, some hundred places of residence can be counted. According to the Harvard papers, a total of 108 "colonies", by I Longuet's estimates, can be counted, that is to say 108 local groups of deportees who identified with the Opposition. Trotsky's young collaborators also earned deportation: Sermuks[56] and VB Eltsin were in Ust-Vym, Poznansky[57] in Kotlas, NV Nechayev[58] in Kolpashevo.

To begin with a sort of political and personal correspondence was established to and from Alma-Ata. Trotsky announced on 28 February 1928 that, of all the deportees whom he had contacted by telegram, only Serebriakov had not yet answered him: in fact, he had simply written a letter,[59] and it would not be long before he capitulated. Subsequently, the organisation was clearly improving. The colonies in European Russia were organised around Rakovsky, those in the North around Mrachkovsky; those in Siberia and Soviet Asia around Sosnovsky. The intermediate "centres" copied the documents which reached them from Alma-Ata by redistributing those which appeared interesting to them.

The political material which circulated thus naturally included the "letters to friends", genuine circular letters from Trotsky or leading people like Rakovsky, Sosnovsky and others, and a mass of documents emanating from individuals or groups of oppositionists. It seemed that the same system was applied in the matter of information, a vital operation, in which new people emerged, friends of Sedov, like YA Kievlenko in Kainsk, Boris N Viaznikovtsev[60] at Tyumen, Vsevolod Patriarkha[61] in Yeniseisk, FS Radzevich,[62] deportee to Termez, or the young Bulgarian Vassil Sidorov,[63] son of a veteran "Narrow Socialist", who led the colony of Rubtsovsk.

The deportees were allowed to work if they could find jobs. The majority did not manage that. It was only the case with some privileged people, with useful skills, reputation or luck. The Leningrad metal-worker Shtykhgold[64] built brick

56. [RH] NM Sermuks: typist secretary and commanding officer of Trotsky's train; arrested at Alma-Ata in 1928.
57. [RH] IM Poznansky (1898?-1938): mathematics student; Trotsky's secretary 1917-27; organiser of red cavalry; shot at Vorkuta in 1938.
58. vNV Nechayev: stenographer in Trotsky's train and member of his secretariat; deported as oppositionist in 1928.
59. Trotsky, circular letter, 28 February 1928. *AH*, T 1161. In fact, Serebriakov had written, but only on 25 February.
60. [RH] Boris N Viaznikovtsev: mathematics student; deported 1928, capitulated 1929.
61. [RH] Vsevolod Patriarkha: Moscow oppositionist; provided information to exiled Trotsky, including a report on agitation in factories.
62. [RH] FS Radzevich: worker-student in Moscow; joined Communist party 1923, expelled 1927, deported 1928, capitulated 1930.
63. [RH] Vassil Sidorov: Bulgarian Communist, took refuge in USSR 1925; arrested 1929, deported and disappeared.
64. [RH] Shtykhgold: Leningrad Communist, close to Zinoviev.

houses. Viaznikovtsev, an engineering student, taught mathematics. His fellow student Kantorovich[65] was in the kolkhoz administration. Rakovsky, like Trotsky, had contracts with Gosizdat, the state publishing house. Finally the best known, Rakovsky, Preobrazhensky, IN Smirnov, Muralov, were employed by the planning organisations. These were in a better material situation. The majority lived with great difficulty, as the allowance of 30 roubles per month, given them by the GPU, was scarcely adequate.

"Literary" activity, as the Russians called it, was important. Many deportees wrote, not to pass the time, but because they finally had the chance to do so. There was for example in circulation a "Critique of the Draft Programme of the Comintern", much admired by Trotsky, written by Dmitri Lapin,[66] of whom we know nothing. We know that Sosnovsky wrote an *Agrarian Policy of Centrism*, Smilga a book about *Conquests of the Proletariat in Year XI of the Revolution*, Preobrazhensky a *Sociology of the Capitalist World*. We know about many works and projects: Dingelstedt,[67] who had done a thesis on the land question in India, was now working on the social structures of that country; Radek had started a major biography of Lenin; Smilga was working on the theories of Bukharin and his "school"; Preobrazhensky was doing research on the medieval economy, VB Eltsin on the French Revolution; Vilensky-Sibiriakov[68] returned to the study of China and Boris S Lifshitz was studying the cycles of capitalist economy.

It seems that Rakovsky was one of those who did most work at the beginning of his exile. Christian Georgiyevich was employed in Astrakhan by the regional commission of the plan administration, as an "economics specialist" at 180 roubles. His most famous writing of this period is his letter to Valentinov[69] in early August 1928, which Trotsky circulated to all the "colonies" and which would later be known as the *Professional Dangers of Power*.[70] There he showed the corruption of that part of the working class which had given birth to the bureaucracy and to the party apparatus, the formation of a privileged layer supported by the possession of power which it usurped while benefiting from the passivity and a certain indifference of the masses. In passing he stressed the decisive role of "the party régime" as one of the main factors in the fight against degeneration.

But Rakovsky did a great deal more general work in Astrakhan, where he also caught malaria. He was working simultaneously on the drafting of a

65. [RH] Kantorovich: student, associate of Sedov, member of Opposition.
66. [RH] Dmitri Lapin: Latvian Communist in Left Opposition: while deported wrote critique of draft programme.
67. [RH] FN Dingelstedt (1890-1938): agitator at Kronstadt in 1917, student at Institute of Red Professors, director of Leningrad Forest Institute; one of most brilliant of younger generation of Left Opposition; organised strikes and hunger strikes at Vorkuta, where he was shot in 1938.
68. [RH] Vilensky-Sibiriakov (1888-1937): Menshevik worker, went over to Bolsheviks 1917; secretary of society of former convicts; member of Left Opposition, deported 1928, capitulated 1929.
69. [RH] GN Valentinov: old Bolshevik, on editorial staff of *Trud*.
70. [RH] See http://www.marxists.org.uk/archive/rakovsky/1928/08/prodanger.htmn

biography of Saint-Simon, an examination of the origins of the utopian socialism, a *History of the Civil War in Ukraine*, works ordered for official Soviet publications, and his memoirs which, according to what he wrote to Trotsky, consisted of his recollections of the main personalities and congresses of the Second International. These works were finished, then seized by the GPU, and no information about their existence was given in February 1988, when the official rehabilitation of Rakovsky was announced.

This rapid outline cannot fail to impress. These men of different generations did not often find enough time in life to put their ideas on paper. Some of them, on the other hand, lived by their pen. But neither group ceased to be driven by ideas and that is undoubtedly what inspired them with confidence in their own abilities.

Perhaps Maria Mikhailovna Joffe[71] was right when she wrote from Moscow to Alma-Ata: "Those who are not making careers for themselves drink vodka. [...] Only the oppositionists continue to really think."[72] In any event, while in exile they thought and they wrote and we can see this process of debate through the documents, generally handwritten, which they exchanged.

It was a letter from Nadezhda Ostrovskaia[73] in Voronezh which first told Alma-Ata the news that Preobrazhensky considered that the leadership of the party had just carried out "a turn to the left".[74] It was the first information about the birth of the tendency of those who were initially called the "conciliators" — Preobrazhensky and Ishchenko,[75] joined a little later by Radek.

His first text, in March, was, to tell the truth, rather careful. The "emergency measures" were the response to the offensive by the rich peasants and the reflection in Russia of the intensifying class struggle in Europe. The "left turn" could rapidly come to an end, which would not be very likely, because it would then be necessary to go much further to the right than the right-wing advocates of a new NEP could even dream about. So in his view the most probable outcome would be a "return to a Leninist agrarian policy" based on "the elevation of the poor and medium peasants against the capitalist elements".

In this second case, it would be necessary, according to him, for "the Left Opposition, collectively, to go ahead of the majority of the party, regardless of the stupidities and baseness from which it suffers". He proposed the drafting of a text in which the Left Opposition, noting the positive aspects of the new policy, would offer its support to the leadership in carrying it through without requiring "the rehabilitation of the Bolshevik-Leninists or mentioning the repression". In order to prepare such a statement, the Left Opposition should ask permission from the leadership to hold a conference enabling them to work

---

71. [RH] MM Joffe (born 1900): wife of AA Joffe; arrested for organising assistance for the deportees; released after 1956 and emigrated to Israel.
72. Undated letter from M. Joffe, *AH*, T 1090.
73. [RH] Nadezhda Ostrovskaia: Bolshevik in 1905, Chekist, deported 1928.
74. Ostrovskaia to Trotsky, 20 February 1928, *AH*, T 1139.
75. [RH] AG Ishchenko: Bolshevik from 1917, trade-union official, member of Left Opposition, capitulated 1929.

together. Preobrazhensky suggested that Trotsky and Rakovsky should take responsibility for this request. Preobrazhensky insisted on the nature of the policy in which Stalin was engaged: the "turn to the left", he insisted, reflected the positions defended by the Left Opposition like a "distorting mirror".[76]

The same point was made by Ishchenko, who insisted that "the struggle in the countryside" had started with "the appearance of a turn to the left". The result of the battle would be decided by the position held by the Opposition at the decisive moment. He emphasised:

> Such a situation makes it possible for us to take a more concrete course to rejoin the party and not to defer this return for an indefinite time. Keeping the opposition outside the party for a prolonged period would be very dangerous for the dictatorship of the proletariat.[77]

Thus the discussion started immediately. Certain responses were very sharp. FN Dingelstedt wrote:

> These measures have been caused by the threat of famine and economic crisis. [...] The rise of unemployment, the deceleration of industrialisation continues: where is this new course? [78]

Smilga, on 4 April, was almost as cutting:

> The current zigzag cannot be regarded as a consistent left turn. The terror that the leadership is using against the Left Opposition cannot bring about a serious correction of the party's line.[79]

Sosnovsky had the same hard line, categorically rejecting the very idea of a turn.

But a new tendency became apparent, intermediary between the first two. Rakovsky, for example, fully accepted the analysis made by Preobrazhensky of the two possible alternatives. For him it meant that the Opposition should "be based on the zigzag to the left and on the workers' activity to turn this zigzag into real left policy". But that point could not be reached by an alliance with the leadership, but only "by work at the base". Criticising Preobrazhensky's practical proposals, Christian Georgiyevich retorted that "rejoining the party today can occur only at the price of capitulation": the necessary statement must be addressed to the workers and not to the leaders.[80]

This was a rather similar position to that put forward by Valentinov. For him, Moscow was preparing "the last act of Thermidor", and Preobrazhensky's practical proposals would lead to capitulation: however the Left Opposition

---

76. Preobrazhensky, "The Left Turn", *AH*, T 1262.
77. Ishchenko to Trotsky, April 1928, *AH*, T 1254.
78. Dingelstedt to Trotsky, 8 July 1928, *AH*, T 1891.
79. Smilga to Trotsky, 4 April 1928, *AH*, T 1273.
80. Valentinov to Trotsky, 14 April 1928, *AH*, T 1309.

could "support the authors of the emergency measures if they turned to the masses and openly broke with the right of the party".[81]

On 30 April however, VD Kasparova[82] made herself the spokesperson of those deported, still pretty numerous it seemed, who "were having difficulty in analysing the situation" and did not really know what point they had reached.[83]

After this a discussion developed whose positions and documents, in particular by Valentinov and Sosnovsky, gave the same picture for the various regions. Trotsky then decided to formulate a position which, while opposing the steps recommended by Preobrazhensky and Ishchenko, did not burn any bridges. His letter of 9 May showed where he was heading.

For him, the measures against the kulaks were an "inconsistent, contradictory, but all the same undeniable" step towards the policy of the Opposition, therefore the right direction. He maintained:

> It should be said clearly and precisely. But, initially, we should not exaggerate the extent of this step — judging from experience, we should be prudent about such turns — , not make unnecessary approaches, and explain succinctly the reasons, the mechanics and the ideology of the turn.[84]

On the question of the origin of the "turn" — he accepted the term — there was an objective need. Who had created it? He answered:

> It goes without saying it is ourselves, in as much as we are only a conscious expression of an unconscious process. If we had not been there, the current economic difficulties would have led to a huge success for Ustrialov's[85] supporters.[86]

Agreeing with the class analysis and the theoretical appreciation of the new policy by Preobrazhensky, he warned against the tendency to think that the kulak question could be dealt with in the countryside alone, whereas it would be resolved by industrialisation, by the correct direction of the International and by the training of cadres. As for the practical approach, he began by saying clearly:

> Are we ready to support the current movement? Absolutely. With all our forces and by all means. Do we consider that this movement increases the chances of cleansing the party, without too large clashes? Yes, we

---

81. Valentinov to Trotsky, 19 April 1928, *AH*, T 1326.
82. [RH] VD Kasparova (1875-1937): Bolshevik in 1904, propaganda secretary of bureau of political commissars, associate of Trotsky; worked in Comintern on woman question in the East; deported 1928, said to have capitulated in 1935.
83. Kasparova to Trotsky, 30 April 1928, *AH*, T 1377.
84. Trotsky, circular letter, 9 May 1928, *AH*, T 3112.
85. [RH] NW Ustrialov (1890-1937): lawyer and journalist, advocate of the NEP as a means of peacefully restoring socialism; returned to USSR 1935; arrested and sentenced 1937.
86. Trotsky, circular letter, 9 May 1928, *AH*, T 3112.

think so. Are we ready to cooperate precisely in this way? Entirely and without reserve.[87]

This is also what he proposed to say, in the calmest manner, in the statement which should be sent to the Congress of the Communist International and in which the Opposition must, according to him, demand to be accepted back into the party because the whole situation confirmed that this was more than legitimate.[88] Did Trotsky convince them? It seems unlikely. At the end of May, Preobrazhensky wrote:

> We based our tactic in 1927 on the worst alternative, we gambled on pessimism. We must now have a different tactic, we must risk something on the side of optimism. If Thermidor has not been carried out, we must be delighted and move towards a rapprochement with the party. If not we shall be transformed into small sect of 'true Leninists'...[89]

A few days later, he declared that it was quite wrong to state, as Trotsky had done, that it was the Opposition's activity which had caused the turn, whereas, obviously, it was the result of the efforts of the "kulaks". He revealed the basis of his orientation by saying:

> The capacity of the majority of the leadership to find a way of getting back to a Leninist policy was shown in reality by its struggle against the kulaks.[90]

VB Eltsin, on the other hand, drew up an indictment against Preobrazhensky and the conciliators which showed that he did not share Trotsky's diplomatic or educational concerns with the latter and those who thought like him. Already, on 16 May, he wrote to Trotsky that "centrism is twice as dangerous when it pretends to be left-wing".[91] A few days later, in a circular letter, he attacked what he considered to be the clear basis of Preobrazhensky's position.

For him, it was not a question of a conflict of ideas in the apparatus and behind the scenes, but of class struggle. The causes of the degeneration of the party and state apparatus, which had led to the politics and ideology of the kulak, were obviously social causes. The slide to the right had not been the result of an evolution in ideas, but of a shift by the leadership of the ruling proletarian party towards the rural and urban petty bourgeoisie and of the pressure of international capitalism. Speaking about the years 1926 and 1927, he wrote:

> Our fight was an attempt on behalf of the proletarian vanguard to oppose this process; and, in this fight, we ran up against the inertia and

87. Ibid.
88. Ibid.
89. Preobrazhensky to Trotsky, end of May 1928, *AH*, T 1497.
90. Preobrazhensky, June 1928, *AH*, T 1593.
91. VB Eltsin, 16 May 1928, *AH*, T 1464.

the passivity of the working masses, which, in their turn, were the result of factors of an internal and international nature.[92]

The worst error would be to believe that the party could be saved without the initiative and the movement of the working class itself. This is why it was necessary to be opposed to everything — obviously he was referring to the "authorised conference" suggested by Preobrazhensky — which suggested any conciliation with the apparatus, with hostile class forces and manoeuvres at the top. It was necessary to support measures in the fight against the kulaks and at the same time to criticise without compromise and denounce the overall policy of those taking them:

> Only a powerful rise of the international labour movement and the increase in activity and in the defensive capacity of the Russian workers will put wind in the sails of the political life of the proletariat and the Russian party.[93]

The definition by VB Eltsin of what he regarded as the correct policy towards the "centrists" appeared as a little more "leftist" than that which Trotsky gave:

> Our task is to fight the danger from the right and to unmask centrism *today* so as to have the awakened mass of workers behind us *tomorrow*.[94]

The divergences appear to widen on another point, that of policy on Germany. In March, the founding congress of the organisation of the "Left Communists" — the members of the United Opposition in Germany, the Leninbund — decided to participate in the elections by presenting their own candidates against those of the German Communist Party. As early as the autumn of 1927 a strong current in favour of this tactic took shape in their ranks, which Trotsky criticised in a letter probably written in January, aimed at what was called "the Fischer-Maslow group". In face of this initiative, which Trotsky regarded as a move towards a "second party", Radek proposed to send to *Die Rote Fahne* a telegram denouncing this candidature and asked Trotsky to co-sign it, which he refused to do.[95] Radek thus sent his telegram alone.

His initiative was very badly received in the ranks of the exiled oppositionists. The deportees of Kainsk wrote a very curt letter to him, reminding him that it was a question, among militants, "of preventing errors before they occurred", whereas he was happy "to judge them afterwards". They reproached him with taking a position with insufficient evidence: while being for their part hostile to the fight for a "second party" and a "Fourth International", they did not think that the candidacies of the Leninbund would necessarily mean

---

92. VB Eltsin, beginning of June 1928, *AH*, T 1587.
93. Ibid.
94. VB Eltsin, beginning of June 1928, T 1587.
95. Radek to Trotsky, 18 April 1928, *AH*, T 1325.

this. They brutally asked Radek what he would say if German oppositionists called on Stalin directly to repudiate him. They held that his telegram did nothing but "demoralise" the ranks of the opposition and questioned him on the rumour that he had written to Zinoviev and Kamenev, assuring him that it would be "treason" to do so.[96]

The camp of the "conciliators" thus got one more recruit, and, this time, they would oppose Trotsky on the question of the Opposition's statement to the Sixth Congress of the Communist International. After his circular letter of 9 May which put forward their positions, a new discussion started among the "colonists".

Preobrazhensky, in a letter to Trotsky of 2 June, insisted that a clear distinction be made between the general world situation of the working-class movement and the negative results directly due to the errors of the Comintern: "It is better to criticise less but better", he wrote, paraphrasing Lenin. The "left turn" must be called what it was, a positive step forward, but at the same time it should be observed that the leadership had maintained its position on the question of internal democracy and that it had exactly the same positions as at the time of the kulak offensive. He was still unwilling to speak about either "readmission to the party" or "democracy" and he proposed to finish the statement thus:

> We want to make peace with the majority of the party on the basis of the new course. We ask the Congress to reinstate us in the party so that we can loyally carry out our tasks, without factional activity.[97]

The response of Trotsky was a vigorous counter-attack. In his "letter to friends" of 24 June, he attacked the idea of the conference, launched by Preobrazhensky, which he thought ridiculous. He quoted Sosnovsky and Rakovsky who both countered Preobrazhensky with their own approach, namely confronting political questions from the point of view of the party régime:

> At this time this is the sole correct and valid criterion. Not because the party régime is the independent source of all the other phenomena and processes [...]. But, insofar as the party is the unique instrument by means of which we can act on the social processes, for us, the criterion of the seriousness and the depth of the movement is above all the refracted image of the turn in the party.[98]

It was at this point that Radek intervened for the second time, in a completely independent way, since, under the pretext that there was no time, he sent a draft to eight oppositionists announcing that, if there could be no discussion, he

---

96. Letter from Kainsk, May 1928, *AH*, T 1404.
97. Preobrazhensky to Trotsky, 2 June 1928, *AH*, T 1606.
98. Trotsky, circular letter, 24 June 1928, *AH*, T 3114.

would send it to the Congress under his name alone. It was a gesture of distrust which would gain him much hostility in the colonies.[99]

As far as the situation in the USSR went, Radek's draft statement seemed less diplomatic than Preobrazhensky's. It must be emphasised, he said, that the crisis in the collection of grain had revealed the nature of official policy. However the CC, according to him, "has recognised the reality of the kulak danger" and "demanded that it be fought", which was important. He proposed to organise the agrarian proletariat, to purge the party and the Soviet apparatus of pro-kulak elements, to change its social composition, to deepen its self-criticism and to reinstate the Opposition in it. On the international level, he wished to change the positions formerly defended in China. For him, the previous theses of the opposition misunderstood the role of the peasantry in countries with "nascent capitalism" like India and China. The Radek draft insisted (in a passage which was finally omitted) :

> If History demonstrates that certain leaders of the party with whom, as recently as yesterday, we crossed swords, are better than the ideas that they defended, nobody will be happier than we shall be.[100]

When he was informed of Radek's draft, Trotsky had just finished his own "statement" to the Sixth Congress and his "letter" which would conclude with a sentence of a very different inspiration to that of Radek's text:

> Well-intentioned functionaries see the solution of the greatest historical tasks in the formula: 'We must change things in a decisive way'. The party must answer: 'It is not you who must carry out the change, it is *you* who must be radically changed and in the majority of cases, be removed from your posts and replaced'.[101]

The difference was considerable. An improvised consultation in the colonies revealed some hundred votes for Trotsky's draft as against three for that of Radek. Bombarded with telegrams and critical letters from the colonies, Radek explained that he had sent his text only because the letter containing Trotsky's draft had not arrived. He withdrew his own text and signed Trotsky's.

Thus the Opposition front was temporarily reunited. The course of the July plenum eased matters considerably. For all the observers and in particular almost all the protagonists in the discussion, this plenum constituted a victory for the right and the burial of the "left turn". Only Ishchenko continued to work for a rapprochement which, in the new context, now seemed to be purely and simply going over to the side of the leadership. The elements who had fought the conciliators triumphed. Dingelstedt wrote:

---

99. Circular Letter by Radek, 24 June 1928, *AH*, T 1780 a.
100. Draft statement by Radek, 24 June 1928, Ibid, T 1780 b.
101. Letter to Sixth Congress of the Comintern.

> The Opposition must reject any illusion of a regeneration of the party apparatus by a compromise with the present leadership.[102]

A letter from Victor Borisovich Eltsin showed that there remained traces of this hard fight:

> The series of letters, draft statements, theses and new theses, by E[vgeni] A[lekseyevich] [Preobrazhensky] K[arl] B[ernardovich] [Radek] and I[var] T[enisovich] [Smilga], etc is starting to go beyond the limits. Our patience has narrow historical limits. We have 'put up with' the first theses of EA, then the letter of KB (which he did not send to me), and finally we tolerated for too long the deeply opportunist theses of EA, which have nothing to do with a Marxist policy.[103]

It was about the same time that Radek wrote his study entitled "Development and Significance of the Slogan of the Dictatorship of the Proletariat",[104] in which he tried to show that Trotsky wrongly interpreted as support for his theory of the "permanent revolution" the shift by Lenin in 1917 from the slogan of the "democratic dictatorship of the workers and peasants" to that of the "dictatorship of the proletariat".[105] It was this long study that Trotsky would start to answer in the text finally published under the title *Permanent Revolution*. But, for the moment, he was above all preoccupied with strengthening the unity of the Opposition, seriously shaken by these disputes.

Trotsky was in fact very keen to calm down the conflict, the more so as he was certain that the July plenum, with a shift to the right, would be followed by a whole series of other zigzags and general delirium. He was convinced of the need to keep Preobrazhensky and, perhaps still more, Radek, in the ranks of the Opposition. He did not even despair of winning back Ishchenko, even when the latter went to Moscow, apparently in the hope of a deal with Yaroslavsky.[106] In a letter addressed to Smilga, Trotsky spoke about the "misunderstandings" which had separated them and about the responsibility of the post office for the multiplicity of "statements" to the Sixth Congress.[107]

In a letter to VD Kasparova, he acknowledged that he had ignored sharp reproaches from the young people for his excessively conciliatory attitude towards Preobrazhensky, and willingly confessed that perhaps he had been too diplomatic. He also recognised that Radek, finally, deserved the good thrashings

---

102. Dingelstedt to Trotsky, 8 July 1928, *AH*, T 1891.
103. VB Eltsin to Trotsky, 20 August 1928, *AH*, T 2310.
104. Radek, *AH*, T 2324.
105. I. Longuet, *op. cit.*, p93.
106. [RH] MI Gubelman known as Emelian Yaroslavsky (1878-1943): party member from 1898; Left Communist in 1918; later responsible for ideology and repression in struggle against Left Opposition.
107. Trotsky to Smilga, 4 September 1928, *AH*, T 2480.

that he was getting from the same young people, assuring her however that he had done all that he could to pour oil on the troubled waters.[108]

The discussion had been very enlightening for him; it had taught him personally a great deal and it had contributed in a significant fashion to the creation of a younger generation of oppositionists. He saw a conclusive proof of this in the growth of the Opposition within the working class and the youth, and also the rallying to the Opposition statement at the Comintern Congress of working-class elements who had hitherto supported the Democratic Centralists. His correspondence with SA Ashkenazy[109] and especially the Ukrainian Rafail[110] (RB Farbman),[111] showed the value which he attached to gaining worker cadres.

Actually, his way of considering matters from the perspective of history gave him an obvious superiority to those he was debating with: his eyes were fixed on a world view and on decades. Moreover, how could he let himself be impressed by men who, in the best of the cases, would only be able to follow in the footsteps of Zinoviev and Kamenev, who were very superior to them? The problems lay elsewhere: it was obviously his support that Bukharin had asked for in July 1928 in Kamenev's apartment, when in panic he poured out his soul to him.

It was on 11 July 1928 that this meeting took place, organised by Sokolnikov,[112] who was trying to prevent Kamenev and Zinoviev from supporting Stalin by getting them to form a "bloc" with Bukharin. Bukharin appeared very disturbed, agitated and tormented: things had gone a long way, and he thought that within two months, either Stalin's group or Bukharin's would look for an alliance with the Zinovievites and the Trotskyists. He spoke about the peasant riots, about the members of the Central Committee who supported the right — including Yagoda[113] — and about those who had betrayed them — like Voroshilov[114] and Kalinin.[115] His reflections on Stalin's personality were those of a man who was hard pressed: he was a "Genghis Khan" who "would cut their throats", who was only interested in power and who was much further away from the other factions than they were from each

---

108. Trotsky to Kasparova, 30 August 1928, *AH*, T 2419.
109. [RH] Trotsky to Ashkenazy, 30 August 1928, *AH*, T 2420. [Revecca Ashkenazy: member of Bolshevik party and oppositionist; wife of KI Grünstein.]
110. [RH] RB Farbman, known as Rafail: tailor, joined party 1910 or 1912; member of Central Committee of Ukrainian party in 1919; Democratic Centralist, expelled and deported in 1928; made false capitulation in 1930, resumed political activity; arrested 1934 and disappeared.
111. Trotsky to Rafail, 10 November 1928, *AH*, T 2874.
112. [RH] GI Brilliant, known as Sokolnikov (1888-1939): doctor of economics, Bolshevik from 1905; People's Commissar for finance, then ambassador to London 1929-32; jailed for ten years in 1937.
113. [RH] HG Yagoda (1891-1938): party member from 1907, statistician; deputy head of Cheka in 1924; People's Commissar for the interior 1934, dismissed 1937; sentenced and executed at time of third Moscow trial.
114. [RH] KI Voroshilov (1881-1969): party member from 1903; organised guerrilla war in Ukraine; incapable of waging modern war, but commanded Leningrad front in 1941.
115. [RH] MI Kalinin (1875-1946): president of Executive Committee of the Soviets; for a long time oscillated between Stalin and the "rightists".

other. It clearly appeared, from the account of this meeting, that Bukharin also wanted to ally with Trotsky against Stalin. Trotsky would answer in an indirect way.[116]

Indeed, he seized the opportunity of a letter from a "rightist" in the party, his former ally YM Shatunovsky,[117] to tackle the problem of the possibility of an alliance with the rightists. At the end of this long screed, he listed the conditions for organising a real congress of the party, up to and including a secret ballot for the nomination of delegates, which led him to recall, as we pointed out previously, that "the centrists" were "the main support and protection of opportunism in the party."[118]

He returned to the question with as much clarity as firmness, after the general outcry caused by his proposal, unexpected by many. At almost the same time a new sign of the worsening crisis in the party appeared. On 22 September, following a chance meeting in Theatre Square in Moscow, Kamenev invited to his home two Trotskyist leaders in the capital. A report arrived a few weeks later at Alma-Ata. The correspondent, who signed this message "Anton", gave an account of what Kamenev had said:

> Everything will be re-examined at the October plenum. The result will be either a step forward directly towards Thermidor or a step forward hidden from the eyes of the masses. He considers that the analysis by LD of the July plenum was completely correct. [...] He says that LD should draw up a document where he would say 'Call on us! We will work together!' But he will not do it and will remain at Alma-Ata unless an express train is sent to get him. But when they send the train, the situation in the country will be such that Kerensky will be at the door.[119]

In a letter of 21 October devoted to general problems, Trotsky merely noted these advances with a caustic irony and concluded:

> That he is singing, without fear of Yaroslavsky, shows that the grip of the apparatus is weakening and that the chances for the Opposition are growing. We will give him the credit. But our only conclusion must be: we must hammer the capitulators two, three, ten times harder.[120]

The day before, he had sent Radek a very curt letter, since the latter had apparently not sent him the text on the dictatorship which he had circulated.

---

116. Notes by Kamenev on his meeting with Bukharin, 11 July 1928, *A.H,*, T 1897
117. [RH] Yakov Shatunovsky (1876-1932): engineer and Left Social Revolutionary; Trotsky brought him into Bolshevik party in 1917; on Trotsky's general staff, in charge of train and locomotives; sympathised with "rightists" in late 1920s.
118. Trotsky to Shatunovsky, 12 September 1928, *AH*, T 3132.
119. Anton to Trotsky, 22 September 1928, *AH*, T 2630.
120. Trotsky, circular letter, 21 October 1928, *AH*, T 3146.

*   *   *   *   *

The last months of 1928 were no longer a time of intense discussion, but months of elaboration and reflection after the storm. Trotsky, already very cut off by the "blockade", reconsidered the need, shown by the discussions, for deepening the analysis, not only of the situation in the party and the apparatus, but even the prospects for the "march to Thermidor" that the Opposition intended to resist. On the consequences of the July plenum, after the elimination of Uglanov[121] from the leadership in Moscow, he wrote:

> After having yielded politically and secured a majority, Stalin is attacking on the terrain of organisation.[122]

For him the fate of the battle between centrists and rightists was settled in advance: the leaders of the latter would recoil before a confrontation. But the question remained of knowing how the "threat from the right" might actually be manifested in the country. Trotsky suggested an alternative which he called "Bonapartism" — a superior concentration of power raising itself above the masses. For the first time, he perceived an alternative to the victory of the right — Thermidor pure and simple — namely, a temporary victory of the centrists, which would result from "the union of the centrist apparatus with the governmental repressive machine". He came to the conclusion that "centrism after all represents only one variety of the tendency [....] seeking reconciliation with bourgeois society which is striving to be reborn".[123]

In the fight at the top which was about to begin, he denounced the illusion of the conciliatory wing of the Opposition: the centrists would undoubtedly seek support from the defectors from the Opposition, and never from the Opposition itself. The latter must go boldly ahead of the masses and above all help them everywhere to smash down the defences put up against them by the bureaucrats:

> The axis of our domestic policy consists in really maintaining power in the hands of the proletariat or, more accurately, restoring to it that power usurped by the apparatus and in subsequently strengthening the dictatorship of the proletariat on the basis of systematic improvement of the conditions of existence of the working class.[124]

Taking one more step towards the abandonment, not yet definitive, of the concept of Thermidor used until now, he considered the question of the nature of what he still called "centrism". He pointed to its social base in the

---

121. [RH] NA Uglanov (1886-1940): Bolshevik from 1907; in Petrograd during insurrection, then party apparatchik; connected with rightists; expelled 1932 for not denouncing Ryutin; arrested 1936, executed in prison.
122. Ibid.
123. Ibid.
124. Ibid.

development of the Soviet bureaucracy which was becoming increasingly independent of the working class and dependent on the bourgeoisie. He reaffirmed the line of the essential independence of the Opposition:

> The Bolshevik-Leninists have only one way to go, to mobilise the elements who live and are capable of living for their party, to unite the proletarian core of the party, to mobilise the entire working class. [...] The current centrist campaign against the right must illustrate to all proletarian revolutionaries the need and the duty to multiply their efforts tenfold to follow an independent line, forged by the whole history of Bolshevism, and which has been proved correct through all the colossal trials of the events of these last years. [125]

* * * * *

Thus the Alma-Ata operation seemed to have been a bitter setback for Stalin. Trotsky had been neither isolated nor muzzled. Not only had he succeeded in preserving, in spite of distance, the unity of the Opposition, but he was able to carry out a political offensive, to galvanise the opponents of Stalin, and to appear more and more as the alternative solution. One of the proofs of the failure of the Stalinist enterprise was without any doubt the introduction of what the deportees would call the "postal blockade": their correspondence was sent to them less and less — except the rare letters from capitulators. "The snow settled on our isolation", wrote Natalia Ivanovna.[126]

On 16 December, a special representative of the GPU, Volynsky, arrived at the house in Alma-Ata. This was the man who had succeeded in finding D, and arresting him, and in preventing any communication between Trotsky and the "centre in Moscow". He brought a message which constituted a real ultimatum, cited from memory by Trotsky:

> The work of your political sympathizers throughout the country has lately assumed a definitely counter revolutionary character; the conditions in which you are placed at Alma-Ata give you full opportunity to direct this work; in view of this, the *collegium* of the GPU has decided to demand from you a categorical promise to discontinue your activity; failing this, the *collegium* will be obliged to alter the conditions of your existence to the extent of completely isolating you from political life. In this connection, the question of changing your place of residence will arise.[127]

---

125. Ibid.
126. [RH] Natalia Ivanovna Sedova (1882-1962): Trotsky's companion and mother of his two sons.
127. L. Trotsky, *My Life* (1930), chapter XLIV at http://www.marxists.org/archive/trotsky/1930/mylife/ch44.htm

Convinced that the ultimatum from the GPU meant that he would be arrested and imprisoned for an indefinite period, Trotsky refused to give a written answer. But on 16 December 1928, he addressed to the Central Committee of the Party and the Executive of the International a letter which was in fact intended for the world and posterity:

> The demand that I abstain from political activity is a demand that I renounce the struggle for the interests of the international proletariat, a struggle which I have been waging continually for thirty-two years, throughout all of my conscious life. The attempt to represent this activity as 'counter-revolutionary' comes from those whom I charge, before the international proletariat, with violating the fundamental principles of the teachings of Marx and Lenin, with infringing on the historical interests of the world revolution, with renouncing the traditions and precepts of October, and with unconsciously, but all the more menacingly, preparing the Thermidor.[128]

He affirmed that he would not give up "the struggle against a strangling party régime", "the blindness of the present direction of the Communist Party", and the "economic policy of opportunism". Evoking the repression which had fallen on the Opposition since 1923, he wrote:

> For six years, we have been living in the USSR under the conditions of a growing reaction against October, and, consequently, of a clearing of the way for the Thermidor. The most obvious and complete expression of this reaction within the party is the savage persecution and routing of the Left wing in the party organization.[129]

He contrasted "the incurable weakness of the reaction headed by the apparatus", of which he said that "they know not what they do", since they were executing "the orders" of the enemy classes, to the "historical strength of the Opposition" which "sees the dynamics of the class forces clearly, foresees the coming day and consciously prepares for it."[130]

He responded to the sentence about the conditions of his existence and the threat of isolation from political life by recalling that he was exiled four thousand kilometres from Moscow, two hundred and fifty from the nearest railway, in a locality where malaria, plague and leprosy were prevalent, and where the newspapers arrived ten days late at the earliest and where letters took months. He pointed to the arrest of Sermuks and Poznansky, guilty of wanting to share his exile, and to the delay to letters bringing him news of his daughters' illness. Recalling the judgment of Lenin on the rudeness and disloyalty of Stalin, he showed the growing harshness of the methods employed against the

128. Ibid.
129. Ibid.
130. Ibid.

opposition, the fatal hunger strike of Butov,[131] the "violence, beatings, torture — both physical and moral — ... inflicted on the best Bolshevik workers for their adherence to the precepts of October."

Recalling the ceaseless efforts, since 1923, to reduce him to silence, in one way or another, he recalled his statement to the Sixth Congress of the Communist International: the requirement to give up political activity could only come from "a completely depraved officialdom". His conclusion was clear:

> To everyone, his due. You wish to continue carrying out policies inspired by class forces hostile to the proletariat. We know our duty and we will do it to the end.[132]

One month then passed in the most total isolation and complete postal blockade. The newspapers which the exiles received gave a prominent place to the polemic against "the right". Bukharin still expressed himself from time to time. His "Notes of an Economist", published in *Pravda* of 30 September, constituted an obvious attack against Stalin. In a speech of 28 November, he made an attack, in terms which recalled those of Trotsky, against "the party functionaries who are turning themselves into bureaucrats", and against the provincial chiefs who had become "bureaucratic idols", having nothing but contempt for those for whom they were responsible.

The decision to exile Trotsky was finally taken at the Political Bureau in mid-January. Bukharin opposed it. According to an official minute of a subsequent Political Bureau, Stalin was reported as having argued in the following way:

> Trotsky must be exiled abroad 1) because, as long as he remains in the country, he is able to direct the Opposition ideologically and its numerical strength keeps on growing; 2) so that he can be discredited in the eyes of the masses as an accomplice of the bourgeoisie as soon as he arrives in a bourgeois country; 3) in order to discredit him in the eyes of the world proletariat: social democracy, without any doubt, will use his exile against the USSR and will fly to the assistance of Trotsky, 'the victim of Bolshevik terror'; 4) if Trotsky attacks the leadership by making revelations, we will be able to present him as a traitor. All these are arguments in support of the need to exile him.[133]

Volynsky remained on the spot in Alma-Ata while awaiting instructions after his visit of 16 December. On 20 January, he again went to the house of the exiles, with an extract from the official minutes of the *collegium* of the GPU accusing Trotsky of "counter-revolutionary activity expressing itself in the organization of an illegal anti-Soviet party, whose activity has lately been directed toward

---

131. [RH] GV Butov (?-1928): engineer, Trotsky's private secretary during the civil war; arrested in 1928, he died following a hunger strike.
132. Ibid.
133. Letter from Moscow, 22 March 1929, *Biulleten Oppositsii* no 1, p3.

provoking anti-Soviet actions and preparing for an armed struggle against the Soviet power", and consequently deciding to expel him from the Soviet Union. The day of 21 January was devoted to packing the luggage: Trotsky and Ljova[134] would not go, as they had envisaged, to hunt the predatory tigers from Balkash, which had come up the Ili River and were approaching Alma-Ata. On 22 January, early in the morning, the interminable journey began.[135]

It would last twenty-two days. A bus took the travellers, their escort and their luggage from Alma-Ata. But the tractor sent to meet them could not get through the pass of Kurday. They had to continue on light sledges as far as Pishpek where they could take the train. It was in the vicinity of Aktyubinsk that Trotsky learned, from one of the senior GPU officials who was accompanying him, that he was to be expelled to Turkey — which he again refused. In Ryazhsk, Sergei[136] and Lyova's wife, Ana, got onto the train for the last part of the journey. But they were stopped: for eleven days and eleven nights, the train was halted, probably in the area of Kursk, in terrible cold, doubtless waiting for instructions. Did Trotsky read Bukharin's article published in *Pravda* of 24 January, 1928 on Lenin's "political testament", a political testament that Bukharin, without saying so, did not contrast to Trotsky's ideas? He made no comment about that. On the other hand, he noted that it was in this period that he learned of the arrest of many oppositionists regarded as "the centre", the Georgians Kavtaradze[137] and Budu Mdivani,[138] the literary critic AK Voronsky,[139] the former Kronstadt sailor VS Pankratov[140], the soldiers Dreitser,[141] Gayevsky,[142] Enukidze: in total 350 arrests in the Moscow area, 350 in several large cities, Leningrad, Kharkov, Odessa, Dniepropetrovsk, not to mention the arrests of deportees.[143] Now the largest number of "Bolshevik-Leninists" were to be found in prison and we have a description of the sordid conditions under which a hundred of them were imprisoned in Tobolsk, while Verkhne-Uralsk, Suzdal, Cheliabinsk were starting to fill up.

Undoubtedly at the time Trotsky also did not know that, on 30 January, the Bolshevik-Leninists of Moscow had published a report of the conversations in

134. [RH] Leon Sedov (see note 35 above).
135. *My Life*, chapter XLIV.
136. [RH] Sergei L Sedov (1908-1938): younger son of Trotsky and Natalia Sedova.
137. [RH] SI Kavtaradze (1885-1971): old Bolshevik, head of Georgian government 1922-23; member of Left Opposition, expelled 1927, imprisoned 1929; rehabilitated in 1940, became Vice-Commissar for foreign affairs, then ambassador to Romania.
138. [RH] Politcarp (known as Budu) Mdivani (1877-1937): party member from 1903; member of Georgian presidium in 1922; opposed Stalin on question of the "Federation"; expelled 1928, readmitted 1930; sentenced to death and shot.
139. [RH] AK Voronsky (1884-1943) party member from 1904, literary critic, editor of *Krasnaia Nov* 1921-27; expelled 1927, imprisoned 1929, released but rearrested, died in jail.
140. [RH] VS Pankratov: Kronstadt sailor, then Chekist, deported 1928.
141. [RH] EA Dreitser (1894-1936): young officer in Red Army; member of party then of Left Opposition; deported 1928, capitulated 1929; defendant at first Moscow trial.
142. [RH] PI Gayevsky: soldier in Red Army, railway worker, Menshevik who became Bolshevik; expelled 1926.
143. *Pravda*, 23 February 1929.

July of the previous year between Bukharin and Kamenev which would enable Stalin to make a new and furious attack against Bukharin;[144] the publication was perhaps a provocation.

The train arrived at Odessa on 10 February 1929, and Trotsky could look from afar at the city where he had gone to secondary school, where he had first armed himself as a militant in his adolescence, and where he had spent quite a few months in prison. After further delays due to the fact that the port was blocked by ice, Trotsky, Natalia Ivanovna and Lyova were finally embarked on the steamer *Ilyich* from which they would disembark in Constantinople on 12 February. On his arrival, Trotsky gave a written statement to the Turkish authorities explaining that he was entering their country against his will.

He would never return to the USSR.

---

144. Stalin "The Bukharin Group and the Right Deviation", 9/10 February 1929, *Sočinenija* , (Moscow 1946-51), XI, p319.

The "Bloc" of the Oppositions against Stalin in the USSR in 1932

PIERRE Broué's 'Bloc of The Oppositions' first appeared in the Cahiers Léon Trotsky, no. 5, January-March 1980. It was significant for a number of reasons. First, the article not only reinforced our awareness of the degree of opposition to Stalin in what for him was the troubled year of 1932 but emphasized its aspiration to unity. Second, Broué documented for the first time that links existed between Trotsky and non-Trotskyist opposition groups inside the Soviet Union. Third, he was able to demonstrate that the later terror had its roots in earlier difficulties: the charges in the Trial of the Sixteen in 1936 were not simply pathological inventions but had some rational basis in the events of 1932. Fourth, the research undertaken by Broué and his team from Grenoble at Harvard confirmed the necessity for continuing archival research. Isaac Deutscher had earlier worked in the closed archive but The Prophet Outcast, while referring to Trotsky correspondence at this time, makes no reference to these matters.

The episode is further discussed in J Arch Getty, *Origins of the Great Purges* (Cambridge: 1985), pp119-123; P Broué, 'Party Opposition to Stalin (1930-1932) and the First Moscow Trial' in ??, *Essays in Revolutionary Culture and Stalinism* (1985); P Broué, *Trotsky* (Paris: 1988), pp700-712; P Broué, *Histoire d L'Internationale Communiste, 1991-1943* (Paris: 1997), pp591-594; VZ Rogovin, *1937: Stalin's Year of Terror* (1998), pp60-66. See also RW Thurston, *Life and Terror in Stalin's Russia* (New haven: 1996), pp25-26 and M Jansen and N Petrov, *Stalin's Loyal Executioner: People's Commissar Nickolai Yezhov, 1895-1940* (Stanford: 2002), pp44-49. The opening of the Russian archives witnessed increasing interest in Ryutin and publication of his platform and documents: see, for example, B Starkov, 'Trotsky and Ryutin: from the history of the anti-Stalin resistance in the 1930s' in T Brotherstone and P Dukes, eds, *The Trotsky* Reappraisal (Edinburgh: 1992). There is a brief discussion of the Riutin circle in I Kershaw and M Lewin, *Stalinism and Nazism: Dictatorships in Comparison* (Cambridge: 1997),pp40-44, where the Russian language literature is cited. Also worth consulting is RW Davies, 'The Syrtsov-Lominadze Affair', *Soviet Studies*, 1, 1981.

Broué needs no introduction to many of our readers: he is the doyen of contemporary historians of Trotskyism. Founder of the *Cahiers Léon Trotsky*, he is President of the Leon Trotsky Institute at Grenoble where he was for many years Professor of Contemporary History at the Institut d'Études Politiques. Much of his work is available in English, most recently and notably, *The German Revolution, 1917-1923* (Leiden, 2004) but it is with regret that we record that his *Trotsky* and *Histoire de L' Internationale Communiste* still await translation.

This article was translated by the late John Archer. We have made small stylistic changes and updated some of the notes.

* * * * * *

Researchers from the Institut Léon Trotsky[1] made an important discovery, while investigating documents in the Library at Harvard College, which were destined to appear in the volumes of the *Oeuvres* for 1936 — 37. They confirmed the existence in the USSR in 1932 of a "bloc" of the Oppositions against Stalin. It was a substantial discovery though it does not for a moment justify the old Stalinist thesis that there was a "terrorist" bloc. Nothing has appeared to support the statements which were taken seriously some years later in the "Moscow Trials", but the discovery does call into question all the non-Stalinist and anti-Stalinist interpretations of the history of the USSR. This is because the counter-statements by Trotsky, his son Sedov and their defenders had hitherto been interpreted as denials that any bloc whatsoever was formed between Communist tendencies at the end of 1932.

The two documents which attracted our notice and which are reproduced in the appendix to this article are, first, a letter by Jean van Heijenoort[2], Trotsky's secretary, dated 3 July 1937 and addressed to his son Leon Sedov[3] in Paris. The second is the copy of an undated letter in German from Trotsky to Sedov, the content of which enables it to be dated towards the end of 1932, in the October or

1. This work-group consisted of Alain Calvié, Michel Dreyfus, Jean-Paul Joubert, Isabelle Lombard, Katia Chitzov and Pierre Broué. It worked in the library of Harvard College at Cambridge, Mass., from 2 January to 29 February 1980.
2. Jean Van Heijenoort (1912-1986) was a student of mathematics and a member of the Communist League when he went to Prinkipo at the end of 1932 to be one of Trotsky's secretaries, a function which he fulfilled for seven years, from Prinkipo to Coyoacán. He was secretary of the Fourth International during the war, and, after his break with that organisation, he was Professor of Philosophy (Logic) at Brandeis University until he retired. He played a key role in the classification and identification of the "exile" papers.
3. Leon Sedov (1906-1938) was the eldest son of Trotsky and Natalia Sedova. He was a member of the Communist Youth and one of the most active members of the Left Opposition in the USSR. In 1927 he chose to remain with his father, whose exile in Alma Ata and, later, in Turkey he shared until 1931. In Berlin from 1931 to 1933, he was in reality responsible for the "Russian Section" of the Opposition, and then for the International Communist League, the brain of its network of correspondence in the USSR. He then migrated to Paris, were he died in highly suspicious circumstances, following an operation for appendicitis on 15 February 1938, taking with him all the details of his clandestine activity, the names of his correspondents in the USSR and all knowledge of where he had hidden parts of his own and of his father's archives.

November. This second letter provides evidence that the bloc existed and that Trotsky regarded joining it as "acceptable", as well as his reasons for this opinion and the immediate objectives which he foresaw for this alliance. Van Heijenoort's letter was written after a conversation with Trotsky; it confirms that the other document is authentic; it provides the elements of a chronology which enables it to be at least approximately dated, and establishes that a link really existed already at that date between the Trotskyist fraction, in the USSR and abroad, and IN Smirnov[4]. Smirnov was an old Bolshevik and oppositionist, who had repented in 1929 as the leader of a clandestine group which opposed Stalin in the USSR and a member of the "bloc". The information which Van Heijenoort sent in this way to Sedov enable us to identify even who was the principal link between Smirnov and Leon Sedov, the old Bolshevik Holzmann[5], one of the accused and of the victims in the first Moscow Trial. In Sedov's secret letters in 1932, he called Holzmann "the informant".

These were the elements with which the Institut Léon Trotsky began after abandoning for a few days its plan of work on 1936-37 to look for the grounds for the existence of this bloc around 1932 and immediately afterwards, through the letters of Trotsky and his son and through the letters from the Soviet Union which were published in the *Bulletin of the Opposition*, the organ of the Russian Left Opposition which appeared in Berlin. The results of these researches were greater than they expected. They discovered, in one of the rare letters which Sedov wrote in invisible ink (citric acid) to his father to send information about the bloc, an undated letter to which Trotsky replied on 3 November 1932. They also found other allusions to the "bloc", a whole discussion about the new conditions which its formation brought about, in the letters between Trotsky and his son, as well as documents, some of which had been published, which shed light on this period in the history of the USSR. Careful study of the minutes of the International

---

4. Ivan Nikitich Smirnov (1881-1936) was a precision engineer, who joined the Russian Social-Democratic Labour Party in 1899. He was a Bolshevik in 1903 and organised the Moscow insurrection in 1905. After years of prison and hard labour, he was one of representatives of the organisations in Russia at the Prague Conference which really founded the Bolshevik Party in August 1912. He played an important role during the civil war in the 5th Army, and then as President of the Revolutionary Committee of Siberia. He entered the Central Committee as a candidate member in 1919 and as a full member in 1920. In 1923 he joined the leading nucleus of the Left Opposition. He was expelled from the Party in 1927 and deported, and, in 1929 he capitulated. He worked as the director of an automobile factory at Nijni Novgorod, where he organised a group in opposition to Stalin, and for this he was sentenced to ten years' imprisonment at the beginning of 1933. He was one of the defendants in the first Moscow Trial, where he agreed to "confess" after a long resistance and was one of the few to defy the prosecutor. He is said to have refused to appeal for mercy because he regretted his confession. He was executed in summer 1936.
5. Edward S. Holzmann (1882-1936) was an Old Bolshevik who had been a member of the Left Opposition in 1926-27. He was a senior official in the economic administration: he had been sent on a mission to Berlin and agreed to meet Sedov there in autumn, 1932 at the request of Smirnov. He was a defendant at the first Moscow Trial in and even confessed to having met Trotsky in Copenhagen with Sedov — who had never been to Copenhagen — in the Hotel Bristol ... which had been demolished in 1917.

Secretariat of the Left Opposition, of which Leon Sedov was a member, contributed some extra insights particularly in the matter of language.

What Groups were Involved?

Sedov's letter in invisible ink reveals that the following groups existed: the Trotskyist Group in the USSR ("Our Group"), the Zinovievists, the group of IN Smirnov, the Sten–Lominadze Group, the "Safar(ov)–Tarkhan(ov) Group, the "right-wingers" and the "liberals". Of course, not all of these participated in the "bloc", but all of them knew of its existence and, according to Sedov, had contacts with it.

The authentic Trotskyist fraction had a very long history, but for all that it seems to have been reduced at this time to its lowest point[6]. As far as we know, the only one of those whom the comrades in deportation regarded as a "leader" and was at liberty in Moscow at this time was Andrei Konstantinov[7], who was not arrested until December 1932. But there is absolutely no doubt that a small group did exist and was in clandestine communication with Sedov at this time. The memoirs of an old German Communist, who died recently, bear witness to the contact which he personally made in Moscow at the beginning of 1933, on Sedov's instructions, with a representative of the Moscow Trotskyists[8]. We should note that Sedov's letter about the bloc mentions that the "old men" had capitulated, but declared that the links with the workers had been preserved.

The "Zinovievists" do not need to be introduced. Zinoviev and Kamenev had capitulated[9] at the beginning of 1928 and had joined in the uproar against the

6. Trotsky wrote, in a letter dated 31 October 1930, to Max Shachtman, one of his comrades in USA (Harvard College Library 10282) that "the organisation as such in Russia had been destroyed", following the repression which Stalin had inflicted on it over several years. It is only in 1932 that we find in his writing the assurance that its reconstruction had begun.
7. Andrei Konstantinov (known as Kostia), a Muscovite, Party member since 1916, is mentioned by Maria M. Joffe in her memoirs (*One Long Night*, London, 1977) as one of the principal clandestine Trotskyist leaders. There is no mention of him, either in the *Bulletin of the Opposition* or in the "exile correspondence", apart from one letter, which Victor Serge was to publish later. This does not say he was a Trotskyist leader, and puts his arrest at the end of the year 1932. He died in 1942, according to Maria M. Joffe, who has sketched a particularly attractive portrait of him.
8. In his memoirs, *Spartakus, Aufstieg and Niedergang*, published under the name "Karl Retzlaw", Karl Gröhl (1896-1979), who had been (under the name Hans Friedberg) the head of the military apparatus of the German Communist Party and (under the name Karl Erde) one of the leaders of the Left Opposition in that party, says (p356) that he had arranged, on Sedov's behalf, a contact with the Trotskyist Group in Moscow, one of the leaders of which he had met in the Tverskoy Boulevard, in front of the Pushkin monument, and another in the hall of the Trade Union building. He never had any response to report, but he found this in Sedov's hands when he returned to Berlin. The *Bulletin of the Opposition* published a letter signed "TT" in its February 1933 issue.
9. Gregori Y. Radomylski, known as Zinoviev, (1883-1936), and Lev B. Rosenfeld, known as Kamenev (1883-1936), were both Old Bolsheviks and close collaborators with Lenin, Kamenev being Trotsky's brother-in-law. As fellow-members with Stalin of the "troika" they had been the first to attack Trotsky, but after their break with Stalin they led the "new"

Trotskyists. But a decision of 6 October 1932 expelled them once again from the Communist Party of the Soviet Union. The letters reaching Trotsky and Sedov from the Soviet Union had for some time indicated that the two former leaders of the "New Opposition" of 1926 were experiencing a kind of recovery. There was talk of Zinoviev criticising Stalin's German policy and reasserting what the policy of the "United Front", laid down in Lenin's time, had been. He was also said to have declared, semi-privately, that his worst political mistake had been in 1927, when he had decided to capitulate to Stalin and to join in the attacks on Trotsky, so as to work his way back into the party[10]. In any case (as Sedov made clear) Zinoviev and Kamenev were expelled in October 1932 at the very moment when the discussions with the Trotskyists were developing[11]. Officially, they were criticised for having failed to denounce certain oppositional activities, which the so-called Riutin–Slepkov Group had been carrying on over several months, and to which we shall return[12].

The group led by Ivan N Smirnov (whom Lenin had called "the conscience of the Party"), a member of the Left Opposition who had capitulated less abjectly than some others, such as Radek[13], was made up of former Left Oppositionists like him. In this connection, Sedov named Preobrazhensky and Ufimtsev[14]. We may

Leningrad Opposition, which then carried on the struggle — in alliance with Trotsky's Left Opposition inside the "Unified Opposition". They had capitulated to Stalin after the defeat of the Opposition, had made a full "self-criticism", denounced "Trotskyism" and been re-admitted into the Party. In September 1932 they were again excluded, at the time of the "bloc", and once again re-admitted in May 1933, after a still more thorough self-criticism. In December 1934 they were re-arrested after the assassination of Kirov, and condemned, Zinoviev after one trial and Kamenev after two, to ten years' imprisonment. They were the principal defendants in the "Trial of the Sixteen" in August 1936, they made the confessions demanded of them, were sentenced to death and were shot.

10. Harvard College Library (4782), an undated letter written in citric acid from Sedov to Trotsky.
11. Ibid.
12. The decision bears the date 6 October 1932.
13. Karl B. Sobelson, known as Karl Radek (1885-1939?), a free-lance in the left of Social-Democracy in Poland and later in Germany before the Great War, had participated in the "Zimmerwald Left" and represented the Bolsheviks in Stockholm in 1917. He had been the delegate of the Russian Communist Party in Germany, and later secretary of the Communist International. From 1923 onwards he was a member of the Left Opposition. He had been deported at the beginning of 1928 and had capitulated in 1929. Rumours accused him of being responsible for the arrest and execution of the Bolshevik, Blumkin, in 1929. The letters from the USSR to the *Bulletin of the Opposition*, as well as the writings of Trotsky and Sedov, mention him after that time only with expressions of the deepest contempt. He was one of the docile defendants in the second "Moscow Trial", where he saved his head.
14. Evgeny A. Preobrazhensky (1886-1938), a Bolshevik in 1904 and leader of the Party in the Urals in 1917, was elected to the Central Committee in 1917 and became its secretary in 1920. He belonged to the central nucleus of the Left Opposition and became its spokesman against Bukharin in the "economic debate" of the 1920s. He was expelled in 1927 and deported in 1928, and capitulated with Radek and Smilga in July 1929. A correspondent in the *Bulletin of the Opposition* at the beginning of 1932 reported that he was content "to drink tea and play the guitar". He disappeared in the Great Purge, without figuring in any of the trials.

NI Ufimtsev was a locksmith and a Bolshevik since 1906. He was expelled in 1928 and re-admitted in 1930.

suppose that there were other former Oppositionists, whom Trotsky categorised as "capitulators", who were part of this group or at least knew of its existence; they had been arrested at the same time as those just named. There was Smilga, who had capitulated at the same time as Preobrazhensky and Radek. There was Perevertsev, who, under the pseudonym of "Peter", had been one of the organisers of the Left Opposition in Western Europe in 1927. There was Boris Livshitz, who had long since been deported to Slavograd. There were the old Bolsheviks, Grünstein, Ter-Vaganian, Mratchkovsky[15] and others. Sedov's letter in invisible ink gave Trotsky some information about how the GPU exposed the group. One of its members, who had lost his mind, was arrested by chance — and talked. Sedov emphasised that Smirnov knew the cause of his arrest perfectly well

15. All the people listed above had played a role in the "Unified Opposition", but had capitulated in the course of the following years. Ivar T. Smilga (1892-1937), a Bolshevik since 1907, of Lettish origin, was the youngest member of the Central Committee in 1917. He had fought against the Left Opposition in 1923, but joined the Unified Opposition in 1926 and refused to follow Zinoviev and to capitulate in 1927. He capitulated in July 1929 at the same time as Radek and Preobrazhensky. At the end of 1932, he was sentenced to five years' imprisonment, and disappeared in the Great Purge.

Nikolai N. Perevertsev, an Old Bolshevik and an early organiser of the Left Opposition in the Ukraine, had been sent to Geneva as a technical expert to join an international commission on railways. Under the pseudonym, "Peter" or "Pierre", he had been one of the organisers of the Left Opposition in capitalist Europe. He was deported in 1928 and interned in the isolator in Verkhne-Uralsk in 1931. He appears to have capitulated about this time, but was re-arrested at the end of 1932 and disappeared.

Boris S. Livshitz (1896-1949), a Bolshevik in 1917, was a political commissar in the Red Army during the Civil War and then a student in the Institute of Red Professors. He was a member of the Left Opposition, and was deported in 1928. Trotsky regarded him as one of the most promising of his generation, but he capitulated in 1929. He was a senior official in external trade, probably linked to IN Smirnov's group, and was arrested at the end of 1932. He was released at an unknown date and served during World War Two as a war correspondent.

Karl I. Grünstein (1888-1937) was a worker of Lettish origin, who did years of hard labour under the Tsar. He was a divisional commander in the 5th Army and, after the Civil War, was director of the national school of aviation. He was the General Secretary of the society of former political prisoners and a friend of Trotsky. He was one of those who signed the Platform of the Left Opposition and the declaration by Rakovsky in August 1929. He was badly treated and probably capitulated in 1932.

Vagarshak Ter-Vaganian (1893-1936) was an Old Bolshevik, Party leader in Armenia, leader of the revolution in 1917 in his country, editor-in-chief of the review, *Under the Banner of Marxism*, member of the Left Opposition since 1923, expelled in 1927, deported in 1928, and capitulated with Smirnov in 1929. At the end of 1932 he was sent into exile. At the first Moscow Trial he confessed to having been one of those who negotiated the bloc, particularly with Lominadze in support of the Smirnov Group. He was sentenced to death and executed.

Sergei Mratchkovsky (1883-1936) was born in a Tsarist prison, where his parents were serving sentences for political offences. He was a Bolshevik in 1905, a partisan leader in the Civil War and then commander of a division. He was arrested in 1927 in connection with the affair of the clandestine "printing works". He was expelled and deported, and capitulated with IN Smirnov in 1929. He then worked on the construction of the Amur-Baikal railway in the Far Eastern province. He figured in the Moscow Trial of 1936, in which he was accused of having been the Trotskyists' go-between with a view to forming a bloc with the Zinovievists. He was sentenced to death and executed.

and had told him in particular that there had "been no weak point which came from abroad". We may feel surprised that Trotsky agreed to contacts with "capitulators", whom he had criticised sharply during the preceding years. He gave the explanation himself, when he wrote, on 3 March 1933, that the arrest of these people enabled one "to draw the balance of the experience of honest, sincere, non-careerist capitulation"[16].

We have less information about the Sten–Lominadze Group[17]. Even the fact that Sedov writes of a "group" and links the two names is new. The generally accepted version distinguished between two groups, made up of former supporters of Stalin and of determined opponents of Trotsky. This distinction was drawn on the basis of the accusations which appeared in the official press in 1930, about the "Sten–Chatzin" Group[18], which was particularly implanted in the Communist Youth, and about the so-called Syrtsov–Lominadze Group[19], which Roy Medvedev says in his book on the history of Stalinism was "non-existent". Medvedev claimed that Lominadze, a long-time favourite of Stalin and first secretary of the Party Committee in Transcaucasia, with the support of his deputy, Nikolai P Chaplin[20], a former leader of the Communist Youth, had secured

16. L. Trotsky, *Signal Trevogi* (The Alarm Signal), *Bulletin of the Opposition*, No 33, March 1933, p7.
17. Jan E. Sten (1899-1937) was regarded as one of the best philosophers among the younger generation in the Soviet Union during the years 1925-1928 and he had the job of giving Stalin private lessons in "dialectics". He was a member of the Central Control Commission, from which he was removed in 1928. He was sent into exile in 1932, arrested in 1937 and executed without trial in the notorious Lefortovo prison.
    Vissarion (Besso) V. Lominadze (1898-1934) was a Bolshevik in 1917; he held important positions in the Communist Youth, the Young Communist International and, then, in the Communist International. He aligned himself with the most determined supporters of Stalin against Trotsky and the Left Opposition: he was sent to China by the Communist International in 1927 and there helped to organise the disastrous Canton insurrection. As Secretary of the Party Committee in Transcaucasia, he secured in 1930 the adoption of a resolution which criticised Stalinist policy; he was removed from the Central Committee and all his posts. He resumed his studies in engineering and was appointed Party Secretary at Magnitogorsk. He committed suicide in December 1934 following a summons from the GPU at Chelyabinsk. He was later mentioned by some of the defendants in 1936 as one of the members of the bloc.
18. Lazar A. Chatzkin (1902-1938), a Bolshevik in 1917, was the first secretary of the Communist Youth from 1919 to 1922 and was secretary of the Young Communist International. As a member of the Presidium of the Communist International, he fought against the Left Opposition. He was accused in 1931 of belonging to a group of Oppositionists led by Lominadze, and lost all his responsibilities. He was expelled from the Party in 1935: official sources indicate that he committed suicide.
19. Sergei I. Syrtsov (1893-1938), a Bolshevik in 1913, was Party secretary in Odessa in 1920-21, and then made his career in the apparatus. In 1929 he became President of the Council of People's Commissars for the RSFSR [Russian Soviet Federative Socialist Republic] and a candidate member of the Politburo. He was then accused of belonging to a conspiratorial group with Lominadze. He was removed from the Central Committee and sent into the provinces to manage a phonograph factory. He was arrested during the Great Purge and died in prison, where he probably was executed.
20. Nikolai P Chaplin (1902-1938) was one of the leaders of the Communist Youth with Chatzkin, and then was Lominadze's deputy in the Party Committee in Transcaucasia. He was arrested during the purge and disappeared in prison.

acceptance of a document which in 1930 had accused the leadership of "neglecting the needs of the workers and peasants" and denounced the party bureaucrats for "behaving like feudalists and nobles"[21]. Syrtsov, for his part, as President of the Council of People's Commissars for the Russian Soviet Republic had drawn attention to the difficulties in the countryside and protested against the announcement of the victory of socialism[22]. As to the philosopher Jan E Sten, who at one time had been giving Stalin lessons in "dialectics", he was said, according to a manuscript quoted by Medvedev, to have forecast in 1928 that Stalin "would do things that would eclipse the Dreyfus and the Beilis affairs"[23]. Since then Sten had been in disgrace. However, a letter addressed to the *Bulletin of the Opposition* in November 1930 gave a quite different version of events, according to which Lominadze and Sten had been associated with the oppositional resolution of the Party Committee in Transcaucasia. They had been summoned to Moscow to see Stalin, had given ground and recognised their mistake — but immediately afterwards had held a meeting at Syrtsov's house. The Moscow correspondent who wrote to Trotsky and Sedov did not mince words about those whom he called "two-faced people", and added that the police had then searched Syrtsov's place and discovered "minutes of meetings which revealed the existence of the bloc"[24]. Another letter from the same correspondent (who signed himself NN) says that the "Group" (Syrtsov and Lominadze as well as Sten) had been denounced by a provocateur named Reznik, and that the secret meeting was held in the house of an important Party member named Nussinov. According to Reznik, Syrtsov had first adopted a provocative attitude in the Politburo, calling Stalin "a stupid man who is leading the country to ruin", and declaring that there was no longer a Politburo, but only a "Group of Four", Stalin, Molotov, Kaganovitch and Ordonikidze[25]. The two men were removed from the Central Committee and transferred to subordinate jobs. In 1932 Syrtsov was managing a factory and is never mentioned, while Lominadze was the local Party secretary at Magnitogorsk. All these pieces of information justify the conclusion that Sedov's version about a Sten–Lominadze Group, which included former leaders of the Communist Youth, such as JC Chaplin and Chatzkin, deserves more credit than that of Roy Medvedev.

We know almost nothing about the "Safarov–Tarkhanov" Group. There is no doubt that Safarov is an old Bolshevik who was well known for his work in France during the war and in connection with Far Eastern questions after the revolution. He was a member of the "New Opposition" in Leningrad in 1926, but did not follow Zinoviev and Kamenev when they broke with Trotskyism in 1927-28. Like

21. A. Ciliga, *Au Pays du Grand Mensonge*, p228. [This passage does not appear in the English translation- see note 31. *RH*.].
22. Roy Medvedyev, *Let History Judge*, p142.
23. Ibid, p225, according to a samizdat by Frolov.
24. *Bulletin of the Opposition*, No. 17-18, Nov.-Dec. 1930, p39. The letter mentions, not the resolution of the Party Committee in Transcaucasia, but "an appeal in the Caucasus".
25. *Bulletin of the Opposition*, No. 19, March 1931, pp17-18.

Tarkhanov, he was deported at the same time[26]. The group seems to have been a product of the historical trajectory of the "Zinovievist" Group which joined the "Trotskyists". They later capitulated, but despite that did not go back to their original grouping.

The group which Sedov calls "the right-wingers", on the other hand, presents greater problems. As we know, that term was commonly used to describe those in the Party who followed Bukharin, Rykov and Tomsky[27], from the time of the NEP up to that of their leaders' "self-criticism". But there is no indication to support the hypothesis that these people carried on any activity in 1932, or even that they maintained a certain oppositional spirit. On the contrary, the minutes of meetings of the International Secretariat of the Left Opposition and some of Sedov's letters make it appear that at that time he applied the term, "right-wingers", to what historians call the "Riutin Group", a new group which appeared precisely in 1932. We have only indirect evidence that it existed and carried on activity. Its documents have never been unearthed. Riutin[28] was an old Menshevik teacher,

---

26. Gueorgui V. Safarov (1891-1942) was a Bolshevik in 1908, who emigrated, returned to Russia in 1912 and then emigrated to Saint-Nazaire in France, which he left for Switzerland in January 1916. He returned from Switzerland to Russia with Lenin. In the course of the following years, he was put in charge by the Communist International of organising its work in the Middle and Far East, as a member of the Praesidium. In 1924 he was a member of the Central Committee and chief editor of the Leningrad *Pravda*. As a member of the New Opposition and then of the Unified Opposition, he was expelled from the Party in 1927 and did not immediately follow Zinoviev in his capitulation in 1928. After being re-admitted to the Party, he was once more expelled in 1934 and deported. He was mentioned several times in the various trials. He spent his last years in Vorkuta, where the sufferings of this broken man are described by Maria Joffe.

    About Tarkhanov, we know only that he had been a Party member since 1917, that he came from Leningrad, that he was expelled and then re-admitted at the same time as Safarov .

27. Nikolai I. Bukharin (1888-1938) was a Bolshevik in 1908. He was regarded as a theoretician and, according to Lenin, was "the darling of the Party". He was the leader of the "Left Communists" against Lenin and then, in alliance with Stalin, developed the themes of the NEP pushed to an extreme, on the enrichment of the kulak, the construction of Socialism at a snail's pace, and so on. He followed Zinoviev at the head of the Communist International. In November 1929 he was relieved of all his responsibilities and made a complete self-criticism. In 1933 he became the editor-in-chief of *Izvestia*. He was mentioned in the second Moscow Trial and was arrested in January 1937. He was sentenced to death in March 1938 at the time of the third trial.

    Alexei I. Rykov (1881-1937) was a militant in 1900 and joined the Bolsheviks in 1903. He led the fraction of the "komitetchiki" against Lenin, and spent many years in prison and exile. He was a member of the Central Committee, and followed Lenin as President of the Council of People's Commissars. He was associated with Bukharin, eliminated and capitulated with him and was sentenced to death in the same trial.

    Mikhail P Tomsky (1880-1936) was a Bolshevik in 1904, a lithographic worker, member of the Central Committee from 1919 onwards and President of the Soviet Trade Unions, was the third of the troika of the right-wing. He was eliminated at the same time as Bukharin and Rykov, and did not wait to be arrested, but committed suicide after hearing that his name had been mentioned in the first Moscow Trial. It appears that the three historic leaders of the Right had absolutely no activity as a group and not a shadow of opposition in 1932, and that the term "right-wingers" applied to a group could not in any case be applied to them.

28. Mikhail N. Riutin (1890-1937) was a former teacher who became an officer during the war. He

who joined the Bolshevik Party after October. He had been a pillar of the "Right" and had particularly distinguished himself in the struggle against the Unified Opposition in 1926-27 by organising "strong arm" squads, to terrorise everyone likely to sympathise with it. However, in 1928 he had been one of the first Stalin attacked during his preparations to eliminate the right; he was relieved of his responsibilities in the Moscow Committee of the Party and as editor-in-chief of *Krasnaya Zvezda*. It was then that he had formed a group, with PA Galkin, the conspiratorial character of which no one denies. In this group were to be found elements from various currents, such as disciples of Bukharin, bright jewels of the Institute of Red Professors, such as Alexander Slepkov and Dimitri Faretsky[29], as well as little known former "Left Oppositionists" and especially, senior members of the apparatus, such, for example, as Nikolai A Uglanov[30], and even prestigious Old Bolsheviks like the metalworker, Kayurov[31], who led the Vyborg district in Leningrad during the revolution. The Group had drafted a voluminous quasi-manifesto of more than 160 pages, about which we have several indirect pieces of evidence. Ante Ciliga says that it declared: "the Right-wing has proved correct in the economic field and Trotsky in his criticism of the system inside the Party"[32]. It sharply criticised Bukharin for his capitulation to Stalin and advocated the immediate re-acceptance into the party of all those who had been excluded, beginning with Trotsky and his comrades. According to the Menshevik historian, Nikolaevsky, Bukharin told him that the text stated that Stalin "was in his way the evil genius of the Soviet revolution: pushed by an appetite for power, he had led the revolution to the brink of ruin"[33]. Victor Serge adds that at the end of a detailed study of the career of Stalin, the manifesto of the Riutin Group recalled the precedent of the agent-provocateur Azev employed by the Okhrana, and his

was first a Social-Revolutionary and then a Menshevik, and joined the Bolsheviks in the Far East during the Civil War. In 1927 in Moscow, where he was leader of a Party branch, he took the initiative in organising violence against the Opposition in party meetings. He was expelled and imprisoned in 1932, and disappeared.

29. Alexander Slepkov (1900-1937) was a historian and one of the most brilliant students in the Institute of Red Professors. He was a disciple of Bukharin. It appears that he broke with Bukharin because he disapproved of the latter's capitulation. He was exiled to Samara in 1932 and rejected the advances of Stalin, who admired his editorial talents. Soon afterwards sentenced to five years' imprisonment, he appears to have hanged himself in the isolator at Verkhne-Uralsk. His comrade and friend Dimitri Maretsky (—) had a similar fate. The Stalinist press referred to the "Riutin-Slepkov" Group.
30. Nikolai A. Uglanov (1886-1940) was the son of a peasant, a Bolshevik in 1917 and member in 1917 of the Petrograd Soviet. He was then a political commissar, then regional secretary of the Party at Nijni-Novgorod from 1921-1924, and then in Moscow , a candidate member of the Politburo in 1925. He led the repression and violence against the Opposition in 1927 in Moscow. His self-humiliation in 1932, did not save him from being deported and disappearing during the purges, after having been "named" in the public trials.
31. Vassili N. Kayurov (1876-1936) was regarded by many as the typical Bolshevik worker. He died in prison. Trotsky frequently borrowed from this worker's memoirs in his *History of the Russian Revolution*.
32. A Ciliga, *The Russian Enigma*, London, 1940, p279.
33. Boris Nikolaevsky, *Les Dirigeants Soviétiques devant le pouvoir*, p21.

role in the Socialist-Revolutionary Party[34], to declare that one could legitimately ask oneself whether Stalin's policies "are not the fruits of an immense and quite conscious provocation"[35]. Bukharin and Serge likewise agree in reporting that the manifesto declared for "the elimination of Stalin", without which (it wrote) "it was impossible to restore its health to the Party or the country"[36]. It was for failing to denounce the existence or the circulation of this manifesto — which did circulate, according to our evidence, in the factories in Moscow and elsewhere — that Zinoviev and Kamenev were officially excluded from the Party again in 1932. The statements of all the witnesses agree in stating that Stalin in the Politburo called for the head of Riutin, whom he accused of working for his assassination, and that the Politburo refused, influenced by Kirov. Riutin kept his head for a certain time but was imprisoned in an isolator where conditions were hard.

There remains the last of the groups which Sedov mentioned in his letter. The role of this particular group was, beyond question, important in the history of the bloc, although the group never was part of the bloc; he called it "the liberals". The historian is here reduced to conjectures, though the question is clearly a key one for the interpretation of the history of the period. Who were "the liberals"? Several hypotheses are plausible, including that of Sedov, who suggested that "liberals" meant "all oppositionists". The one hypothesis which it seems possible to sustain — though with reservations, because the data is lacking is that we have here members of the apparatus who were hostile to the policy of terror. Did they include Kirov himself? His positions have frequently been stressed by official historians in the Khrushchev period and there is an unverified report that he made contact with Sedov in Paris in 1934, through a trusted agent[37]. Or, without implicating Kirov himself, did the Group include "this important number of Party leaders ... including essentially the secretaries of regional committees and secretaries of non-Russian Central Committees", who in 1934 under the leadership of IM Vareikis[38] formed an "illegal bloc", which attempted to replace Stalin by Kirov during the XVIIth Congress of the CPSU?[39]. The question marks are necessary here. May I be permitted to add that, if the "liberals" whom Sedov mentioned were not these people, then at any rate they must resemble them like brothers?

34. Victor Serge, *Memoirs of a Revolutionary*, Oxford, 1967, p259. Evno F. Azev (1869-1918) is the most famous agent-provocateur in the workers' movement in the world. Between 1903 and 1908 he was at the head of the combat organisation of the Social-Revolutionaries, organising and directing terrorist operations — such as the one which took the life of the Minister Plehve — and continuing to inform the police and betray militants to them by denouncing some of the preparations in advance.
35. Victor Serge, ibid.
36. Nicolaevsky, op cit, p21-22.
37. In *Le Réfractaire* for April 1978, the old French militant Marcel Body tells of how an emissary from Kirov, a member of the Central Committee and brother-in-law of Dr. Levine, had recourse to his services in order to meet Sedov in Paris and sound him about the attitude which Trotsky might adopt towards proposals to re-admit those who had been excluded from the Party — which according to him figured in Kirov's programme.
38. Iossif M. Vareikis (1894-1939) was a Bolshevik in 1913. After the revolution he made his entire career within the Party apparatus.
39. Roy Medvedyev, op cit, p155.

Moreover, for an "illegal bloc" to have been able to reveal itself during the XVIIth Congress, it must have had earlier origins and solid foundations.

The Short Lived Bloc

Sedov's letter in invisible ink reveals unambiguously that three groups joined the agreement which enabled the bloc to come into existence, the Group of Smirnov and the ex-Trotskyist "capitulators", that of the Zinovievists and that which Sten and Lominadze led. According to Sedov, discussions were going on with the Safarov–Tarkhanov Group, and he expected that these discussions would lead it to join the bloc soon. Trotsky questioned Sedov about the attitude of the bloc to what remained of the former "leftist" oppositions, the "Decist" Group[40] and the Workers' Opposition[41], but we do not have Sedov's reply on this point. The materials as a whole show that the "bloc" or at least one of its constituent parts was in contact with the Riutin–Slepkov Group, the "rightists". But they acted independently of each other, as Trotsky's remark shows: "The opinion of the allies that one should wait until the rightists are more involved does not have my agreement, as far as concerns our fraction." He added at once: "From the political point of view, that would mean leaving the field open to the rightists"[42].

The problem of the "liberals" was far from clear. In this connection too, Trotsky wrote to Sedov on 12 October (1932): "As far as the liberals are concerned, it is necessary to be very, very careful. Apart from having to fulfill any promises to them, we have not the slightest interest in rejecting them. Even in a modest way, they have given us more than anyone on a 'practical' line, to be sure, and not politically"[43]. What is the meaning of this phrase, which only documents that we have not yet discovered at Harvard, which in all probability were destroyed, can illuminate? Which of the "liberal" bureaucrats gave practical help to the Left Opposition? Who were those, some of whom really turned towards the others who initiated the "bloc" and the Trotskyist fraction? We have to resign ourselves for the present to leaving these questions unanswered.

In any case, it cannot be denied that there were discussions between the Trotskyists and the "liberals". Trotsky noted in his letter of 30 October 1932: "That the liberals and their nearest neighbours today find us too conciliatory is in the normal order of things ... The liberals say 'We must wait for the rightists to act': that means that they are in fact choosing the road of passivity. And, to us, they will say: they are too moderate: they do not turn enough to the masses, etc."[44].

40. The "Decist" Group was so named from the fact that its initials (DC) corresponded to its title, "Democratic Centralist". Its principal leaders, Vladimir P. Smirnov and Timotei F. Sapronov, were deported.
41. The Workers' Opposition was an Opposition group which went back to 1920, when it had been led by Shlyapnikov and still counted some dozens of supporters in the camps and the isolators.
42. Harvard College Library, un-dated German text (1932), (10110).
43. Harvard College Library, (4777).
44. Ibid (10047).

What was the content of the "bloc"? We must note first that we are dealing with distinct, independent groups. In the letter which caught van Heijenoort's attention in 1937, and which attracted ours in January 1980, Trotsky wrote: "The proposal for a bloc seems to me to be perfectly acceptable. I stress that we are dealing with a bloc and not a fusion". And he writes, specifically: "The bloc does not exclude reciprocal criticism. Any propaganda by our allies in favour of capitulations (such as Grünstein, etc.) will be inexorably and pitilessly resisted by us."[45].

This was the setting within which, as Van Heijenoort wrote to Sedov in 1937, after questioning Trotsky on the subject: "The content of the bloc is strictly laid down... and amounts to no more than the exchange of information." In 1932, Trotsky was writing: "How is the bloc going to express itself? For the moment, principally in the field of exchange of information. The allies keep us informed about what concerns the Soviet Union, while we do the same for them as far as the Communist International is concerned. We should reach an agreement about very exact means of corresponding. The allies should send us letters for the *Bulletin*. The *Bulletin* undertakes to publish the documents of the allies, but it reserves the right to comment freely on them"[46]. And he sent to his son the political questions to raise: "what does the ally think of the draft programme published in the last issue of the *Bulletin*? What does the ally think of the problem of the Communist International (we regard this problem as no less important than that of the USSR)?"[47].

From this viewpoint, we have a possibility of testing whether the agreement really worked. The "informer" unquestionably provided Sedov with at least one document from the pen of one of the leaders of the groups forming the bloc. This was the article published in *Bulletin of the Opposition*, No. 31, (November 1932) entitled: "The Economic Situation of the Soviet Union" and dated from "Moscow, end of September". This bears the signature "*Ko*". Sedov said at the time of the first Moscow Trial that it served to indicate IN Smirnov. This is confirmed in Van Heijenoort's letter of 1937, which states: "The Kol mentioned must be Kolokolnikov, the pseudonym which Sedov gave to Smirnov". An attentive examination brings out other points which unquestionably reveal the contributions of the "allies" to the correspondence which appeared in the *Bulletin of the Opposition*" even before the alliance.

To begin with, there is the letter signed "MM", in *Bulletin* No. 28, (June 1932). It is probably a disguise or a "working over" of the very similar letter which we found in the Trotsky Archives, in the Safrys folder, signed "Svoi"[48]. The

---

45. Ibid.
46. Ibid (13095).
47. Ibid.
48. We found a letter signed "Svoi" — very similar to the letter which is signed MM in the *Bulletin* — in one of the dossiers of Trotsky's correspondence with the Pole in Czechoslovakia, Safrys, known as Zvon. We are dealing, from all the evidence, with an error by a librarian unfamiliar with the Russian alphabet, who has mixed up "Svoi" with "Zvon". The fact remains that S can mean also S(mirnov) — and that Smirnov could have signed Svoi.

correspondent of the *Bulletin* is in fact remarkably well informed about what was happening, not only in the apparatus, but at its summits. For example, he says (this would hardly be likely if he were a "Trotskyist") that he was present on 23 February, when Stalin's entry at the Bolshoi Theatre was received "in glacial silence". He reports on discussions in the corridors between delegates to the XVIIth Party Conference (January-February 1934) about Stalin's persistent silence there. He mentions the impact which Trotsky's article, *Germany: the Key to the International Situation*, had *in the bureaucracy*. He mentions the disagreement of Molotov with a possible restoration of the internal market. He describes the welcome which NI Muralov[49] gave to notable capitulators. Still more decisively, he describes "the Grünstein couple", as well as Veronika S Kasparova[50], as "irreproachable old-Bolshevik revolutionaries" whereas Trotsky, as we know, regarded Grünstein as a "capitulator" and, in his reply to Sedov's information, stressed that all propaganda in favour of people like him should be "inexorably and pitilessly" fought[51].

The phenomenon is still clearer in the letters which appear in the *Bulletin* of November 1932, No. 31, and those which follow it. The Trotskyists in the USSR would have to enjoy the privilege of being everywhere at once if they could be the informants, or even the recipients, of most of the details which appear in this correspondence. A letter signed N. mentions several bureaucratic jokes about Stalin, conversations at the beginning of the Plenum of the Central Committee (January 1933) and in the corridors at the Executive Committee of the Communist International, and even a courageous intervention by the Pole, Lensky, about the situation in Germany[52]. In issue No. 32, another correspondent reports on the atmosphere in a meeting of the Society of Old Bolsheviks and on the reactions of its members to a speech by Piatnitsky. The same correspondent describes what happened in a meeting of the bureau of the Moscow Committee of the Party, and the debates about constructing a skating rink on Red Square, about which no public statement was made. *Bulletin*, No. 33, publishes a "Letter from Moscow", which gives precise information about how a top trade union leader, Nemchenko, was arrested. It discloses the identity of the provocateur (Nikolsky) who betrayed to the police the clandestine group in the Commissariat of Agriculture, which

49. Nikolai I. Muralov (1877-1937), the son of a peasant, an agronomist, a Bolshevik in 1903, had played an important role in the 1905 Revolution in Moscow. In 1917 he was the leader of the Moscow Soviet and led the Red Guards who took possession of the palace. He held important commands during the Civil War, especially on Trotsky's staff. He was a member of the Left Opposition from 1923 onwards and was expelled and deported in 1928. He was one of the rare opponents to Stalin who were not persecuted down the years and who were allowed to work without having "capitulated". He was arrested in 1936, tried, sentenced to death and executed with the other defendants in the second Moscow Trial.
50. Veronika Kasparova (1875-1937) was an old militant in Russia and emigration held important responsibilities in the Communist International in the category of "women's work". She was deported with her son in 1928, and must have capitulated in 1935 or 1936 and disappeared during the purge. Grünstein had capitulated earlier, probably in 1932.
51. Cf, n.43.
52. *Bulletin*, No. 31, November 1932, p23.

included Eismont, Tolmachev and the former rightwinger and ex-People's Commissar, AP Smirnov[53]. The same document gives an echo of what happened at the Plenum of the Central Executive Committee, how Voroshilov[54] treated Rykov there, as well as what Kirov said in a "restricted, and closed" meeting of Communists in Leningrad.

None the less, by the time these articles appeared in Berlin in the *Bulletin*, the "bloc" whether or not it had really been able to express itself in other ways and, for example, to hold formal meetings had already been terminated by the arrest of those principally concerned. The letter from Sedov which lists the components of the Bloc mentions at the same time the arrest of the leaders of the Smirnov Group and of Smirnov himself and the collapse of the "old members" of the Left Opposition. . A letter from Moscow, dated 6 December 1932, mentions the arrest on 24 and 25 November of oppositionists from the "Eismont group": Eismont, Commissar for Supplies in the RSFSR, Tolmachev, head of road transport, and AP Smirnov himself. It mentions the fate of other "allies" or "contacts" of the bloc, who had already been arrested earlier: "Kamenev was deported to Minussinsk, Slepkov to Taron, and Riutin was held in the isolator at Chelyabinsk. It had been suggested to Smirnov that he should leave Moscow."[55] Another letter, signed TT, dated February 1933[56], which seems to all appearances to have come from an authentic member of the Trotskyist fraction, listed the personalities who had been arrested in the preceding few months, people who had belonged to the groups which made up the bloc or were in contact with it.

The fate of anyone whose name was mentioned from that time as having connections with the "Bloc of the Opposition" was immediately sealed. Among them, Lominadze committed suicide in 1934 at Chelyabinsk, after receiving a summons from the GPU[57]. Ivan N Smirnov, Ter-Vaganian and Mratchkovsky, on the one hand, and Zinoviev and Kamenev on the other, as well as their principal

53. Nikolai B. Eismont (1891-1935), a lawyer, a party member in 1907 and then a member of the Inter-Borough organisation in St. Petersburg, returned to the Bolshevik Party in the fusion in 1917. He then served in the railway administration and had been People's Commissar for Commerce in the RSFSR from 1926 to 1930 and for Food Supply from 1930 onwards. He died in unknown circumstances in 1935.

   Alexander P Smirnov (1877-1938), son of peasants, a textile worker and a militant in 1895, was several times delegated to congresses, a member of the Bolshevik Central Committee before the war, was deputy commissar for the Interior and then Commissar for Agriculture and a member of the Central Committee from 1924 onwards. He was expelled in 1933 and died in prison.

   Vladimir N. Tolmachev (1886- ?), Party member since 1904, disappeared in the same circumstances.
54. Klementi E. Voroshilov (1881-1969), a metal worker, a Bolshevik in 1903, volunteered for the army in 1914 and became a sergeant. He was a partisan leader in the Civil War and associated with Stalin, forming the "Tsaritsyn Group". He was a member of the Central Committee in 1920, Commissar for War in 1925, member of the Politburo in 1926; he survived Stalin and was President of the Supreme Soviet of the USSR from 1953 to 1960.
55. *Bulletin*, No. 32, December 1932, p28.
56. *Bulletin*, No, 33, March 1933, p23-26.
57. Roy Medvedyev, op cit, p167. For information about the end of the life of Lominadze, see Margaret Buber-Neumann, *Von Potsdam nach Moskau*, p413-415.

collaborators, were defendants in the first Moscow Trial, were sentenced to death and were executed. Jan Sten, Chatzkin, Chaplin, Riutin, Uglanov, Kayurov, Preobrazhensky, Smilga, Ufimtsev, Perevertsev, Grünstein, Kasparova and Safarov disappeared, most of them arrested in 1937 at the latest during the Great Purge. Doubtless no one can explain why a single one of them, Boris Lifshits[58], survived until after the war.

We know that all these ex-oppositionists had shared the fate of the group of the "liberal bureaucrats" in this period. The standard-bearer of the latter, Kirov, was assassinated in 1934, and we must not forget that Khrushshev said that the tracks of the assassins of Kirov led up to Stalin himself. Kuibychev[59], who, according to Medvedev, "supported" Kirov in the Politburo, like Orjonikidze, died in suspicious circumstances — assassinated by the Trotskyist–Zinovievist rightists, said Stalin while Ordjonikidze committed suicide[60]. The head of the "illegal bloc" which appeared at the 1934 Congress, Variekis, disappeared in 1937, like most of the apparatchiks, who, like him, had played the game of the "liberals" against the terror. The bloc of the Oppositions was consummated in common graves. But the point is this: it had at first been a real threat and, by the very fact of having been formed, had been a political reality. We cannot believe that it did not have a very great influence on the policy of repression, which Stalin directed against the Old Bolsheviks and the generation of the companions of Lenin who had begun to coalesce in 1932.

Trotsky and the Slogan: "Get Rid of Stalin"

The correspondence between Trotsky and Sedov between October and December 1932 the period of the "bloc" constitutes an extraordinary set of documents. They enable us to follow almost from day to day the efforts of Trotsky to cling as closely as possible to what was really happening in the Soviet Union, and to grasp the full significance of the "bloc", the cement of which precisely was hostility to Stalin, and the desire to drive him out of the General Secretary's position.

Trotsky opened the discussion about whether the slogan, "Get Rid of Stalin", was appropriate on 17 October. "Get Rid of Stalin", he wrote, "is correct in a well-defined, concrete sense", but contrary to the "allies" and the "right-wingers", he

---

58. Trotsky preserved in his archives a photograph of the front page of *Pravda* for 30 July 1936, in which figured two "old" Oppositionists, Livshitz and the Georgian, Kavtaradze, the only one to return from deportation without making a "declaration", by the mercy of Stalin, and who died a vice-minister.
59. Valentin V. Kuibychev (1888-1937), the son of an officer, a medical student and, in 1904, a Bolshevik. During the Civil War belonged to the "Tsarytsin Group" and after 1927 was a member of the Politburo. He died in 1935, and Stalin blamed the defendants in the third Moscow Trial for his death.
60. Grigori K. Ordjonikidze (1886-1937), a male nurse and a Bolshevik in 1903, was a friend of Stalin in Georgia. He was elected a member of the Central Committee in 1912. He was Party secretary in Transcaucasia and brutally led the "Russification" of Georgia. He was a candidate member of the Politburo in 1930 and joined it in 1934. He seems to have belonged to the group of the supporters of Kirov; his death in 1937 was a suicide.

did not think it an appropriate one. In fact, he wrote that this slogan would not be dangerous "if we were strong". But did it not risk being supported by the émigrés, by the Mensheviks and by the "internal Thermidoreans"? He went on: "It is always possible that in a few months Stalin will be obliged to defend himself against the Thermidorean pressure, and that we shall be obliged to support him momentarily". Indeed, "this stage is not yet past and, consequently, this slogan does not correspond to the needs of the movement"[61].

He returned to this question in another letter, dated 24 October. In it he stressed the importance of what "S(voi)" had communicated about what is being said in the bureaucracy: "If Trotsky comes back, he will shoot us all one after another." According to Trotsky, they should avoid any slogan, any formulation, which could be interpreted as an intention to get rid of everybody and everything and to settle old scores, etc." He explained: "The nearer the denouement approaches, the more we must act in a supple, conciliatory way without for all that making the slightest concession of principle"[62].

He returned on 30 October to the question of the "liberals" who would regard the Trotskyists as "too moderate". He repeated: "We must pay the greatest attention to the middle-rank bureaucrats, who say that, if Trotsky comes back, he will start up a cruel repression. That is today the principal weapon of the Stalinists. Our platform is entirely turned towards the masses. Our next tactical step must be to take account of the wall which separates us from them"[63].

On 7 November, Trotsky discussed the question of knowing "when and how" they would be able to "raise the apparatus against the master", He insisted: "Raising it consists in giving to the hesitant apparatus the opportunity of saying, in opposition to the master: 'Those whom he persecutes and hounds are ready to work even with him. These are honest, useful people. The course which the master has taken is, therefore, a bad one'. He developed this idea: "We do not change our criticisms by one iota. We wage a ruthless, courageous campaign against the policy of the master on the international plane, and at the same time we declare: 'We are ready to work in a common organisation even with the master; this demonstrates, on the one hand, our devotion, to use an elegant word, and on the other hand, our firm confidence in our own strength. To have a more radical position today would create a confusion of slogans with hostile groups"[64].

Finally, he wrote on 27 December 1932, an article in the form of an interview, which shows that he intended it for publication:

Q. Is the ruling Stalinist fraction not going to give way to yours?

A. The future will show. It is the Party which will declare what it wants. We shall content ourselves with demanding that the Left Opposition be re-admitted into the Party. We are ready today, as we have been in past years,

61. Harvard College Library (10248).
62. Ibid.
63. Ibid.
64. Ibid.

to collaborate fully with the fraction which today is in power, and in every task.

Q. If I understand you rightly, then, you agree to collaborate with Stalin?

A. No doubt whatever of that. As a fraction, we have often made declarations on this matter. In the *Bulletin of the Opposition*, for October 1929, you can read: "The Opposition places the basis of the question on a higher level than the form, the interests of the revolution above the ambitions of an individual or a group. It is ready to occupy the most modest place in the party. But on condition that it remains itself." It is not about Stalin, but of something which is of greater significance than the personal destiny of everyone of us.[65]

It is likely that, by this date, he had managed to convince Sedov, who had strongly protested against the distinction which Trotsky had drawn between the slogan "Get Rid of Stalin" and the slogan "Get Rid of the Rule of the Individual", in his letter dated 12 October 1932. Sedov declared: "Before everything else we have to drive out the present leadership and get rid of Stalin nothing but their liquidation can bring victory". This was the position, in the last analysis, of Riutin and his associates in the group of "right-wingers", if not of the "liberals".

The Turn in 1933

The problem of understanding how the situation — aspects of which were the regroupment of Stalin's adversaries, a profound discontent among party cadres and a loss of confidence in the leadership by those who until then had been its supporters — could be transformed in a relatively short space of time remains to be solved. In fact in 1934 it was the Trotskyist Old Guard who capitulated and bowed their heads before Stalin. Rakovsky, Sosnovsky[66] and, soon afterwards,

---

65. Ibid (T 3485).
66. Khristian G. Rakovsky (1873-1941) was born in Bulgaria. He was educated under French influences, a socialist from his youth, a personal friend of Trotsky, jailed during the war, freed by the revolution and joined the Bolshevik Party in 1917. He was President of the Council of People's Commissars for the Ukraine from 1919 to 1925, and was a member of the Left Opposition from its beginning, which resulted in his being sent as ambassador, first to London and then to Paris. He was the spokesman of the Left Opposition at the XVth. Congress of the CPSU in 1927, and was then deported to Saratov, to Astrakhan and finally to Barnaul in terrible conditions. He escaped and was recaptured. He capitulated in 1934 and was arrested in 1937, to be one of the defendants in the third Moscow Trial. He died in a concentration camp.

Lev S. Sosnovsky (1886-1937) was a Bolshevik in 1903, an underground militant, who was deported and then exiled. He was one of the most popular journalists in the Soviet Union because of his attacks on the bureaucrats. He was a member of the Left Opposition, was expelled in 1927 and deported in 1928. In 1929 he had been imprisoned in an isolator and subjected to a regime which was all the more rigorous because he was seriously ill. He also capitulated at the beginning of 1934 and disappeared in the Great Purge, but without appearing in a trial.

Kasparova after years of desperate resistance in appalling conditions. In December 1934 Stalin rid himself of the embarrassment of Kirov. The preparations began in the prisons of the GPU for the trial of Kirov's "murderers" — in fact of the members of the "bloc". These people appeared, broken, and confessed to the cynical accusations of the prosecutor, Vishinsky, to the catcalls of the public[67]. The indictment mentioned the "bloc" of 1932. We know that Stalin dissatisfied with the results of the trial of the "Sixteen" telegraphed to his colleagues in the Politburo, on 25 September 1936, that the GPU had been "four years behind". The figure "four" was not there by chance. It showed clearly that, in Stalin's eyes, everything had begun precisely in 1932[68].

We think that the reversal of the situation cannot possibly be explained simply in terms of the repression, which began in the later months of 1932 and which the Plenum of the Central Committee confirmed, in limited forms, in January 1933. For precisely at this date, it was still a question of limited repression. Blood was not spilled in 1933 because the "liberals" opposed this course. Ivan N Smirnov was found guilty of "contacts abroad" his personal meeting in Berlin with Sedov in 1931 and his sending Holzmann to Sedov in 1932 but was only sentenced to ten years in prison. Riutin was convicted of writing the document which treated Stalin as a "provocateur", but he was only sent back into an isolator. Others, especially the members of the groups that were betrayed by an informer the Smirnov Group, for example, were likewise sentenced to terms of imprisonment. Most of the oppositionists, however, were merely deported. Lominadze was not arrested; he was to be arrested only in 1934, as we know. Sten was deported; he was to be arrested only in 1937. Most of the people who were linked in one way or another with the bloc and with the discussion in autumn 1932 were arrested only at the end of 1934 and in the early months of 1935. That is the date after which the militants, who had been expelled from the Party and had been arrested either in deportation or while they were still at liberty, began to be tortured and to be scientifically prepared by the GPU with a view to their "confessions" What had happened in the interval?

Jan Van Heijenoort, who was Trotsky's secretary from Prinkipo to Coyoacán, recorded in his memoirs the deep physical and (doubtless) moral change in Trotsky in the early months of 1933[69]. He confided in the present writer something which he did not write in his book, namely that Trotsky became aware at this period that he would never return to the Soviet Union. He had already suffered the blow of

67. Andrei Y. Vyshinsky (1883-1955), a socialist lawyer, a Menshevik in 1903 and until the Civil War, at the end of which he joined the victors. He was Professor of Law in Moscow, Public Prosecutor of the RSFSR in 1931 and in 1935 of the USSR, and presented the prosecution in the Moscow Trials with unequalled cynicism, against those who had always been his political adversaries! He was vice-minister of Foreign Affairs from 1940 to 1949, minister from 1949 to 1953 and once again vice-minister from 1953 to his death.
68. The existence of this notorious telegram was revealed by Nikita Khrushchev in his notorious "secret speech" at the XXth. Congress of the CPSU. No one, as far as we know, has established the relationship between the "four years" of delay to which it refers and the real existence of the bloc of 1932.
69. Jean van Heijenoort, *With Trotsky in Exile*, Harvard UP, 1978, pp41-42.

the death of his daughter, Zinaida, by suicide. The exile was doubtless even more deeply affected by the brutal reversal in the world situation which the unopposed victory of Hitler's gangs in Germany signified and the destruction in a few weeks of the organised workers' movement and of the chances of revolution for a generation. The victory of Hitler opened the door to the defeat of the working class throughout all Europe, and marked the beginning of the inexorable approach of World War II.

And the Soviet Union was not outside this world which the defeat marked in this way. The destruction of the German workers' movement meant the destruction of all the apparatuses of the Communist International in that country, and the disappearance of that network which Leon Sedov had patiently woven within them, and which had enabled him to keep up contacts with the Oppositionists in the Soviet Union. After 1933 Trotsky and Sedov were formally cut off from the Soviet Union. This is a fact of enormous importance, and they had no answer to it. Isolation, the fascist threat and false appeals for "unity" broke Christian Rakovsky more surely, we cannot doubt, than had the hellish cold at Barnaul or the dreadful conditions of his unsuccessful attempt to escape and his recapture. It was despair in the face of such a defeat which delivered the Old Bolsheviks into the hands of Stalin's executioners; nothing else could have forced them to bend, as long as they retained hope. Many Oppositionists who sincerely desired reforms no longer accepted the risks to which a political crisis would henceforth expose the country, under the threat from Germany. From that time onwards, no one could reasonably hope to "get rid of Stalin", whose position was consolidated by Hitler's victory, at precisely the moment when that position was becoming critical.

None the less, Stalin had still to manoeuvre for a long time before he could mount the counter-attack to wipe out those who had thought even for a moment about removing him or striking him down. Concessions to the "liberals", who were always wrangling with him at the top of the apparatus? Awareness of the need to avoid re-unifying the front of his adversaries in any other way? The Oppositionists who had been expelled and arrested in 1932 had been accused of having formed a secret organisation to restore "capitalism" and the kulak in particular. It is true that Zinoviev and Kamenev, who had been denounced as accomplices, were none the less allowed to come back to Moscow in March 1933 after an acceptable self-criticism. On 8 May, Stalin and Molotov signed a circular denouncing what it called "a saturnalia of arrests"[70]. In the days following the XVIIth Congress (January-February 1934) at which the "illegal bloc" of the "liberals" tried to remove Stalin to replace him with Kirov, if we are to believe what Khrushchev wrote and the memoirs which Roy Medvedev[71] quoted the liberation began of thousands of political prisoners. But the German defeat handed the initiative back again to Stalin; he seized it, and with murderous determination he struck after December 1934 and the assassination of Kirov ....

70. Merle Fainsod, *Smolensk under Soviet Rule*, p263.
71. Roy Medvedyev, op cit, p155-156.

The Bloc and the Moscow Trial

When we re-examine the Moscow Trials in the light of this recently discovered information, we find another problem raised. The indictment dates the conclusion of the bloc in 1932 as the starting point of the "terrorist activity" of the accused[72]. From their side, Trotsky and Sedov denied that the bloc even existed.

Let us look back first to the report of the first trial. Here the terms "bloc" and "unified centre" are used inter-changeably, when the term "unified centre" should rather be used to mean the leadership of the bloc. This does not make our enquiry easy. According to the indictment, "the unification of the Trotskyist Group and the Zinovievist Group, who organised a unified centre" had taken place at the end of 1932[73]. The term "Trotskyist Group" here means those who presented themselves as such at the trial, namely IN Smirnov, Ter-Vaganian and Mratchkovsky. The verdict corrects the date and places the origin of the bloc in autumn 1932[74]. Several meetings are mentioned in the course of the trial. One of them took place in the country house of Zinoviev and Kamenev at Illinskoye[75], another at Zinoviev's house[76], and then one in Kamenev's house[77] and the last in Mratchkovsky's carriage[78] When Zinoviev was questioned about whether he had received terrorist "directives" from Smirnov, he replied that he had "had negotiations with him on two or three occasions"[79]. According to the indictment, Smirnov made a full confession at his examination[80], and replied to the question, when had he "left the centre" that "he had no intention of leaving it"; "there had been nowhere else to go"[81]. On the subject of the makeup of the "unified centre", the indictment and the verdict both state that it was composed of seven persons, Zinoviev, Kamenev, Yevdokimov and Bakayev, for the Zinovievists, and Smirnov, TerVaganian and Mratchkovsky for the Trotskyists[82]. The confessions of the defendant Reingold mention an additional member, Sokolnikov[83], about whom Kamenev specified, under the pressure of the prosecutor, that he was a "secret" member. Kamenev likewise added to the leaders of the "Zinovievists" the

---

72. The Trial of the Trotskyist-Zinovievist Terrorist Centre, p11
73. Ibid.
74. Ibid, p178.
75. Ibid, p48, 66.
76. Ibid, 19, 55.
77. Ibid, 47.
78. Ibid, 47-48.
79. Ibid, 54.
80. Ibid, 37-38.
81. Ibid, p81.
82. Ibid, p11, 178.
83. Ibid, 54, 67. Grigori I Brilliant, known as Sokolnikov (1888-1939), student, a Bolshevik in 1905, in prison and emigration. He was a member of the Central Committee from 1919 to 1927, Commissar for Finance in 1917 and from 1922 to 1926. He belonged to the New Opposition and then, during the several months of the Unified Opposition, was ambassador in London, where he remained until 1933. He then became Deputy Commissar for Foreign Affairs. His denunciation in the trial led to his being arrested and found guilty. He was condemned to ten years' imprisonment in the second Moscow Trial in January 1937.

name of the Old Bolshevik, Kuklin[84]. Smirnov mentioned the participation of "the Group of Lominadze" in the "bloc", and Mratchkovsky that of the "LominadzeChatzkin Group", while they were definite that Lominadze had been "a member of the centre"[85]. Bakayev, however, included two other Old Bolsheviks in the "centre", Kuklin (already mentioned) and Charov[86]. The names of other militants from all the Oppositions and every period, are mentioned several times in connection with the linkages in the "centre" and its "negotiations with a view to joint activity"[87]. Let us notice also the role which the confessions of several of the accused attribute to the Old Bolshevik, Gaven, who is presented as an agent who is in touch with Trotsky but who was not in the dock[88].

84. Ibid, p67. Alexander S. Kuklin (1876-193?) was one of the longest serving Petrograd worker-Bolsheviks to be a member of the Central Committee. He was a Zinovievist, a member of the Unified Opposition; he was excluded in 1927 and capitulated in 1928. He was sentenced to ten years' imprisonment in the first trial of Zinoviev and Kamenev in January 1935.
85. Ibid, p17.
86. Ibid, p60. Ivan B. Charov (1884-1938) was also one of the veteran workers in the party in Petrograd, a member of the Zinovievist Group, the destiny of whom he shared, when he was sentenced in 1935 to eight years' imprisonment.
87. Two persons mentioned in the course of the trial were charged and arrested immediately: these were Sokolnikov and Serebriakov, who were to meet again in the dock in the second trial. It was officially announced that an enquiry would be opened into Tomsky (who committed suicide), Radek and Piatakov (who were sentenced in the second trial in January 1937), Rykov and Bukharin, (who were sentenced in the third trial in March 1938). Among the militants mentioned as participants or accomplices, who died during the late nineteen-thirties, without being publicly tried, let us mention IT Smilga, NK Uglanov, the "leftists" Sten and Chatzkin (without including Lominadze, who committed suicide in 1934), Shlyapnikov and Medvedyev, former leaders of the Workers' Opposition and several military chiefs who were all shot, Schmidt, Putna, Estermann, Gaievsky and Kusmichev.
88. The Gaven "case" remains a mystery.The man was presented in the trial, by the indictment and by certain confessions, as an emissary sent by Trotsky, into Russia. This was not just anybody. Yuri P Gaven (or Gavenis) (1884-1937), known as Dauman or Donner, was of Lettish origin and had been active in the Russian Social-Democratic Labour Party and later in the Lettish Party, of which he had been a member of the Central Committee. He spent long periods in prison under Tsarism; in 1917 he led the revolution in Minussinsk and later presided over the revolutionary committee in the Crimea. He had been a member of the Central Control Committee and one of the directors of Gosplan, His arrest goes back to 1934. Though he was a central point in the indictment and the confessions of the principal defendants, he did not appear in any public trial and all trace of him is lost after the trial of August 1936. There are several possible hypotheses: perhaps he was an agent-provocateur, who made convenient confessions and was spared. This is not likely. Other provocateurs had appeared among the defendants in the dock. A more probable hypothesis is that he had so resisted torture, blackmail and pressures exerted on the accused, that he was not presentable in public. But in that case why would he play so important a role in the scenario of the accusation? The only explanation is that, after having confessed, he retracted his confession too late for the script to be rewritten or for his resistance to be broken. But the question still arises as to why a man, who was an authentic Old Bolshevik and without doubt a man of strong character, was presented as having played such a key role. The most probable hypothesis is that he had effectively played a role, if not in the Trotskyist fraction, at least in the bloc, and that, therefore, there was in the role which the accusation attributed to him one of those "grains of truth" which tend to be overlooked when the lies are so great.

As we know, the indictment, which started from the existence of the "bloc" in 1932, and relied on the confessions extracted by torture and blackmail from broken men, declared that Trotsky had then given "terrorist instructions and directives" to his supporters and, in particular, had organised the assassination of Kirov. Trotsky's friends, following the line of Sedov and of Trotsky himself, had no difficulty in showing how improbable and stupid was the argument about a "centre" which functioned when practically all its members were in exile or in jail. The first reaction of the French Section, the Parti Ouvrier Internationaliste, took this line, in a statement of 17 August 1936, which could not have been drafted without Sedov's agreement, even if he did not draft it with his own hand; it confined itself to the charges that "a bloc" had been formed, which had then functioned, with people who were under arrest and could not possibly have communicated with each other.

Perhaps it is the very stupidity of this charge which has concealed from the eyes of historians the few grains of truth on which it tried to rely to get people to believe in the terrorist character of the "bloc" and the "criminal" role of the accused. But there can be no doubt that the defence of the accused, as Leon Sedov presented it in *The Red Book of the Moscow Trials*[89], has very much contributed to convincing researchers that there never was a bloc in 1932, not even a political bloc. When Sedov sifted the various reports of the trial which he possessed, he left not a stone standing of either the indictment or the confessions. He examined the contradiction between the indictment and the verdict as to the date when the bloc was formed[90]. He demonstrated that, of the meetings which the accused "admitted" if they really did ever take place the first three were meetings of the Zinovievist Group and the last was of the Trotskyist Group[91]. He stresses that no element in the indictment and no confession ever mentions any meeting whatever of the "unified centre", and shows that the answers of Zinoviev and Smirnov are equivalent to a denial even that it had existed[92]. He was ironical about the conflicting accounts of the different defendants about the makeup of the centre, and about the absurdity of the statement that the secret centre could have secret members[93], stressing that men whom some of the accused name as leaders of the "centre" such as Sokolnikov, Kuklin and Charov or as its agents such as Gaven, do not figure among the accused, any more (moreover) than does any member of the LominadzeChatzin group, Sten and others[94].

Sedov mentions the difficulties which the Stalinist regime encountered in the years 1930-32, the rise of popular discontent and the growing anxiety and mistrust in the party apparatus. He writes:

---

89. When Trotsky was interned by the Norwegian Government, he had no means to reply to the accusations which were launched at him at the time of the first Moscow Trial. Reluctantly, Leon Sedov was, therefore, obliged to take up his pen and to write this remarkable work, which absolutely demolished the Stalinist thesis.
90. L. Sedov, *Livre Rouge sur les proces de Moscou*, p59.
91. Ibid, p59.
92. Ibid, p61.
93. Ibid, p62.
94. Ibid, p58ff.

Therefore, in 1932, we can observe a certain re-awakening, though a pretty feeble one, of the groups which previously had capitulated to Stalin: the group of Zinoviev and Kamenev, the group of the former Stalinists of the left of Lominadze–Chatzin–Sten (those whom they called the 'leftists'), of Smirnov and his friends, and also several right-wingers, Riutin-Slepkov and others. But we must not exaggerate this re-awakening. For the majority, it had no more than the character of discussion in the family circle. They would go no further than "frank" conversations, dreaming that it would be good to have a new policy and a new leadership. It would seem that people from different circles and different groups were seeking some personal contacts and links with each other. The most daring perhaps said that it would be good to form a 'bloc'. But it is probable that they did not go even so far as to say that. Today — four years later? — Stalin extracts a 'bloc' and even a "unified terrorist centre" out of all this.

It is evident that the Russian BolshevikLeninists did not join any bloc with one of these groups. All these groups at one moment or another had capitulated to Stalin.

That is why they were irreconcilably opposed to the BolshevikLeninists, who regarded and continue to regard their capitulation to Stalin as one of the greatest crimes against Communism and the interests of the working class. On this question, the Left Opposition took a particularly intransigent stand. In the eyes of the Bolshevik-Leninists, the groups and these people did not and could not have any political or moral authority.

The Left Opposition welcomed the re-awakening of these groups — the "Party liberals" as it called them — as having an essentially *symptomatic* significance. Of course, it *could* serve as a point of departure for the return of Zinoviev, Kamenev, Smirnov and the others to the old banner of the Bolshevik-Leninists. But nothing came of it.[95]

This document, written on the morrow of the first Moscow Trial, is in complete contradiction to the document in invisible ink which Sedov wrote in 1932, bearing witness to the negotiations with the "Trotskyists" in the USSR, as well as to Trotsky's letter which approves the formation of the "bloc" as an alliance and not a fusion, with the comments by Trotsky which have been quoted above[96]. Sedov's statement of his case about the "bloc" of 1932 carries conviction only on one point, that of the "centre", or the collective leadership, of the bloc. He wrote, in fact, in a note to his chapter on "the formation and the activity of the 'unified centre'":

> The fact remains that the centre was organised and at the same time ceased to be active. It was organised, no doubt, for the special purpose of ceasing to do anything [97].

95. Ibid, p65-66.
96. See the Appendix, Document n.2.
97. L. Sedov, *Livre Rouge*, p59, note 6.

We believe that the truth is that the "hardlyorganised 'bloc'" could not provide itself with a real centre — because of the repression, because it is the same letter from Sedov to his father that explains the make-up and the aims of the bloc that reports that the GPU has destroyed Smirnov's group. The conclusions follows: there was a "political bloc", though not a "unified centre" — and not at all a "terrorist centre", which simply does not arise.

Let us come straight to the point. We see nothing in Sedov's attitude that is not extremely normal — it is an attitude which Trotsky shared — of denying in 1936 that a bloc had been formed in 1932. Some of the reasons for this are self-evident; there are others. What was to be gained in 1936 by acknowledging the existence in 1932 of an ephemeral bloc? Historical truth perhaps would have been served, but that could wait. Would it have helped to explain that this was a purely political bloc, and not a terrorist bloc, as the Moscow prosecutors and judges claimed? It was of no interest, and could only have provided the world-wide propaganda machine of Stalinism with supplementary arguments and head-lines, such as "Trotsky's Son Confesses: He was in touch with the Terrorists", etc. Finally, it seems clear to us that Trotsky had no interest whatever in admitting, in the face of the gaze of these people, who claimed that they were guilty of terrorism, that he had believed, four years before, that he could conclude an alliance with them. But there are other arguments which justify the denials by Sedov and Trotsky. The men in the dock in Moscow were the people who confessed, to be sure. But they did not confess everything, and others in the hands of the GPU continued to hold out, because that was their duty as antiStalinist fighters. No doubt there were Trotskyists among them, but there were others, such as, for example, members of the Lominadze Group, none of whom appeared in a trial. To acknowledge in 1936 that a political bloc had existed with Zinoviev and Smirnov in 1932 would have been to collaborate with Stalin and to help him to strike at everyone who had taken part in the alliance and could not be broken or had not yet been "unmasked". On that point our conclusion is clear: Trotsky and Sedov did not tell the truth about the bloc of 1932, but at that moment it was precisely their duty not to tell the truth about it. Today the problem is completely different.

One point remains, and it must have caused Trotsky and Sedov a good deal of embarrassment at the time: first, the contacts between Smirnov and Sedov and, secondly, the contacts between Sedov and Holzmann, who was Smirnov's emissary. We know that Trotsky totally denied these episodes, in his first reactions. His companion Natalia reminded him that Sedov had met Smirnov in Berlin, and had told him about it, in July 1931, and, of course, about the visit by Holzmann. Trotsky corrected himself. From that moment onwards, Sedov and Trotsky both stuck to what was to be the Trotskyist version of this episode right to the end — that it was initially an accidental street meeting in Berlin in July 1931, several personal discussions by appointment, the promise by Smirnov to provide information, the despatch in autumn 1932 of Holzmann to Berlin, when he handed to Sedov some notes on the economic situation (the article signed Ko.) and a series of verbal statements, from which Sedov manufactured a "Correspondence with Moscow", which appeared in *Bulletin*, No. 31[98].

When, in 1937, Van Heijenoort discovered Trotsky's letter of 1932 in a "confidential" file, he recognised its importance, and wrote the letter to Sedov which put us on the track of this affair. Van explained in particular that, for the moment and before a reply from Sedov, he had not informed the Dewey Commission[99], which was meeting in New York, about this document. We have not found either Sedov's reply or any letter to the Dewey Commission on this subject; moreover, the report of the Commission contains no trace of information about it. The fact remains that the affair was no doubt embarrassing, and that Sedov took it seriously enough to check again that the official record contained nothing which would oblige the "defence" to change its position on this point[100]. According to all appearances, he finally decided to leave matters as they stood. Indeed, it is not certain that making this document public might possibly have called into question the work of the Commission, through which lies of far greater amplitude and significance were being ground to dust[101].

A Fresh Source of Light

The attitude which Sedov and Trotsky took in 1936, about what had happened in the Soviet Union in 1932 could not lessen the effectiveness of what Trotsky was publishing, without any ambiguity, immediately after the events. For example, he described the political situation in the following terms in his letter of 16 December 1932, addressed to the sections on the state of the Left Opposition:

> In the past year very important changes took place in the status of the Russian Opposition. Their general direction can be characterised by the word 'ascent'.
>
> Many hundreds, perhaps even thousands, of former capitulators, particularly workers, have returned to the path of the Opposition; these are the elements which in the spring of 1928 honestly but prematurely believed in the principled change of the official course. The places of exile and imprisonment are being constantly filled with such 'backsliders'. It is unnecessary to say how much this fact strengthens the authority of those Oppositionists who never abandoned their banner for a single hour.
>
> Among the older generation of Bolsheviks, including those who only yesterday were ardent Stalinists, can be observed the complete decay of the authority of Stalin and his group and a decided turn towards great attention and estimation of the Left Opposition. It is most significant that precisely the Old Bolsheviks, who took an active part in the life of the Party under Lenin

---

98. Ibid, p98.
99. See the Appendix, 3, above.
100. Manuscript note on the document No 2 in Appendix.
101. The report of the commission over which presided the famous educationalist and philosopher, the American John Dewey, both concluded that Trotsky was innocent, as also was Sedov, and was published in English in 1938 under the title, *Not Guilty*, but regrettably it has not been translated into French to this day.

but later let themselves be scared by the spectre of 'Trotskyism', now, after their experience with the Stalin regime, begin to discover where the truth lies. That is a very important symptom!

But incomparably more important is the process which is going on among the workers, especially the youth. Just as in its time the Czarist bureaucracy called all dissatisfied workers, protestors and strikers 'socialists', sent them to prison or to Siberia, and made it possible for them to meet real socialists there, so the Stalinist bureaucracy now arrests and exiles in ever-increasing numbers dissatisfied and protesting workers, declaring them 'Trotskyists' and pushing them on to the road of the Left Opposition.

As far as the illegal organisation of the Bolshevik-Leninists in the USSR is concerned, only the first steps have been taken towards its re-organisation[102].

These were not empty phrases. The isolation of the Left Opposition was drawing to an end, after years of severe repression. It was evidently a phenomenon of the first importance — and one which, quite understandably, Soviet historians of the Khrushchev period were careful not to reveal — that Old Bolsheviks, who had been authentic Stalinists, had drawn their conclusions and, from that time onwards, were turning towards an alliance with the Trotskyists. Such a phenomenon was inconceivable without a pressure from the mass of the workers; it was precisely about this that the correspondence and the *Bulletin* were accumulating the information for anyone who knew how to recognise it. One letter, in September 1932, tells of "sit-down strikes" in the Urals[103]. Another, in August, mentions strikes and street demonstrations in Ivanovo-Vosnesensk, where Kaganovich and Molotov saved the situation by sacrificing local scapegoats to the workers' wrath[104]. During the final months of 1932, the letters from the USSR to the *Bulletin* gave more and more examples. More than a hundred workers were arrested at the Amo plant after leaflets from the Opposition had been distributed, and several dozen at Charkopodshinsk, at the Calibri factory, and at the Baltic plant in Leningrad. A leaflet (not produced by the Opposition) had been distributed in a factory at Kovrov, and it took up the slogans of the Opposition[105]. During the October commemoration, in a factory which produced brakes, a portrait of Stalin had been posted up, and turned into one of Trotsky. The editorial of the wall-newspaper in the *Proletarian Labour* factory for 22 January 1933, devoted to the death of Lenin, was made up entirely of extracts from articles by Trotsky[106].

The correspondents of the *Bulletin* had only very limited resources, under a regime so dominated by censorship and by the police. What do the archives of the State and of the GPU conceal on this subject? Doubtless, on an infinitely more vast scale, what

---

102. Harvard College Library (T 3481). Published in French in the *International Bulletin of the Communist Left Opposition*, No. 19, December 1932, and, in English, in *Writings of Leon Trotsky: 1932-33*, p24ff.
103. Letter signed "Z", in *Biulleten Oppositsii*, No. 31, November 1932, p24.
104. Extract from a letter of 20 August 1932, in *Biulleten Oppositsii* No. 29-30, September 1932, p13.
105. Letter from Moscow, of February 1933, signed "TT", ibid No. 33, March 1933, p24-6.
106. Ibid.

the Smolensk archives have revealed to us. The portrait of Trotsky that was discovered on a collective farm; the wood-worker who declared for pluralism in the USSR, denounced bureaucratic exploitation and paid tribute to Zinoviev and Kamenev in a debate on the Constitution[107]; the worker who, when called upon by a party agitator to give the name of an Old Bolshevik, replied "Trotsky"[108] — all these in the few months preceding the first Moscow Trial.

This deep movement — whatever its level may have been in 1932 and which only the files of the GPU may some day reveal — imparts a rhythm to the history of the Soviet Union, as to all human societies. This is the major fact, of which our findings at Harvard come at an appropriate time to remind us. The Old Bolsheviks and party cadres, who had so recently been ferocious Stalinists, were seeking an alliance with the Left Opposition which they had so recently denounced, were forming a "bloc" about which they asked Trotsky's opinion and which they invited the Trotskyists to join, and tried to work out a programme for public safety jointly with them ... were astonished when Trotsky did not go along with their slogan of "Get Rid of Stalin". The victory of Hitler enabled this movement in the bureaucracy, which had not ceased to exist deep in the working class, to be crushed. The Moscow Trials, like the Great Purge, were the instrument of an unprecedented terror against anyone who expressed or even might have expressed the aspirations of the masses in some way or other. The rhythms of the history of the Soviet Union too are the rhythms of the class-struggle.

This is the significance, it seems to us, of this first discovery which we made, almost by chance, in Trotsky's archives in exile at Harvard. There will be others.

APPENDIX

Document No.1

The letter from Van Heijenoort to Sedov, 3 July 1937[109]

Dear Friend

I am sending you a copy of a letter which was found in the archives. The sheet was in a "confidential" dossier with various other things. The letter, of which I have made an exact copy for you, bears neither a date nor the name of the person to whom it is addressed. It is an original, rather badly typed: it seems likely to be a copy made from a manuscript letter. Here are some indications which my uncle has dictated[110]:

---

107. M. Fainsod, op cit, p322.
108. Ibid.
109. Library of Harvard College 13905 with the permission of the college. The original is in French.
110. "My uncle" meaning Trotsky

1. The letter must have been written by me and addressed to LS in Bn[111].
2. The Kol. mentioned must be Kolokolnikov, the pseudonym which LS gave to Smirnov.
3. The question of the bloc was considered in the letter on the basis that some of the capitulators were becoming dissatisfied again with the official policy, without also joining the Left Opposition, far from that. The content of this "bloc" is strictly defined in the letter and basically is reduced to exchanges of information.
4. The date of the letter can be established from that of the meeting with Hn[112] and that of the publication, in "Soc. V."[113], of the declaration of the 18[114].

Would it be possible to recover the original? Naturally, before we receive information from you, we shall make no use of this document in connection with NY. [115]
Very cordially
J. v. H.

NB Sedov wrote several notes by hand on this letter:

in Russian: "Find LD's letter"
in French: "Me to check the English text or copy the most important American extracts"

Document No.2

The letter from Trotsky to Leon Sedov[116]

Dear Friend
1. My letter to my native land[117] was already written before I received your letter about the information concerning Kol.[118] My letter is evidently intended for the Left Opposition in the true sense of the word. But you may show it to "the informant"[119], so that he may have an idea of how I see things.

---

111. Leon Sedov at Berlin
112. ES Holtzmann
113. The Menshevik paper, *Sotsialistitcheskii Vestnik* (Socialist Courier) then published in Berlin and edited by Boris Nikolaievsky.
114. What the Menshevik paper called a declaration of eighteen Bolsheviks seems to have been the platform of Ryutin.
115. New York which was where the Dewey Commission was examining the two Moscow Trials.
116. Library of Harvard College 13905c and 1010, with the permission of the college. Translated from the German by Alain Calvié. This document is not dated, the two examples we have seen are the same, both copies. It seems that Sedov was unable to find the original.
117. This is about a circular to the Russian Bolshevik-Leninists that we do not have.
118. Kolokolnikov (from "Kolokol" the clock) was what Sedov called IN Smirnov
119. The source was ES Holzmann who had met Sedov and had passed on to him news and

2. The proposal for a bloc seems to me to be completely acceptable. I must make quite clear that we are dealing with a bloc and not a fusion.
3. My proposed declaration is evidently intended for our fraction of the Left Opposition in the strict sense of the term (and not for our new allies). The opinion of the allies, according to which we should wait for the rightwingers to involve themselves more deeply, does not have my agreement, as far as our fraction is concerned. One fights repression by means of anonymity and conspiracy, not by silence. Loss of time is impermissible: from the political point of view, that would amount to leaving the field to the right-wingers.
4. How is the bloc going to express itself? For the moment, principally by the exchange of information. The allies keep us informed about what concerns the Soviet Union, as we do for them about what concerns the Communist International. We should agree on very precise arrangements for correspondence.

The allies must send us correspondence for the *Bulletin*. The editors of the *Bulletin* undertake to publish the documents of the allies. But it reserves the right to comment freely upon them.
5. The bloc does not exclude mutual criticism. Any propaganda by the allies on behalf of the capitulators (Grünstein, etc.)[120] will be inexorably, mercilessly resisted by us.
6. The question of the economic programme is outlined in the last number of the *Bulletin* and (will be) developed in the succeeding issues.

Some questions:
1. What does the declaration of the 18 (Sots. Vestnik)[121] mean?
2. Where do the Decists, the Workers' Opposition and other ultraleft groups stand?
3. What does the ally think of the draft programme published in the last issue of the Bulletin?
4. What does he think about the Communist International? (We attribute the same importance to this problem as to that of the USSR)?

As concerns the general situation in the country, the information does not differ much from the picture which I had formed from an attentive reading of the Russian newspapers.

documents from Smirnov.
120. Cf N.15, pp9-10.
121. See note 6 above.

Document No. 3

Letter from Sedov to Trotsky[122]

The (...) is organised [123] it includes the Zinovievists, the Sten–Lominadze Group and the Trotskyists (former "...")[124]. The Safar–Tarkhan Group [125] have not yet formally entered they have too extreme a position; they will enter very soon. The declaration of Z. and K. [126]on the very grave mistake which they made in 1927 was made at the time of the negotiations with our people about the bloc, just before Z. and K. were deported.

The collapse of the IN (...)[127]Group, Preobrazh.[128]and Uf.[129] (these three groups formed part of the centre) was provoked by a sick, partly insane man. They arrested him by chance and he began to talk. They have certainly found no document in the homes of IN or the others that could be "Trotskyist literature". Some days before IN was arrested, he told our informant: "X. has betrayed and I am expecting to be arrested from one day to the next." Thanks to the presence of his Markovkin[130], who had provided him with all the information, he was prepared. Unfortunately IN did not have time to pass it on[131].

The informant says that there was *no* weak point whatever coming from abroad or in general connected with abroad.[132]

The collapse of the "old men" is a heavy blow[133], but the links with the workers have been preserved...

---

122. Library of Harvard College 4782, with the permission of the college. Translated from the Russian by Isabelle Lombard. We only give an extract, the part that deals with the bloc. The rest deals with the "special journeys" in Russia and unwillingness of Sedov to leave Germany which was the wish of his father. We want to publish this in No.6 of the *Cahiers Léon Trotsky*, whose theme is the Russian Left Opposition. The letter, written in citric acid and not dated is the only evidence of a reply to document no.2. We have followed here the order of the discoveries.
123. The missing word has been cut out with scissors. It seems to be the word "bloc"
124. The missing word has been carefully erased. It seems to be "capitulators".
125. This is about Safarove and Tarkhanov.
126. Z and K are obviously Zinoviev and Kamenev.
127. The missing word has been carefully erased. It seems to be "Smirnov"
128. Preobrazhensky
129. Ufimtsev
130. Was this an individual? We have not identified him even if it could be about the policeman who informed Smirnov.
131. We do not know what this was about.
132. The word *no* has been underlined by Trotsky.
133. We do not know to whom this refers: Grünstein?

The Socialist Youth in Spain (1934-1936)
(When Carrillo was a Leftist)

TROTSKY wrote about Spain and about the positions which Andres Nin adopted towards the proposal to enter the Socialist Youth, in a letter of 16 July 1936. This letter was a polemic against his comrade, Sneevliet, and was addressed to the leadership of the Dutch RSAP. He wrote:

> The splendid Socialist Youth came spontaneously to the idea of the Fourth International. To all our urgings that all attention be devoted to the Socialist Youth, we received only hollow evasions... The Socialist Youth then passed over almost completely into the Stalinist camp. The people who called themselves Bolshevik-Leninists and who calmly saw this happen, or better yet, who caused it, have to be condemned for ever as traitors to the revolution.[1]

In the documents recently published in the *Oeuvres* [French edition of Trotsky's writings], from 1934 onwards, there are abundant references to and remarks about the entry which Trotsky advocated into the Socialist Youth and the Socialist Workers' Party (PSOE), and the refusal of the Communist Left (Izquierda Comunista), which ended in 1935 in its fusion with Maurín's Workers' and Peasants' Bloc within the POUM. In *La Révolution espagnole*, I tried to throw all the light I could on the content of Trotsky's proposals — the text of which we do not have — and on the successive refusals of the Spanish Trotskyists, and I was content to mention as an important element in the context the "radicalisation", which has sometimes been called the "revolutionisation" of the PSOE, as well as some external signs of the evolution to the Left, even to "Leftism", of its youth organisation, the Federación Nacional de Juventudes socialistas (FNJ).

---

1. *Writings of Leon Trotsky: (1935-36)*, Pathfinder Press, NY, p368. [There is a very brief discussion of this question in Broué & Témime, *The Revolution and Civil War in Spain*; see note 4 below — note added by *Revolutionary History*.]

Recent developments in post-Franco Spain have had positive results in the field of historiography, because they have finally given access, not merely to the collections of books and journals of the 1930s, but also to the documents in the archives which were seized on a huge scale by Franco's army between 1936 and 1939 and were preserved at Salamanca[2]. Consequently it has now become possible to study in itself the evolution to the left of an important fraction of the Socialist Workers' Party of Spain, under the authority of Largo Caballero, and notably that of its most active wing, the Federation of Socialist Youth, one of the leaders of which was to have a long political career — because he was, quite simply, Santiago Carrillo. In the course of the last five years, important works have been devoted to this question from various standpoints,[3] and a first review of the question is now possible, based on printed sources as well as on hitherto unknown archives.

The Radicalisation of Largo Caballero

The pressure to the left within the socialist parties from 1933 onwards is not, of course, a purely Spanish phenomenon, as some experts on Spain believe and certain political writers maintain. The phenomenon was due in general both to the economic crisis and its socio-political consequences and to the defensive reflex provoked by Hitler's victory without a struggle in Germany; it was a world-wide phenomenon. The special feature in Spain was that the radicalised left wing of the Socialist Party was to have as its spokesman and its principal

2. The Archivo Historico Nacional, Civil War section, in Salamanca, the former archive section of the Civil Guard, which helped the repression during and after the civil war, is today under the control of the Ministry of Culture and is run by an archivist. The earlier indexing, which was certainly helpful in police investigations, is very inadequate for scientific research nowadays, but the documentation is of exceptional quantity and quality.
3. Among these studies, I shall first mention the work of the British historian Paul Preston, *The Coming of the Spanish Civil War*, London, 1978, which closely studies the internal life of the PSOE, of the UGT and of the Socialist Youth, simultaneously, in the dialectic of development, of the CEDA and of the JAP. We must place on the same level a very important study in the history of ideas, the book by Marta Bizcarrondo, *Araquistáin y la Crisis Socialista en la IIIa República: Leviatán 1934-1936* (1975) (while we await her thesis on the PSOE in those years); the interesting essay by Ricard Viñas, "*La Formación de las Juventudes Socialistas Unificadas 1934-1936)* 1978 to which it would be right to add the two works by Santos Julía, "*La Izquierda del PSOE (1935-36)* (1977), and *Origines del Frente Popular en España 1934-36* (1980). Marta Bizcarrondo has produced and annotated a new re-printed edition of *Leviatán*, the review of the Left Socialists, and Paul Preston has made an anthology of the same *Leviatán (Antología)*. Many of the important documents used for this study have likewise been republished, and we have used here the new edition of the *Discursos a los Trabajadores* of Francisco Largo Caballero and the anthology of the speeches of Indalecio Prieto prepared by Edward Malefakis under the title *Discursos fundamentales*, as well as the anthology of the discussions about the revolution of October 1934 prepared by Marta Bizcarrondo under the title *Octubre del 34: Reflexiones sobre una Revolucion*, which reproduces the text of the pamphlet of the Socialist Youth *Octubre: Segunda Etapa* [October: The Second Stage]. We have also used other, older works, notably the second volume of the memoirs of the former secretary of the PSOE, Juan-Simeón Vidarte, *El Bieno Negre y la Insurrección de Asturias* (1978), which includes many documents and useful pieces of information.

leader a man who until then had been correctly regarded as one of the most hardened reformists in the Second International, Francisco Largo Caballero.

He was a former plasterer, who only had learned to read and write at the age of twenty-four, and was one of the best-known leaders of the party and of the union which he controlled, the General Union of Workers (UGT). He was one of the most stubborn opponents of affiliation to the Communist International and one of the active supporters of the PSOE, and then, under the dictatorship of Primo de Rivera, the determined supporter of collaboration which would allow the UGT to grow. He favoured the alliance with the republican bourgeois parties to bring down the monarchy, and since the coming of the Republic had been Minister of Labour in the Socialist-Republican coalition government, accepting the responsibility for measures of repression as severe as, for example, the famous "law for the defence of the Republic".[4]

But in the middle of 1933, at the moment moreover when the Socialists entered the government, several factors combined to pressure Largo Caballero to use more sharply left language — as much directed to the bourgeoisie as to the workers. He noticed with great bitterness that the social legislation of which he was the author continued to be sabotaged by functionaries high and low, while the employers were resuming the offensive everywhere and in every field. Moreover he was greatly impressed by the victory of Hitler and the destruction of the entire German workers' movement and of its social conquests, as well as by the analysis of these events by his comrade, Luis Araquistáin.[5] Like thousands and thousands of others he was convinced that the leader of the Popular Alliance, José Maria Gíl Robles[6] was taking the road of fascism in Spain and acquiring power by legal means, so he thought that the very existence of his party was now at stake.

The first indication that he was turning to the left was given in a speech which he delivered on 23 July in the Pardiñas Cinema in Madrid, to the Socialist Youth of the capital. He defended the participation of the Socialists in the republican government; when he pointed out that fascism was the last resort of capitalism in its extremity, he advanced some daring formulations, in particular declaring that he preferred "the socialist dictatorship" to "the bourgeois dictatorship or to fascism"[7]. Some weeks later he returned to the charge when

4. The text in French of this repressive law of October 1931 is included in my book, *La Revolution espagnole: 1931-1939*, Paris 1973, pp105-106. [This book has not been translated into English. The document referred to does not appear in P Broué & E Témime, *The Revolution and the Civil War in Spain*, London, 1972. — note added by *Revolutionary History*.]
5. Marta Bizcarrondo, *Araquistáin...*, pp124-14.
6. José Maria Gíl Robles (1898-1980), lawyer, was the head of the Acción Popular, which was trusted by the Catholic hierarchy, and was the leader of the "accidentalistas", the supporters of playing the parliamentary game within the constitution, in order to block reforms and take back power. From 1931 onwards he was the leader — known as "The Boss" — of the CEDA (Confederación Española de Derechas Autonomas). This was the bloc of the Right, the youth organisation of which, the JAP (Juventud de Acción Popular) gave itself the airs of a fascist militia.
7. *El Socialista*, 25 July 1933.

addressing the students at the Socialist Youth summer school, held at Torrelodones, where the interventions of Besteiro, followed by those of Indalecio Prieto, provoked much dissatisfaction.[8] Largo Caballero, for his part, did not disappoint his young audience. Speaking of participation in power, he said that he did not make this a question of principle, but that today less than ever did he believe in the possibility of achieving socialism within the framework of bourgeois society. He declared that the aim of socialists must be to conquer power, and that a socialist republic must put an end to the exploitation of man by man. He also recalled the formula of Engels about "the dictatorship of the proletariat".[9]

Was the President of the PSOE really calling into question his old reformist thinking and practice? Most writers today strongly doubt this; they declare that Largo Caballero was quite happy following — from a safe distance and in words only — the working masses and the youth in an ever-stronger orientation towards the left since 1931. In any case, from that day onwards the alliance was made between the Socialist Youth and the old leader of the Party and of the UGT, whom they made their "honorary president". He gave his first interview to their weekly journal, *Renovación*, after the Socialists left the government. From that time onwards, after the experience of these years, he was doubtful of possibility of winning even the most minimal demands of the proletariat within the bourgeois republican framework. He believed that Spain was on the eve of the social revolution, and set before the youth the mission of encouraging the indecisive and of driving out of the party the passive elements that were no use to the revolution.[10]

It was on this line that Largo Caballero flung himself into the electoral campaign in November, at the head of a Socialist Party which, this time, did not have an alliance with the bourgeois republican parties. His meetings came to seem like popular referenda and, as Paul Preston emphasises, "his language grew more revolutionary as he travelled", in obvious response to the furious attacks

---

8. The summer school of the Socialist Youth met in tents in August 1933, with some 150 students from all over the country, of whom a dozen were girls. In the Archivo Nacional Historico de Salamanca, Sección Guerra Civil, Politico-Social, "Madrid", Legajo 1460, there is an important file devoted to the sessions of 1932 and 1933. The level of theoretical education of the students was very weak; nearly all of the seventeen written replies to the question, "What is Socialism?" made of socialism a moral ideal. Largo Caballero had not been previously announced as a speaker, but the students felt frustrated and were and dissatisfied by the speeches of Besteiro and Prieto. This dossier in particular tells us that the young Santiago Carrillo, the son of a supporter of Largo Caballero, named Wenceslao Carrillo, was an apprentice printer, then an apprentice journalist on *El Socialista*, who was just beginning his political career, was the secretary of the summer school and responsible in particular for inviting the speakers.
9. This speech was published in the form of a pamphlet, entitled *Possibilismo en la democrácia socialista*. The part in which the old Social-Democrat presented himself to his young listeners is reproduced in *Discursos a los Trabajadores*, in the 1979 edition, pp27-31.
10. *Renovación*, 23 September 1933.

of the right, but also and above all "to the unrestrained enthusiasm of the crowds, who cheered his speeches long after they were over."[11]

The PSOE was defeated; it won only 58 seats, though it received 1,627,000 votes, more than any other party ever before. This was thanks to the electoral law, which favoured broad coalitions so twice as many votes were needed for a Socialist candidate to be elected. The anarchists abstained from voting, denouncing Caballero for participating in repressive governments. But, in addition, beyond the slightest doubt, the propertied classes, confident of getting away with it, massively employed methods such as pressure on the working people, threats of loss of employment in the countryside, violence and sometimes terror and in any case organised fraud: sufficient reasons to convince the Socialists that they had nothing more to expect from bourgeois democracy. The Socialist Youth identified themselves with the new course and with the President of the Party and launched a campaign of propaganda and enlightenment. It was in this way that they came to publish in pamphlet form a speech which Araquistáin delivered on 29 October 1933: Araquistáin, Largo Caballero's adviser, explained in it, on the basis of the German experience, through part of which he had lived, that only the socialist revolution, by destroying the bourgeoisie, could really bar the road to fascism.[12]

At the end of December Largo Caballero reached the conclusion that an insurrection had to be prepared "to save the republic". Supported by an agreement with Prieto, he was active, at the end of 1933 and in the early months

---

11. P. Preston, op cit p90. According to the pamphlet attacking Caballero in 1936 by the reformist journalist G. Mario de Coca, *Anti-Caballero: Una crítica marxista de la bolchevización dal partido socialista obrero español* (republished in 1975, with introduction by Marta Bizcarrondo), it was at the start of his campaign in the provinces that he was called "the Spanish Lenin", a title against which he politely protested (p86). Gabriel Mario de Coca also gave an account of Largo Caballero's campaign: on 30 October, at Zafra, he foretold the opening of a new revolutionary period, which was not that of 1931 which had culminated in the Republic: "The new period will culminate with the establishment of the social republic". On 9 November, at Don Benito, he declared that Spain was nearing the social revolution and that the bourgeoisie had to be expropriated by violence. It would be necessary to fight until "the red flag of the revolution floats over all the public buildings". On 10 November, at Azuaga, he said that if a movement arose in the army, it would not be a movement of generals, but a movement of "soldiers and sergeants", to "install the social Republic". On 13 November, at Elbacete, he said: "It is true, if legality does not serve us, if it obstructs our advance, then we shall leave bourgeois democracy on one side and shall go to the revolutionary conquest of power". On the 14th, in Murcia, where he was frantically applauded by the Socialist Youth, he ended: "A period of transition to socialism will be needed by us, and this period is the dictatorship of the proletariat, towards which we are headed". op cit pp88-90.
12. L. Araquistáin, *Una lección de historia: El derrumbamiento alemán.* (1933). Luis Araquistáin Quevedo (1886-1959) was a brilliant intellectual who moved to the left. He was ambassador in Berlin from February 1932 to February 1933, where he drew the conclusion that both the Communist Party and the Social-Democratic parties were bankrupt. The only way to overcome fascism, or "open bourgeois dictatorship", was by "open socialist dictatorship". Bourgeois democracy was of interest to the proletariat only to the extent that it enabled the proletariat to "strengthen its positions in its struggle for power".

of 1934, in removing the opposition within the PSOE and even within its leadership.

One of the bastions of the resistance to the new course was obviously the Executive of the UGT, presided over by Julián Besteiro[13]. The battle for control began in the leadership of the UGT when Gíl Robles, the Parliamentary leader of the CEDA,[see Note 6] who had emerged victorious in the elections, publicly declared his determination to establish a "Corporative State" in Spain in the near future. Amaro del Rosal, a leading member of the Socialist Youth and leader of the union of workers in banks and finance, proposed to the national council of the UGT a resolution in favour of "the immediate and urgent organisation, in agreement with the Socialist Party, of a revolutionary movement of a nationwide character to win total power for the working class". It was defeated by 28 votes to 17. In response Largo Caballero then got a decision to create a joint committee of the PSOE and UGT, with himself in the chair, and which had the task of studying the practical aspects of creating a revolutionary movement if the CEDA took over the government. On 27 January 1934, the programme for this possible uprising, drafted by Prieto, was submitted to the national committee of the UGT, which approved it[14], a decision followed by the immediate resignation of the former Executive, which firmly opposed what it called "adventurism". It was immediately replaced by a new team devoted to Largo Caballero, who was once more general secretary under the presidency of his comrade Anastasio de Gracia[15], a leader of the building trades' union. Those in agreement with the new

13. Julian Besteiro Fernández (1870-1940) was a veteran of the party, a university professor, with a reputation as a theoretician. He had been chairman of the strike committee in 1917 and advocated that the Socialists should leave the tasks of governing to the republicans alone and especially the tasks of the "democratic revolution", without trying to "skip stages". He was President of the Cortes in 1931; his base in the PSOE was in Madrid, and in the UGT it lay in the support of the railway workers and the agricultural workers. He was regarded as the leader of the "reformist" wing.
14. *Boletín de la Unión General de Trabajadores de España*, December 1933-January 1934, for the debates as a whole and their various sudden changes. The text of the programme drafted by Prieto is in *Guerra y Revolución en España*, by Dolores Ibárruri and others, pp52-54. It included ten points: nationalisation of all the land; financial priority to irrigation works; reform of public education; dissolution of the religious orders and the confiscation of their property; dissolution of the army and a new army on a democratic basis; dissolution of the Civil Guard and formation of a people's militia; reform and purging of the state bureaucracy; improvement of the material and moral condition of industrial workers; reform of the tax system; rapid application of all these measures by new legislative organs which the people will create. This programme was only known about *fifteen months later*, long after the insurrection which was to apply it had been checked! Largo Caballero moreover got decisions about action voted on (ibid, p54), to (1) organise an "undisguisedly revolutionary" movement, (2) to launch such a movement at the opportune moment independent of the initiatives of the enemy, (3) the PSOE and the UGT to make contact with elements ready to take part in this movement, (4) in the event of victory, the formation of a PSOE — UGT Government open to all organisations which had taken a direct part in the battle, and (5) this government carrying out the above programme. Indalecio Prieto y Tuero (1883-1962), was linked with business men and had a very "liberal" style. For many years he was the great rival of Largo Caballero in the PSOE.
15. Anastasio de Gracia Villariabia (1890-1981) came from Toledo. He was for many years a leader in the union of building trade workers, of which he had recently become the President. He

secretary-general of the UGT included leaders of the important metal-workers' unions, those like Pascual Tomás, who led the building trade workers, the Young Socialist, Carlos Hernández Zancajo, who led the transport workers' union, and the leader of the bank employees. They now became the majority, and took the leadership of the very important Federación Nacional de Trabajadores de la Tierra, the agricultural workers' union, which was now in the hands of the team led by the teacher Ricardo Zabalza, the supporter of Largo Caballero from Navarre[16].

The "Besteirist" leadership of the Socialist organisation in Madrid, the role of which was always a key one in the Party, likewise fell into the hands of the supporters of Largo Caballero, among which were many members of the Socialist Youth[17].

The Federation of the Socialist Youth

Soon after the Russian Revolution in 1917, it was the Socialist Youth who, as in many other countries at that time, formed the first nuclei of the future Communist Party. After that, during the 1920s, the re-constructed Socialist Youth had hardly been conspicuous for boldness or audacity; they were a small organisation mostly composed of the children of leading comrades or active members, and were, until 1932, led by people known for their moderation and reformism without any problems. But this state of things changed completely after 1932 and especially in 1933.

When the PSOE and the UGT decided at the beginning of 1934 to launch an insurrection if the CEDA became the government and, in a word, defend the Republic and the work of the Constituent Cortes and of the Socialist-Republican government, an important component of the Party and especially of its left wing, the FJS — which also occupied positions in the UGT — openly proclaimed that this insurrection would be nothing else than an insurrection for power, for the installation of the dictatorship of the proletariat.

---

was to become a minister in the Largo Caballero government in 1936-37. He died in exile in Mexico in the early 1980s.

16. The agricultural workers were at one and the same time the most wretchedly paid and those whom unemployment hit hardest. The FNTT (Federación Nacional de Trabajadores de la Tierra) had had a mushroom-like growth since the proclamation of the Republic; in June 1932 it had 445, 414 members out of a total of 1, 041, 539 in the UGT. It was the very strong pressure from its very combative militant base which had driven out of its leadership Lucio Martínez Gíl, the supporter of Besteiro, and was to dictate its policy to his successor, Ricardo Zabalza (died 1939), one of the leaders of the PSOE in Navarre.

17. *El Socialista*, 28 January 1934. Gabriel Mario de Coca, op cit p101, says that on this occasion there was no political discussion and no confrontation of ideas, but that votes were taken only on purely procedural questions. He states moreover that the meeting was "fixed" in advance by the Socialist Youth. Among the new leaders of the Agrupación Socialista Madrileña, we find particularly the names of Wenceslao Carrillo, the father of Santiago, and of Carlos Hernández Zancajo.

After 1932 the activity of elements "of the left", whose views began to cause anxiety to some gentlemen, appeared in the Socialist Youth Federation. From summer 1933, the speech at the Pardiñas cinema and especially the intervention of Largo Caballero at the Socialist summer school, the "leftist" current behind Largo Caballero gained great strength. Already *Renovación*, the Federation's weekly, was defending the most extreme positions being expressed anywhere in the Socialist milieu. This current — which had all the features of an organised fraction — took control of the leadership of the Socialist Youth at its 5th Congress in April 1934, when the organisation had 20,000 members, which it was to double in a few months[18]. This new leadership won an overwhelming victory on the basis of a political report presented to the congress by a former student leader, José Laín Entralgo, which stressed the need to break with the bourgeoisie and its parties in order to start immediately to prepare for the seizure of power by the proletariat, i.e. the Socialist Party.[19]

The new president of the Federation, Carlos Hernández Zancojo, who had been politically active for years, belonged to the "older" generation and was nearer to the upper age-limit of 35 than to the 20-year-olds who were the majority of members[20]; he was well known, in addition, for his leadership of his transport workers' union and his work in the Socialist organisation in Madrid. But the new leaders around him were really very young. Santiago Carrillo, the new secretary-general, was just nineteen. He was the son of a faithful supporter of Caballero, brought up in the circles of the apparatus, apprenticed to typesetting at thirteen, then an apprentice-journalist on *El Socialista*; in 1933 he was the general secretary of the summer school. At *Renovación*, which he had been editing for a year, he was replaced by a young militant student, Segundo Serrano Poncela, aged twenty-two. Around this secretariat, there was an equally youthful administration: José Laín Entralgo, of course, but also Federico Melchor, José Cazorlá, Alfredo Cabello, Rafael Cuadrado.[21]

18. Until 1933 the leadership of the Socialist Youth was drawn from the so-called "reformist" wing of the PSOE, the leader of which was Besteiro. The supporters of the last named were Juan and Mariano Rojo, José Castro, Felix García, at the head of the Socialist Youth. For the figures, see Santiago Carrillo, *Demain l'Espagne*, p31.
19. Jose Laín Entralgo had been one of the main leaders in Madrid of the student organisation, FUE. His report to the Congress, entitled "Posición política de las Juventudes", was published in *El Socialista*, 21 April 1934.
20. The upper age-limit for admission to the Socialist Youth was 35. But the overwhelming majority of the members were very much younger. In the PSOE there was a very important generation gap, because the recruitment of youth had practically died away during the dictatorship of Primo de Rivera, and had speeded up in 1930.
21. Segundo Serrano Poncela (1912-1976), then a student of literature, had been (according to the Archivo Historico Nacional, Madrid, 1460) one of the students at the summer school of the Socialist Youth in 1932 at El Pardo. Federico Melchor belonged to the group which attended the school the following year. His written reply to the set essay, "What is Socialism?" (cf footnote 8), in which he displayed his knowledge, mentioning the utopians, Hegel, Marx and the dialectic with a touch of pedantry, contrasted with the candour and modesty of the work of his fellow-students.

The new team hid neither its intentions nor its ambitions. It wanted to make use of the youth organisation as a faction in the internal struggle in the party, as the spearhead of the "revolutionary" tendency of Largo Caballero, which the whole leadership backed. We may note this interesting point: while Caballero's young supporters constantly referred to the authority and the prestige of Largo Caballero, at the head of the Federation of Socialist Youth, inside the party they nonetheless posed the question as one of generations. The congress had not yet closed when Serrano wrote in *Renovación*, under the significant title "Crisis of Confidence", that the men of the generation which held the reins of the party were in reality "crushed by so many years of erroneous reformist interpretations of the Marxist tactic"; he counterposed to them the principled firmness of the new arrivals:

> The new socialist generation will oppose everything which signifies an alteration of Marxist purity in its conception of power.[22]

The political thought of these young people was certainly far from being perfectly clear. Their adversaries could often, and without great difficulty, detect their contradictions and sudden reversals of line. But the axis of their orientation was very clear. They believed that the proletarian revolution was on the immediate order of the day in Spain, and that as a result of the facts of history and the present consciousness of the masses the instrument of this proletarian revolution could only be the PSOE which they believed had to be swept clear of its reformist elements and reinforced by revolutionary elements from outside.

Already in 1933, in a series of articles in *Renovación*, the young Federico Melchor, fresh from the summer school, was stressing important points of agreement with the organisations which had just declared for the Fourth International: the "struggle against fascism, the conquest of political power by revolution, the imminence of the revolution, the necessity to destroy reformism, the internal democracy of the party", and declared that their role would be even more important inside the existing Internationals. Then he declared that the Trotskyists and the Socialist Youth were fighting the same struggle to break with "Stalinism and revisionism", but that he did not believe in the construction of the Fourth International and wanted the support of the Trotskyists to help to defeat the reformist faction in the Socialist Party.[23]

---

22. *Renovación*, 18 April, 1934.
23. Fed-Mel, "Hacia la IVa Internacional?", *Renovación*, 30 September 1933; F. Melchor, "La IVa Internacional", ibid 11 November and 9 December 1933. We may also look at "Posición de los jovenes trotskistas", ibid 27 January 1934, and "A los jovenes trotskistas", 3 March 1934, discussion articles on the policy of the United Front which the Left Communists in Spain were advocating. In his book, *Jalones de derotta, promesa de Victoria* (1948), the Trotskyist G. Munis emphasises the great influence which the Trotskyists of the Communist Left had in the ranks of the Socialist Youth and the prestige which their leaders enjoyed. He gives some examples of this, such as the vote of a provincial federation, that of Old Castile, to join the Fourth International which was being built, the constant references to Trotsky by the leaders and their appeals to the Trotskyists to "enter", as well as the pressure which was put on him

The German experience — which had first been made known by Araquistáin — had informed them of Trotsky's positions as well as of the double "failure" of the two equally erroneous tactics, "the reformist, petty-bourgeois social democratic tactic" and "the intransigent, sectarian tactic of the Communist International"[24]. This is what Santiago Carrillo explained in July 1934 to a delegation of Communist Youth. The important thing in his eyes was that the movement of the masses was forcing the workers' organisations to form a united front, to take power through the formation countrywide, of Workers' Alliances[25]. The Socialist Youth refused to accept the demand of the Communist Youth that the Trotskyists should be excluded from the joint activities[26]. On this point Carrillo did not spare the Communist Youth his criticisms. He said that he was certain that the mass movement would oblige the Communist Party of Spain to join in the Workers' Alliances which it had been slandering for months.

The Socialist Youth were not yet ready to join the Communist Youth in a "People's Anti-Fascist Bloc" as the latter proposed. Carrillo mentioned ironically the recent conclusion in France of the unity agreement between the SFIO and the PCF:

personally to join the Socialist Youth without in any way renouncing his political ideas. Andrade says that political portraits of Trotsky could be found in the offices of the Socialist Youth leaders.

24. For the account which follows, which is a synthesis of the ideas of the leaders of the Socialist Youth in the middle of 1934, reference is made throughout to the minutes of the discussion with the delegation from the Communist Youth of 26 and 30 July, published in *Renovación*, 28 July and 4, 11 and 18 August 1934, a document which Ricard Viñas published as an appendix to his work, to which we refer the reader. The delegation of the Socialist Youth was composed of Santiago Carrillo, Serrano Poncela and José Laín. Carrillo was the only member of the delegation to speak (Viñas, op cit, p78).
25. Ibid p81. The "Workers' Alliances" were united front organisations, the initiative for which had been taken by the Workers' and Peasants' Bloc led by J. Maurín and by the Communist Left led by Andres Nin: the Workers' Alliance in Catalonia came into existence at the end of 1933. That in Madrid had been formed in May 1934, apparently on the initiative of the Socialist Youth. The CNT joined the Workers' Alliance only in the Asturias. The Communist Party opposed the "Workers' Alliances", which it regarded as the worst form of "social fascism" and called them "the Holy Alliance of the counter-revolution"... until September 1934, when it decided *in extremis* to join them.
26. Among others, Victor Alba, *El Partido Comunista de España*, p170, states that Trifón Medrano, the secretary of the Communist Youth, having laid down in advance that the young Trotskyists were to be excluded from the Workers' Youth Alliance which was being formed, Santiago Carrillo, in the name of the Socialist Youth and with the support of the Libertarian Youth preferred to drop the project. Nonetheless it seems that the Madrid leadership of the Socialist Youth was not always firm in opposing expulsions of the Stalinist type, and agreed to joint demonstrations from which the Trotskyists had been excluded in advance. This was notably the case in the huge demonstration, "The Meeting in the Stadium" on 10 September 1934, where over 100, 000 young people protested against a governmental decree which attacked their civil rights, prohibiting anyone under 23 from joining a political body without previous authorisation by their parents.

They say that they renounce systematic violence. But we must unite in order to organise violence![27]

Moreover the Socialist Youth allowed criticisms and did not go in for insults. Carrillo said that it was not the use of insults which would make them decide to adopt a policy of the so-called "anti-fascist front", for they believed it impossible to form a front against fascism with people who, like the Radicals, were clearly engaged in opening the way for fascism.

For all that, they defended — particularly against the Trotskyists, but also against other formations — what appears at first sight to be a rather surprising conception of the "united front", which was apparently only possible, according to them, for preparing to seize power: this was the role which they ascribed, at any rate in theory, to the Workers' Alliances. In 1934, in any case, and as soon as the decision for the possible insurrection, which they wished to make the start of the dictatorship, had been taken, they subordinated everything to this one objective. Santiago Carrillo declared to his questioners from Communist Youth, "The proletariat has nothing to gain in skirmishes: it wants to give battle in a definitive way"[28]. He therefore strongly opposed any partial action, any strike which could risk drawing the proletariat into a premature battle, because according to him not even the General Strike itself could be any more than the complement "of the insurrectional action of the armed bodies for the conquest of power."[29]

This rejection of partial actions, described as "the will to conserve the forces of the proletariat" for "D-Day" was put to the other workers' organisations with all the confidence of an organisation which was seriously preparing, if not "the great social revolution", at least an insurrection in all the workers' regions in Spain, and which was conscious that it was benefiting from the immense popularity of Largo Caballero, who at this time was the incarnation of the deepest aspirations of the workers and of the masses of toilers in the countryside, and whom the Socialist Youth began to call "the Spanish Lenin".

Military Preparations for the Insurrection

The technical preparation of the insurrection evidently involved the delicate problem of arming, forming and training militias which would be the spearhead of the insurrection. On these points we have a certain number of documents

---

27. Viñas, op cit, p80. Carrillo at the time was diametrically opposed to the line of the Communist International on this point.
28. Ibid, p79. Despite these peremptory statements and at least partly under the pressure of their own rank and file, the leaders of the Socialist Youth agreed to the organisation of large united demonstrations, which were extraordinary factors in mobilising in this period, at the time of the funerals of the Young Socialist militant Juanita Rico, murdered on 10 July, and of the young Communist leader, Joaquín de Grado, who was assassinated on 29 September.
29. Ibid, p104.

and some valuable statements about the specific activity of the Socialist Youth in particular.

The search for arms seems to have begun fairly early in 1934. The largest deal was to be the purchase of an important stock which some Portugese conspirators collected, part of which was to be seized with the steam-ship *Turquesa*, which had tried to land the arms on the coast of the Asturias[30]. A report from the head of the Security makes clear that the Socialists also succeeded in making several "purchases" of arms under the cover of foreign governments, in particular of the government of Ethiopia, the cargoes being redespatched secretly to another destination, in Spain, soon after having been landed to be sent on to their destination in East Africa. Moreover, substantial stocks of guns were acquired by thefts which the workers themselves organised in the arsenals where they made them. (La Trubia, Toledo). When the time came, they counted on seizing in the first hours of the insurrection arms held in the stores of the arsenals, — in the Asturias they got 17,000 rifles — and the arms from a certain number of police stations, Assault Guards and civil guards, with the complicity of Socialists in the army or the police[31].

30. M. Tagüeña, *Testimonio de dos Guerras*, p52, gives the explanation about the arms purchase by a secret Portuguese organisation, as does B. Diaz Nosty in, *La Comuna Asturiana*. (*The Case of the 'Turquesa'*, pp108-113), and Santiago Carrillo in *Demain 1'Espagne*, p35. They all claim that the Civil Guard got only part of the cargo. There are many obscure aspects in the episode of the *Turquesa*, the organising of which was believed to have been done by Prieto. According to the judicial enquiry in 1934-35 (AHN "Madrid", Legajo 721), the arms had been paid for by the leader of the UGT miners' union (SMA), Amador Fernández: the investigators believed that this union had obtained the funds simply by a bank loan contracted by the management of the San Vicente mine, which belonged precisely to it. Santiago Carrillo says (op cit p35) that, if his memory does not betray him, the Socialist Party obtained the money in question by successfully forging a cheque of the Marquis de Villapadierna "for a million pesetas and a little over", and getting it cashed by a well-dressed comrade. Manuel Tagüeña Lacorte (1913-1972) a student of mathematics and physics at Madrid had at first belonged to the Communist Youth. But he joined the Socialist militias and refused to leave, abandoning the Communist Youth for the Socialist Youth; he had important responsibilities in the militias in 1934 on the eve of October. He was jailed for several months after the insurrection, did his military service and in 1936 joined the leadership of the United Socialist Youth. He organised the first militia units of the JSU in 1936 and joined the Communist Party of Spain in 1937. In 1938 he was in command of the 5th Army on the Ebro front with 70, 000 men. He emigrated to the USSR in 1939 and studied at the Frunze Academy, then was an instructor in an officers' school until 1946, and then was in Yugoslavia until 1951. At that date he became a research worker in a medical laboratory in Czechoslovakia, a country which he left, at the same time as he left the Communist Party, in 1955, to go to settle in Mexico. He refused to return to Spain when the Franco regime invited him to do so.

31. Tagüeña mentions (p53) a plan to attack the barracks of the motorised group of the Civil Guard of Guindalera in Madrid, where the conspirators counted on the complicity of lieutenant Fernando Condés, a member of the PSOE, who was to play in 1936 an important role in the kidnapping of José Calvo Sotelo, which led to his murder, and was killed at the very beginning of the civil war. It seems that, among the officers on whose support Largo Caballero had counted was Rodrigo Gil, who in July 1936 was to play an important role, as the lieutenant-colonel in command of the artillery park, in the distribution of rifles. Tagüeña tells (pp45-50) in detail of a long-range expedition — to Valladolid — to seize a stock of arms belonging to the right; he describes (p52) how the constant moving of stocks of arms could

As to the militias, the Security report already quoted includes two circulars from the leadership of the Socialist Youth in Murcia, dated respectively 6 June and 28 July, as well as a general report of 30 May 1934, about the military preparations of the Youth and of the Socialist "Militias".[32]

The Socialist Youth circular of 6 June refers to earlier directives about the immediate creation of militias, indicating that many already exist and are functioning perfectly. It insists that the militiamen must not carry their arms unnecessarily, must hide all documents which could be compromising and must immediately form an underground alternative leadership. It stresses that the preparation properly so-called — exercises and handling of weapons — must be carried out as far as possible in the country, under the cover of excursions of a "scouting" type, in order to protect the militiamen from being caught by surprise by the police. It insists on the importance of "surveillance" and even "espionage" of the enemy camp — the "fascist" organisations and the police — and insists that this be undertaken where it is not already being done, as quickly as possible and, of course, in the strictest secrecy. It pointed out, finally, that it is necessary to form in every locality a "chemical" section, with the duty of making bombs and explosive devices; this to be rigorously separated from the rest of the organisation. Finally, it repeated the necessity for the strictest discipline and on the decision, already taken, to punish with death any who might betray or be detected in giving information.

---

not fail to attract attention and revealed a dangerous amateurishness, with the precious parcels deposited on the doorsteps of the people for whom they were intended! In this way is explained, no doubt, how so many arms came to be seized before D-Day and the biggest haul of all was made during a search of ... the Casa del Pueblo, about which the right-wing press constantly alleged that it was crammed with arms. Among the collections of weapons which the police discovered, which are mentioned in the works of Amaro del Rosal (*Historia de la UGT*, vol. I, pp390-396) and Juan Simeón Vidarte (*El Bieno Negro*, pp214-219 and 158-159), were those in apartments rented by Socialist deputies or other personalities, as for example Gabriel Morón in Madrid, Juan Lozano, a deputy for Jaen, Rodriguez Vera and Professor Rafael de Buen. Certain aspects of this technical preparation were so obviously improvised by amateurs that they are completely incomprehensible. On the other hand, there is still a real problem concerning the officers who were involved in preparing the insurrection. All the authors speak of complicity among the officers, republicans or Socialists, whose intervention in the insurrection at the head of their troops would have been decisive. The names are often mentioned of the officers of the Assault Guards, Moreno and Castillo, of captains Benito Sánchez and Carlos Faraudo, of the lieutenant of the Civil Guard, Fernando Condés, and, of course, of sergeants. However, it is hardly likely that Prieto, who was responsible for contact in the armed forces, failed to make contact on this point with the generals who belonged to the freemasons in the army, such as Miguel Cabanellas, Riquelme, Nuñez del Prado, and Gómez Caminero or with the brigadiers, Llano de Encomienda, Miaja, Pozas, Martínez Cabrera, Martínez Monje, etc. Alvarez del Vayo says that the movement counted on "certain officers", who should have brought out their troops but did not move. But no one has offered any explanation of this "defaulting": perhaps it is one of the factors in the violent antagonism in later years between Prieto and Caballero. The only soldier who was really compromised was sergeant Vásquez, who was shot on 1 February 1935.

32. AHN. "Madrid", Legajo 721, Salamanca.

The organisation of the militias itself was the subject of an eleven-point summary. To be admitted to it were members of the Socialist Youth and those of the PSOE and of the UGT, while the two latter categories could be "allocated by quota", in order to avoid the leadership of the militia by the Socialist Youth being questioned. The militiamen were organised in groups of ten — known as "tens" — commanded by a "leader", nominated like the local leader of the Socialist Youth, by its local committee. Preference was to be given to members who had done their military service and possibly had training as officers or non-commissioned officers. The members of the "tens" would learn to handle their rifles within the framework of the "ten". Preparing explosives, holding stocks of them and handling them would be reserved for a special section. Each of the men admitted to the ranks of the militias must have a weapon. The local committee of the Socialist Youth had a free hand to nominate people for tasks, for training and for judging and punishing traitors on occasion. The order to mobilise, on the other hand, as well as strategic directives, were to come from the Provincial Federal Committee and the "senior leader" appointed by it.[33]

The circular from the same provincial committee on 28 August was more laconic and already had a smell of gunpowder about it. The local and provincial committees of the JS were dissolved. Authority on a local level was with the weekly meeting of the leaders of tens with the local leader who was now responsible to the senior leader who had to have means of contacting all the local leaders. Were the JS really dissolved into their own military organisation, thus becoming semi-clandestine? We may feel legitimate doubt as to how radical this transformation was in a framework in which public political activities — distribution of *Renovación*, mass meetings — and trade union activity were being carried on legally. There was doubtless at least a certain division of labour.

The national leader of the militias was José Laín. We have a fairly complete report on the militias in Madrid, by Manuel Tagüeña, who at the time was a student of science, aged 21 and a member of the Communist Youth:

> At first there were almost public mass meetings in the Socialist Club in the West; these were followed by small meetings in squads of ten men who belonged to a secret organisation.[34]

It was actually in a building belonging to the Casa del Pueblo that he learned, from the leader of his squad, how to handle a Mauser. The first interventions by these militias took place at the time of the General Strike in Madrid, which was the response to the gathering of the fascists planned by the extreme right CEDA at the Escorial for 22 April.[35] Tagüeña left the Communist Youth when it

33. AHN. "Madrid", Legajo 721, Salamanca.
34. Tagüeña, op cit, p47. The *Ten Commandments* of the young Socialist explain that the group of ten must move in three ranks of three, with the leader marching alone on the *left*. See *Renovación*, 17 February 1934.
35. The Juventud de Acción Popular, the youth organisation of the CEDA, with fascist style and

wanted to make him give up the socialist militias, and he made rapid progress in them: with his militant friends, the medical student Federico Coello, and the law student Francisco Ordoñez, he entered the "General Staff" of the real military command of the militias, with José Laín, the bank employee Victoriano Marcos Alonso and the Italian militant Fernando De Rosa[36]. At the beginning of September, he received the command of a "company" formed of ten squads of ten men each, plus a command unit, the members of which lived in the quarter of Glorieta de Quevado. Ordoñez told him at the beginning of September that the insurrection was now inevitable and would in all probability be started at the beginning of October.[37]

It was within this framework of preparing an insurrection which the majority of the leaders of the UGT no doubt wished with all their hearts to avoid, but for which the Socialist Youth were consciously and enthusiastically preparing, that the discussion, within the UGT, the PSOE and the Workers' Alliance of Madrid took place on the situation of the agricultural workers and their strike at the beginning of the summer — a discussion which Paul Preston has decided to locate in a political setting independent of the preparations for insurrection[38].

---

methods, decided to organise a gigantic meeting at the Escorial on 22 April. For several weeks in the Workers' Alliances in Madrid the Socialist organisation opposed the proposals for action against this meeting which came from the delegate, G. Munis, of the Communist Left, (see Munis, *Jalones...*, pp114-115) In the end Munis and his supporters wrung from the Workers' Alliance a slogan of a twenty-four hour General Strike, on the evening of 21 April. The strike was a total success. The workers opposed the gathering at the Escorial by every means — including the intervention of armed Socialist militiamen. Only some ten thousand managed to get there, and these included a number of peasants who were forced to go by their local employer. Faced with this success, the leaders of the Communist Youth and of the Socialist Youth both began to claim the credit for the initiative which had not come from either of them. (On these claims, see Viñas, op cit, pp73, 81, 83!)

36. Tagüeña, op cit p48. Fernando De Rosa (1908-1936) had done his military service and was a second lieutenant in the Italian military reserve. He emigrated to Belgium, where he organised — unsuccessfully — an attack on the life of the Crown Prince Umberto of Italy. He was a member of the maximalist Socialist Party of Italy. He emigrated to Spain, where he was a member of the Socialist Youth. In the plan for the insurrection, he had received from Largo Caballero and from the "revolutionary committee" the mission of arresting the President of the Republic. He was sentenced to nineteen years in prison. When released in February 1936 under the amnesty, he again became head of the organisation of the Socialist militias, with the officers who were connected with the conspiracy of 1934, the captain of engineers Faraudo, the Assault Guard lieutenant José Castillo and the Civil Guard Condés. In July 1936 he organised the 11 October battalion, of which José Laín was the commander and was in conflict with Santiago Carrillo. He was killed by a bullet in the head on 15 September 1936. Among the other militia commanders, JS Vidarte mentions Enrique Puente.
37. Tagüeña, op cit p52. The revolutionary committee, which was formed of six people (Largo Caballero, Enrique de Francisco, Juan-Simeón Vidarte, Felipe Pretel and the leaders of the Socialist Youth, Hernández Zancajo and Santiago Carrillo) had approved the formation of a government, but had not yet decided whether it would consist of "ministers" or of "people's commissars".
38. See the account and analysis in Preston, op cit, pp112-120.

1934 was in fact the year of the great offensive of the proprietors of the large estates to bring down wages and get rid of the organised farm workers, following the notorious formula: "You are hungry? Go eat the Republic!" We have seen that, on 28 January 1934, under the pressure of the members who wanted to fight, the leadership of the powerful UGT trade union, the Federación Nacional de Trabajadores de la Tierra — with half a million members — passed into the hands of the team of Ricardo Zabalza. The trade union leaders exhausted all legal means and methods of propaganda and had accumulated proofs of violations of legality and of violence and provocations by the landed proprietors, and ended by deciding to call the strike, under the threat of being removed from office by their followers.

They did not call the strike lightly, as Paul Preston emphasises. A first warning was issued on 31 March, in the journal *E1 Obrero de la Tierra*. But the Executive Committee of the UGT advised the leadership of the FNTT against issuing the strike call: the harvest was not at the same time all over the country, the small farmers risked being hit by it and, especially, the strike would lead to an inevitable confrontation. During March and April, Largo Caballero and the Executive Committee of the UGT did their utmost to convince Zabalza and his comrades not to call for a strike by agricultural workers which the UGT would not be able to support in the other sectors. The joint PSOE–UGT committee, which was commissioned to study the insurrection, repeatedly warned the provincial organisations and emphasised that the strike of the agricultural workers had nothing to do with the proposed insurrection and, in this way, indicated that it was premature!

However, the union members were dying of slow starvation; they demanded the strike, which in the end they imposed on the leaders who could no longer hold them back. After a final attempt to negotiate, the National Committee of the FNTT, meeting on 11-12 May, announced the strike, which would begin on 1 June on a programme of truly minimal demands[39]. The reply of the government was a decree which made harvesting a "national public service" and the strike a "revolutionary conflict": all meetings, demonstrations and propaganda in connection with the strike were prohibited and a severe censorship imposed for several weeks. There were thousands of arrests and the local leaders were mostly sentenced to years of imprisonment without remission. The agricultural workers were left isolated and were crushed. The harvest was brought in by the army: two years and the electoral victory of 1936 were needed for the union to raise its head and come back to life...

Indeed, the policy of Largo Caballero and the UGT leadership is heavy with responsibility; when it warned the strikers, it was, in effect tipping off the government that it would have its hands free to hit out at the strikers. The attitude of the Socialist Party led to lively discussions in the Workers' Alliance in Madrid. On the evening of 1 June, Munis, who represented the Communist Left ("Izquierda Comunista") in the Workers' Alliance in Madrid, called for a

---

39. *El Obrero de la Tierra*, 19 May 1934.

solidarity strike of 48 hours, to show the Government that the peasants were not alone. The delegates of the Socialist organisations, the PSOE, the UGT and the Socialist Youth retorted that the matter concerned the peasants alone, who had been warned in good time. They declared that the "time to act had not yet come" and that they could not run the risk that the government might decide to close the Casa del Pueblo. In order to be better understood and, no doubt, for lack of arguments, the Socialist leader and supporter of the UGT, Rafael Henche de la Plata, without speaking, pulled a gun out of his belt and laid it openly on the table in front of him[40]. On 31 July, at the National Committee of the UGT, Ramón Ramírez, the young secretary of the Federación de Trabajadores de la Enseñanza ("Teachers' Union") — and who better than teachers to feel the need of the alliance of workers and peasants? — vigorously criticised the leadership of the UGT, which he accused of having brought the defeat on the striking agricultural workers and handed them over to repression. Largo Caballero in person undertook to reply to him; he spoke ironically of the "infantile leftism" and "verbal revolutionism" of his young comrade who quoted Marx and Lenin, and explained to him that Spain in 1934 was not Russia in 1917 ....[41].

In Paul Preston's opinion, an analysis of the way in which Largo Caballero behaved in the face of the strike which the FNTT called reveals clearly that the old leader had not definitively broken from his longstanding reformism. Moreover, this behaviour constitutes a decisive argument for those who believe that the president of the PSOE and secretary-general of the UGT was talking about the coming insurrection merely in order to frighten his political opponents and, especially, to make sufficient impression on the president of the Republic to discourage the latter from calling in the CEDA. The interpretation seems to be a good one. Can we apply the same conclusions and give the same explanation for the attitude of the Socialist Youth? At this time they too were not sparing of adopting "leftist postures" and playing at "verbal revolutionism", to use the expressions of Largo Caballero, but none the less they were unconditionally on the side of Largo Caballero against his teacher-critic and against the land workers who had been guilty of an "untimely" strike. I do not think so. Their work was entirely round the axis of the technical preparations for the coming insurrection; they were convinced that a strike in solidarity would lead to a premature confrontation, in which the armed force of the proletariat could not have been sufficiently prepared. The leaders of the Socialist Youth made the mistake of what we may call "military leftism" — though, it is true, this came in useful to cover up a profoundly opportunist policy[42].

40. Munis, op cit, pp120-122.
41. *Boletín UGT*, August 1934: summarised in Preston, op cit, pp197-198.
42. Juan-Simeón Vidarte speaks of the "rage" which Largo Caballero felt against Zabalza, the teacher from Navarre who led the strike (which he himself believed to be a pointless action), but emphasises nonetheless that it was supported by over 90% of the workers concerned. We can refer to the declarations of Santiago Carrillo in his meeting with the leaders of the Communist Youth (Viñas, op cit pp78-79); according to him, they should not "start off partial

Nonetheless, such as they were in this summer of 1934, with their absolute rejection of all class-collaboration, their refusal to form any lasting alliance with the bourgeois republican parties and their double condemnation of the Second and the Third Internationals, the Socialist Youth of Spain were one of the most advanced sectors which were emerging from European Social-Democracy in crisis. We can understand how Trotsky, who correctly understood that the organisation of the Socialist Youth was only expressing, to be sure in a deformed way, but none the less directly, the revolutionary aspirations of the working-class youth in Spain, came to take it upon himself to advise his comrades in the Communist Left in Spain to follow the French example and to enter the PSOE and especially the Socialist Youth. In other words, that he conceived of an operation which could, in the best case, have enabled the best elements of the Socialist Youth to be won for the Fourth International, and, in the worst, have inoculated the great majority of the latter against the virus of Stalinism, against which they incorrectly believed themselves to be immune.

The Socialist Youth in October and What Followed

There can be no question in this article of retracing the unfolding of the "October Revolution in Spain", from the struggle in the Asturias to the defeat in Catalonia, by way of the aborted insurrection in the other centres of the country, which demonstrated yet again the primacy of politics in the framework of proletarian military policy.

Trotsky had believed that a bold policy on the part of the Catalan revolutionaries in favour of the independent republic of Catalonia could have formed the first step in the proletarian revolution in the peninsula[43]. The timidity

---

battles, the immediate aim of which was not the taking of power". He explained: "The peasants have made a very great sacrifice to get very little, because, if they were to win their demands, the struggle would have had to have the taking of power as its main aim." The history of the workers' movement in the 20th century shows at least one more example in which the workers' leaders saw fit to restrain "partial struggles" in order to "preserve the forces intact" for "the Great Day" in preparation: it is that of the leaders of the German Communist Party in September 1923 in the course of preparing for an insurrection — also in October — which also came to nothing (cf Broué, *The German Revolution 1917-1923*, pp766-778.) Was not the underlying idea of the military policy of the Socialist Youth that they must fight "for" the masses, whose own movement was therefore not taken into account, even in the plans for insurrection? Therefore, the peasants were abandoned and, some weeks later, the officers who had undertaken to lead their troops into the streets having defected, the leader of the Socialist militias, del Rosal, came to explain to the leaders of the insurrection that "things were going badly, the troops from the barracks had not come down into the streets" (Alvarez del Valo, op cit, pp174-178). They had made the workers wait until then. They were still waiting. But from then on they had nothing to wait for but the repression that was to strike them.

43. This document is published in French in Léon Trotsky: *Oeuvres*, Vol 4, April 1934-December 1934, pp182-186. [The French-language text here is a translation from a somewhat indifferently translated English-language text, undated, which was found in the archives of the Communist League of America. It appears to have been a letter addressed to the International

and opportunism of the organisations which made up the Workers' Alliance in Catalonia at the time explain the defeat without a struggle of the Workers' Alliance at least as much as the abstention of the CNT, which remained outside the struggle. In the Asturias, the realisation of total workers unity with the adherence of the CNT to the Workers' Alliance and the adherence of the Communist Party at the last minute gave, on the contrary, an extraordinary energy to the workers' struggle.[44] The Asturias insurrection, in the words of Luis Araquistáin, "was the work of the working-class youth, an irresistible movement from below of a mass which did not mean to miss its battle against fascism... in which this working-class, which hitherto had rejected violence, demanded its baptism of fire as the beginning of a new historical period"[45].

In the rest of Spain the grand design of the Socialist Youth came to nothing: Manuel Tagüeña has left us the account of his wanderings at the head of his company. His men were mobilised on 4 October and told at 9 o'clock to move to a bar in the La Prosperidad quarter which they had difficulty in reaching .... because of the general strike: these armed men ran into patrols of assault guards or civil guards who did not ask them to account for themselves. Several companies found themselves in the same place without instructions. At midnight he took the initiative of occupying the Socialist club in the district and putting armed sentries outside it. Soon after, a messenger brought the order to move to Cuadros Caminos, where they would put on uniforms of civil guards, before attacking the barracks at Guindalera, where a Socialist guard would let them in: an order, as he wrote forty years later, which could not be carried out in a city with a general strike going on and in a state of war. Nonetheless, he was preparing to move when he was surprised by the arrival of a truck-load of assault guards; after a brief exchange of fire, the militiamen were completely surrounded, and surrendered.[46]

The analysis which Munis gives does not differ from the impression which we form from the story by Tagüeña; he writes that the workers were ready to fight and had sufficient arms to begin the insurrection. On the evening of 4 October, the streets were filled with crowds of strikers waiting for the slogans of

Secretariat, the contents of which enable it to be situated approximately between July and September.][Sentences in brackets added by John Archer.] The title in the *Oeuvres* is "Le Conflit catalan et les tâches du prolétariat": the article contains very striking formulations, including an extraordinary anticipation of 1936, the role of the central committee of the militias, etc.

44. We find in the AHN Madrid (Legato 721) a report from the civil governor of the Asturias, Fernando Blanco Santamaria, entitled, "Notes on my management"; it is the justification of a sacked man. He says there: "The enormous masses of workers who people the Asturias — not less than 120, 000 — all members of the organisations, the UGT, the PSOE, the Communist Party and the CNT, when they agreed to work together in what was called the 'Workers' Alliance", made this province a unique case of extreme danger in Spain".
45. L. Araquistáin, "La Revolución de Octubre en España", *Leviatán*, February 1936, p33.
46. Tagüeña, op cit, pp53-55. It seems that the events in which Tagüeña took part in the Prosperidad quarter are the same as Munis (op cit, p135) situated in the Guindalera, namely the essential of this failed insurrection in the capital.

"a peaceful strike". There were some exchanges of fire on 5 October and some lightning operations by commandos of Socialist militiamen against the Ministry of the Interior, the Telefónica Company and the Capitanía General. In the afternoon of the 5th several thousand workers tried on their own initiative to get possession of the barracks at Moncloa, but were driven back by the officers alone, for lack of weapons[47]...

However, the revolutionary spirit of the Spanish proletariat was such in these years that neither the inglorious defeat of the rising in Madrid and elsewhere, nor the crushing in a desperate battle of the Asturian miners interrupted their advance, quite the contrary. October 1934 was for the proletariat a defeat rich in promise. It proved that the strength of the proletariat lies in its unity, and that this unity required the workers' organisations to put an end to their divisions. In this sense, the Socialist Youth, who had made themselves among other things the defenders of the "Workers' Alliances" and supported them against the Communist Party could now claim for themselves what was effectively a political victory.

However the practical unfolding of the revolution brought them little satisfaction. The heroes of the Asturias insurrection were the traditionally moderate leaders of the Asturian miners, like Ramón González Peña[48]. The Socialist Youth had played no role in Catalonia, which was natural enough, because their implantation there was weak. But in the regions where the militants had taken charge of the preparations for the insurrection — in Madrid, where it was to be "commanded" by Amadeo del Rosal[49], but not only in Madrid — the insurrection had misfired in an often pitiable way. Moreover, part of its leadership had been arrested and imprisoned in the *Carcel modelo*, for instance, Carrillo, De Rosa, Del Rosal, Hernández Zancajo, without counting Largo Caballero himself. Others had taken refuge, like Serrano Foncela, in France, or, like José Laín, in the USSR.

The faction whose strengths and weaknesses in 1934 we have described was without doubt now threatened by the political counter-offensive of the right and the centre, taking advantage of the destabilisation provoked by repression which struck principally at the left. The representatives of the ruling classes were quite

---

47. Munis, op cit, pp134-139
48. Ramon González Peña (1889-1952, a working miner, had been in 1910 one of the founders of the Union of Miners in the Asturias (SMA), had been the leader in 1920 of the famous strike at Peñarroya and then organised the strikes in Rio Tinto. He was condemned to death for his role in 1934 and pardoned in 1935 after an international campaign. It was he who, when in prison, had launched the first attack on the Socialist Youth in an interview. He became president of the UGT in 1937 when Largo Caballero and his supporters were eliminated.
49. Amaro del Rosal Díaz (born in 1904) was a leader in the Socialist Youth, of the Federation of Bank Employees and a member of the Executive of the UGT. According Álvarez del Vayo, he was the principal leader of the socialist militias(op cit p175), and it was as such that he went to the apartment of the painter Quintanilla where the members of the revolutionary committee were hiding, to account to them for the failure of the undertaking. Munis (op cit, pp136-7) is particularly severe in his criticism of him, and Largo Caballero was not less so, according to certain unverified reports.

clear on this point. One high functionary, sent in March 1935 to the Asturias, wrote in his report:

> The young people in all the revolutionary organisations are united in a desire for subversion, and the leaders and senior figures in the CNT and the UGT are engaged in splits and tactical changes which ought to be taken into consideration and may produce excellent results.

Moreover, he added:

> The dangerous potential of the working class, it seems to us, should be combated very soon, by means of division.[50]

It is probably this delicate situation, which the leadership of the Socialist Youth — or that part of it which was imprisoned in the Carcel Modelo in Madrid — were taking into account. In fact they went over to the attack in public with a pamphlet entitled, *October: The Second Stage*. The second edition of it was signed by the president of the Federation, Carlos Hernández Zancajo, but it appears to be the work of Santiago Carrillo in collaboration with he fellow-prisoner Amaro del Rosal[51]. In a few pages, the authors sketched a history of their own fabrication: the revolution of 1917, defeated in Spain, victorious in Russia, a split which could evidently be explained by the enthusiasm for revolution of the Socialist Youth of the period but which was above all the responsibility of the Communist International of Lenin which imposed the "21 Conditions" on a Spanish Socialist Workers' Party which then quite legitimately refused to give up its independence and internal democracy, and which, alone on the extreme left of the Second International, pursued a revolutionary policy — including within the Azaña government in the first years of the Republic[52]...

---

50. This report, signed D. Vicente Santiago, dated 9 March 1935, is to be found in AHN Madrid, Legajo 721. We do not know whether it was addressed to the Minister of the Interior or to the head of the Government.
51. Marta Bizcarrondo (cf her introduction to *Octubre del 34*, p50) states definitely that Amaro del Rosa, in May 1976, declared to her that he was the author of 36 of the 98 pages of the pamphlet.
52. I have already touched on this question, in an article entitled "Santiago Carrillo, the USSR and History", which appeared in No. 9 of *Nueva Politica* in Mexico in 1979. This study dealt with the explanations which the Secretary-General of the Communist Party of Spain gave at that time of the history of the Communist movement since 1917, and, especially, with the "historic antecedents" of what he called "Eurocommunism". This examination of both the writings of the first years of his career and of those of what, no doubt, will be its last years reveals that, in this man who never hesitated to contradict himself or to deny that he contradicted himself, there exists at least one consistent element. This element is a colossal contempt for History, which, in fact, he manipulates in one presentation or another to suit his particular political needs at the moment: it is an element which we cannot call anything other than cynicism. It may seem difficult to claim, in 1935, to be a "Bolshevik" and, at the same time, to denounce the "Twenty-One Conditions". Yet at that same time he was, on the one hand, complaining about the "independence" of the parliamentary fraction of the PSOE and even of the absence of control over the party's press, while, on the other hand, he was saying that the party's policy

Then the Socialist Youth, who regarded themselves as the finest fruit of this revolutionary party, had just noticed, through October and their preparations for it, that they were under threat from within. They recalled the attitude of Besteiro and his friends of the "reformist" current in 1930 and their hostility to the revolutionary plans to bring down the monarchy. They recalled also their role at the head of the UGT from 1932 onwards when they opposed the policy advocated by Largo Caballero. The authors of *October* took pains to show how those whom they called "the chiefs and little chiefs" resisted the insurrectional line and at best ignored or most often sabotaged the directives. They wrote about the UGT, with its structures too rigid to meet the needs of the times, with its parliamentary group that spread confusion by defending in the Cortes its own policy in opposition to that of the Party — not to mention the local leaders, who had not lifted a finger in October, the "moderate Socialists", whom a Government circular said had to be humoured. They should all be unmasked, removed from their positions and eventually expelled. This purge, to which the Socialist Youth at the time applied a name with a really provocative implication, "Bolshevisation", was to be carried out from the bottom to the top, without weakness and especially without fear of a split, because the reformists had no real basis in the party — at least outside its apparatus.

But matters were not the same where the "centrists" or "middle of the road people" were concerned. The role which the leaders of this tendency, Indalecio Prieto and González Peña played before and during the insurrection is well-known, and won them a great increase in prestige. In the period which opened immediately after the October defeat, it is clear that "centrism" was preparing systematically to defend the reformists against the revolutionaries, in the name of "unity". Furthermore, it was to try to put forward, along with the perspective of new elections, the renewal of the alliance with the bourgeois republican parties, this "Popular Anti-Fascist Bloc" which had just found a place at the centre of the agitation of the Communist Party. On this point, the supporters of "Bolshevisation" were sharp and unambiguous:

> This slogan will find people to defend it in our party: the centrists. Every militant must be ready to prevent them from having their way. Centrism will try on this occasion to join battle against the revolutionary faction and to become the axis of the party. The fight will be hard. Our revolutionary capacity will be put to the test... We must disarm the

---

of collaborating with the regime of the dictator Primo de Rivera and its later policy of actually participating in the Azaña government from 1931 to 1933 were "revolutionary". He did, indeed, declare, on the one hand, that the PSOE was a revolutionary party, the only one in the Second International, and, at the same time, on the other hand, that it needed to be "Bolshevised". Let us note that in 1933-35 Carrillo permitted himself the liberty of criticising Lenin, but never mentioned Stalin. The common element between Carrillo in 1935 and Carrillo in 1978 is this: like every anti-Communist, he treats Bolshevism and Stalinism as the same. During the intervening years, he has been an authentic "Stalinist", in the sense in which Thorez used the term when he boasted of that "honour".

Communists who on this question agree with the right of the party, by showing that it is we, like real Bolsheviks, who issue the slogan of the Alliance of the Proletarians against the slogan of the Popular Anti-Fascist Bloc.[53]

The authors of *October* conducted a long and bitter polemic against the leaders of the Communist Parties, whom they called, like Trotsky, the "epigones", recalling their slanders and insults and their bitter struggle against the Workers' Alliances, which they were finally to join at the eleventh hour.

But they dwelt at perhaps still greater length on what they called "the second stage of Bolshevisation", by which they meant the question of the International.

"Our aim", they said, "is not only the Spanish revolution but the world revolution, the dictatorship of the proletariat in all countries."[54]

They proposed not only to break immediately from the International of Socialist Youth, but that the PSOE should break from the Second International, which they described as "a corpse". A first element of their response should, according to them, be to construct a new centre to regroup Socialist Youth internationally, which they could construct quickly with the Socialist Youth of France, the Socialist Young Guard of Belgium, the Italian and the Austrian youth.

The Fourth International — from which they had not been very far in 1933 — was now, on the contrary, "an unfortunate slogan". They regarded it as possessing no real base and therefore no possibility of development, precisely since the Third International had abandoned its sectarian policy which had led to the disaster in Germany. Moreover, they believed that Trotsky himself had "tacitly renounced" the slogan — apparently since he advocated the policy of "entrism" into Social-Democracy.

For all that, the Socialist Youth did not think it possible for the PSOE to join the Third International, although it had a fundamental programmatic agreement with it. In fact they were not only in total disagreement with its policy of a "Popular Anti-Fascist Bloc" in Spain and elsewhere, but, even more, with its constitution, which signified "the dictatorship of the Executive" and the

---

53. *Octubre*, according to Bizcarrondo, op cit, p126. Caballero and Prieto had been in agreement, it seems, during the period of preparation of the insurrection, when the latter agreed that it should be organised by the PSOE with the collaboration only of workers' formations. On the reasons advanced by the two tendencies later on, see Vidarte, op cit, p409, who summarises them as follows:

> We (i.e. Negrin, Prieto, etc.) had drawn the following conclusions from the October movement: it is impossible to conquer against an organised State and we must, therefore, create an electoral bloc in order to win back the Republic as the only road... The friends of Caballero drew other conclusions and very different ones: the Asturias had taught that the people could win, even against an army and all the organisation of the State". Of course, other factors were involved: the desertion of the officers with whom Prieto had organized connections, certain declarations by Prieto abroad, his criticisms of the imprisoned leaders' refusal to claim responsibility for the strike, a decision which had been reached earlier with the support of his vote, etc.

54. Ibid, p126.

strangling of all internal democratic life. To be sure, a development was certainly possible and desirable, and that would then permit the PSOE to join the Third International, since, as the authors of *October* stressed, "Russia is the first Socialist country, the Mecca of the proletariat, and in her and her alone can rest the centre of the world proletariat as long as the revolution has not conquered in other countries".[55] We may observe that the word "Stalinism", which occurred with some frequency in the articles of the writers in *Renovación* in 1933 and 1934, does not appear a single time in *October: the Second Stage*.

Moreover, it is not without interest to reproduce the conclusions of the brochure of the "Bolshevisers" of the Socialist Youth who were jailed in the Carcel Modelo, at the moment when in Moscow the general turn was being prepared towards the policy of the Popular Front, one of the first consequences — or, if you prefer it, one of the first aspects — was in France to be the support of French national defence advised by Stalin in his conversation with Pierre Laval[56] and the abandonment of anti-militarist work:

> For the Bolshevisation of the Socialist Party!
>
> For the transformation of the party structure in the direction of centralisation and with an illegal apparatus!
>
> For the political unification of the Spanish proletariat in the Socialist Party!
>
> For anti-militarist propaganda and the penetration of the State Forces!
>
> For the unification of the trade union movement!
>
> For the defeat of the bourgeoisie and the victory of the Revolution in the form of the dictatorship of the proletariat!
>
> For the reconstruction of the international workers' movement on the basis of the world revolution!
>
> To realise these slogans, the Socialist Youth must demonstrate their superiority and their spirit of sacrifice in order that the workers will entrust to them the responsibilities of leadership.
>
> The Federation of the Socialist Youth of Spain, today more united and stronger than ever, draws its inspiration, in issuing these slogans, from the revolutionary history of our country, from the best traditions of Russian Bolshevism and from the two great champions of classical socialism: Marx and Lenin.

---

55. Ibid.
56. Pierre Laval, the French Minister of Foreign Affairs, had been to Moscow to sign the Franco-Soviet non-aggression pact. He had met Stalin there and had declared to the press on 15 May 1935: "M. Stalin understands and fully approves the policy of national defence adopted by France to maintain its forces at the level needed for its security". The Communist Party, which until that time had been resolutely opposed to the very idea of "national defence", had covered Paris with posters headed "Stalin is Right".

The Socialist Youth regard Comrade Largo Caballero as the chief and inspiration of this revolutionary rebirth; today he is the victim of the reaction which sees in him its most determined enemy.[57]

The entire ambiguity of the Socialist Youth is to be found in this document: legitimate ambition alongside the manoeuvres of politicians, the pressures exerted by the masses alongside the concerns of men of the apparatus. Yet nothing was settled: the historic fate of the leadership and of the Socialist Youth of Spain was not yet sealed. The Trotskyist militant Enrique Fernández Sendón[58], who in September 1934 had moved at the Central Committee of the Communist Left of Spain a resolution, agreed unanimously, which haughtily rejected Trotsky's proposals of "entrism", now found himself imprisoned in the Carcel Modelo with the militants of the Socialist Youth and their leaders. Convinced by his daily contact with them, he became in turn a supporter of "entrism" and succeeded in convincing the majority of the Executive of the Communist Left, including Nin, that this solution should apply to the whole organisation with the exception of Catalonia, where the fusion with Maurín's Bloc and a number of small organisations was in hand. But, on the demand of the Madrid organisation, which saw in such a decision a *de facto* split, the question was submitted to a referendum, which rejected the solution of the Executive: in September the Communist Left of Spain dissolved itself into the POUM. There was to be no "entrism" in Spain.

None the less the developments of the following months would further strengthen the arguments of the supporters of "entrism". The centrists were counter-attacking. Prieto, who was in exile in Belgium, wrote in *El Liberal* in Bilbao and in *La Libertad* in Madrid at the end of May a series of articles in which he disputed the right of the Socialist Youth to express their views in public as they had, accusing them of both indiscipline in relation to the party and of "the cult of the leader" with regard to Largo Caballero.[59] The very journals which published these articles refused the right of reply to the prisoners in the Carcel Modelo: the leaders of the Socialist Youth could reply only thanks to the hospitality which the columns of *La Batalla*, Maurín's weekly organ in Barcelona, offered to them.

Once again Santiago Carrillo issued an appeal for help directed to the oppositional Communists in the Bloc and in the Communist Left, who were preparing to unite in a new organisation. He ended an article entitled "The Bolshevisation of the Socialist Party" on 28 June as follows:

---

57. *Octubre*, pp155-156.
58. Enrique Fernandez Sendón was a member of the Communist Left under the pseudonym of L. Fersen.
59. The most important of these articles, "Socialist Positions: My Right to an Opinion" (*El Liberal*, 22 May), "Socialist Positions: the Amnesty, the basis for the electoral coalition" (Ibid, 23 May), "Socialist Positions: The Value of Parliamentary Action" (Ibid, 24 May), "Socialist Positions: The Remorse of Defeat" (Ibid, 25 May), "Socialist Positions: The Exotic Plant of Caudillism" (ibid, 26 May), are reproduced in the anthology *Discursos Fundamentales*, pp228-254.

We have a correct theory and we have faith. But in order to win we need the support of every real Marxist. Without this support our efforts run the risk of being sterile. According to our classics, we must seek the masses where they are. And today they are in the Socialist Party, which has an unequalled history and capacity for struggle. You must come into our ranks to fight against those who, if we do not stop them, will lead these masses on the road to defeat. The gentlemanly revolutionaries who look down from on high at the way we work, instead of taking part in our tasks, these people are assuming a very heavy historical responsibility.[60]

Here we can feel the contradiction between the extent and the urgency of the task to be accomplished and the obstacles which were encountered by these leaders of the Socialist Youth, mostly in prison or in exile, or even reduced to semi-clandestinity. Maurín, who polemicised with Carrillo because the latter rejected the idea of a "unification" and called upon the "Marxists" to enter the PSOE in order to fight there, evidently did not understand that the stake in this battle between internal factions in the PSOE, which was going on in the full light of day, was quite simply the class independence of the Spanish proletariat expressed through the orientation of its principal political party. In another article in *La Batalla*, it was the task of Carlos Hernández Zancajo to demonstrate very clearly the connection between the accusations of Prieto directed at the Socialist Youth and his intention of imposing on the PSOE the policy of alliance with the republicans which Manuel Azaña, from his side, had taken up.[61] For this policy to succeed, two conditions were needed: the PSOE must "bury its arms" and, likewise, it must silence its Youth.

Towards the United Socialist Youth

It was the Communist Party which was to carry through, to its profit, the operation which the PSOE was striving to achieve, without success. The Socialist Youth were disarmed — by their inadequate political education and, in particular, their total ignorance of the history of Stalinism and their profound failure to understand the nature of Stalinism. Even more than Largo Caballero, but in precisely the same way, they were caught in the trap of the turn in the Communist International in 1935, which implied, for a whole period, the alliance between the Communist Party and the Socialist right wing, which the Socialist Youth claimed to be getting rid of by means of "Bolshevisation". Moreover, concretely, the powerful appeal to sentiment of the argument that there must be an amnesty for the 30,000 political prisoners of October 1934[62] was to ensure

60. Santiago Carrillo, "Habla el secretario de la Juventud socialista", *La Batalla*, 28 June 1935.
61. C. Hernández Zancajo, "En defensa de las Juventudes socialistas: Posiciónes socialistas", *La Batalla*, 12 July 1935.
62. Some examples taken at random in Legajo 2371 give an idea of the scope and severity of the repression, including the regions where one might feel that nothing happened. According to a

that every formation would accept, if only in a forced manner, the "Popular Anti-Fascist Bloc", of which Azaña was to be the standard-bearer; once more the workers' parties would be the auxiliaries and the working people the infantry.

The Socialist Youth alone, despite their principled position, were no doubt in no position to prevent this development, which Largo Caballero never thought of confronting head on. Nonetheless, opposition on their part, a split on this question, the split of the Left from the PSOE of which it had been the driving force, would have formed a terrible obstacle to the new policy of Stalin and the generalisation of the Popular Front. In any case the Communist International spared no effort to win the most important leaders of the Socialist Youth by one means or another. In this connection the small colony of socialist refugees in the USSR appears to have played an important role. It appears that Margarita Nelken had been won to the Communist Party[63], which she was to join officially later on. José Laín, the former leader of the socialist militias, a member of the leadership of the Socialist Youth, had taken refuge in the USSR. He was present at the Seventh Congress of the Communist International and then at the Congress of the Young Communist International. Thirty-five years later, Fernando Claudín, the former leader of the Communist Youth, was to write that the Seventh Congress gave a striking confirmation "of the way the national sections of the Comintern were totally subordinated to the policy of the Soviet state", and that the point of departure for the new, Popular Front policy was "a pragmatic response to the urgent requirements of Soviet foreign policy".[64] José Laín wrote, for the new weekly organ of the Largo Caballero Left, that the Seventh Congress had definitively responded to the hopes of the Socialist Youth by the transformation of the Communist International and its recognition of "national roads", and by opening the perspective of organic unity in every country[65].

---

letter from someone imprisoned at Pamplona, dated 17 August 1935, there were in that town 175 charged of whom 145 were imprisoned while the same correspondent tells of heavy penalties inflicted by the court at San Sebastian: two were condemned to 20 years, two to fourteen years, two to ten years, and seven acquittals after ten months of preventive detention.

63. AHN "Madrid", Legajo 2371 contains a significant exchange of letters between Indalecio Prieto, who was then in exile in Ostend, and a Socialist militant from Bilbao who had taken refuge in the USSR, Miguel Segurajauregui. In a letter dated August 23, the latter reports a violent incident which had just taken place between Virgilio Llanos and Margarita Nelken, when the latter boasted of having prevented Prieto from being invited to the USSR. Prieto replies on August 26 that he is not in any way surprised; his answer conveys that he believed that Margarita Nelken had already been won to the Communist Party and that she was playing the role of a "sleeper" in the PSOE. Margarita Nelken, who was elected a deputy in February 1936, formally joined the Communist Party in the December of the same year.

64. Fernando Claudín, *The Communist Movement from Comintern to Cominform*, London, 1975 Part One, pp187 and 182-3. Ricard Viñas, in a book which elsewhere is very interesting, refers on this point to the work of Fernando Claudín, and at the same time offers an analysis of the Seventh Congress of the Communist International about which the best one can say is that it is astonishing in its... candour; moreover it does not even take the trouble to refute the analysis of Claudín, to which it refers while it is the opposite of his own (op cit, pp39-43).

65. Cf the comments sent from Moscow on the Seventh Congress by José Laín, in *Claridad* of 17

The pressures to which the young leaders, and sometimes also old militants, were subjected in the USSR can be detected between the lines in the letters which they wrote from Moscow to the West or to Spain. While the letters in 1935 written in "Spanish" speak about the problems of Spain and the PSOE, those written in 1936 in jargon think only of celebrating "the socialist fatherland and its beacon" and make the attitude towards the USSR as a whole — Stalinism included — the touchstone of being a "revolutionary"[66].

Inside Spain the conditions of detention in the Carcel Modelo for the "politicals" were flexible enough to permit a similar rapprochement. The young Socialists and the political prisoners who supported Largo Caballero were the object of the attentions of the Communist Party. Its General Secretary, José Diaz, had just visited Largo Caballero to propose to him that their two parties take equal responsibility for the insurrection[67]. Codovilla, the representative of the Communist International in Spain,[68] could, we are told, count on the

August and of 12 and 19 October 1935.
66. José Laín and his comrades wrote on 2 February 1935 to Álvarez del Vayo — for Largo Caballero — that it was necessary at once to carry out a purge of the PSOE and to form the Workers' Alliance on a national scale. On March 1935, they took up these points again and insisted on the need for a campaign of trade union unification which would include the UGT, the CGTU and the CNT. The same file (AHN, "Madrid", Legajo 2371) includes two letters from the same group of Socialist refugees in the USSR, from Moscow and from Voroshilovgrad, dated January 1936, one of which speaks of "the leadership of the Bolshevik Party, which has made it the centre and shining light", while the other declares that "the revolution, the Soviet Union and the Bolshevik political line are indivisible". At this time there was no longer a Workers' Alliance, and the Communist Party, along with the Socialist right-wing, had imposed the Popular Front on the Republicans. But the letters of the "Bolshevisers" of yesterday merely sing the praises of the USSR and its leaders. We should likewise take note of someone who writes to Prieto in August 1935 to tell him about a stay by Dr. Juan Negrín in Moscow and the Crimea. An undated list, which may be from January 1936, gives the names of 36 Socialist refugees in the USSR, 14 of whom belonged only to the PSOE, 13 only to the Socialist Youth and 9 to both. The figure is confirmed by a letter from the USSR by Enrique de Francisco, a devoted follower of Largo Caballero, who states, in connection with the "Open Letter to Largo Caballero" — published in *Mundo Obrero* but not in *El Socialista* — which was signed with 28 names, that eight members of the Socialist colony had refused to sign it: this letter was a apology for the USSR in the most tedious Stalinist style.
67. D. Ibarruri, op cit, vol. I, p62. The Socialist leaders, including Largo Caballero, had denied before their judges the role which was imputed to them and refused to take the responsibility for the insurrection.
68. Vittorio Codovilla (1894-1970), was born in Italy. He was a leader of the Communist Party of Argentina and worked for the Communist International, especially in Spain, during the 1930s, under the name of Medina. On his visits to Carrillo in prison, see Viñas, op cit, p36, note 30, who mentions the evidence of Pere Ardiaca and Fernando Claudín. In fact, Carrillo has recorded it himself in *Demain L'Espagne*, pp43-46. He says: "Codovilla worked very well with me. I partly have him to thank for having become a Communist. But I had not yet had any contact with the leaders of the Party apart from Uribe [...] It was the International which, with the leaders of the Communist Youth, maintained direct relations with us." He mentions only one single visit by Codovilla in prison, but indicates that he had several discussions with him after leaving prison before he departed for the USSR. On his political "transition", he says: "We, like many young people, were 'leftists'. Our visit to the Soviet Union marked a decisive turn in our orientation".

unconditional support of Araquistáin's brother-in-law, Julio Álvarez del Vayo, a member of the entourage of Largo Caballero. Codovilla was to visit Santiago Carrillo in the Carcel Modelo and have a long political discussion with him. Was it really Jacques Duclos, the leader of the French Communist Party, as people assert, who convinced Largo Caballero not to oppose the "electoral bloc of the Left" which prefigured the Popular Front — a new version, barely varnished over, of the policy of collaboration which Prieto advocated and which the old "Lenin of Spain" had wanted to reject for ever? In a book which he wrote in Paris and which the POUM published in Barcelona, *El Partido Socialista y la Conquista del Poder*,[The Socialist Party and the Conquest of Power] S Serrano Poncela, a member of the secretariat of the Socialist Youth, showed that he saw in the turn of the Communist International most of what José Laín saw in it in Moscow, but not what Araquistáin had guessed in Madrid[69].

Finally Andrés Nin was quite right to judge the attitude of the left socialists totally "incongruous" with regard to the Seventh Congress of the Comintern, of which they approved and even celebrated its results boasting of democratisation which was entirely imaginary without apparently understanding that it had revived for reasons relating to the foreign policy of the USSR, the policy of class collaboration which they had fought for years and which was that of their unshakeable adversaries on the right wing of the PSOE.[70]

But perhaps we should look elsewhere than in political analysis for the reasons for an incongruous attitude which ignorance alone cannot explain. To begin with, it is clear that the imprisonment of Largo Caballero and the exile or imprisonment of a number of his supporters enabled Prieto and his political friends to win back some of the ground which they had lost, and that the "Bolshevisation" project of the Socialist Youth appeared quite unrealistic to the extent that it became clear that the policy of Prieto was going to coincide more and more with that of the Communist Party, which was more than ever in pursuit of a "Popular Anti-Fascist Bloc". In any case, for the leaders of the Socialist Youth, the reasons which they advanced were what they believed to be a new element in the problem: according to them, the Seventh Congress of the Communist International opened the prospect of organic unity enabling the historic split in the workers' movement since the beginning of the 1920s to be

---

69. S. Serrano Poncela thought that the Communist International could accept the "Left Socialists" without immediately changing its constitution because its new policy corresponded to their aspirations: Araquistáin believed, for his part, that the Congress had increased the freedom of the national Communist Parties and lessened the centralisation of the Communist International: nonetheless he believed that the new policy was inspired by the immediate interests of the USSR.

70. Cf Andrés Nin, "El Congreso de la Internacional comunista y las socialistas de izquierda. Una incongruencia", in *La Batalla*, 30 August 1935. Nin analysed the policy of the Left Socialists as positive and progressive and the Stalinist turn as a considerable retreat and a turn to the right. He asked how the Left Socialists could envisage organic unity with the Communist Parties which were precisely in the process of accepting the positions of their "reformist" and "centrist" adversaries in the PSOE. The analysis was excellent, but there were no proposals which could have assisted in clarification.

overcome in a positive way. On this point, Santiago Carrillo wrote in October 1935:

> Our ambition cannot be limited to occasional unification in the struggle. We must go further. We must advance towards organic unity, towards reuniting the Marxist proletariat in one party and one youth movement. We must recognise with pleasure that we have made giant strides in this during the last few months... In our country, this unity must take place within the old, the glorious Socialist Party. Because it has the strength, because it has the quality, because it has the prestige... The fusion of the Marxist workers on the national scale under our banners is necessary. On the international ground, where then we shall all decide freely and democratically. On this point, I have my criterion. It is in Russia that the basis of the world unification is situated, as long as the working class has not trodden down bourgeois institutions and begun to construct socialism in other countries.[71]

Carrillo could speak out loud. The Congress of the Socialist Youth which met at Ruzafa on 1 September had approved by an overwhelming majority the perspective of fusion for the organic unity of the Youth and had endorsed the pamphlet *October*. The new element was what he called his "personal criterion". Already in Paris Serrano Poncela had written that the constitution of the Communist International should not be an obstacle to a union between socialists of the left and the Third International. Marta Bizcarrondo notes very rightly in this connection that "The Russian Revolution and the USSR played from that time onwards a mythical role which was absent from *October*".[72]

In September the Congress of the Young Communist Internationale was held in the wake of the Seventh Congress of the Communist International. José Laín was, of course, present. The Congress came out in favour of organic unity with a view to forming a very broad youth organisation, "an organisation of the masses of non-party youth", according to the official formula. The majority of the leadership of the Socialist Youth in Spain were won to this proposal, but on the condition that the unification should be carried out by the entry of the Communist Youth into their ranks. In parallel the return of the CGTU, the trade union centre controlled by the Communist Party of Spain, into the ranks of the UGT was prepared. On 6 December 1935, Santiago Carrillo hailed "the forced march towards organic unity": the Third International at last had "come round":

> We cannot lose sight of the fact that this turn, this return to the postulates of Marxism by way of the corrections of the Third International places us now on the same political plane as the Communists... We cannot hesitate to define our position. We have

71. "Unidad de acción y unidad orgánica", *Asturias*, 25 October 1935.
72. M. Bizcarrondo, op cit, p62.

organic unity; we want it and we shall have it by forced marches, because we also are communists like Marx, Engels and Lenin, because the Chinese walls which separated us from the Communist International have crumbled and because we are going to achieve their final destruction by extirpating the bureaucratic and petty bourgeois residues which cemented them.[73]

Was the die cast? Had the "personal criterion" which Carrillo mentioned in September definitively carried the day in the Socialist Youth? Doubtless not yet. The discussion was lively, even in the leadership, and critical opponents were going to express themselves in public. Serrano Poncela, for example, returned from exile, was to attack the proposals of the Young Communist International's Congress with some vigour:

> Fusion of the Socialist Youth and the Communist Youth into one body which puts its strength at the service of socialism, but which is structured in such a fashion that other organisations, which are not yet in the service of the working class, can be absorbed into it... that it fights for democracy and against fascism, but at the same time for workers' power, which is eminently anti-democratic. A Youth movement without a party, without a programme, without concrete objectives... It is correct for the working-class to form a ring of iron round the Soviet Union, undertake the struggle against its enemies, but there is no basis in a materialist interpretation of history for these enormous efforts to make the entire international workers' movement rotate around the defence of the USSR, however important that may be... In my opinion, the Congress, the International and its youth appendage have responded in the first place to the defence of the Soviet Union and only in the second place to the interests of the proletariat of countries other than the fatherland of socialism. This means that Russia is doing what is right for it when it creates in the West democratic and petty bourgeois alliances instead of working-class alliances, account being taken of the threat of the front from Central Europe to Japan, but the national working class also is doing what is right for it when it does its best to defend the sacred interests of the land of socialism without harming its own sacred national interests.[74]

---

73. "Hacia la unidad orgánica a marchas rapidas", *Claridad*, 7 December 1935.
74. *Rebelión*, 11 January 1936. *Rebelión* was the organ of the Socialist Youth in Elda. The article is reproduced in Viñas, op cit, pp140-143. Serrano Poncela, who was director of the daily paper *Ahora* during the civil war, taught in American universities after the war. In fact at this time there was a tendency forming in the Socialist Youth which was again raising the banner of "leftism", with José Bullejos, Luis P. García Lago (a former supporter of the Fourth International in 1934), Grigorio López Raimundo, who later became the underground chief of the Communist Party of Spain.

The struggle was becoming more poisonous within the PSOE between the partisans of Largo Caballero and those of Prieto, particularly with the resignation on 15 December 1935 of Largo Caballero from the presidency and the Executive of the party and the campaign for a congress which would give the party a homogeneous leadership. In this context the orientation of the Socialist Youth towards "organic unity" with the Communist Youth in fact diverted them from the internal struggle in the PSOE and gave solid arguments to their adversaries.[75]

Shortly after he was released from prison, at the beginning of March, Santiago Carrillo went for a week to the USSR with Trifón Medrano in a joint delegation intended to settle with the Young Communist International the final details of the joint text entitled "Bases of Unification".[76]

The "unification meeting" — in anticipation of a congress which was planned but never took place because of the civil war — was to take place in Madrid, Plaza de Las Ventas, on Sunday 5 April 1936, under the effective chairmanship of Largo Caballero, of whom it is known that he had expressed in private strong reservations about the unification of the Youth organisations and in any case had totally rejected a break by the PSOE with the Second International, though he was no less on the line of "organic unity". The new organisation — which was called in a slightly improper way the Unified Socialist Youth — seems, on good evidence, to have had much greater material resources than hitherto, which cannot be explained simply by the fact that its membership quickly doubled.[77] The first issue of its weekly, *Juventud*, in a new and very

---

75. On the reasons, which continue to be hotly debated, for this resignation, see Preston, op cit, pp237-239 and Santos Julía, pp81-86. Largo Caballero had resigned a first time on 1 October, but then withdrew his resignation. On 16 December, he confirmed it. The pretext was a technical one, but it appears that he did not want to go on sharing power in the Executive and thought that a congress would give him the homogeneous leadership which he needed. Did the masses support Largo Caballero as he believed? It is probable. But the apparatus was for Prieto. The Socialist Youth — were they still advocates of the "Bolshevisation" which implied that they must remain within the PSOE? This is doubtful. Certain elements displayed tendencies to split away, and Paul Preston sees them as being behind the attack on Prieto at Ecija, which at the time would have been a kind of provocation to split.
76. The secretary of the party, Juan-Simeón Vidarte, in *Todos fuimos culpables*, vol. I, p58, says that at the end of 1935 Jacques Duclos had visited Hernández Zancajo in prison and made advances to him to join the Communist Party, mentioning a visit to the USSR as soon as he was released. Hernández was indignant. This is the reason why, in March 1936 and even though he was President of the Socialist Youth, he refused the invitation and was then replaced by Federico Melchor, who went with Carrillo to Moscow.
77. Viñas, op cit, p61. Curiously, the author does not ask himself the question why the material means at the disposal of the United Socialist Youth were immediately — as he remarks — infinitely superior to those of the Socialist Youth before: he contents himself with noting that the Socialist Youth were "boycotted" by the press of the PSOE, *Claridad* apart. We can understand the legitimate concern of Ricard Viñas not to explain the rallying of the Socialist Youth leaders to Stalinism in terms of "shady manoeuvres", political treachery, disloyalty, corruption, etc., but his lack of curiosity on this central question is astonishing. It seems likely that the United Socialist Youth, the most precious means of Stalinist penetration in Spain, received substantial material help from Moscow.

unpolitical style, abundantly illustrated, had a print-run of 100,000 copies. The history of the Socialist Youth was ended. The history of the Unified Socialist Youth had begun. It was not only a new chapter; it was a new book.

By way of a Conclusion

Was the Unified Young Socialists already won to the Stalinist policy when it came into existence? All the evidence suggests that Trotsky thought so — or estimated that, at least, the men of the Communist International believed that they controlled the leadership, which implied that a certain number at least of the old leaders of the Socialist Youth had secretly joined them. The official version of the history of the Communist Party of Spain would have us believe that Carrillo and the other leaders of the JSU came and asked to enter the Communist Party en bloc at the most dramatic moment of the siege of Madrid, at the time of the departure of the Largo Caballero government for Valencia and of the formation of the Junta for Defence of Madrid: this is the date which fits in best with the explanation that the valiant fighters of the JSU joined the most courageous and far-seeing formation of fighters. In fact, we know that Santiago Carrillo, months before, was already taking part in the work of the Central Committee of the Communist Party[78]. And a speech delivered on the day before the unification meeting by the general secretary of the Socialist Youth warned his members against internal criticisms voiced by the "Trotskyists", which, at the time of the first Moscow Trial, presented his true visiting-card and displayed his political colour[79].

The history of the JSU still remains to be written. Manuel Tagüeña, who went back to the Communist Party with his comrades, points to the powerful tension which existed at the national level in the leadership, between Carrillo and Cazorlá on one side and Laín, Melchor and Fernando De Rosa on the other. The political career of Santiago Carrillo in the apparatus of the Communist Party of Spain is well known. Many of the other leaders of the 1934-1936 period were all pushed more or less rapidly to the side-lines[80]. In 1937, when, with Largo

78. P Preston, op cit, p308, gives several references to Carrillo's participation, as someone invited. What was Carrillo's real status at this time? JS Vidarte (op cit, pp58-59) writes that Carrillo "began to work for fusion" as soon as he returned from the USSR. This is obviously false: Carrillo was working for the organic unity of the youth organisations for months before. What is true, and what Carrillo confirms in his *Demain l'Espagne*, p45, is that he decisively finished his balancing act while he was staying in Moscow at the beginning of 1936. Vidarte, (op cit, 595) says that the leaders of the Socialist Youth, which had become the United Socialist Youth, had already by that period "become Communists and faithful servants of Moscow".
79. *Mundo Obrero*, 1 May 1936. Santiago Carrillo had professed great admiration for Trotsky in the past, but he was no longer ignorant of what it meant in the USSR to be called a "Trotskyist".
80. Tagüeña, op cit, p90 indicates the existence of these rivalries at the top He makes clear, moreover, (p98), that after the death of Trifón Medrano, the former leader of the Communist Youth, Carrillo took the leadership with no competition, closely followed by Claudín. Among the leaders of the former Socialist Youth, the "marginalisation" of whom he mentions, let us quote the cases of José Cazorlá (after his brief passage as deputy to Carrillo in charge of public order in the Madrid Junta), José Laín (who was first director of the training of commissars and

Caballero had been eliminated thanks to Carrillo's efforts, the coalition of moderate socialists and Stalinists which gathered round the Negrín Government undertook to liquidate the positions of Caballero's supporters, especially in the press and in the UGT, a resistance formed itself in the JSU. Its spokesman was the former president Carlos Hernández Zancajo, and he grouped round himself a certain number of provincial leaders who refused to go to the Communist Party, such as José Grigorí, Juan Tundidor López, from Valencia, and Rafael Fernández from the federation of the Asturias. In reality, one last stand by Largo Caballero's supporters demonstrated their personal loyalty to the old leader who all now rejected and expressed their refusal of being Stalinised under the banner of anti-fascism. No doubt this opposition was not as dangerous as the leaders of the Communist Party themselves seem to have believed.[81]

These were in reality the last twitches of a current which was finally worn down by capture and which formed the "mass basis" of the Spanish Communist Party. What a master stroke this capture was, the possibility of which was not evident at the outset. Can we believe — as Trotsky was convinced — that the fate of the Socialist Youth would have been different if in 1934 and still more in 1935 the militants of the Communist Left had taken the step which Trotsky suggested to them? Personally, at the end of this study I believe that it would. The contradictions, the oscillations and the uncertainties which the Carrillo current displayed were never in fact subjected to the fire of serious internal criticism or the test of coherent contradiction — which would have been the case if the Trotskyists had entered and which was purely a matter of their

> then a civil governor) and Federico Melchor. Serrano Poncela remained a journalist in the leadership of the daily *Ahora*. Tagüeña himself was the only important military chief to emerge from the ranks of the Socialist Youth. On the other hand, we find several of them in the police services, the lawyer Ordoñez and especially Santiago Garcés, who was the head of the Servicio de Investigación Militar (SIM), who was reputed to be linked to the Soviet secret services. He took refuge in Mexico, where he was investigated after the attempt on Trotsky's life on 24 May 1940, but was later held not to have been involved. Tagüeña does not lay any emphasis on the role of the former members of the Socialist Youth in the repression against the other workers' organisations. Sometimes his personal animosity against Carrillo warps his judgement: for example, it is not true that all the other leaders of the Socialist Youth were "marginalised". José Cazorlá, the deputy Delegate and later the Delegate for Public Order in the Madrid Junta, held a post of confidence: he joined the Central Committee in 1937. We know that he was unable to leave Madrid in 1939 and there he led for some time under illegal conditions a "delegation" of the Central Committee, which left him no hope when he was arrested and sentenced to death. Moreover, at the time when Tagüeña was finishing his memoirs, Federico Melchor Fernández, the former admirer of Trotsky who had become one of the specialists in denouncing Trotskyists, was still a member of the secretariat of the Communist Party of Spain. Segundo Serrano Poncela distanced himself. One case of a "fall" is certain: it is that of José Laín, who took refuge a second time in the USSR and there became .... a primary school teacher. He was to return to Spain during the life-time of Franco.

81. In AHN "Madrid", Legajo 2371, there is a report by Manuel Delicado, in the name of the Central Committee, delivered to the members of the cells of the collaborators with the Central Committee on 1 September 1937, in which he states: "The supporters of Caballero and the Trotskyists, the malcontents and the capitulators... could succeed in putting together a bloc, which would create a difficult situation."

choice. It seems to me especially that the companions of Carrillo displayed, in relation to the history of the Soviet Union and of Stalinism itself, a lack of comprehension and of knowledge so profound that we may rightly suppose that they would never have offered any insuperable barrier to the analyses of the Trotskyists.

It is of course useless to imagine what could have happened but did not happen. Therefore we have to content ourselves with observing that as early as 1934 the leaders of the Communist Left had given up on the Socialist Youth, the leaders of which they regarded as perfect little bureaucrats, who had very quickly learned in the closed circle of the organisation how to manoeuvre like politicians, how to lie and even to slander. They were convinced — correctly — that the "radicalisation" of Largo Caballero came above all from the realm of talk and threats, but did they not understand how powerful would be the pressure with which the working-class base responded to this "verbal revolutionism"? Did they not know that, in order to construct a party which "wants and is able to make the revolution", as Esteban Bilbao wrote in 1934, it was necessary to be able to go and seek, where they were, the elements who, in tens of thousands, were allowing themselves to be misled by a Socialist Party capable only of "brandishing threats".[82]

This is what Trotsky, in any case, criticised especially in his Spanish comrades; they observed and commented, without intervening, and in this way allowed this considerable, generous, devoted militant force, which was ready for every sacrifice, to fall in the end into the hands of Stalin and of the fresh young Stalinists as the instrument which betrayed the Spanish revolution in the name of "the defence of democracy", which, precisely they had rejected at the outset as a deception!

Juan Andrade, who was an opponent of "entrism", wrote about the Socialist Youth that they were "a confusionist Jacobin current", and that its propaganda was nothing but "shouts and phrases", but that it had "extraordinary importance" as arousing an echo among the youth. He agrees that he does not know why the leaders of the Socialist Youth limited themselves to the fusing of the youth organisations. But likewise he stresses that the Socialist Youth contributed to the Communist Party "the great complementary force which it lacked" and that this aid was fundamental. Finally, he mentions that it was the former militants of the Socialist Youth "more than the old Communists, who were to lead the repression against the other working class tendencies". He observes: "The phenomenon of the conversion of these young Socialists, their

---

82. Estaban Bilbao, "Algunas consideraciones ante la situación", *Comunismo*, April 1934, p168. Estaban Bilbao Urruza (1896-1954), was a member of the Socialist Youth in 1913, one of the founders of the Communist Party in Bilbao in 1920 and was excluded in 1929. He organised the Left Opposition in Bilbao and in Astillero. He had been the first to advocate "entrism" in the Socialist Party and the Socialist Youth. He himself entered the PSOE but remained isolated there. During the Civil War he joined the GBL of Munis. He died in exile in France.

activity and their conduct during the civil war, would be worthwhile studying thoroughly from every point of view."[83]

This article has no other ambition than to stimulate a reply to his appeal by opening a discussion.

---

83. Juan Andrade, *Apuntes para la Historia del PCE*, pp72-74. This is essentially the summary of a lecture delivered in Paris on 25 May 1966. Juan Andrade Rodríguez (1898-1981), was a Socialist in 1916 and in 1919-20 was one of the organisers of the Spanish Communist Party, a member of its Executive and the editor of its weekly journal, *El Comunista*. He was one of the principal leaders of the Communist Party of Spain and was expelled in 1928. He then became one of the leaders of the Left Opposition and then of the Communist Left, and a member of the Central Committee of the POUM when it was founded. He was arrested in June 1937 and sentenced to 15 years in jail in 1938 at the time of the POUM trial. He escaped in 1939, got to France and was sentenced in 1941 by a military tribunal to five years' imprisonment, but was liberated by Spanish members of the Resistance. After a long exile in Paris, he went back to Madrid in 1980 and died there on 1 May 1981.

Kurt Landau
Also known as Agricola, Wolf Bertram, and Spectator

Born on 29 January 1903 in Vienna (Austria); disappeared in Barcelona (Spain), September 1937. Member of the Austrian Communist Party, then of various Left Opposition groups in Vienna, Berlin and Paris. Member of the POUM in 1936.

THE son of a prosperous Viennese wine merchant, Kurt Landau had a Bohemian student youth similar to that of many young people from the Jewish intelligentsia in the imperial capitals: but it is also said that he attempted various circus jobs and for a time was a lion tamer at the Hagenbeck Circus. In 1921 this educated and cultured adolescent joined the new-born Austrian Communist Party, already shaken by fierce factional struggles and in 1922 became leader (*Leiter*) of the Warring district (*Bezirk*) in Vienna. Early in 1923 he supported the left-wing criticisms made by the Italian Bordiga[1] of the new line of the International, which was described as "opportunist". In 1924, still in Vienna, he made the acquaintance of Victor Serge, who was part of a group of Comintern emissaries and who worked on its press bulletin *Inprekorr*.[2] It seems that Serge gave him the first solid items of information about the factional struggle in the USSR. The same year Landau took charge of the CP agit-prop department and became an editor of its main publication, *Die Rote Fahne* (Red Flag), with responsibility for cultural matters. In the discussion on culture he adopted the arguments developed by Trotsky against "proletarian culture".

Originally he kept aloof from the struggle between the two rival oppositions of Josef Frey and Karl Tomann, but he moved closer to them after their unification in September 1925. In March 1926 he joined this "united opposition" which he seems to have considered as the Austrian equivalent of the Russian United Opposition.[3] Expelled along with most of his comrades in late 1926, he was, in early 1927, one of the founders of the Kommunistische

---

1. Amadeo Bordiga (1889-1970): Italian left Socialist, opposed World War I, supported Third International, but within Italian Communist Party was totally opposed to parliamentary participation; expelled 1930, but remained active with his own current until his death.
2. *International Press Correspondence* was the weekly organ of the Communist International, published in Germany in several languages, including English.
3. The alliance formed in 1926 between Trotsky, Zinoviev and Kamenev.

Partei Oesterreichs-Opposition (KPÖ-O — Austrian Communist Party Opposition), led by Frey, which published *Arbeiterstimme* (Workers' Voice). Originally he supported the view that the KPÖ-O should not work for the reform of the Austrian CP, but should itself aim to become the real Austrian Communist Party. However, the KPÖ-O continued to reproduce the fierce internal factional struggles of the Austrian Communist Party with its regroupments, its shifts of alliance and its bitter personal conflicts. Following a heated theoretical debate with Frey, Landau and some of those close to him were expelled from the KPÖ-O in April 1928 for an "ultraleft deviation" (according to the historian W Wagner,[4] this involved sympathy for the ideas of Karl Korsch[5]). He then founded a rival organisation, the Kommunistische Opposition-Marxistisch-Leninistische Linke (Communist Opposition, Marxist-Leninist Left), whose support was based in the city of Graz, and he began to issue his own publication, *Klassenkampf* (Class Struggle), then *Der Neue Mahnruf* (The New Warning Cry).The conflict between Landau and Frey then reached new heights of invective and personal accusations. He met Rosmer at the station when he visited Vienna in July 1929, and made the best impression on him.[6] Trotsky and Rosmer considered transferring him to Paris to support Rosmer in international work. Landau, in an article which was reproduced notably in the publication of the Leninbund,[7] *Die Fahne des Kommunismus* [The Flag of Communism], and then in *Contre le Courant* [Against the Stream],[8] supported Trotsky's position against Urbahns[9] and Maurice Paz.[10] This marked the beginning of a correspondence with the exiled Russian. Impressed by the talent and clarity of expression of this young militant — Landau was only twenty-six — and anxious to get him away from the overheated factional culture in Vienna and make full use of him in work appropriate to his abilities and of enormous importance, Trotsky had no difficulty in persuading him to go and settle in

4. The reference is to Winfried Wagner's thesis on *Trotskyism in Austria*, Salzburg, 1976.
5. Karl Korsch (1886-1961): Joined German Independent Socialist Party 1917, German Communist Party 1920; Minister of Justice in Thuringia in 1923; expelled from Communist Party 1926 as ultra-left; emigrated and settled in USA; now best known for philosophical writings.
6. Alfred Rosmer (1877-1964): Revolutionary syndicalist, opposed World War I, active in Comintern and Red International of Labour Unions; expelled from French CP 1924; 1929-31 organiser of Left Opposition, but broke with Trotsky. For Rosmer's account of the meeting see *Revolutionary History*, Vol. 7, No. 4, pp119-122.
7. Leninbund (Lenin League): Formed 1928 by expelled left-wing members of the German CP; sympathetic to Trotsky's positions; included prominent former CP members such as Maslow, Fischer and Urbahns.
8. Journal in support of Russian Opposition launched by Maurice Paz in 1927, but ceased publication in 1929 when Trotsky ended his collaboration with it.
9. Hugo Urbahns (1890-1947): Joined Spartacus League 1918, became leading figure in German CP; expelled as leftist in 1926, became a leader of Leninbund; developed view that Russia was state capitalist; emigrated to Sweden in 1933.
10. Maurice Paz (1896-1985): Lawyer, member of Communist Party from 1920; in 1927 launched *Contre le courant* in support of Russian Opposition; expelled from CP; Trotsky ended cooperation with him in 1929; joined Socialist Party 1931; withdrew from political activity for health reasons after 1940.

Berlin with his partner (Katia Lipshutz had been living with him since 1923). Trotsky took responsibility for meeting his material needs out of the money he received for copyright in Germany.

Contact with the militants of the Leninbund sympathetic to Trotsky proved very difficult. Landau presented himself as a "representative of the Russian Opposition" — that is, of Trotsky — and seemed unwilling to allow any discussion. Seeing that the Leninbund did not offer him favourable ground, he turned to the small Berlin group known as the "Wedding Opposition", which had been in contact with the Russian Opposition for a long time, and which was at this time led by the young Hans Schwalbach[11]; he was thus able to have his own political force at his disposal. It seems that Trotsky was not able to keep him to a path which no longer meant winning over the Leninbund, but rather splitting it; nor could he improve his relations with the German nucleus of veterans who made up the "Leninbund minority". After the expulsion of the latter group, he came under renewed pressure from Trotsky and from the insistence of visitors to Constantinople, Pierre Naville[12] and Max Shachtman,[13] to commit himself to progress towards unification; this was concluded on 30 March 1930 by the formation of the Vereinigte Linke Opposition (United Left Opposition — VLO) in the KPD (German Communist Party) Bolshevik Leninists, the German section of the International Opposition which was being built. As a member of the Executive of the VLO from its creation, and editor-in-chief of its publication *Der Kommunist* (The Communist), and elected a member of the International Bureau a few days later, Landau seemed destined to become one of the main international leaders of the Left Opposition — in fact he was only passing through. To begin with there was his unconditional support for his Austrian comrades in *Der neue Mahnruf* in their factional struggles and the excessive accusations made in support of their cause, and the political conflict with the Leipzig organisation of the VLO, being manipulated at this time by Stalin's agent Ruvin Sobolevicius, who was using the pseudonym of Sobolev or Roman Well. Moreover his pursuit of international alliances was dubious in Trotsky's eyes, and finally his own policy of removals from office, expulsions and forcible takeovers within his own organisation made a split inevitable. Landau's opponents described him as a "psychopath" and insisted that no cooperation with him was possible because of his "methods". The split was finalised on 31 May 1931, following the visit of Pierre Frank.[14] Kurt Landau

11. Hans (Johann) Schwalbach (1905-1994): German Trotskyist.
12. Pierre Naville (1904-1993): Surrealist; joined French Communist Party 1926; met Trotsky in Russia in 1927; expelled from CP 1928; pioneer French Trotskyist; organised founding conference of Fourth International in 1938; withdrew from Trotskyist movement in 1939, but wrote copiously on Marxist theory; leading member of PSU in 1960s.
13. Max Shachtman (1904-1972): Leading US Trotskyist from 1928; in 1940 split with Trotsky, rejecting defence of Soviet Union; founded Workers' Party; later moved to right.
14. Pierre Frank (1905-1984): Joined Communist Party 1925, Trotskyist from 1929; founder member of Ligue Communiste; secretary to Trotsky 1932-33; in 1935 he and Molinier launched *La Commune*, leading to dispute with Trotsky; after World War II leading figure in Fourth International and French section.

then kept control of *Der Kommunist*, and transformed the faction of the organisation which he had kept under his control into the Linke Opposition der KPD/Bolshewiki-Leninisten (Left Opposition of the German CP/Bolshevik-Leninists). Its sole basis seems to have been a shared hostility to Trotsky's "methods". Landau, who still had good relations with Rosmer, was also in contact with the Gauche communiste (Communist Left) of Claude Naville[15] and Michel Collinet,[16] and, it appears, with the Izquierda comunista (Communist Left) of Andrés Nin.[17]

The organisation led by Landau — at most three hundred members — continued clandestine activity in German until spring 1934 when it was destroyed by Gestapo infiltration and the arrest of militants. Kurt Landau had emigrated to Paris in March 1933 with Katia. He pioneered the denunciation of Trotsky's "betrayals" and "capitulations": this was how he described the latter's orientation in 1933 towards "a new communist party" in Germany, then towards "a new international", and subsequently his policy from 1934 onwards of "entrism" in the Socialist Parties and the "French turn". From May 1933, he had printed in Vienna and published in Paris *Der Funke* [The Spark], organ of the Marxist-Internationalists, of which he was the main and often the sole member of the editorial team. But this paper was to be killed off in Austria in 1934. Henceforth Landau was reduced, in the words of Hans Schafranek,[18] to "circle work", and duplicated publications. Shortly after his arrival he had grouped around him a certain number of oppositional members of the Communist Party [PCF] who were in process of breaking with Trotsky, and he began to orient himself towards work inside the PCF. He considered that the Left Opposition had been destroyed by "Trotsky's liquidationist current", but insisted that it had "laid the ideological foundation for the oppositional tendencies of the future"; for him now the only perspective was "the struggle to win over politically the Stalinised vanguard of the proletariat" through the building of a clandestine "internal faction" capable of giving life to "spontaneous oppositional tendencies" within the PCF. On the basis of this line he made contact and merged with the small internal opposition group in the PCF led at this time by André Ferrat,[19] a member of the Political Bureau, and the Pole Georges

15. Claude Naville (1908-1935): Brother of Pierre Naville, Communist from 1926, Trotskyist from 1929; broke with Ligue communiste in 1931 and formed Gauche communiste.
16. Michel Collinet (1904-1977): Developed towards Trotskyism in late 1920s; founder-member of Ligue communiste in 1930; opposed to Frank-Molinier leadership; split in 1931 to form Gauche communiste; in 1935 joined Revolutionary Left of Socialist Party; became member of POUM and published POUM's French journal; after World War II wrote a number of books on socialist theory.
17. Andrés Nin (1892-1937): Supporter of Left Opposition; returned to Spain 1931, formed the Communist Left, which in 1935 merged with the Workers and Peasants Bloc to establish the POUM (Workers Party of Marxist Unification); kidnapped, and murdered on Russian orders.
18. Hans Schafranek (born 1951): Austrian historian; biographer of Landau — see *Revolutionary History*, Vol. 4, Nos. 1/2, pp54-72.
19. André Ferrat, pseudonym of André Morel (1902-1988): Joined French Communist Party 1921; member of Political Bureau 1928-36, but expelled 1936; became open member of *Que faire?*; active in Resistance, leading member of Socialist Party after Liberation.

Kagan/Lucien Constant[20] who was in charge of agit-prop. From 1935 Landau became one of the members of the nucleus and of the editorial team of the journal *Que Faire?* (What is to be Done?) published by the group in question, in which also participated the former oppositionists Pierre Rimbert[21] and Hipólito Etchebéhère and his wife Mika Etchebéhère.[22]

Landau began his collaboration with this review with a startling article entitled: "From the Fourth International to the Second International. The Path which led Leon Trotsky to Social Democracy". In this he stated in particular: "Revolutionary Marxists must follow their own road both within the Party and in the Communist International. They must group together within the Party to help the Party and the International find the right road, Lenin's road." In September-October he published another article in *Que faire?*, a polemic against "comrade Bréval" (André Ferrat), who had cautiously envisaged the use of "defeatist" slogans in the event of a war in which the USSR was France's ally. Landau, for his part, declared that everything should be done for the defence of the USSR, writing: "The defeatist slogan does not take account of this double and complicated problem: it is correct in the case of a war between two armed imperialist groups, but not for the Soviet-imperialist bloc, which is a bloc full of contradictions."

Kurt Landau was profoundly shaken in August 1936 by the trial of the Sixteen in Moscow, following which Zinoviev, Kamenev and other old Bolsheviks were sentenced and executed. He tried to organise a joint protest in Paris by the émigré oppositional Communist groups, and he made vain efforts to convince Brandler, the leader of the KPO[23] and the leaders of the SAP.[24] He ended up merely with a joint action with the German section of the ICL,[25] the IKD,[26] and with the International Group of Ruth Fischer[27] and Maslow.[28] But he

20. Georges Kagan, known as Lucien Constant (1905-1943): Polish Jew; expelled from France 1927 for CP membership; returned to France 1931, involved with Ferrat in *Que faire?*; left CP 1935; went to US 1940, became academic.
21. Pierre Rimbert, pseudonym of Charles Torielli (1909-1991): Joined French Communist Party 1925; expelled 1932 for supporting electoral agreement with Socialist Party; member of Ligue communiste and Gauche communiste before joining Socialist Party; active in Resistance; after war rejoined Socialist Party, later in PSU.
22. Hipólito Etchebéhère (1900-1936): Born Argentina; anarchist, then Communist and Trotskyist; came to Europe 1931; was in Germany when Hitler came to power; died fighting with POUM at Atienza. For a biographical sketch by his wife Mika see *Revolutionary History*, Vol. 5, No. 1, pp33-37.
23. Communist Party Opposition, formed in 1929 by Brandler and his followers after their expulsion from the German CP.
24. Socialist Workers Party of Germany, centrist split from German Social Democratic Party in 1931; dissolved in 1945.
25. International Communist League, name of the International Left Opposition from 1933 onwards.
26. International Communists of Germany, German section of the International Left Opposition from 1933.
27. Ruth Fischer, pseudonym of Elfriede Eisler (1895-1961): Founder-member of Austrian Communist Party 1918, then leading figure in German Communist Party; with support from Zinoviev reached leadership of German CP in 1924, but expelled in 1926; founder of the

also polemicised against Trotsky and Sedov[29] and their opinion that the accused Olberg[30] was a GPU agent who had played the role of police spy in the trial. Olberg, a former member of the German Left Opposition, had followed Landau at the time of the 1931 split, and the latter preferred to see him as a victim of the GPU. On this occasion he entered into correspondence with the oppositional group in the Czech CP around Josef Guttmann[31] and Záviš Kalandra.[32]

After the relative failure of his attempts to mobilise action against the Moscow Trial, Kurt Landau turned to Spain where he saw an authentic proletarian revolution with the potential to regenerate the Communist movement. His friends Hipólito and Mika Etchebéhère had already gone there, and the former had died on the Madrid front. Landau arrived in Barcelona with Katia in November 1936. He rapidly won substantial influence with the leaders of the POUM which he joined — without abandoning his general strategy of "reforming" the Communist Parties. He contributed to *La Batalla*[33], and coordinated the POUM's international relations, especially in connection with the preparation of the international conference in Barcelona being planned by the POUM leadership. He still envisaged "a new Zimmerwald" of which the POUM would be the axis, and in this perspective he drew up programmatic bases for the international regroupment which was to be created. This activity drew him into a sharp polemic against the Brandlerites and the SAP supporters, and particularly against the young Willy Brandt,[34] who was at this time a defender of the Popular Front policy. But this battle of ideas against the supporters of the POUM "right" did not prevent him from presenting in his articles and pamphlets a defence and celebration of the POUM's policy which formed a permanent and particularly sharp polemic against Trotsky and the

Leninbund and other oppositional groupings. Exiled in France in 1933, moved to USA in 1941 and naturalised as American.
28. Arkadi Maslow, pseudonym of Isaac Chereminsky (1893-1941): Active in German Communist Party from 1920, supported March Action; in 1924 leader of German CP with Ruth Fischer, but expelled 1926; co-founder and leader of Leninbund; emigrated to France in 1933 with Fischer; unable to enter USA, settled in Cuba where he died in road "accident", which Fischer attributed to Stalin's assassins.
29. Lev Sedov (1906-1937): Elder son of Trotsky, active in Left Opposition; exiled with father; Berlin 1931, Paris 1933; probably murdered.
30. VP Olberg (1907-1936): Active in German Opposition in 1930, follower of Landau; one of the accused in the first Moscow Trial.
31. Jozef Guttman (1902-1958): Joined Czech CP in 1921; became editor of *Rude Pravo* in 1929 with Klement Gottwald; critical of German Communist Party in 1932, formed faction which fused in 1938 with Trotskyist groups; later emigrated.
32. Záviš Kalandra (1902-1950): Surrealist poet and historian, joined Czech CP 1923; member of Guttmann's faction in 1933, broke with CP over Spain and Moscow trials; deported to Mauthausen; returned to Czechoslovakia after war; arrested 1949, tried and hanged.
33. Newspaper of the POUM.
34. Willy Brandt, pseudonym of Herbert Frahm (1913-1992): Member of SAP in 1930; journalist in Spain during civil war; after World War II leading figure in German Social Democratic Party; Chancellor of West Germany 1969-74.

Fourth International. Landau's activity against the POUM could not fail to draw him to the attention of Stalin's agents who knew that this militant did not enjoy any diplomatic protection. He had to go into clandestinity after the days of May 1937 and the outlawing of the POUM.[35] We do not know why he left the relatively safe shelter which the Catalan CNT[36] had obtained for him at the request of Augustin Souchy.[37] He lived for some weeks in the suburbs of Barcelona, at the home of a veteran woman activist of the Spanish opposition, the Izquierda comunista and the POUM, and it was there that he wrote in particular his article against Trotsky "Bolshevism, Trotskyism and Sectarianism". The police or at least the Soviet intelligence services were actively looking for him: we know from the interrogations of other prisoners that he was accused of being a member of the Executive Committee of the POUM and the instigator of a "terrorist group" for which Stalin himself was a target. He was arrested on 23 September at the home of the POUM militant, Carlotta Durán, who was hiding him, by three policemen — two in plain clothes and one assault guard in uniform — who came at 7.30 p.m. Nothing more was heard of him. On 30 September, the General Delegate for Public Order in Catalonia, Paulino Gómez, officially denied that the police service had anything to do with his arrest. It is probable that he had been arrested by officers who were members of the intelligence services, or that he was immediately handed over to them and held captive in one of the "chekas"[38] that they controlled. Kurt Landau was never seen again. Neither protest movements abroad, nor the heroic efforts of his partner could shed any light on the route that led to his death. One version that circulated in the jails claimed that he had actually been tortured and put to death in the cellars of the Colón Hotel in Barcelona. Others say he had been seen in the premises of the cheka at 299 Corcega Street in Barcelona. Katia Landau did not rule out the possibility that he was taken to the USSR with a view to a "Moscow Trial", and that he was executed there.

Kurt Landau's partner, Julia Lipshutz, known as Katia (born in 1905), who shared his life and struggles from 1923 onwards, was arrested in Barcelona while he was in hiding; in prison she went on hunger strike from 8 to 22 November 1937 to demand information on her husband's fate and to know whether she herself had been imprisoned with a specific charge or as a hostage. She was released following numerous representations made by French socialists, especially Marceau Pivert.[39] Remarried to Benjamin Balboa (1901-1976), the

---

35. Fighting in Barcelona 3-8 May 1937 with Communist Party forces against POUM and anarchists; the POUM was outlawed the following month.
36. National Confederation of Labour, Spanish anarcho-syndicalist trade-union confederation, founded 1911; participated in Republican government 1936.
37. Augustin Souchy (1898-1984): born in Germany, went to Sweden in 1914 to evade conscription; active as syndicalist in Germany from 1919; moved to France 1933, then Spain, where he was an adviser to the CNT; interned in France 1940, but escaped to Cuba and Mexico, where he remained active in the anarchist movement.
38. By analogy with the "The All-Russian Extraordinary Commission for Combating Counter-Revolution and Sabotage" in post-revolutionary Russia.
39. Marceau Pivert (1895-1958); leader of the "Revolutionary Left" in the French Socialist Party

man who had enabled the crews of the Spanish fleet to forestall the officers' rising in 1936, she emigrated with him to Mexico in 1940 and settled in Cuernavaca where she was still living in 1984.[40] She continued trying to cast light on the murder of Kurt Landau.

from 1935; expelled 1938 and founded PSOP (Workers and Peasants Socialist Party); after World War II returned to Socialist Party.

40. We have been unable to get any information about Katia Landau after this date.

In Germany for the International
Excerpt from *Leon Sedov*[1]

THE nature of the developments dealt with in this chapter required Broué to display a sensitivity to character that was not frequently required in his work. It is particularly noteworthy that he was prepared, where the documentary evidence required it, to shed an unflattering light on Trotsky. Sedov, having left Russia, had become absorbed in the affairs of the nascent Fourth International, based in Germany amid the deteriorating conditions of the Nazi rise to power. The conditions of his work were appallingly bad and were hugely exacerbated by the exigencies of the Trotsky family's difficulties, especially the suicide of his half-sister Zina and the need to make arrangements for the upbringing of her son. These burdens would have been sufficient to exhaust even a person of extraordinary capacities, but for Sedov there was also the stressful relationship with Jeanne Martin de Pallières, whose attachment switched back and forth between him and Molinier.

Broué devoted two issues of the *Cahiers Léon Trotsky* (Nos 13 and 14 March and June 1983) to Sedov, including an extensive selection of Sedov's writings. The "Red Book on the Moscow Trials" (New Park 1980) is the only text available in English. Further information on this period can be found in the article "German Trotskyism in the 1930s", *Revolutionary History* Vol 2 No 3, by Wolfgang Alles, now available on the RH website.

* * * * *

When trying to convince Sedov to go to Germany to complete his studies, Trotsky had been very insistent that he should not give up the "Russian work" which he alone was capable of carrying out. However, he could turn his back neither on German nor on international work. The Nazi offensive against the Weimar Republic was also an attempt to destroy the most advanced labour movement in continental Europe.

1. Chapter 5 from Broué's book *Léon Sedov, fils de Trotsky, victime de Staline*, Les Éditions Ouvrières, 1993.

At that time, the German Communist Party (KPD) was following a suicidal policy, which Stalin had dictated to it in person through the agencies of the International. Whereas the Social Democrat Party (SPD) satisfied itself with haranguing the State and begging the government to repress the Nazis, the KPD identified the SPD as its enemy number one, stating that it had become "social-fascist" and that "the Nazi tree must not hide the social democrat forest". It made its main attacks on the Socialists, proclaiming that no alliance was possible with their chiefs. This policy, which it cynically called the "united front from below", was actually a policy of division and rejection of the united front at a moment when such a defensive front was the only means of standing up to the Nazis and of supporting the leftwards evolution of the German Socialists and the workers whom they influenced.

The ultimate future of the revolution, as well as that of the Soviet Union, was being played out in Germany. As Sedov saw it, it required the construction of a solid German section of the Left Opposition capable of "rectifying"[2] the line of the KPD and of involving it in real united front actions, demonstrations needed to convince the German workers. Some of its militants gained important local successes in this way, such as Helmut Schneeweiss[3] who had organized workers' defence groups in Oranienburg uniting the SPD, the KPD and the newly formed SAP (Socialist Workers' Party)[4] born from a rightward split from the Socialists and reinforced by former Communists. It was also necessary to build solid sections of the International Opposition everywhere so as to carry on the fight against Stalinist counter-revolution on a world scale. Liova devoted himself to it.

2. [RH] It was not until 12 March 1933 that Trotsky announced to the International Secretariat in Paris that he considered the KPD to have failed as a revolutionary party, and that a new party was required in Germany. It would not be until 15 July that he published the generalised conclusion that the same line applied globally, that new revolutionary parties were required everywhere and that they should be led by a new, Fourth, International. Until that change of line was completed, the sections of the International Left Opposition followed the policy of seeking to bring the parties of the Comintern back to a revolutionary approach.
3. [RH] On 30 January 1933, the workers defence organisation in Oranienburg, led by the Trotskyist Helmut Schneeweiss opened fire on the Nazis who had come to "triumph" in a workers' district, and put them to flight. The weaponry had been hidden and maintained since the "German October" of 1923. The core of the organisation (56 members of the KPD) had been expelled from the KPD for oppositional activity — differences over the United Front — and took with them the core membership of the Anti-Fascist League of Struggle, about 100 active supporters. Schneeweiss's group had been approached by a number of currents but was quick to ally itself to the Left Opposition. See Wolfgang Alles, *German Trotskyism in the 1930s* in Revolutionary History, Vol.2 No.3, Autumn 1989. After WW2 suspicions circulated about his involvement with the Stasi.
4 [RH[Broué's characterisation of the origins of the SAP is open to dispute. It was formed in October 1931 led by left figures in the SPD, Kurt Rosenfeld and Max Seydewitz. Paul Lei merged his own journal with theirs, after which they were often known as the Klassenkampf group. Its membership was certainly heterogeneous, politically, but it included a substantial proportion of the revolutionaries who found no basis or possibility of working in the SPD or KPD.

*   *   *   *   *

Nothing was easy for him: He lived with Jeanne[5] on money sent by his father — who was not rolling in it. Second hand clothes, sordid, cold rooms in wretched lodgings, poor man's food and long journeys on foot were his daily lot. Tobacco tormented him greatly because this heavy smoker did not like German cigarettes, and anyway they were too expensive for him. This forced him into a perpetual hunt for Russian cigarettes, adding a torment — and a danger — to all the others. He knew such moments of poverty that he even sent his father — he apologised for it later — an unstamped letter, because he did not have the wherewithal.

He was however a studious and punctual student at the Technische Hochschule, a large polytechnic school, where he was admitted for the academic year 1931-1932, where he had to restart his engineering studies from the beginning. He scrupulously signed the attendance sheets there. A visit to Paris for surgery on an awkward squint caused his only absence. This business, carried through by Gérard Rosenthal[6] and his father Dr. Georges Rosenthal, a leader of the Radical Party, was not easy to bring about. The French police authorities were not keen to accommodate in France this young Communist who was bound to be a convinced revolutionist.[7]

They gave way however, perhaps as a result of Dr. Rosenthal's Masonic friendships and they could not fail to have been impressed by the people who were his guarantors: Madame de Saint-Prix,[8] daughter of the former President of the Republic Emile Loubet[9] and mother of the poet — a Communist ahead of his time — Jean de Saint-Prix,[10] prematurely dead, the physician Paul Langevin[11]

5. [RH] Jeanne Martin des Pallières (1897-1961) expelled in 1929 from the French communist party for oppositional activity. Married to Raymond Molinier, but undertook a relationship with Lev Sedov while working for Trotsky at Prinkipo in 1929. After the death of Sedov she took care of Vsevolod ("Sieva") Volkov, Sedov's nephew and Trotsky's grandson. Eventually an acrimonious dispute arose over the arrangements for Vsevolod when Jeanne rejected Trotsky's demand that he should live with him in Mexico, which was eventually settled in Trotsky's favour by the French courts. Jeanne resumed contact with Sedova and provided some important reminiscences about the life of Trotsky and his entourage in Prinkipo, in letters to Jean van Heijenoort (in *Cahiers Léon Trotsky* No 4, October 1979).
6. [RH] Gérard Rosenthal (1903-1994) founder member of the French section of the Left Opposition. Visited Trotsky in Prinkipo in 1929, thereafter representing his legal interests in France. Author of *Avocat de Trotsky* 1976 . Left the Fourth International and joined the Socialist Party in 1945.
7. Files of the Prefecture of Police force, Paris
8. [RH] Pacifist and humanitarian, later called for an alliance with the USSR against Hitler. (1870-1964)
9. [RH] Émile François Loubet (1838-1929), 7th President of the French Republic, 1899-1906. Succeeded to the Presidency at a key moment in the Dreyfus affair. By remitting the sentence opened the road to the defeat of the charges against Dreyfus. Was a central figure in forming the 'Entente Cordiale' in 1904, and the 'Triple Entente' of France, Britain and Russia in 1907.
10. [RH] Pacifist (1896-1919), associated with the revolutionary circles of Marcel Martinet and Romain Rolland.
11. [RH] Paul Langevin (1872 –1946) a prominent French physicist. One of the founders of the

and the president of the Ligue pour les Droits de l'Homme[12], Professor Victor Basch[13]. The operation went well. His stay in Paris made it possible for Liova to win back Jeanne who had temporarily left him.

Their relationship had not left the storm zone. The love remained, but so did the crises, the estrangements, and the violent disputes. Liova knew the pangs of jealousy when Jeanne left again for Paris for some weeks because her husband blackmailed her with the threat of suicide, or when Molinier[14] announced his next trip to Berlin, en route to Constantinople. Later, in the middle of 1931, came the break. Jeanne went back to Paris — but "not to Molinier", he insisted. According to the confidences of Liova to his mother, the relationship was on its last legs and Liova started to make acid comments about the Molinier brothers[15] and their relationship with Jeanne. He considered that a final break with her, although difficult to live through, would be "salvation" for him, but added that she would never get over it He assured his mother that he kept his "joie de vivre" despite everything.

Some months later, Jeanne was again in Berlin. "for a long time", he assured his mother, specifying however that "that can change from one day to the next". They arrived together from Paris after his eye operation. He wrote that they were happy, with no plans for the future. But two months afterwards, he started to despair again: Raymond did not cease calling Jeanne on the telephone to entreat her to return, and she was "dying" before his eyes, terrified by the thought of opening a letter from her husband. He feared the strain was too great and might drive her to suicide.

    Comité de vigilance des intellectuels antifascistes, in 1934.. Removed from his senior position by the Vichy government for outspoken anti-Nazism. President of the Ligue de Droits d'Homme from 1944 to 1946 and a member of the French Communist Party at about the same time..

12. [RH] Ligue Pour Les Droits de l'Homme. League for the Rights of Man. Formed in 1898 by Ludovic Trarieux in defence of Dreyfus. Played an honourable role in defence of Victor Serge against Stalinist repression but failed to support Trotsky and the Trotskyists in the international campaign against the Moscow trials.
13. [RH] Victor Basch (1863-1944), philosopher and university teacher in France, but of Austrian Jewish origin. Co-founder of the LDH in 1898 and its fourth president in 1926. Murdered in 1944, with his wife Ilona, in Marseilles by the Milice on Nazi orders. They wrote on his body "The Jew always pays". Author of numerous books on aesthetics and individualism.
14. [RH] Raymond Molinier (1904–1996) founder of *La Verité*, the journal of the French section of the Left Opposition. Gérard Roche gives a valuable summary of the political disagreements between Trotsky and Molinier in *La Rupture de 1930: "Affaire Molinier" ou Divergences Politiques?* in Cahiers Léon Trotsky, No 9, January 1982. For details of the complex factional activity in which he was later to be involved see Trotsky's *The Crisis of the French Section [1935-1936]* Pathfinder Press, New York, 1977. In the same issue of the *Cahiers*, Broué in his article *La "reconciliation" avec Raymond Molinier* presents correspondence between Trotsky and Molinier in 1940, found in the Betty Hamilton archive. In this document his main role is that of the dispossessed husband of Jeanne (which is in no way to underestimate the importance of his political activity.
15. [RH] The second Molinier brother was Henri (1898-1944), who used the *nomme de guerre* d' Audouin

On his arrival Liova turned, following his father's advice, to the Pfemferts. Franz[16], an expressionist poet and "Left Communist", had from time immemorial kept up personal relations with Trotsky, and his wife Aleksandra Ramm[17] had translated Trotsky into German. Liova was careful to have infinite patience with them. Although they did not look kindly on his competition, which broke the exclusiveness of their relationship with Trotsky, they rendered him great service on every level. Liova assured his mother later that in two years he had been the only person not to quarrel with the Pfemferts, for whom quarrelling was a speciality, and to have repeated to himself in French, while champing at the bit: "What's the point?"

He then made contacts in the Russian milieu with the student Oskar Grossmann[18], whom he recruited to the German section of the Opposition, the Left-Menshevik Grigori Bienstock and some others. He established an invaluable relationship with the Menshevik Boris Nicolaievsky[19], already one of the men whose documentation on the USSR was without equal. He rediscovered a Russian friend, Dîna Mânnhof, who had married a Berliner and become a psychoanalyst.

He worked mostly within the German section and allied himself particularly with Eugen Bauer, Dr. Erwin Ackerknecht[20], whom he brought from Leipzig to Berlin to help him when he realised that he would have to concern himself with the German section, and also Otto Schüssler[21], a packer of art books, whom he was to send to his father as secretary.

16. [RH] Franz Pfemfert (1879-1954) former leader of the journal *Die Aktion*, one of the founders of the KAPD, which he left together with Otto Rühle to establish the AAUE — the "General Workers Union Unity Organisation" which rejected any direction by any political party.. Obliged to leave Czechoslovakia after Hitler's rise to power, later living in Mexico.
17. [RH] Alexandra Pfemfert, née Ramm (1883-1963) was the main translator of Trotsky into German during the 1930s. After the death of Franz she returned to Germany.
18. [RH] Oskar Grossman (????-????) a soviet student in Berlin who would become the leader of the youth in the German Left Opposition and would undertake the struggle in clandestinity after 1934 under the *nomme de guerre* of Otto. In his article *Ljova, le "Fiston"* Broué points out that the date of Grossmann's condemnation by a Nazi tribunal mysteriously preceded that of his expulsion from the Soviet Union.
19. [RH] Boris Nikolaievsky (1886-1966), a Menshevik in exile at the time, editor of their main journal, and eminent historian
20. [RH] Erwin H. Ackerknecht, often known as Eugen Bauer (1906-1988) first joined the revolutionary movement in a student group in Fribourg in 1924, under the influence of Pfemfert and *Die Aktion*. Joined the communist youth organisation in Berlin in 1926 where he quickly drew close to the positions of the Russian opposition. Joined the KPD in 1928. A founder of "Bolshevik Unity" and a collaborator with Roman Well. By 1932 however was a determined opponent of Well and collaborator with Sedov. Became the leader of the clandestine German section of the Left Opposition.
21. [RH] Otto Schüssler, known as Oskar Fischer (1901-1982), employed in Leipzig as a packer of art books, a militant in the KAPD until joining "Bolshevik Unity" in 1928. His great qualities as an autodidact and writer carried him into the leadership of the group and then of the unified opposition. Suggested by Acklerknecht to Sedov in 1932 as a potential secretary to Trosky in Prinkipo. From there he went to Prague to lead the work on *Unser Wort* until this work was taken on by Walter Held. Eventually became part of Trotsky's entourage in Mexico.

He also made the acquaintance, naturally, of the foreign militants whom he had not known previously, and from whom he received visits, the Frenchman Pierre Frank[22], and also the Spaniard Juan Andrade[23], who went on holiday in Berlin, to the great scandal of Trotsky; the Greek Mitsos Yotopoulos[24] — Witte or Vitte — sent by the archeiomarxists (or "Marxists of the archives", a group which had broken with the Comintern in 1924 and recently joined the Left Opposition) to the International Secretariat. In Vienna, he had renewed contact with the widow of his friend Kliatchko[25], Anna Konstantinovna. He wrote:

> A serene 'old lady', like Anna Konstantinovna, is worth more than thousands of youths! I fell in love with her on the spot.[26]

At that time, Anna Kliatchko was living with one of her daughters. Lina Semionovna. Liova also found Raïssa Epstein[27], a comrade of his father's in his youth, wife of the psychoanalyst Dr. Alfred Adler[28] and also J. Frank-Graef[29]

22. [RH] Pierre Frank (1905-1984), son of Russian émigrés, a chemical engineer, joined the PCF in 1924 and the Left Opposition in 1927. Visited Trotsky at Prinkipo in 1932. With Molinier, opposed Trotsky's line on exiting from the SFIO and with him founded the *La Commune* group when they were expelled from the Fourth International. Travelled to Britain to maintain production of *Inprecor* during WW2 where he was supported by Betty Hamilton but otherwise was very little in contact with the Trotskyists. Returned to France after the war to join the leadership of the Parti Communiste Internationaliste. Elected to the International Secretariat of the FI in 1963 and edited *Intercontinental Press*. On the breakup of the PCI, took a role in the leadership of the new Ligue Communiste until his death. Author of *The Long March of the Trotskyists*.
23. [RH] Juan Andrade (1898-1981). Member of the Spanish Young Socialists from 1916, editor of their paper *Renovacion* from 1919 to 1920. Sympathiser with the October revolution, met Borodin and M.N. Roy when they visited Spain and took part in the foundation of the Spanish Communist Party (PCE). He became a member of its Executive Committee and leader of its weekly *La Antorcha*. Expelled in 1027 for supporting the LO, participateds in the foundation of *Izquierda Comunista* and the review *Communismo*, which was banned in 1934. In 1935, he took part in the foundation of the POUM, characterized as "centrist" by Trotsky. During the civil war, arrested by the Stalinists and held in prison from mid-1937 to the end of 1938 along with other leaders of the POUM. Went into exile in France where he was promptly imprisoned again until 1944 when he resumed a leading role among the POUM in exile. Returned to Madrid in 1978 where he died.
24. [RH] Dmitri Yotopoulos (1901-1965), known as Vitte and Witte. A chemist by profession. From 1924 a leader of the "archeiomarxists", a split-off from the Greek CP, named after their journal *The archives of Marxism*, which was recognised in 1931 as a section of the LO. Living at this time in Berlin and acting as a member of the International Secretariat.
25. [RH] Semyon Lvovich Kliatchko (????-1914) is warmly remembered by both Trotsky and Sedova in the text of *My Life*. A strong friendship developed between the families of Trotsky and Kliatchko during the former's exile in Vienna.
26. AIHS Amsterdam. L. Sedov: letter of 28 February 1931.
27. [RH] Raissa Timofeievna Adler, wife of the famous psychiatrist Alfred Adler. The Adlers became friends of Trotsky during his period in Vienna before the First World War, through contact with his friend Adolf Joffe who was receiving psychoanalytic treatment at the time.
28. [RH] Alfred Adler (1870 –1937) An Austrian medical doctor and psychologist, founder of the Society of Individual Psychology in 1912. Served in the Austrian army in WW1. Had to leave Austria in 19323 because of his Jewish heritage, and moved to the USA. Died in Scotland during a lecture tour in 1937.

who had been called "Esquire" in Prinkipo in his time there. He went to pay a visit to Max Adler[30] who received him very warmly.

* * * * *

A little less than a year after his arrival, he had to look after his sister Zinaïda[31] in Berlin, who had come for the sake of her lungs. The attentive care of Dr. May brought to an end the damage done by the doctors in Constantinople who had caused a pneumothorax by mistaking one lung for another. But while her physical condition improved symptoms of mental disorder appeared.

Trotsky did not take the real situation into account, settling medical questions that he knew nothing about, in an authoritarian, pedagogic manner, sending letters which made Zina's condition worse. Liova himself felt sincere pity for her and his letters to his parents, whom he did not manage to convince, were imbued with an immense and distressing compassion for his fragile elder sister. And yet, what could he do, a political activist for up to 15 hours per day while studying his course and textbooks at night?

After the disappearance of Zina, he had to take care of her little boy, his nephew Vsevolod Volkov[32], known as Sieva, only 7 years old. He liked him because he was "nice and sweet", but, after the death of his mother, the child had health problems and soon had to be sent to a Vienna boarding school under medical supervision. Liova did not need these burdens, which overpowered him morally.

The Berlin police added to the tension by frequently summoning him to undergo close interrogations, and threatening to expel him and especially by subjecting Jeanne and Zina to the same treatment. Zina was deeply upset by this kind of treatment. Liova was distressed by the hatred which these police showed for his father.

Other long and difficult tasks arose unexpectedly. Thus the proposal for Trotsky to travel to Czechoslovakia for treatment at a spa kept Liova busy for

---

29. [RH] Jacob Frank known as Max Gräf Economist of Lithuanian origin. Led an internal opposition within the Austrian CP, which briefly unified with Landau's group in 1931 before returning to the CP, after seeking to disrupt the Left Opposition. For some months had served as Trotsky's secretary in Prinkipo Had warmly recommended Roman Well (Ruvin Sobelovicius) to Trotsky as a trustworthy man.
30. [RH] Max Adler (1873-1937), leader of "Austro-Marxism"
31. [RH] Zinaida (Zina) (née Bronstein) (1901-1933) Trotsky's first daughter by his first wife, Aleksandra Sokolovskaya. After Trotsky's escape from Siberia in 1902 she was brought up in the main by Trotsky's parents. Married Zakhar Moglin in 1917 with whom she had her first child Aleksandra Moglina (1923-1989). Subsequently married Platon Ivanovich Volkov with whom she had a son Vsevolod in 1926.
32. [RH] Vsevolod (diminutive Sieva, then Esteban) Volkov, born in 1926 to Zina and Platon Volkov. Traveled to Turkey and then Berlin with Zina, who had only been allowed to bring one of her children into exile with her. Following Sedov's death was taken care of by Jeanne for some years until Trotsky obtained custody and received him in Mexico. Currently, under the name Esteban Volkov, is the custodian of the museum of Trotsky's last house.

several months because the frontier crossing into Bohemia by land posed inextricable problems for Trotsky. And so, there was Liova, thrown into the world of aviation, private aircraft, air transport charges and international regulations. Finally, the Czechoslovakian government refused the visa which it had half promised: what lost time and effort!

To these must be added worries which, if they are not always in the forefront, are nevertheless lastingly devastating whenever one's mind is not preoccupied with something else. Anna[33] did not write any more. According to a letter which he wrote to Natalia Ivanovna, it seemed, though it was not certain, that she had remarried. Of course, he assured her that it did not bother him particularly since he was living with Jeanne. He repeated that it was a tragedy for him to be deprived of news of Liulik[34] who was now five years old and whom for a time he had hoped his mother would agree to put in his care in the West.

Now there was no possibility of that happening. Van[35] told me that Anna had re-married, to a Stalinist.[36] Liova was in despair. He repeated it in his letters to his mother. He loved his little one and missed him. He was worried about the education he was getting; wasn't he likely to undergo deformations which could not be put right? In other words, if he found him again one day, would he not be a stranger to him? Moreover, Anna's sister[37] had married Aleksandr Poskrebychev[38], a right-hand man of Stalin. Liova would confide later to a close friend that he was afraid they had taught his child to hate him.

33. [RH] Anna Metallikova, Sedov's wife whom he met and married in Moscow as a student.
34. [RH] Diminutive for Lev, the son of Sedov and Metallikova.
35. [RH] Jean Van Heijenoort (1912-1986), long time collaborator with Trotsky from the exile in Prinkipo to Mexico One of the secretaries of the Fourth International.
36. Mrs Vilgelmina Slavoutskaia, a former full timer for the Communist Youth International (KIM), told me she had met Anna Metallikova in a Moscow prison in 1936.
37. [RH] Bronislava ("Bronka") Poskrebysheva (1910-1941) née Metallikov. A doctor of Jewish-Lithuanian origin. Previously married to a lawyer, with whom she had one child before marrying Aleksandr Poskrebychev. Her brother, also a doctor in service at the Kremlin, was arrested in 1937 because of his remote family connection to Trotsky. Bronka made an unsuccessful appeal to Stalin for her brother's release. In 1939 she appealed in the same cause to Beria, whereupon she was herself arrested. Stalin is supposed to have joked with Poskrebychev "Don't worry. We'll find you a new wife." Despite this, Poskrebychev remained loyal to Stalin and Beria. Bronka was shot, with numerous others, in 1941 as the German army drew near to Moscow.
38. [RH] Aleksandr PoskrEbychev (1861-1965) is mentioned by Sudplatov in *Special Tasks*, London, 1985 (p 95) as "a short, dumpy-looking man in a green tunic" whom he later learned was "Chief of Stalin's secretariat". He showed Sudoplatov and Beria in to the meeting with Stalin where the order was given for the assassination of Trotsky. This description is untypically mild, and Poskrebychev is usually described in terms of personal loathing. Appointed in 1929 as Deputy Head of the Secret Section of the Secretariat of the Central Committee, he led that body from 1930 to 1952. In this capacity he controlled to a large extent access to Stalin and the flow of material from secret agents to him. His dismissal from this post has been seen as part of a campaign by Beria to erode the dying Stalin's capabilities. Poskrebychev appears to have attracted sadistic treatment from Stalin; the Medvedyev's report an occasion at a New Year's Eve party when Stalin made him wear burning tubes of paper on his fingers in place of candles. Alleliyuva reports that Stalin frequently forced him to drink more than anybody else at dinner parties for the leadership.

* * * * *

The first decision taken at the time of his arrival had been the transfer of the Bulletin of the Opposition[39] to Berlin under his direct control. He began to work on it but a few days later, the news of the fire which had devastated the villa of Prinkipo in the night of 28 February to 1 March 1931 imposed additional tasks on him. Most of the library had been destroyed by the fire. It was necessary to reassemble the collections of books and working material — dictionaries, encyclopaedias, handbooks. Trotsky obviously did not have the means to bear such expenditure and it was up to Sedov to find solutions, almost from scratch, to request external aid without giving the impression that Trotsky was begging, yet without paying. He met this challenge. But on April 21, three months after his arrival, he wrote to his mother that "from the point of view of amusement", he was living as if he were in Turkey and that he had not made a single trip out yet and that he did not know Berlin.

Trotsky had asked him not to get involved in German work. However, as Liova sent news to him of his meetings, his experiences and his knowledge of the militants, he was driven into it. The German section was in a sorry state: two factions were opposed to each other; that of the majority of the leadership was inspired by Landau[40]. Liova met him, estimated that he did not understand anything and that a split with him was inevitable. Trotsky, apart from this business, seemed particularly worried by the behaviour of his former secretary, Jakob Frank called Graef, and by what he called "the Leipzig group", the former "Communist Unity Group" led by the two Sobolevicius[41] brothers, Abram and Ruvin, called respectively Adolf Senin[42] and Roman Well[43], later exposed as

39. [RH] *Biullen Oppozitsii*, the Russian language journal, founded by Trotsky in 1929. At first printed in Paris, then moved to Berlin. Banned by Hitler in early 1933 and removed to Paris, then to Zurich in 1934, again to Paris in 1935 and eventually to New York in 1939 where it ceased to be published in 1941. The complete text in Russian is available from Pathfinder Press.
40. [RH] Kurt Landau, 1903-1937, a leading member of the Communist Party in Austria, then of a number of oppositional groupings in Vienna, Germany and Paris, including for a short time of the Left Opposition, where he led the German section between 1929 and 1930. Disappeared in Barcelona, widely believed to have been assassinated by the Stalinists
41. [RH] Abraham SoboloviClus (1903-?) and Ruvin (1901-1962) sons of a Lithuanian industrialist who owned a factory in Leipzig. Together they formed a small oppositional group "Bolshevik Unity", which joined the Left Opposition in 1929. Eventually they assumed the leadership of the German section of the Left Opposition which they endeavoured to destroy by publishing a statement of *rapprochement* with the Moscow line in *Die Permanente Revolution* not seen by Sedov before publication.
42. [RH] Senin was one of several pseudonyms of this individual. As Jack Soblen, in 1957 he told a US Senate Committee that he had been a GPU agent during his time as a member of the Left Opposition.
43. [RH] Ruvin Sobelovicius (1901 –1962). After studying agronomy in Germany spent a year in Russia where it is likely he joined one of the secret services. Returned to Leipzig in 1927 where he studied economics and joined the KPD. Became a leader of the Left Opposition and pressed towards a split with the Landau group despite Trotsky's cautions. Established himself in Berlin as a medical student in 1931, from where he was involved in the despatch to Russia

GPU agents as was Frank-Graef. In both cases, he did not feel suspicion but rather uneasiness in the face of analyses which ran counter to those of the international Opposition and his own and especially their policy of a deliberate and rapid split with Landau. It was for Liova to look more closely and to see more clearly.

At the end of March. Liova informed his father of the arrival of the two brothers in Berlin and one could foresee that Roman Well would take over the leadership of the section after the split. He seemed in a great hurry in any case. Liova made more and more contacts; on the question of the books, he had met the famous "Comrade Thomas"[44], the former executive secretary of Western Europe (WES) of the Comintern, who opened up contacts for him with the left socialist party SAP, in which he would ally himself with Boris Goldenberg[45], a promising young man, and the economist Fritz Sternberg[46]. He had a very serious discussion with the veteran Spartakists Paul Frölich[47] and Jakob Walcher[48] who were the left wing of the Brandlerite[49] KPO (Communist Party Opposition) and would join the SAP the following year.

of the Bulletin of the Opposition. By the end of 1931 Sedov was becoming concerned about his political differences in evaluation of the KPD and the Stalinist line. As Dr Robert Soblen, committed suicide in 1962 faced with prosecution as a Soviet spy.

44. [RH] See *Revolutionary History Vol 9 No 2* for a full discussion of "Comrade Thomas"
45. [RH] Boris GOLDENBERG (1908-1980) known as R. Frey, Gilbert and Bernhard Thomas. Son of a Jewish attorney, attended high school in Berlin, studied in Freiburg and Heidelberg. Joined the SPD in 1924, expelled two years later for having secretly conducted fractional activity on behalf of the KPD. Supporting the "right" line of Thalheimer and Brandler he joined the KPO and subsequently the SAP, where he adhered to the line of Walcher and Frölich. In Berlin he met Sedov and allowed him the use of his apartment for an office. Arrested and tortured by the Nazis in 1933. On his release traveled to Paris where he worked with the revolutionary left of the SFIO until 1935. By 1941, after further travels, he was in Cuba where he worked as a university teacher and journalist until 1960. Lived in London until 1964 and then returned to Germany where he was active as a translator, editor and journalist. Author of several books on Cuba and Latin America.
46. [RH] Fritz Sternberg (1895-1963). A socialist university teacher, recognised as one of the most capable of Marxist economists in his time, joined the SAP in 1931. Despite his personal support for Sedov, declined the opportunities to meet Trotsky in Prinkipo and Copenhagen. Subsequently visited Trotsky in France in 1933 or 34. Emigrated to Czechoslovakia and subsequently settled in Basle.
47. [RH] Paul Frölich (1884-1953) best known today as a biographer and editor of Rosa Luxemburg. A militant among the young socialists and the left of the social democrats before the war and an internationalist during it. Allied to Radek. A leader of the IKD in Bremen which joined the KPD(s) on its foundation. From this "leftist" position moved towards Brandler in 1922. Then followed the same evolution as Walcher through the KPD, KPO and SAP. Interned in France between 1939 and 1941 awaiting a visa for the USA. Returned to Germany in 1950 and undertook educational work in the SPD and the unions.
48. [RH] Jakob Walcher (1887-1970). Before WW1 organised a left social-democrat group in Stuttgart, joined the Spartakists during the war, a founder of the KPD(S) and one of its leaders until 1923. Supporter of the "right" line of Brandler . Called to Moscow where he worked for the Red International of Trade Unions until 1926. Expelled in 1928. With Frölich a founder in turn of the KPD and the KPO. Joined the SAP with the KPO Minority in 1932. Went to France where he operated under the name Jim Schwab. Went to New York in 1941 and

He had the good fortune to benefit from the protection of a German social democrat professor, Hermann Heller, who, he said "although a social democrat and a professor", was a "marvellous guy", who straightened out all the administrative difficulties for him about his studies. He became acquainted with former leading German CPer. Werner Scholem[50], a man of high quality, according to his father. He convinced him to collaborate with the press of the Left Opposition, which he was to join in 1933. He met Karl Korsch[51], but without result. He also very quickly got to know all the militants who counted in the German section. I spoke above about his immediate connection on the political level, then quickly on the personal level, with Dr. Ackerknecht. It was under his influence and the authority of Trotsky that in the German section a "buffer-group" was constituted, a conciliating centre, which involved some of those who previously followed Landau.

Relations with his father seemed unchanged. In spring 1931, Liova thought he was annoyed with him. He assured Natalia Ivanovna of his goodwill and entreated her confidentially to tell him with what his father reproached him but would not say to him. In the course of the year, quarrels returned on several occasions between them and Liova did not give ground. Liova thought that nothing could be done in Austria with Josef Frey[52] a real eccentric. Trotsky wanted at all costs that Liova should find the means of associating him with the work of the international Opposition. Trotsky thought that Liova was putting too much time into contacting Scholem whereas, for Liova, it was Scholem who was in no hurry to meet him, or even to resume political activity. Trotsky, on the

---

returned to Bremerhaven in 1946. He was accused in footnote to Pathfinder Trotsky 1932-3 of returning to Stalinism. In fact he joined the SED and lived in the Soviet zone, aiming to improve the situation and build socialism. Sacked from his post as editor of a union journal in 1951 and rehabilitated after the "secret speech". His memoirs were seized by the Stasi and refused publication — parts of the MS remaining missing.

49. [RH] Heinrich Brandler (1886-1967), a building worker, he was one of the rare working class leaders of the Spartakist nucleus, and, after election to the KPD Central Committee in April 1920, he became chairman of the party in February 1921, and took over the party leadership during the March action. Imprisoned from July to November, he stayed for several months in Moscow as a member of the Praesidium of the Communist International. As General Secretary of the KPD in the autumn of 1923, Stalin blamed him for the October defeat.

50. [RH] Werner Schloem (1895-1940). SPD in 1913, USPD in 1917, KPD in 1920. CC and Politbureau in 1924 under Fischer-Maslow, where with Grylewicz was involved in purging the "right". Also under the name Gershon Scholem a scholar of Jewish mysticism. Killed in Buchenwald.

51. [RH] Karl Korsch (1886-1961). Author of *Marxism and Philosophy* and *Karl Marx* (Leipzig 1923) Former minister in the communist-socialist government in Thuringia of 1923, expelled from the KPD for "Trotskyism" in 1929. Led a small, "ultra-left" group.

52. [RH] Josef Frey (1882-1957) a founder of the Communist Party in Austria and organiser of soldiers' councils, thereafter a leader of the Left Opposition there. Expelled from the CP in 1927. Trotsky's document *The International Left Opposition: Its Tasks and Methods* turned his back on Frey and his supporters, calling for a new and independent section to be formed there. There was a complex history to the oppositional communist groups in Austria, characterised by a reluctance to join the International Left Opposition.

basis of information from Paris, was exasperated with the American Becker[53], whom he accused of being an agent of demoralization of the Opposition because of his relations with some Russian capitulators. Liova continued to employ him and to take responsibility for him.

Trotsky had sent the American section a large sum of money taken from his advance royalties, whereas the Americans owed a considerable sum for the Bulletin of the Opposition. Liova did not mince his words: in Berlin there were some comrades who had nothing to eat because they were keeping the Bulletin alive, it was "shameful" to give money to the American section. Trotsky, who Liova thought, in a general way, lacked a "sense of proportion", which he however recommended on every occasion to everybody, offered himself the luxury of a lesson in détente:

> My dear boy, excuse this rebuff. But we are engaged in such a fight on the terrain of principles that in all other relationships we can and must show a spirit of conciliation and attentiveness, and in all cases abstain from haughty attitudes and excessive hardness.[54]

Liova excused himself too, but held to his view, writing in a letter to Natalia Ivanovna:

> Don't be upset at my "American" letter. I am deeply, unshakeably convinced that it is I who am right.[55]

Four months later, on 11 March 1932, Trotsky had the grace to write to Liova that indeed, in spite of the advance of his subsidy, the Americans had not paid their debt and that it was inadmissible.

We know nothing about the meeting between Liova and his parents, in the train which crossed France at the end of 1932. Both were returning from Copenhagen, where Trotsky had been invited by the socialist students to speak about developments in Russia, and where he had met a number of his supporters. We know only that they had one disagreement of a practical nature about how to continue the journey in spite of sabotage by the French authorities. One may guess, since we do not have any written documents on these two points, that they spoke about the visit of Smirnov's[56] envoy and about

---

53. [RH] John Becker (????-????), a widely travelled American engineer who provided Sedov with information from the oppositionist Mratchkovsky, who after capitulation (later recanted) had become a factory director. In editing the *Biulleten* Sedov would transform Becker's information into communications from inside Russia
54. AHLH, Trotsky: letter to Sedov, at the beginning of December 1931.
55. AHI, Sedov: letter of 1 January 1932.
56. [RH] Ivan N. Smirnov (1881-1936), Bolshevik from 1903, worked as a mechanic, hero of the civil war, nicknamed "the conscience of the Party". Member of the Left Opposition until 1929 when he re-entered the Party. Met Sedov by chance in Paris and agreed to provide him with information for the Bulletin of the Opposition.

the death of Zinoviev[57], about which a rumour had been spread; or that they simply went on with their quarrel!

On 1 January 1933, Sedov wrote a letter of apology in a humble tone because his mother had sent a sharply reproachful letter to him: Trotsky had not received the books he needed and he was wasting his time, not being able to work any more. Everything showed that Liova had a bad conscience. He however had sent the books in the usual way and the delay or disappearance could not be blamed on him.[58]

Following the split and the reorganisation of the International Secretariat, it was Trotsky himself who had raised the prospect of moving the organisation to Berlin and involving Liova in it. It was undoubtedly one of the most difficult periods of Liova's political life. The situation in Germany was worsening daily and the Nazi danger, in the street and the ballot box, continued to grow. Liova experienced it in his institute. The Nazis gathered some 70% of the students to howl "Jews out".

The division that the leaders of the social-democrats and the Stalinist Communists kept up, made impossible any reaction in a society terrorized by the violence of the "brown plague": The Nazis were marching towards power. However, they were not simple reactionaries: their goal was to crush the German labour movement and the democratic movement for decades, and the installation of a racist, terrorist dictatorship. Attentive, Liova suggested in September 1932 that they had reached their apogee and that they would have to to seize power in the short term if they wanted to preserve their cohesion. The offensive was therefore close.

The German Left Opposition was numerically weak: a few hundreds only. But it included personalities of great value, veterans, worker militants, courageous and lucid intellectuals, they would fight with all their strength "to rectify" the line of the KPD, to mobilize the Communist workers in favour of the united front of workers' organisations, to galvanize resistance, to prepare the masses for the recourse to arms which was becoming essential. Some, like Ackerknecht and some others, went from meeting to meeting, others fought in their cells, others finally, like Schneeweiss in Oranienburg and the young Held[59]

57. [RH] Grigori Zinoviev (1883-1936), nomme de guerre of (Ovsei-Gershon Aronovich) Radomyslsky.
    Old Bolshevik and supporter of Lenin from early days. First President of the Comintern. Supported Stalin's campaign against Trotskyism and later united his supporters with those of the Left Opposition to form the "United Opposition". Expelled 1927, capitulated and was readmitted in 1933, framed in the first "Moscow Trial" of 1936 and executed.
58. International institute of social history. Amsterdam, Sedov: letter to N.I. Sedova, 1 January 1933.
59. [RH[Heinz Epe, known as Walter Held (1910 –1941), a member of the LO in Germany as a student. Went abroad to escape the Gestapo by whom he had been condemned to death. From Prague he led the new journal *Unser Wort* (Our Word), and for a time occupied a midway position, supporting Trotsky on the need for a new German party but not for a new International.

in the Ruhr, organised workers' defence groups, militias to defend the workers' districts from the raids and parades of the SA.

But the Opposition also included — and at its head — GPU agents, with all the consequences for its internal life. Too many militants were only interested in the factional fights which were tearing the party asunder, in the fight for power inside this tiny organization. The enemy for them was the man of the opposing tendency. The majority of sympathisers, dismayed by these sectarian factional affairs, kept their distance. The weight of the degeneration of the USSR and the Comintern bore down heavily on the shoulders of this discouraged generation.

The German Opposition did not have enough strength and could not have had the authority which would be needed to organise a real resistance to those whom Trotsky sometimes called the "liquidators" and to wrench from them the power in the Communist Party. Only perhaps Sedov — who was called Ludwig, Alex, and at the end Schwarz — seemed to still believe in it. He personally recruited not only Werner Scholem, the former leader of the German Left wing, but also Karl Ludwig, a remarkable militant, a former journalist with *Volksville*, who succeeded in creating an independent clandestine opposition group in one of the large Berlin suburbs, with more than twenty members. He kept contact with Friedberg-Retzlaw[60] of the M-Apparat (the military apparatus) of the CP.

Liova did not have any disagreement with the line recommended by his father -propaganda for the united front, the achievement of segments of this policy, the fight to win over the militants of the KPD, to fight inside to "rectify" its policy. He sent him news on his own contacts and the achievements of the Opposition. Many of his newspaper cuttings were from the working class press, but also up-to-date information on the negotiations between the right-wing, a speech by Hitler who announced the offensive, a word of von Schleicher[61] on which it was necessary to hammer out propaganda, etc. He seldom gave his opinion on the German situation as such, writing however that it was very serious in a letter to his father of April 1932, then in July letting his rancour explode against those whom he called "the little bosses" of the workers parties in a letter to his mother:

> What a vile band this social-democracy is! In all my life I have never seen anything like it (except in the books) and such irresponsible, criminal stupidity from the Communist. Party. Thälmann[62] (CP) should be hung beside Severing[63] (SPD), but it will not be for a long time yet.[64]

60. [RH] Real name Karl Gröhl. For details see Revolutionary History Vol 8 No 4, where chapters of his memoirs are translated
61. [RH] Kurt von Schleicher (1882-1934) General. Chancellor between December 1932 and January 1933, murdered by the Nazis in June 1934.
62. [RH] Ernst Thälmann (1886-1944), Chairman of the KPD from October 1925 until arrested in March 1933. Shot in Buchenwald August 1944.
63. [RH] Carl Severing (1875-1952) Prussian Interior Minister (1920-26, 1930-32) and also German Interior Minister (1928-30). In 1921 sent troops against workers in the Halle district, leading to the March Action.

At the same time, the crisis was brewing within the international opposition. The Russian Pavel Okun, known as Mill or Obin, was brought onto the IS (international Secretariat of the Opposition) because of his knowledge of languages and so that he could translate the Russian documents emanating from Trotsky to his comrades in the IS. Was he an agent? Ambitious, disturbed a little? A disorganised megalomaniac? During his period in the IS, he meddled in everything and created extraordinary confusion. Finally, he would negotiate with the GPU in the rue de Grenelle and gave them information and documents in exchange for a visa to return to the USSR. It was a repetition of the Kharine[65] business. He was to be found signing a "declaration" in Pravda of 19 December 1932. Everyone, finally, was surprised.

But the Opposition was not at the end of its difficulties. Its two leaders Senin and Roman Well were both long-standing GPU agents, trained for this task in the USSR, and inserted into the international League to try to destroy it from within. More dangerous therefore than people like Kharine, Frank-Graef who joined them, or Mill, who undoubtedly became the playthings of the GPU only at the end of a process of decomposition. Roman Well was the leader of the majority of the German section and the strong man of the IS. Faced with him, not really taking him seriously, Liova temporized, with the blessing of his father, while Bauer-Ackerknecht launched awkward and repeated attacks. The agents had their faithful around them, Büchner, of Leipzig, Horst Sprengel of the Berlin organisation, more "ultra" and more aggressive than them. Trotsky, suspicious, had a long discussion with Senin in Copenhagen in November, from which he concluded that he was confused, but honest.

Stalin sensed that the Nazis were likely to come to power soon. He knew that the Opposition would accuse him of betrayal, because his policy had been constructed and criticized in the full light of day. So he wanted to have his hands free, to be disembarrassed, at least in Germany. At the beginning of December 1932, Well was broadcasting his criticisms, describing as "radically false" an article by Trotsky on the USSR. Then he developed in the International Secretariat of 15 December a line which amounted to asserting that the International was in process of rectifying itself, that the Left Opposition had disappeared in Russia, that Sedov and Bauer had misinformed Trotsky and tried to prevent the necessary rapprochement with the official line.

Trotsky immediately called for their expulsion, but when his message arrived in Berlin, the partisans of Well unmasked themselves by publishing a special number of *Die Permanente Revolution*, which announced the rallying of the

---

64. AHLH, Sedov: letter with N.I. Sedova, 27 July 1932.
65. [RH] Solomon Kharine, known as "Joseph", a Russian supporter of the International Left Opposition, and a member of the commercial delegation in Paris, was apparently influenced by Radek's statement of capitulation to Stalin in 1929, and offered to provide information to the GPU. He provided addresses and documents, including the complete text of the first issue of the Bulletin of the Opposition. See Broué's article *Un capitulard à Paris : l'affaire Kharine* in the Cahiers Léon Trotsky Issue 7/8, 1981.

Opposition to the Moscow line, and its decision to dissolve itself. Therein they proclaimed "the bankruptcy of Trotsky's perspectives on Germany and the Soviet Union". The text was followed by several hundred signatures of Opposition militants, the majority of whom never knew of its existence.

Trotsky's anger exploded ... against Sedov whom he accused of not having taken Well seriously and of having allowed the sabotage to proceed without ever seeking to stop it. Sedov retorted that he had certainly been a conciliator, but he was not the only one and that his father had more than once preached moderation with regard to the two brothers, which was a fair point. In fact the operation came to a sudden end in the organisation, which did not follow Well. On the other hand it had thrown a real discredit on the Left Opposition at a time when it certainly did not need this new blow. On the specific ground of organisation, Liova was optimistic. There were now 750 active militants. The Sudeten German Fritz Bergel, known as Barton, had been just sent to reinforce the apparatus because he was a specialist in financial questions. Fritz Belleville[66], a recognized theorist and notable speaker, an esteemed veteran, had come from the Leninbund to join the Left Opposition. Contacts increased with the militants of the SAP, themselves in favour of a workers united front against Nazism. Karl Ludwig and Werner Scholem were to become leaders of weight. New leaders had appeared in the recent combat and the young Heinz Epe. known as Walter Held had been called from the Ruhr to lead the policy with regard towards the SAP and towards its communist wing which it appeared possible to win over.

But this January of 1933 was to open with the first of a series of catastrophes which were to strike Liova hard — and from which his father never really recovered.

According to Liova's letters to the family, Zina grew better at the end of the year 1932. The tuberculosis seemed to be finished and she had no more pneumothorax. The psychiatrist judged that her state was improving. She still had odd behaviour, but as a whole, she was starting to control her life. Unfortunately clarity returned with the cure and with it an infinite sadness. She had hoped, by leaving the USSR, to find this father whom she cherished. These reunions had been brief. Since her illness, he had not ceased to lecture her, to accuse her of being irresponsible, egotistical and hysterical. In fact, he did not understand what she was suffering from and he presumed to control the illness by moral precepts of behaviour. Especially, now that he judged her to be "cured", he demanded that she should return to the USSR to live near her mother, which she did not want at any price. Finally she reproached her father

66. [RH] Fritz Belleville (1903-1994), proofreader and researcher in social sciences at Frankfurt. Joined the young communists in 1919 and the KPD in 1922. Became part of the "Left" and was their spokesman at the 1926 Franfurt Congress, for which he was expelled. A member of the Korsch group until its dissolution, and then of the Leninbund, where he joined the leadership in 1932. In September of the same year he joined the Left Opposition and was co-opted onto the leadership. Emigrated to Basle shortly after and founded the Marxist Students Group, and then the Swiss section of the LO, but split from them over policy differences. Took no further part in organised politics but lectured in workers education programmes..

for what she saw as a betrayal — handing over their utterly personal correspondence, to the psychiatrist, Dr. Kronberg.

She concluded that he did not love her — which was obviously false — and especially that he no longer had confidence in her — which was inevitable given the nature of her illness. She had come to take part in her father's combat as her little brother Liova had had done years before and she had been rejected: she conceived of this with great bitterness and envy, and with the feeling of being a victim of an injustice. Since he was in Berlin, it was Liova himself who took on the role of torturer involuntarily, not proposing any task for her, never involving her in his Russian work. He knew why: he had to defend himself sharply against the very vigorous accusations not only from his father, but also his mother, because he had made her type documents referring to a secret enterprise — which, he assured them, she could not have understood, but which they saw as a grave misjudgement.

Zina was not at all an inexperienced young woman however. At sixteen years old she had been the editor of the newspaper of the Petrograd Komsomol. As a member of the Party, she taught in one of its schools, before fighting in the ranks of the Opposition with her husband P.I.Volkov. She understood the German situation perfectly, and the progress of the Nazis towards power. She read her father's articles with passionate interest, and dreamt of taking his side in this struggle which she could foresee and which she thought could and must, starting with the long awaited reaction of the workers, lead to the proletarian revolution in Germany. However she thought that she was excluded from it in advance. Liova understood but could do nothing about it.

The arrival of her little Siéva[67], whom she loved tenderly, would not divert her from her black thoughts. She took care of him of course, but continued to brood upon her misfortune, of which her psychic disorders, as she understood, were not the smallest part. Terrible blows came to her now from outside. She was deprived of her Soviet nationality, which closed the door of return to her, definitively separated her from her husband, her mother and especially from her small daughter, Aleksandra, born before Siéva, from a short union with a member of the Opposition. She was informed that she would be expelled from German territory and that her visa would not be renewed (the Russian Volkogonov has just informed us that this measure had been taken by the von Schleicher[68] government under pressure from the Soviet embassy).

The idea of leaving German territory filled her with horror, like a desertion. Liova flogged himself, badgered lawyer friends and obtained a deferment. He knew that he could get nothing more. She furiously rejected his suggestion of going to Vienna: she would have nothing to do there. And on top of everything, she discovered that she was pregnant — nobody knows by whom. She had

---

67. [RH] Diminutive for Vsevolod Volkov (b 1926), son of Platon Volkov and Zinaida
68. [RH] Kurt von Schleicher (1882-1934), the last Chancellor of the Weimar Republic. Shot during the "night of the long knives" 20 June 1934

confided about her pregnancy only to Jeanne, without any more detail, and it is clear that, there too, she was alone.

In the morning of 5 January 1933, she prepared Siéva for school, finished the letters which she intended for her own people, carefully blocked up all the exits and turned on the gas. Liova was informed of the discovery of her body; distracted, he could not prevent the police from taking away all the papers, except for the sealed and addressed letters. He could not bring himself to inform his father and thus telegraphed his mother, entrusting to her the task of announcing the overwhelming news to him:

> ZINA HAS TAKEN HER OWN LIFE. ALEKSANDRA LVOVNA AND PLATON MUST BE INFORMED I HAVE NOT SAID ANYTHING TO THEM STOP SIEVA DOES NOT KNOW ABOUT ZINA'S DEATH. HE IS WITH US.[69]

I had the task of explaining personally, on 17 November 1988, to Aleksandra Zakharovna, the daughter of Zinaïda, half-sister of Siéva, the circumstances and the date of her mother's death.

And so, Liova was responsible for a family. This little boy, his nephew, whom he loved though it was not easy, was to deprive him of a few more hours in his life, which was already tragically short of them. The death of Zina monopolised Trotsky's attention for a few days while he wrote his open letter showing that Stalin, who had removed her nationality, and von Schleicher, who expelled her, had pushed his daughter into suicide. Then he turned against Liova, who, it seemed to him, had a tendency, in the texts that he devoted to the death of his sister, to dissimulate the fact that she committed suicide, i.e. to blur the responsibility of the culprits. He returned then to his "negligence", his "underestimation" of the activity of Well and others. He spoke about his "criminal passivity". Neither he nor Liova knew yet that they were dealing with Stalin's agents infiltrated into their ranks.

Liova wrote to his mother on January 24:

> Papa sent an unjust, almost monstrous, letter to me, written with spite (why?) as if he were trying to find in my person the only one responsible for what occurred, completely forgetting all the history of this business, his own behaviour, etc. Jeanne and I were completely devastated by this little letter — I will not reply to him. A polemic could only worsen the situation, and under these conditions, what good is a polemic. I will still write on these questions, but only to you personally. [70]

Far from congratulating him for successes in recruitment that he had announced — a group of a score of militants in Dienslaken, tens in all the cities of the Ruhr, cadres everywhere — Trotsky said to him that he feared the entry into the

---

69   AHLH, Sedov: Telegram of 5 January 1933.
70. AHI, letter to Sedova of 24 January 1933.

section "of new elements, untested and hastily recruited, and among them some Stalinist agents".

That same January, Ivan Nikitich Smirnov[71]. E.A. Preobrazhensky[72] and 87 members of their group, including R.I. Baranov, his companion in the Urals, Tcheslav Kozlovsky, his former rival in love, were arrested. It was the end of the group of the "former Trotskyist capitulators" and all the "Block of the Oppositions" in the USSR.

The same January, the President of the Republic Hindenburg[73] called Hitler to power. The Nazi gang leader became Chancellor of the Reich. It was the litmus test for the German Party and for the Communist International. Trotsky's verdict was pitiless: the "German catastrophe" is their bankruptcy, and they are the cause of "the tragedy of the German proletariat", beaten without having fought.

In the "dialogue" with his father, it was from now on the voice of Liova which dominated, the cold voice of an analyst which reflected both the despair of millions of men and also his own human sensitivity.

On 3 February he wrote:

> The party shows total impotence. What we are living through resembles a surrender of the working class in face of fascism. The Party, exhausted by its false policy, is very close to adding a cardinal failure in these historic days. At the top — disorientation, nobody knows what to do: at the base — they do not believe in their own strength. A great fatalism. perhaps especially in the SPD. I believe that we are now in the decisive days and weeks. If a vigorous action of the working class — which in its development can not be anything but the proletarian revolution — does not occur now, an appalling defeat is inevitable. Such an action is not excluded yet, but in my opinion it is hardly probable from now on. And it is precisely because of the revolutionary character of an action against Hitler, which the SPD wants at all costs to prevent, that the "perspective" of the SPD is something incredible. "We will await the elections in March. If Hitler has the majority, we will see. If he takes action against the constitution, then (!) we will begin to act". The banning of the SPD's demonstration. It would be stupid to think that Hitler will

---

71. [RH] Ivan N. Smirnov (1881-1936), Bolshevik from 1903, worked as a mechanic, hero of the civil war, nicknamed "the conscience of the Party". Member of the Left Opposition until 1929 when he re-entered the Party. Met Sedov by chance in Paris and agreed to provide him with information for the Bulletin of the Opposition.
72. [RH] Yevgeni Preobrazhensky (1886-1937), old Bolshevik, member of the Party secretariat during the civil war, the main economic thinker of the Left Opposition until he capitulated to Stalin in 1929.
73. [RH] Paul von Hindenburg (1837-1934), Field Marshal and former commander in chief of the imperial German army. Played a central part in the repression of the workers revolution of 1918-1919. Elected president of the republic in 1925 as the right wing candidate. Re-elected in 1923, with the support, in the second round, of the SPD against Hitler. As president he called Hitler to take the Chancellorship.

employ the same methods with the SPD and the KPD. He is going to divide them, initially to beat the KPD more easily and to allow the chiefs of the SPD to reiterate 4 August. The Nazis march, with music in the streets. There are no police. They themselves are the police. They are already arresting people in the street (for the moment, they are only isolated incidents but in any event we are only at the beginning) and taking them along to the police station. Schneeweiss, for example, in Oranienburg — one of the rare places of Germany where the Nazis demonstrations were dispersed — the Nazis went to the police station and demanded his arrest. When the police did not arrest him, the Nazis answered: "Good. We will break his head ourselves". A comrade spoke to me about his factory (1200 workers, the majority under Communist influence): at the factory committee, 7 Communists and 5 SPD: 12 members only in the cell: the Communists, on instructions from above, proposed a half an hour long token strike; the SPD answered: "We do not engage in isolated actions: address yourselves to our centre": The Communists, in spite of their dominant influence, were not able to achieve this half an hour strike; the instructor of the KPD committee came to accuse the cell of trailing behind the SPD.[74]

Other letters were devoted to the restructuring of the organisation. With the move to clandestinity, the lack of money became a bigger problem. It had been possible to print a leaflet in 10,000 copies and to distribute it clandestinely, but only because a consignment had been seized. On 12 February he gave good news of the organisation: Karl Ludwig had brought over ten Party workers and hoped to win another 30 to 40. A circle of young people of the communist opposition was created in Berlin. The news was coming in, contacts were being made.

He gave details on the mortal crisis of the KPD:

> The German Party — according to well informed people — has a million marks deficit for its press section alone. Half was wasted on futile expenditure. In some districts they are sacking their sixth or seventh treasurer, one after the other — thieves. It is characteristic, of course of the extent of unemployment but also of demoralisation inside the party.
>
> An anecdote: in a district of Berlin, the Party organises an "alarm exercise"; out of 70 people, 14 come. They conduct a campaign of criticism, organise a second "alarm": 12 of them turn up.
>
> One of the most famous fighters of the party [Erich Wollenberg[75] — PB] (a year in prison for agitation in the army) was on the point of

---

74. AHI, Sedov: letter of 3 February 1933.
75. [RH] Erich Wollenberg (1882 -1973). After volunteering for the German army in WW1, became disgusted with the slaughter and joined the revolutionaries in 1918 and supported the KPD. Led military activities for the Munich Council Republic and subsequently in other parts of Germany. For a brief biography, see the introduction to his book *The Red Army*, New Park,

coming over to us, having apparently guessed what was happening, he was summoned "over there". He went and was forced to stay there.⁷⁶

The news of 25 February showed a worrying development of repression. He wrote in French:

> The Newspaper is not yet prohibited, but the printing works is always occupied by the police and, so it appears, they can occupy it until the elections — to destroy it all afterwards or to prohibit it? Today I have just learned — it must still be verified — that the *Vorwärts* has been occupied: the speed is amazing. This speed and the vigorous action against the SPD gives everything, in my opinion, a forced aspect. "Normally", it would be advantageous, in my opinion, for the Nazis to liquidate communism first and then to deal with the SPD. The fact that they are in such a hurry and take action of such a large scale must probably have its causes within the coalition. The Nazis must have a quite immediate aim of liquidating the German nationalists. It is probably especially that which leads them into this forced acceleration. Unfortunately, nobody has information on the internal affairs of the coalition. It is said that Papen⁷⁷ threatened to resign if they continue with this campaign against the Centre, banning the Catholic newspapers, brawling, etc. and because of that that they undertook a certain retreat with regard to the Centre.⁷⁸

A little later, the same day, he wrote, in German this time:

> The last two issues of *Permanent Revolution*, nos 7 and 8, were confiscated. Number 7 had already been dispatched and they found only a few copies. On the other hand, Number 8 was confiscated at the printing works (only a thousand copies had already left). The plates were probably destroyed. Functionaries were installed in the printing works yesterday evening until this afternoon. The paper was confiscated without them knowing its contents, just on the basis of what it is (...) the existence of *Biulleten* is also in danger.⁷⁹

The same day, in a letter in Russian to his mother, he complained that his father did not write. He wrote:

1978, which however has been modified by later research not yet available in English..
76. AHI, Sedov: letter of 12 February 1933.
77. [RH] Franz von Papen (1879-1969), Deputy of the catholic Centre Party, subsequently of the German nationals. Chancellor of the Reich from June to November 1932.
78. AHI, Sedov: letter of 25 February 1933. in Russian.
79. AHI, Sedov: letter of 25 February 1933. in German.

> Papa does not seem to have any clear idea at all about what is going on here. I do not even know if I will be able to put out the *Biulleten*. The printing works is occupied (...) It is the same question with *Permanente*: its existence is no more than a question of days.[80]

On 3 March, after the Reichstag fire, he informed his parents that he would take essential decisions without consulting them, in particular to leave Germany if he considered it necessary, He explained again:

> From Istanbul, do you and Papa feel all the tension of emotion here? The waiting for a Nazi rising, and a counter-coup by the German nationalists with the assistance of Reichswehr; pogroms; arrests, on a large scale now, of various opponents. Scholem but also Ossietsky[81], do nothing but worsen the tension. There were some losses in the German organization: Hippe[82] and two of his group. Schöler, some members of the organisation in the provinces too. It is only the start.[83]

He continued to deal with the books which his father needed. Here or there he put a note which showed what Germany was living through: the lynching of a rabbi by the SA, torture in the police stations, the hatred which the Nazis had for Trotsky, the infiltration, which had been uncovered, of Nazis within the cadres of the KPD. He obtained a French visa, this time through the intervention of the minister Anatole de Monzie[84,] "de Monsieur" as they called him among themselves. He sent Jeanne — she had returned in the interim — to reconnoitre, dressed in her most beautiful finery. Some of the archives of the IS were quite simply wrapped in silk lingerie bought specially for the circumstance and placed in the bag. She herself was "papered"-, "stuffed", she was to write[85], with documents that it was necessary to save at all costs, which gave her an unusual stoutness which did not attract the attention of the German police.

80. AHI, Sedov: letter of 25 February in Russian with his mother.
81. [RH] Probably a reference to Carl von Ossietzky (1889-1938), a leading pacifist and anti-militarist organiser and writer, founder of the Republican Party, exposed Germany's secret re-armament in violation of the Versailles Treaty . arrested following the Reichstag fire, mistreated in concentration camps, won the Nobel Peace Prize in 1936, died in civilian hospital but still under guard in 1938
82. [RH] Oskar Hippe (1900-1990), metalworker and trade unionist in 1916 when he became associated with the Berlin Spartakists. Called up in 1918. A founder of the KPD, and member of its left wing in the 1920s. A founder of the Leninbund in 1928, and together with Grylewicz led the left wing to become the German section of the International Left Opposition. Led the Berlin-Charlottenburg group of the LO. Well falsely claimed his support. Imprisoned for two years by the Nazis, and sentenced to twentyfive by the Stalinists in East Germany. Released in 1956
83. AHI, Sedov: letter of 3 March 1933.
84. [RH] Anatole de Monzie (1876-1947), member of the Republican Socialist Party (PRS), held a total of 18 ministerial posts during a long career. Campaigned in 1922 for French recognition of the Soviet Union, and worked with Rakovsky to that end.
85. [RH] Jeanne Martin de PallIères, "Letters to Jean van Heijenoort". Cahiers Léon Trotsky No 4. October 1979.

The last days had been dangerous and Liova narrowly escaped on several occasions. Erwin Ackerknecht told me in particular of a meeting in his office (he was the chief psychiatric doctor of a hospital), with Frankel[86] and Liova. The SA arrived without warning, pointing guns at everyone. The chief doctor started barking in the purest Prussian officer style at the boors who were disturbing him in his important work and sabotaging the health service of the great German nation. Intimidated, the SA withdrew. Liova telegraphed on 24 March that he was leaving.[87]

On the 25th, he was in Paris. The correspondence of his mother and father betrayed an immense relief. They had until the end trembled for their little boy, awaited in anguish the telegram announcing that he had crossed the border and that he was in Paris. However Liova continued the polemic against his father in a long letter to his mother of 7 February — the most complete he wrote:

> I have just received your letter. What a calamity! You absolutely did not understand me (...). I do not want to make a ridiculous, imbecilic figure of myself: "Papa does not appreciate me", because that is not the question. But, for example, that famous night in Marseilles, Papa sought advice from everyone but not from me, and yet I was the "first" and only one, as far as I remember, to propose the return voyage via Italy. There are innumerable facts of this kind. I remember, at the time of the return from Alma-Ata, when I had for the first time advanced a suggestion relating to Istanbul, Papa shot me down in flames... And yet what was necessary was more patience with regard to others. Nobody can learn anything by submission alone. But all these questions which are in themselves and for themselves, questions of organization, are secondary: it is possible and quite admissible to have differences of opinion. If I am not convinced by arguments, you have to let me be convinced by myself and not to drop me overboard with a load of bricks; even without bricks, in fact, I will continue to defend Papa's point of view (as in the Frey business where I did not agree with him and where, exceptionally, it was me who was right). But I return to the question. It is completely incorrect, written in the spirit of somebody who seeks a scapegoat, what Papa wrote to me about matters in Germany. It is that and that only I meant.
>
> Papa accuses me not only dilettantism, but of disorganization, in a certain number of factual questions which simply do not correspond to reality. Erwin and I did all that we could and without our presence, the things would have been much worse. That Well published a forgery, was not in our power to prevent (...) The charges against us are 90% baseless. I can prove it without difficulty. By reading Papa's letter written with

86. [RH] Jan Frankel (1906-1984), joined the Czechoslovak CP in his youth, associated with a dissident tendency that eventually became the Trotskyist movement. An important organiser of the International Left Opposition.
87. AHI, Sedov: telegram 24 March 1933.

poison and spite, I felt once more what I had more than once felt before: that it is on the head of "the best" and those most "worthy of confidence" of those close to him that he places the mark of failure; that can hardly be a good method and does not contribute to the cause (because it oppresses "the best" instead of enabling them to raise themselves up). And in the given case, the tone itself was simply monstrous (precisely in relation to the one who had done the utmost (...) All that, Mama, undermines relationships. That is how it is. All that, for me is in the past. I am obliged to write it since you did not understand me.[88]

Arriving in Paris, at the Gare de l'Est, in the early hours of 5 March, Liova was about to rediscover all the problems of his studies, poverty, Jeanne, the International Opposition, was going to plunge into the French section and to continue to bear the heavy burden of his father's reproaches. That is how it is, he said to himself. But he had not yet reached the end of the journey.

How long your road is, how far, Papa!

---

88. AHI, Sedov: letter of 7 February 1933.

Van Heijenoort
A Trotskyist in New York in the Second World War

IN the obituary that I did for my old friend Van I touched on for the first time the question of his rôle in the analysis of the Second World war and his position in particular on this matter in the IV International.[1] In the past the *Cahiers Léon Trotsky* has published an article of his from 1942 on "The National Question in Europe" which enabled one to emphasise the originality of his political analyses.[2] Lastly the international Spartacist tendency with the characteristic irresponsibility in its method of analysis and its taste for amalgamating positions has attributed to both of us similar positions throughout the period.

In fact Van and I had long conversations in the eighties about the Second World War. From 1939 to 1945 Van was a foreign resident in the United States, living in difficult circumstances and sometimes in penury[3], semi-clandestine because of his position as a political emigré,[4] kept away from influence by the leaders of Socialist Workers Party, in spite of, and perhaps because of, the part which he had played close to Trotsky and of his membership of the International Secretariat[5]. French in origin, he tried desperately during all those years, to find out what was happening in France, the shifting politics, the major movements in the working class and youth, watching for signs of the rise of the revolution. It was not simple curiosity: convinced of the accuracy of the "proletarian military policy" of which Trotsky had started to present the broad outline before his assassination, he sought the means to apply it in the European

1. Pierre Broué, "Van, le Militant, l'Ami, l'Homme", *Cahiers Léon Trotsky*, no.26, June 1986, pp7-14.
2. Marc Loris, "La Question nationale en Europe", *Cahiers Léon Trotsky*, no 23, September 1985, pp88-110. For the originals in English see all these articles on the web at http://www.marxists.org/history/etol/writers/heijen/index.htm.
3. He lived by "moonlighting" and doing odd jobs for comrades.
4. The American Army called up for military service a man who went under several pseudonyms, and who eventually took a female pseudonym to make his life easier.
5. Trotsky's correspondence expresses the fear that his old colleagues, Jan Frankel, and Van, would be regarded as his "spies". In their correspondence from New York, both hid neither their difficulties nor their severe judgements on the American leadership.

situation on the basis of which Trotsky had defined it. He did it with all the more ardour in that he was convinced he was the only one to have understood its spirit and that, as leader of the IS in New York, he clashed daily with Cannon and his representative Bert Cochran (ER Frank): forty years later, he still did not know if he had met with total incomprehension or a sectarian bad faith.

During this same period, I was then a young lad fourteen years younger than him, my perception sharpened by observing the crisis of French society, the collapse of the Army and its traditional values, the loss of prestige of "the elite" and the arrival in power of what seemed to me the worst militaro-clerical reaction in the wake of the military defeat. A teenager, initially attracted by Gaullism, then Stalinism, and, in both cases, put off by their organisational practices, I was won only to the idea of armed struggle with the masses against the occupation and the collaborators in Paris and Vichy; anti-fascist, as I said, I however refused to be or to let myself be called an anti-German and these were the "contradictions" which led me into the ranks of the Trotskyists in 1944.

This itinerary fascinated Van and I had to tell him, going over the extra details and unceasingly describing networks, groups, cadre schools, maquis frequented, operations carried out, which made me recollect my state of mind for him, my vision of the war, and also that of my companions in the struggle and my clandestine leaders, and what I had learnt through my personal experience, of the relations between Gaullists and Stalinist, for example. For him I was a past which he still wanted to decipher, a witness to be cross-examined and, it seemed to me, to provide evidence, somewhat despairing, that he had been right when he was silenced, which revived his regrets, his curiosity and sometimes his incredulity.

Undoubtedly these long conversations in the evenings by the side of the Charles river, at Cambridge, or on the paths bordered by eucalyptus on the Stanford campus, left me with the obligation to try today, in this article, to locate and identify his position on the war through his articles in *Fourth International* for the period when the SWP allowed them to be expressed without too many qualifications: I used for a great part of the period, relatively abundant material, a dozen articles which would undoubtedly occupy a little more than two-and-a-half issues of the *Cahiers*.

The sources of information on which he based his analyses were nothing extraordinary: the main ones consisted the big American national dailies, the European newspapers until 1940, then only the English ones, afterwards the rare letter from France, brief messages, sometimes the official reports which were confidential but available, a few meetings with someone who had come recently from Europe, reports also from England and Portugal based on bits of information, direct or indirect, from France.

Van was not a contributor to *Fourth International* who enjoyed the authority of a James P Cannon. Only one "official" text was from his pen: the manifesto of the executive committee of November 1940 devoted to France under Petain and Hitler. All the others carried the signature of Marc Loris except for the last ones, which are signed Daniel Logan[6][6.]

The *Manifesto* gave a progress report on the world situation after the defeat of France. It rejected all the "technical" explanations for the defeat of the French Army. According to him the key resided in the fact that the bourgeoisie never defends the fatherland for itself, but only for private property, privileges and profit, and that it becomes "defeatist" when they are threatened. It was the fear of unleashing, while resisting to the limit, "a revolutionary war against Hitler", which turned general Weygand into an advocate of capitulation and led him to request an armistice.

He began with the objective fact that the French revolution had not taken place. For him, the opportunity of June 1936 was deliberately snatched away by the sociaist and communist parties, whose policy was to bar the road to the proletarian revolution while opening the way to war and Fascism.

Hitler had left to Petain — that was, to the Army high command, supported by "some anglophobe politicians" and the central core of the bourgeoisie — the "free zone" with its capital at Vichy and the job of dealing with the refugee problem and maintaining order cheaply, while enabling him to concentrate his forces for the invasion of Great Britain. The policy of collaboration and the denunciation by Vichy of Great Britain, again given the status of hereditary "enemy" were an invaluable lesson for the French workers:

> The bourgeoisie .... everywhere and always curbs, in the name of "national" interests, the struggle of the proletariat for its emancipation. The experience of France shows once more that "national" considerations serve only to mask the interests of the bourgeoisie which is always ready to change sides when it is a question of preserving its privileges.[7]

The fate of England had not yet been settled in a conflict which was still spreading. Laval was hoping for a German victory as a result of which he hoped that the French bourgeoisie would be able to participate in the "reconstruction" of Europe. The Manifesto continues:

> The struggle for democracy under the flag of England (and the United States) will not lead to a noticeably different situation. General De Gaulle struggles against "slavery" at the head of colonial governors, that is to say, of slave masters. In his appeals, this "leader" uses, just like Petain, the royal "we." The defense of democracy is in good hands! If England

---

6. We have used here one unsigned article, twelve signed Marc Loris and two signed Daniel Logan; fourteen published in *Fourth International* and one in *Quatrième Internationale*.

   The Manifesto appeared in *Fourth International*, I, no.7, December 1940, pp179-182, under the title "France under Hitler and Petain. Manifesto of the Fourth International". For the original in English see http://www.marxists.org/history/etol/writers/heijen/index.htm.

7. Ibid, p180.

should install De Gaulle in France tomorrow, his regime would not be distinguished in the least from that of the Bonapartist government of Petain.[8]

It was not on the military chiefs that van Heijenoort focused. For him, the class struggle continued:

> The big French bourgeoisie has already succeeded in arriving at an understanding with Hitler. National resistance is concentrated in the poorer sections of the population, the urban petty-bourgeoisie, the peasants, the workers. But it is the latter which give the most resolute character to the struggle and will know how to connect it with the struggle against French capitalism and the Petain government.[9]

An act of faith? Van enumerated the evils which were starting to hit them: food shortages, unemployment, inflation and price rises and control of the economy by the large companies. After having drafted the broad outline of a programme of transitional demands (workers control of food supply, sliding scale of working hours and wages, workers' control of the production, elected factory committees), he continued:

> The present situation will scarcely last long. Up to now Hitler's successes have been due above all to the weakness and decline of the democracies. The real test of the Nazi system has only begun.

He predicted "the inevitable revolts" whose outcome would be determined by the existence of a revolutionary leadership and the Manifesto ends in a statement of faith in the victory of the IVth International in the new period, "that of the struggles and the convulsions of the death agony of capitalism".[10]

The second article by Marc Loris related to Europe and its prospects[11]. The author's youth had been marked by the German occupation of the North of France and he was aware of the people's feeling of hatred against the foreign occupier. He noted as a prominent feature the similarity of the situation everywhere in the various occupied countries, and everywhere the decline of national fascist movements under the German occupation. He stated on the other hand that the upper bourgeoisie was most deeply involved in collaboration and that the advent in France of Admiral Darlan, who derived his influence from his fleet, a major element in the situation, had made Vichy what he called amusingly a "naval Bonapartism".

On the prospects, he was categorical: Hitler could not unify Europe because the national feeling, which had initially helped him, had come back with a

8. Ibid.
9. Ibid.
10. Ibid, p182.
11. Marc Loris, "Perspectives for Europe", *Fourth International*, II, no.6, July 1941, pp179-182.

tenfold strength in the occupied countries. The European revolution which was coming would be led by the proletariat and would be characterised by the appearance of Soviets and a more or less long period of dual power. The question of the revolutionary leadership could only be settled if the candidates for this rôle recognised the rising wave of hatred against the occupier and drew the consequences by a declaration of the right to national self-determination.

Criticising the conception according to which the fight against national oppression would force the proletariat to make an alliance with the petty bourgeoisie on the basis of the latter's demands, he vigorously emphasised that the socialist transformation of society was the only guarantee of the end of national oppression.

Noting that there was developing among both the petty bourgeoisie and even the workers in France a pro-English feeling, he dealt with the question by insisting that it was only necessary to envisage the types of struggle which were coming and to prepare for them. That meant in particular firmness against the petty-bourgeois methods of individual terrorism and sabotage. He concluded:

> Throughout Europe the proletariat is now submerged in the troubled waters of chauvinism. But the socialist solution, so remote today, obscured by nationalisms of all shades, tomorrow will be placed on the order of the day at once. The lessons of yesterday, the situation today and the tasks of tomorrow must be explained patiently to the advanced workers. The cadres of the party of the revolution must be gathered together. But this preparation is neither possible nor worthwhile except by participating in all forms of mass resistance to misery and oppression, by working to organize this resistance, to co-ordinate and broaden it. It is a task demanding the greatest efforts. But they are worth it, for tomorrow they will bear fruits a hundredfold.[12]

It was in October 1941 that Marc Loris saw "the first signs of the storm in France". The conditions in his opinion, had radically changed in the past months: Petain, whose base was weakened, was dedicated to "loyal collaboration", and the terrorist attacks, like that directed against Laval, were, despite of their futility, an indication of crisis. He wondered whether there was a relationship between the growth of individual terrorism and the Stalinist policy of defense of the USSR by all means, admitted that he was not able to settle the question, but repeated that the coming explosion was approaching and that it was necessary to build the revolutionary party before then.

The article "Europe under the Iron Heel", dated 28 January 1942[13], was a remarkable attempt to describe and analyze resistance in Europe. It described the various armed "resistance" activities, attacks against soldiers of Wehrmacht,

12. Ibid p182. For the original in English see http://www.marxists.org/history/etol/writers/heijen/index.htm.
13. Marc Loris, "Europe under the Iron Héel", ibid, January 1942, pp52-57. For the original in English see http://www.marxists.org/history/etol/writers/heijen/index.htm.

attacks against their buildings, sabotage of the telephone installations, the railways and the bloody response of the Nazis leaders — executions of hostages. He stressed the importance of industrial sabotage, ranging from passive resistance to poor manufacture, continual misunderstanding of orders, which caused many "accidents" to materials.

Then he studied the clandestine press in which he first of all distinguished the newspapers that he called "national-bourgeois", which called for a union of the "men of goodwill", but were very guarded about their intentions at "liberation". He stressed that some avoided too much criticism of Petain and that others said openly that they blamed him, above all, for opening the road to revolution. He showed that some of them sharply criticised the Communist Party by pointing out the desertion of Thorez in 1939. He spoke about the ambiguous attitude of the CP and the clandestine *Humanité* to Germany until the attack of 22 June 1941 and indicated in a sentence the new line of the "National Front". In a few words he described the attitude of the churches, all the more divided since they were rooted in society and, he pointed out, in this last case, that the mass of the faithful were hostile to the occupation. For him, the hierarchy in general was playing into the hands of the collaborators. Once more he emphasised the decomposition and accelerated decline of the "indigenous" Nazis groups totally compromised by their links with the occupier, more hated than them if that were possible. He was very cautious about the state of affairs among the occupying troops and the rumours of mutinies and executions, but on the other hand he made a solid analysis of the economic situation, the draining of resources by the occupier, the shortages and inflation, the development of black market, together with the social consequences for France of the mass of prisoners of war kept in Germany. He thought that the reports of real hunger riots in several large French cities at the end of 1941 were to be believed.

The sequel to this analysis was in the July 1942 article entitled of Washington's "New Order"[14], in which he analysed the declarations by the Secretary of State Summer Welles and in particular his comment on the "Atlantic Charter". He wrote:

> Today Hitler's "New Order" has already shown its real face. It is something old — oppression, misery, exploitation. But the "democracies" as well have nothing else to bring to the world. American imperialism is unable to develop the wealth of the globe by making fantastic promises. Far from raising China and India to the material level of the advanced countries, it can only reduce Europe to the level of India. [....] the *pax americana* will be, in the final count, as unstable as

---

14. Marc Loris, "The Washington "New Order", ibid, III, no.7, pp211-214. For the original in English see http://www.marxists.org/history/etol/writers/heijen/index.htm.

the *pax germanica*. The union of the workers will be the peace of the world.[15]

The two long articles on "The National Question" and "The Tasks of Revolutionaries under the Nazi Boot"[16] constitute in a sense the core of Jean van Heijenoort's thoughts after the three years of war and two of occupation. It is a veiled polemic against those in the movement, who treated the national question with contempt and did not understand the fantastic revolutionary power that came from generalised hatred of national oppression under the Nazi jackboot, and he also asserted the progressive character of a number of small bourgeois groupings of resistance which he stated should not be confused with "the Gaullists". For him, the latter used the national feeling to chain resistance to the imperialist camp. A more educational approach was needed with other groups which were turning towards socialism but remained very confused. And van Heijenoort insisted on the value and the importance of the democratic slogans during the coming period, in particular that of the Constituent Assembly, which many Trotskyist leaders saw both as a concession to opportunism and at the same time as something counterposed to soviets. The elements of the conflict which would oppose van Heijenoort and his allies, Goldman and Morrow, to Cannon and the SWP leadership were now in existence.

However it remained to deal with the political aspects of the allied landings in North Africa. Van saw a clear confirmation of his world analysis in the decision to keep the admiral Darlan[17], the heir-apparent of Petain and chief of government of "the French State" in Algiers in power. The account he gave, derived from the reports in the *New York Times* was very appropriate, as was his assessment:

> Now, this ex-democrat turned fascist has become an ex-fascist democrat and he works to "free" France.[18]

And van Heijenoort stressed that the American generals, to explain the confidence that they had in the Admiral, invoked "non-interference" in French politics, a supreme hypocrisy, however, since one the first things they had done was to recover the weapons which had fallen into the hands of Algerian peasants.

The conclusions of Van about this episode are very optimistic, because he considered it revealing.

15. Ibid, p215.
16. Marc Loris, "The National Question in Europe ibid, III, no.9, pp264-268 & "Revolutionary Tasks under the Nazi Boot", ibid no.11, pp333-338, both published in French in *Cahiers Léon Trotsky*, LT no.23, cf N.2. For the originals in English see http://www.marxists.org/history/etol/writers/heijen/index.htm.
17. Marc Loris: "North Africa, A Lesson in Democracy", ibid III, no.11, pp359-362. For the original in English see http://www.marxists.org/history/etol/writers/heijen/index.htm.
18. Ibid, p361.

He wrote:

> The American collaboration with Darlan must have tremendous political repercussions, not only in France but throughout all Europe. For years millions of men have known intolerable suffering under the Nazi iron heel. A great number of them imagined that their liberation will come through the Anglo-American troops. The first act of the commander of these troops after the first landings was to collaborate with a lackey of the Nazi executioners, who finds a few hours enough to pass from one camp to the other. The people who are now still suffering and struggling under their own Darlans will learn quickly and well — we can be sure of that — the political lesson that must be drawn from this ignoble event.[19]

His last comment showed that he believed that the forecast of Trotsky was now close to becoming reality:

> On both sides of the stage the masks are falling off. This means we are approaching the final act, where a new figure enters the scene: the revolutionary proletariat.[20]

In fact, he would recall again on several occasions the Darlan business which he regarded as extraordinarily revealing of the war aims of the allies, or, if one preferred, of the character of the war. In "Political Misadventures of the French Bourgeoisie" (March 1943)[21] he reconsidered the role of the working masses in the resistance to the occupation, showing the pressure which they exerted, in France, on the so-called "Resistance" organisations and the alliance of the Gaullists and of Stalinists to keep this movement as a sacred union for war. Thus he stressed that reluctantly both because he broke army discipline and because he opposed Vichy which, for the French, embodied reaction, the monarchist Charles de Gaulle embodied a certain kind of "left".

As for its character, he defined it in a quotation taken from a broadcast speech by de Gaulle, where he criticized the American policy of support for Darlan, on 6 December 1942:

> The nation will not permit that these men, having failed in foreign war and feeling themselves condemned, should save themselves by creating conditions from which would spring civil war.[22]

His comment struck like a blow from a fist:

---

19. Ibid, p362.
20. Ibid.
21. Marc Loris, "The Political Misadventures of French Bourgeoisie", ibid IV, no.3, pp76-79. For the original in English see http://www.marxists.org/history/etol/writers/heijen/index.htm.
22. Ibid p78.

Thus, according to the general, the deal with Darlan is dangerous because it revives class antagonisms. Since then, several spokesmen of the Gaullist movement have underlined the fact that Washington's policy in North Africa increases the danger of communism in France, against which the Gaullist movement is a much better guarantee than Darlan or Giraud.[23]

A few weeks later, still in *Fourth International*, still under the name of Marc Loris, van Heijenoort studied the conflict between Giraud, the man of the Americans and de Gaulle, who, he said, was in this matter not in the pockets of the British.[24] For him, this conflict is full of lessons, because it marked what he called "this political rebirth of the French bourgeoisie", ... "in the very special conditions of a colonial milieu".

According to him, Giraud, the personification of the military chief, had no other program but that of Vichy whose rule in Africa he had maintained, but the general outcry which followed the agreement with Darlan obliged him "to take a democratic mask" and he had to throw out some ballast by dismissing the too well-known Vichyites: which did not prevent him from stressing that he had "no wish to revive the follies that led to the catastrophe in 1940.", an allusion, in the purest Vichyite style, to the strike movement of June 1936 and the working-class upsurge.

De Gaulle, at the beginning represented a "purely national-military" opposition, but had covered himself since then with a programme of "democracy" and "restoration of republican legality" to preserve contact with and to gain, if possible, control of the Resistance in the interior. The fact that he succeeded in getting foothold in Algiers, against the will of the American government, illustrated the instability of the pax americana. In July 1943, van Heijenoort was astonished that the French upper bourgeoisie did not yet seem to have chosen "the most intransigent bourgeois" nationalism" this Gaullism which, in North Africa, succeeded in bringing together officers of high rank, youth, the students and the "left" petty bourgeois, and which among the working class enjoyed the support of the CP.

His conclusion is a remark of long term significance with which a historian of colonial wars could not fail to be struck.. He stressed how difficult it was for a ruling class to reconstruct its national unity after a military defeat, especially if it had broken the officer corps, like that of 1940 which led to the demand for an armistice and de Gaulle's broadcast of 18 June, indications of a rupture which would last a long time.

The last contribution of van Heijenoort on the European question in the columns of Fourth International is an article entitled "Whither France?", signed Daniel Logan, and dated 17 September 1944.[25]

23. Ibid.
24. Marc Loris, "The Giraud-de Gaulle Dispute", ibid IV, no.7, pp199-202. For the original in English see http://www.marxists.org/history/etol/writers/heijen/index.htm.
25. Daniel Logan, "Whither France?", V, no.9, pp267-270. For the original in English see http://

He started with the observation that a real insurrection had just occurred in France against the German occupation. The press reports of American correspondents enabled him to show that this insurrection was in the majority of cases preceded by strikes in the factories and forced on by the pressure of the masses. He stressed that this insurrection, "whose immediate objective was to destroy the German yoke", had thus a "popular" and "unanimous" nature which made it resemble the revolutions of the 19th century.

Power was in the hands of insurgents and, even more important than the presence of armed civilians in the streets, was the fact that the factories passed into the hands of the workers as was shown in an article by David Anderson in the New York Times of 7 September. How would the question of property be dealt with? He thought that it could only be by a workers' government:

> The first necessary conditions to go along this road are already here: a firm will among the workers not to go back to the past, a deep contempt for the ruling classes, a great confidence in their forces. That's what the mere existence of the workers' committees means. They will gradually fully understand the implications of their position and draw the revolutionary conclusions. The obstacles will not be lacking, the most dangerous of them being the treacherous policy of the Stalinist Party. But the French workers are on the march.[26]

The article by the American journalist led van Heijenoort to a certain number of remarks on points which he thought of greatest importance: the Parisian FFI [French Forces of the Interior] were in fact, according to him, the armed working class, the workers militia in the factories. He stressed their political heterogeneity while indicating the great weight of the CP. He wrote:

> On the whole, a leftist spirit must dominate, — a great thirst for freedom, a deep distrust for authority, a complete contempt for the old ruling classes, with their industrialists and bankers compromised by collaboration, a strong desire for something new.[27]

He explained De Gaulle thus:

> De Gaulle's program is, nationally and internationally, the restoration of bourgeois France. Nationally, his first aim is the reestablishment of "law and order." The present objective of De Gaulle is to stifle the uprising against the Nazis and Vichy in the noose of "republican legality", —

---

www.marxists.org/history/etol/writers/heijen/index.htm.
26. Ibid p268.
27. Ibid p269.

which, of course, would not prevent the general from using in the future, if need be, the Bonapartist sabre.[28]

For the rest, he could make only hollow promises, and announce elections eventually while immediately nominating prefects who came into conflict with against the liberation committees.

For the first time since he had been writing for the American journal, van Heijenoort finally tackled the question of Stalinist influence. The bad state of relations between Gaullists and Stalinists, at the time when he wrote, he explained by the removal of the French Communists from the government and the will of the latter to channel the present discontent against the "men of Algiers". He did not underestimate them, and wrote:

> The Stalinist influence among the Parisian workers is very great .... The party has strong positions in the FFI. In fact, the Stalinist Party is the strongest organised political force in France. It has avoided outright collaboration with De Gaulle and is, at the present time, in a kind of opposition, which cannot fail to increase its influence.[29]

The conflict on the horizon was that of the arming of the people:

> After the first "popular", "unanimous" stage of an uprising is over, a problem inevitably rises up: what to do with the arms that brought victory? Today in France hundreds of thousands (maybe over a million) have arms in their hands. The De Gaulle government cannot tolerate such a situation for long, so fraught with dangers for the bourgeois "law and order." It can do, and is probably attempting to do, two things: either outright disarming the FFI groups or incorporating them into the regular French army. In the second case the question of the discipline would immediately rise up. The FFI elected or chose their own leaders. In the regular army they have to obey officers imposed upon them from above.
> [...]The problem of disarming the population will occupy a large part of the political arena in the coming period.
> [...]De Gaulle has obviously not the force at the present time to imitate Thiers. His first task is the regrouping of the bourgeoisie. He will eliminate its most discredited and hated representatives, soothe its divisions, try to give it back its internal strength and cohesion and an honest face. He needs time.[30]

This time, van Heijenoort did not conclude with the need for "the revolutionary party" and for the victory of the revolution.

28. Ibid.
29. Ibid.
30. Ibid p270.

He concluded:

> Victory will not be easy. But the French workers have made a good start: coming out of the political primitivism of German oppression, they have immediately started to storm capitalist society. We are entitled to place our highest hopes in them.[31]

In the meantime, Jean van Heijenoort had devoted an article to the Italian situation: "Problems of the Italian Revolution" dated 9 July 1944, which did not appear in Fourth International like the preceding ones, but in the *Quatrième Internationale* of the European secretariat in January-February 1945[32]. It was already clear that he had differences with the SWP leadership and even with the European secretariat.[33]

The author started by recalling that Italian Fascism, for a long time the "herald of the reaction" appeared "one of the weakest links" of capitalism. With the fall of the Mussolini regime, "like a rotten apple" Italy has entered a period "of revolutionary instability":

> The Italian revolution is still in its infancy, but it will grow, will fight, will educate itself and will win. Nobody has any more illusions in the stability of the present regime.[34]

The primary question in his eyes was that of monarchy: whether it was that of the king or the crown prince recently proclaimed the lieutenant-general of the kingdom with the blessing of Togliatti's CPI, the monarchy remained the centre of reaction, as in the time of Mussolini, which it had borne in its arms for so long. Van Heijenoort wrote:

> To all the monarchists, to the ambulating corpses of liberalism and to the stalino-royalists, the revolutionary party must answer by the slogan: Immediate proclamation of the Republic, arrest of the king, the crown prince and the royal family, immediate confiscation of all their goods for the benefit of the people![35]

He commented:

> The party that during present weeks would untiringly diffuse these slogans among the large masses would infallibly draw their attention and thus prepare their ears to receive more advanced slogans. At a further

31. Ibid.
32. Marc Loris, "Problèmes de la Révolution italienne" in *Quatrième International*, janvier-fevrier 1945, no.14/15, pp19-22.
33. An introductory note to Loris's article expressed reservations because of the date at which it was written, six months earlier. It should be remembered that the Loris article can be found in almost its entirety in that of Logan cited below.
34. *Quatrième International*, no.14/15, p19.
35. Ibid p20.

stage it would enjoy the authority of having foreseen the march of the development and of having been with the masses in their most elementary struggles.³⁶

To the primary slogan of the "republic", he added that of the "constituent assembly" together with elections of officials by the people as the only correct way of "purging", the rights of assembly, freedom of press, meeting, of association, the separation of the Church and the State and the confiscation of Church property.

Breaking with a position which had been his at the beginning of the war, he proposed, on the question of the Soviets, to push the idea in a more "Italian" form. Continuing what was apparently an internal polemic within the SWP, he wrote: "The opposition between the national assembly and the Soviets is at present completely artificial. It becomes a reality only at a higher level of struggle — in fact with its conclusion. If Soviets make their appearance in Italy in the immediate future, it will be by mobilizing the masses on the basis of democratic watchwords [...] the formula should not be "Constituent assembly or Soviets" but to "create Soviets and develop their political consciousness". ³⁷

His work on the problems of the Italian revolution ended in a long warning against "the danger of ultra-leftism" and a warning which showed where the core of the discussion was:

> History puts *all* the teachings of Bolshevism on the order of the day more imperatively than ever. And one of these lessons is Bolshevism's contempt for mere enlightening propaganda about the virtues of Socialism, its ability to feel the aspirations of the masses, to seize upon the progressive side of these aspirations and on that point to drive a wedge that would detach the masses from their conservative parties and leaders. Can this lesson be forgotten in the present time?³⁸

So it is no surprise that the last article signed Daniel Logan to appear on this general area in 1945 was a piece dated 1 October 1944 entitled "On The European Situation And Our Tasks", a closely argued critique of the SWP congress resolution from November 1944, presented by the editorial board as a discussion article from a member of the minority.

It was a timely intervention. It allowed the author at least to emphasise some inconsistencies and show that the line which underlay them was not particularly clear. Moreover he attacked with devastating irony the assertion of the SWP leadership according to which the coalition government of Ivanoe Bonomi in particular, including Socialist and Communist ministers, would only be a cover for the "open military dictatorship" of the Anglo-American occupation.

36. Ibid.
37. Ibid p21.
38. Ibid p22.

He also stressed the confusion which prevailed in the majority resolution on the possibility of seeing the re-appearance in Europe of bourgeois democratic regimes, the only real alternative after the war being, according to it, either the dictatorship of the proletariat or the most brutal police or military dictatorships.

Pointing out that the majority resolution spoke neither about the slogan of "republic", nor of that of "constituent assembly", limiting itself to "the election of officials" and the "freedom of the press" he suggested the launching of the slogan of a "Togliatti-Nenni Government" (PC-PS).

He explained:

> Thousands, tens of thousands can learn through direct propaganda. [...] But millions, tens of millions have to come to Socialism through their own experience. They have to discard, one after the other, regimes about which they have had illusions. They have to discard false leaders in whom they have put their confidence. The task of the revolutionary party is to speed up and facilitate that process as much as possible, but it cannot jump over it. This is precisely what programs of democratic or transitional demands are designed for.[39]

The amendments presented by Van at the national congress were rejected by 51 votes to 5. A few weeks later, he declared himself in favour of transferring the powers of the IS [International Secretariat] in New York to the ES [European Secretariat] in Paris, putting an end to this situation. His struggle in the SWP minority with Goldman and Morrow belongs to another chapter of the history of IV International.

The best analyst of the SWP, Alan Wald, in the few allusions which he makes to Goldman, Morrow and van Heijenoort, is very severe towards them, recognising however that they were largely correct when they opened the discussion and when they raised the problems of methods, but criticised them for having deviated seriously and having become hostile, adopting methods that they themselves had condemned.[40]

Such as it was, with its breaks, imperceptible turns, interruptions, and with the gaps in our knowledge, the route of Jean van Heijenoort between 1940 and 1944 is enthralling. In conclusion one finds there very little incantation and acts of faith, of hollow formulae and set language, but on the other hand a permanent attempt to analyse the facts under development as Trotsky would have done. In this respect, this reflection is rather impressive, opening horizons of which professional historians and political commentators seem to have been unaware.

His thought seems to have become more concrete as the formulae and references, which were not justified by reality but which at first he considered essential to convince people of his orthodoxy, disappear. From this point of

---

39. Ibid p31.
40. Alan Wald, *The New York Intellectuals*, NY, 1987, pp254-256.

view, it seems that van Heijenoort evolved while moving away from and even opposing Cannon, whose more rigorous formulations were often scarcely compatible with a complex reality.

There remained a terrible gap. The ritualistic references of the early years were followed at the end of this period by the recognition, which was not completely disillusioned, that the "revolutionary party" did not exist; the revolutionary crisis had not waited for it, and without it, it was fated to go into decline.

Like all the Trotskyists of his generation, wasn't Van convinced that, without such a party, the revolution had not least chance of being successful?

Was this, in the last analysis, the cause of a certain despair observable both in his writings and in later remarks made in confidence? The last political text of van Heijenoort, his farewell to Marxism, placed the responsibility for the "bankruptcy" of the revolutionary cause on the working class which had failed to play the role of a revolutionary class, and thus forced the revolutionaries who had expected too much to recognise that their beliefs had been illusions and their analyses abstract constructions.[41]

Under these conditions, indeed, one cannot long continue an effort in the political field, if one has a feeling, which undoubtedly van Heijenoort had, that he could "be useful" in and develop his enthusiasm in another area. But I maintain the conviction that the isolated French Trotskyist in New York who tried to disentangle and get a grasp of the chain which led from national oppression to proletarian revolution, did not waste his time and that his effort to understand the course of the war will one day, in one way or another, help to understand and to change the world.

---

41. Jean Vannier (JvH), "A Century's Balance Sheet", *Partisan Review*, March 1948, pp288-296.

Obituaries

Ted Grant (1913-1006)

THE death of Ted Grant marks the passing of one of the last of that generation who came into revolutionary activity in the aftermath of the Russian revolution. I got to know him well over the past 40 years, as a member of the Socialist Party, since my first involvement with *Militant* in 1964. Unlike many of his contemporaries, however, Ted Grant remained firmly convinced in the ideas that had led that revolution until his death. It is impossible to write an obituary of Ted Grant without also writing a history of the Trotskyist movement, so completely was the story of his life also the story British — and international — Trotskyism.

It is also impossible, when writing an obituary, not to look back on the life of an individual and find in their youth the seeds of what they were to become. And so it is with Ted Grant.

Grant was steeped in the ideas and primarily the method of Marxism, and it was this understanding that enabled him to make his great contribution to the arsenal of Marxism, the application and development of those ideas to the situation the world found itself in after 1945.

For the revolutionary movement, that world was vastly changed from that it had worked in pre-war. The assassination of Trotsky had removed the last great thinker from the International, and the movement found itself rudderless in a rapidly changing world. Trotsky had indicated that the end of the war would see a revolutionary wave sweep the world, as had happened after 1918; its failure to materialise in precisely the way Trotsky had suggested threw the International completely off balance. The leadership turned in every direction in an attempt to understand the situation. For some, capitalism had solved its problems — the old cycle of slump and boom were gone. For others, the Chinese revolution was a victory for the Chinese bourgeoisie, and had ushered in a new period for capitalism. Still others saw in countries like Yugoslavia healthy workers states, and urged the youth of the International to go there to help build the new society.

In the International, only a few lone voices stood out. In America, a minority with Morrow and Goldman argued against a simple repetition of Trotsky's perspectives. In England, it was Ted Grant and the Revolutionary Communist

Party majority who recognised that the revolutionary wave had indeed taken place — the movements in Eastern Europe, the victory of the radical-sounding Labour Party in the UK, the independent movements of the working class in Paris and Italy, the Chinese revolution, the movements against colonialism throughout Africa and Asia — but that these were in the process of being derailed by Stalinism and social democracy. Yet this also brought out another aspect of Grant's make-up — his refusal to acknowledge the contribution others made to the development of theory. There can be no doubt that others in the RCP leadership, such as Jock Haston and others, played an important part in developing the Party's theoretical direction after the war, but no credit to them was ever given by Grant. Even his analysis of the period as being "counter-revolution in democratic form" draws on Morrow's writings. I personally came across Morrow's writings by accident; never did Grant attempt to develop and broaden the theoretical level by encouraging the youth to read others from the Trotskyist tradition and never was recognition given to the theoretical foresight of others.

From this period, Grant's *The Marxist Theory of the State* (1949) was his first and probably most important contribution. After a false start, where he convinced Tony Cliff that the USSR was state capitalist, Ted looked over the edge and saw the abyss to which this idea could lead the movement. In one of his favourite phrases, he "went back to the books" and produced a major contribution on the question of the nature of the state, the dynamics of Stalinism and the processes of the colonial revolution. It is, of course, an irony that it was through this discussion in the RCP that Tony Cliff developed his theory of state capitalism. It was this method he used to analyse the Chinese revolution, being one of the first to hail it as the greatest event in the history of the working class since the Russian Revolution, an overthrow of landlordism and capitalism that took, however, the deformed form of Stalinism from the outset.

To those who argued that capitalism had changed its spots, he produced *Will there be a Slump?*(1960), restating the cyclical nature of capitalism and the dynamics of the capitalist economy. Taken as a whole, it was this body of work that armed the movement here and enabled the rebuilding of international Marxism in the years to come, the theoretical bedrock on which the *Militant*, the *Socialist Party* and the Committee for a Workers International (CWI) would be built.

An obituary, however, is not a eulogy; it must examine an individual as a rounded out human being, warts and all. The tragedy of Ted Grant's life was that, despite the enormous contribution he made to the movement and despite the lasting importance of the body of work that he left behind, he was often a stumbling block to the very movement he had helped build, unable, towards the end of his life, to repeat the role he played in the 1940s of understanding the new world situation.

Others have written here about the post-war world. This was a difficult time for Ted. His party had been reduced to a handful of individuals, and there was the desperate need to rebuild and develop. Ted took various jobs — a door to door salesman, a telephone switchboard operator — to try to raise the money to finance the rebuilding. But if theory was the strongest weapon in Ted's arsenal, organisation certainly was not. Objectively and subjectively, the post war years were a long and painful period.

The first requirement of a revolutionary leader is historical honesty; in all his writings, Trotsky was meticulous in recording accurately the truth of the events he took part in. For Ted Grant, unpleasant memories just did not happen. An example is the role he took at the end of the war. The RCP had been a high point for Marxism in the UK, yet the post war period saw its collapse into a number of competing factions. Where to work was the prime question; Gerry Healey and his group had left the RCP in 1947 and entered the Labour Party on a completely opportunist basis. However, towards the end of 1948, Jock Haston, then General Secretary of the RCP, began to argue for working in the Labour Party despite there not being any immediate prospects for large scale gains through this work. There is no doubt that work outside the Labour Party would have been more productive in that period — and there is also no doubt that Ted Grant knew this. Instead, he resolved to stand with "a tested leadership" against the newer, younger RCP members — the Open Party faction — calling for an open party to be maintained — and capitulate to those in the Labour Party. Rapidly, however, once the RCP had dissolved itself and all were inside the Labour Party, most of the old "tested leadership" fell away and the "unified" Trotskyist group in the Labour Party was purged of dissidents under the tender ministrations of Gerry Healey. Throughout his life, Grant argued that this had not been a mistake — either in or out of the Labour Party, he claimed, would have made no difference. Only towards the very end of his life did Grant finally admit that his stand had been a mistake.

After the collapse of the RCP, these were lean years for Grant and the small group around him. But to talk to him about these years, to try and discuss the development of International Socialism or *Socialist Current* — both short lived ventures in the 1950s — was an impossibility. It is hard not to draw the conclusion that the reason for this was that the group that continued to publish *Socialist Current* after breaking with Grant was composed of many of those who had been in the Open Party faction. For Ted though, the period between the high spot of the RCP and founding of the *Militant* had hardly happened.

Engels once commented that it was better to split an organisation and have a small group that turned itself out to the wider labour movement than a large organisation riven by internal dissent and paralysed from doing any real work. For Ted Grant and the supporters around him, though, the years of uphill struggle took their toll, and in the early 1960s attempts were made to ally with first with the youth of the International Socialists (forerunners of the SWP) in *Young Guard*, and then, under pressure from the Fourth International, with the International Group around Pat Jordan and Ken Coates. These attempts reflected the despair of sections of the group around Grant — and both were doomed to failure. Both mergers had been opposed by the comrades in

Liverpool, at that time including Tony Mulhearn, Ted Mooney and Peter Taaffe. Indeed, the Liverpool comrades walked out of the unity conference. That Liverpool continued to produce a youth journal, along with the recruiting of fresh new supporters in other areas, was a significant factor in the decision to found the *Militant* in 1964.

It was that event, the founding of *Militant*, that changed the future for British Trotskyism. Objectively, the situation was ripe. Labour looked likely to win the election after years of Tory corruption and scandal. The comrades in Liverpool had built up a strong base for the tendency in the Labour Party through their work in the youth field the publication of *Rally*, the activity in Walton CLP and the, often haphazard, publication of *Socialist Fight* in London. At the same time, they had recruited a number of new comrades through their leadership in the area of the 1960 apprentices' strike.

Virtually from the beginning, though, a question mark hung over Grant's attitude towards work in the Labour Party. All the writings of Trotsky, all the documents that provided the theoretical grounding for work in the mass party, discussed this as a tactical issue, to be re-discussed and evaluated as other opportunities presented themselves, as the class struggle developed and changed in character. Yet for Ted Grant, this was becoming a mantra: work in the Labour Party was paramount and should be protected at all costs. This was in complete contrast to the great flexibility regarding the Labour Party shown by the WIL, the organisation Grant helped found in 1937, and later by the RCP. Already, in the 1950s, Grant had abstained in the vote when Bill Hunter was expelled from the Labour Party, in order to protect his own position. Honesty, principle and the ability to openly work for the ideas of Marxism were in danger of being sacrificed to the "principle" of work in the Labour Party.

In many respects, the work went on despite him, combining the tactic of work in the Labour Party with open work and campaigning struggle. A tremendous base was built for the ideas of Marxism, grounded on the theory that Grant brought to the movement. But theory without the ability to turn it into practice can lead to disaster. For years, Grant had armed the movement with the tactic of working in the Labour Party; convincing local Labour Party workers to support the ideas of *Militant* and select Marxist candidates, and the victory in getting three MPs elected, was a great success for Trotskyism in Britain. But this tactic became a principle writ in stone — nothing could be done that might endanger the position of the MPs. So Grant clashed on tactics during the Liverpool struggle, the campaign against the expulsions, during the fight against the poll tax — everything was subservient to keeping our position in the Labour Party, even to the extent of suggesting that our MPs pay the poll tax to prevent their expulsion from the Labour Party! Where would the name of Terry Fields now be in the history of the Liverpool labour movement if he had taken that road rather than go to prison as other working people did, let alone the 34 *Militant* supporters who were imprisoned? What had started out as a tactic was now an unchanging principle.

So too, that flexibility of thought and tactics that had been Grant's hallmark in the 1930s and 1940s turned into mantras that could not be changed, with dire consequences for the development of the movement. The science of perspectives turned into repeated dogma. For example, the forced fusion with the International Group in 1963-1964 could have been a disaster; the first few issues of *Militant* bear testimony to their influence, and, as indicated above, nearly split Grant's group. However, the long-standing political disagreements with the Fourth International led to the predicted split — or, rather, with the behind-the-scenes manoeuvring that was the hallmark of the USFI, the *de facto* expulsion of the British section and the recognition of the International Group as their new representatives in 1965. What could have been seen as a tragic isolation was seen instead by both Ted Grant and Peter Taaffe, *Militant's* delegates to that World Congress, as a blessed liberation, the freedom to really start the building of Trotskyist internationalism. Turning their back on the old organisations, what Grant called the "groupscules", they turned the face of the *Militant* towards the youth and the new, fresh layers of the organised labour movement.

But, if Grant inculcated these new recruits with an orientation towards the mass movement, he combined with it a dogmatic refusal to believe that anyone other than the accepted leaders of Marxism could make a contribution to ideas or knowledge. Books were dismissed out of hand, unread, whether historical written by a member of the SWP or scientific written by university professors. Even novels which had not had the seal of approval were rejected as "rubbish" — again, unread. That broadness of thought that so characterised Trotsky, that led Marx, echoing the Roman dramatist Terence, to say "nothing human is alien to me", was missing from Ted's make up.

In the realm of theory, Ted Grant's *Will there be a Slump?* was one of the *Militant's* basic propaganda documents; it answered those who argued that capitalism had solved its problems, whether Keynesian or "permanent arms economy". Yet, for Grant, every turn in capitalism was a sign of this devastating slump to come. The harshest effect of this was in October 1987. Rather than soberly analysing the various factors at play, and thus preparing the movement for the different possibilities of what might occur, Ted predicted that Black Monday would lead to a 1929-style slump. When this failed to manifest itself, it had a major effect on the membership and supporters of the paper. Why had it not happened? Would it ever happen? How could a leader of the movement be so wrong? It was clear that others in leading positions had disagreed sharply with Grant over this; more and more *Militant* supporters were becoming aware of Grant's increasing dogmatism and his increasing separation from the reality of the movement's work.

The defeat of the Liverpool struggle, the defeat of the miners, the collapse of Stalinism, the fundamental change in the nature of the Labour Party — Ted Grant was unable to meet these new challenges. Instead, he retreated into stale repetitions of old tactics, old characterisations. For years, Grant refused to accept that capitalism had been restored in former USSR, in 1997 an introduction to his *Russia: from revolution to counter-revolution* still talked about "the attempt is being made to restore capitalism in Russia."

The clash, when it came, came as in 1949 — between what Ted regarded as "old guard" — i.e. himself — and a large majority of the "younger" members of the party. To him, the "youth" could not be trusted with the ideas of Marxism — only he could show a correct way forward; this reflected itself in the increasing difficulty in getting Grant to keep to his time when he spoke at meetings. Often, deep political differences first manifest themselves as minor, seemingly secondary issues; the split in the Russian Social Democratic Labour Party first arose over an obscure clause on Party membership. In the *Militant*, it was over who should speak at a European meeting, a "young" member (somewhat long in the tooth even then) or an "older member". This apparently unimportant issue rapidly developed into major political differences — on the Labour Party, on how to build, on the Soviet Union. Discussing with Ted Grant during that period, it was often difficult not to see him as an old man being used by others with their own particular agenda. It was clear his best days were behind him. Even an analysis of the state of the movement in the past few years was beyond him; in one of his last interviews, he still blamed the decline in the position of *Militant* not to objective factors, but to the mistakes of one man — Peter Taaffe!! Grant simply kept repeating that there was no "political life outside the Labour Party", just ignoring the fact that today the Socialist Party has 24 elected members on trade union national executives, far more than the *Militant* ever had.

A constant feature of Grant's outlook was his contempt for the other so-called Trotskyist groups. He was fond of describing the post war years, when he spoke of them searching the world for new heroes — first Tito, then Ben Bella — that they could fawn on as the new leaders of world revolution. This reached its pinnacle when the official leadership of world Trotskyism dubbed Castro as an "unconscious Trotskyist" and Cuba as a healthy workers state. Hegel, Marx and Trotsky wrote of things turning into their opposite; how tragic and how ironic that Grant and the grouplet he led are now doing precisely that as they fawn at the heels of new, modern day "heroes" — in Venezuela but also, irony of ironies, Cuba.

One of the real tragedies of Ted's later years was that he lost the respect and support of the very youth he saw as being so important for the future. If anything showed his inability to adapt to new conditions, it was war in Iraq and the Middle East. At the time of the Second World War, when there was mass revulsion at Nazism and a general mood amongst the working class to go to war, the Trotskyist movement opposed the war — but also argued that Marxists should go with their class into the army and carry out propaganda there, to turn the war into revolutionary struggle; the bourgeois were incapable of waging a war on Nazism. Fifty years later, the 1991 war in Iraq was clearly seen by large sections of the working class as a war for imperialism — "No Blood for Oil" — and any attempt at conscription would have led to mass refusal from the youth, a movement which the Marxists had a duty to intervene in and lead in a revolutionary direction. This was true even more so than in the US during the Vietnam war. For Grant, though, the old mantras held: if there was conscription, the youth would simply have to go and fight. When this was met with gasps of astonishment at one particular meeting, Grant reassured the youth: for every one of them that died, the movement would recruit ten more.

If this has been mostly a political obituary, it is also important to remember Ted as a human being. I first met him at the age of 15, just after the first edition of *Militant* was published. What impressed me most was the patience with which he explained things to me, a young, headstrong youth from a London East End Jewish Communist Party background. I learnt more about the fundamentals of Marxism from those early discussions with Ted than through years of reading and experience. I must have disagreed with something he said — now lost in the mists of time — but he called me a Doubting Thomas. From that day on, for the next 28 years, he continued to call me Thomas, although I am certain he knew my real name.

Then there were his eccentricities. His love of cowboy movies — "bang bangs" — was legendary; there is also the story of how he missed a vital meeting, only to be seen creeping out of the early Steve McQueen horror flick *The Blob*! He was adept at mangling English; for years I had the vision of the leader of Greek social democracy as an avuncular old gentleman called Pappy Andrew.

Other writers have commented on how he never lost his South African accent. He was once on a visit to Merseyside, and the mother of new young comrade in the wilds of Cheshire invited him round for a meal. "A cup of weak tea, please, dear" he asked. "Oh" she said, hearing his accent, "I never realised you were a colonial".

For those of us who came into revolutionary activity in the period from the 1960s, Ted Grant was an important figure, the link with the past directly to Trotsky and the Russian Revolution, a bedrock for the ideas of Marxism. New, young recruits to the revolutionary movement should read his works, learn from them — above all their method — and apply the flexibility of thought and tactics that the young Ted Grant was able to apply, and in this way rebuild the movement he spent his life building. This would be his greatest memorial.

Tony Aitman

We present here a document found in the late John Archer's files (for access to which we are grateful to Bob Archer). It takes the form of a draft letter to Bob Pitt. Cde Pitt has confirmed that he never received a letter from Archer about Militant, so we must assume the project was dropped, or redirected, perhaps at an audience within the "Lambertist" current (we use this personalisation merely as a convenience and not in a derogatory manner – their organisational names have changed a number of times and in recent years have declared themselves to be "The Fourth International", which we think some readers may find confusing.) There are other documents among Archer's papers that show he wished to contribute to work in the "Lambertist" current analysing the particular history of the Militant tendency and of Ted Grant.

Although clearly incomplete, the document brings to bear on the question of Militant and the political history of Ted Grant, Archer's decades of experience of the political issues and the personalities through whom they are brought to life. The notes are undated but clearly refer to a period after the split in Militant that separated Grant and his supporters (Socialist Appeal/IMT) from Taaffe and his (now known as the Socialist Party, and their affiliates, and which Archer refers to as the majority tendency). Some sections dealing with these discussions have been omitted.

As to how "Militant" developed

It would be unbalanced and wrong to make Grant the demon of the story. At the same time, his participation has been so inseparable that we have to write a political biography of him if we are to understand the "Tendency". His political biography requires not merely that we trace what has changed and what has remained the same in his political outlook, but also that we trace his principal role as "ideas-man" to activist groups.

For this purpose, I think that we have to describe — necessarily with a broad brush but, I hope, with a minimum of distortion or subjectivity, not merely the experience of the Trotskyists in the 1940's (to which leading elements in the "Majority" tendency of Militant have realised already that they have to go back), but even earlier, to the early 1930's, if for no other reason than that otherwise there will be confusion about the 1940's.

However remote the 1930's and 1940's may seem, this is not too formidable a task today. A good deal of the necessary preliminary research has been done. That a systematic analysis has not yet been achieved has to be blamed on the objective difficulties more than the shortcomings of the leaderships of the relatively larger groups, since the mere task of holding these groups together in a world situation in which for many years Stalinism and Social Democracy dominated the workers' organisations have not only restricted the possibilities of intellectual work but led them into triumphalist claims . . . To recognise this does not at all mean that we deny or forgive the disastrous mistakes which we must conclude that they have made. All we need is to see what these were.

The central purpose of these notes is to raise the prospect that some of us who regard ourselves as life-long Trotskyists may effectively achieve a political intervention in the present confusion in the "majority" tendency in order to promote the necessary development towards a workers' party in Britain, the British Section of the Fourth International which Trotsky helped to found in 1938.

The "majority" in the former "Militant Tendency", which split away under the leadership of Peter Taaffe in 1991 from the "minority", with which Grant remains associated, appears to me to represent an advanced though far from wholly healthy tendency. I regard the split as progressive and, in any case, inevitable. It appears to me to open up serious political possibilities in the direction of laying the foundation for the future workers' party. However, the "majority" took the step of splitting from the Grant circle empirically, under the influence of the layers of militant youth and of workers whom their activity mobilised in the Anti-Poll Tax Campaign. If the "majority" does not acquire the political means to clarify its position and to find the means which its members are seeking to go forward, then it will break up. The two fundamental problems, which underlie the multitude of episodic questions which these comrades are trying to discuss, are, not unsurprisingly, first the question of Stalinism and its collapse in the USSR and the world, and, secondly, (which is our immediate concern here) is centred round the British Labour Party.[1]

... believed that we must locate ourselves. Consequently, we believed that the class-struggle, in which correct work on our part would be an indispensable component, would break up the Labour Party, possibly isolating its reformist, right-wing and creating a mass centrist movement in which we would play a part. It was recognised that the "Militant Group" could not call openly in its press for the Fourth International at that stage, even while in their local work its members could raise in general terms the necessity for a new workers' international.

In 1936 the "Militant Group" took the point of view that everyone who accepted this perspective should individually join the Labour Party. This was because at that time everyone who opposed "entry" also opposed the above perspective, in the belief that "openly raising the banner of the revolutionary Party" would "attract the masses". In 1938, however, a serious possibility of combining "open" with "entry" work on the basis of the above perspective actually offered itself for a few months. In the unfavourable conditions of downturn in the class struggle, of defeat in France and Spain and of the rising threat of war, the Revolutionary Socialist League managed to produce simultaneously two modest monthly journals, one, "Militant" addressed to the workers inside the Labour Party around our fraction there, while the other, "Workers' Fight", could report on the Founding Conference of the Fourth International and publish its documents.

CLR James and others who rejected any "entrist" perspectives in Autumn 1936, did so because they disliked what it involved — unconditional electoral support for the LP. Trotsky thought this out very clearly, as the report shows, in his conversation with CLR early in 1939. Many others, who were to form the "Marxist Group" in Nov 1936 shared these views, which CLR then expounded.

The "Militant Group" and the RSL did not advance their conception of "entry" as some kind of supra-historical "law", to operate outside space and time, and today, in the light of more than fifty years' later experience, it may be

---

1. A page is missing from the document. It would appear that Archer begins an examination of the roots of Grant's "Militant" in the RSL and the "Militant Group" led by D.D.Harber, of which Archer was a leading member.

thought unwise to try to forecast in advance one form of break-up of the Labour Party rather than another. One possibility is that the extreme right could be driven out and that a centre would then be consolidated against the left, as has happened since the last fifteen years or so. We do not discuss here whether the Trotskyists could have gained more from the crisis in the Labour Party which led to driving out those who were to form the "Social-Democrats". Alternatively, the left could lead out of the Labour Party, to form some new, more "independent" political expression of the class struggle. Thirdly, the Labour Party leadership after purging their internal critics on the Left — and those who could influence the selection of candidates for seats which Labour could expect to win, could be drawn into an alliance with the Liberals or even, in time of crisis, into a coalition with the Conservatives, which, if it had broken its links with the trade union membership, would mean that it could no longer claim to speak in the name of the working class. Nor can we exclude the possibility that the central apparatus could collapse, under the impact of financial crisis and successive electoral defeats; we would then go back to the pre-1900 days of separate local candidatures claiming the workers' votes.

It would be absurd today to suggest that the "Militant Group" in 1936 could have pronounced the last word on "entry". No one foresaw that, at the end of World War Two, Stalinism and Social-Democracy would between them substantially dominate the workers' movement. At the same time, there can be no doubt that the "Militant Group" ruled out any notion of advancing itself as a ready-made "alternative leadership" to that of the reformists, or of short-term destructive "raids" on the Labour Party in order to pull individual militants out into "open work". (Healy and Banda were to try this, with little success, in Clapham in 1961).

The "Militant Group" refused likewise to lay down in advance any precise date by which "entry" was to be terminated. That would depend on circumstances which could be neither foreseen nor fully controlled by it. But in any case it was not likely to lie decades ahead. It expected that "entry" would end when the tensions within the Labour Party had reached the point that a substantial force of militants was ready to follow a lead, to break out of the organisational constraints imposed by the Labour Party. It saw in its own work, one essential element in creating such conditions. Moreover, the first step by the new "independent" organisation must be to turn its back on "leftist" illusions and campaign for a united front with the Labour Party.

The "Militant Group" leadership saw themselves as undertaking the politically demanding task of maintaining its orientation towards the conflicts in the Labour Party in which those expressing the historic interests of the working class clashed with the agents of the bourgeoisie. To do so successfully meant avoiding opportunism on the one hand and sectarianism on the other.

Therefore, if the apparatus succeeded in driving some or all of its people out of the Labour Party, they would not thereupon assert that the Labour Party was "finished" or had "sufficiently exposed itself" (as Healy was to claim in 1964).

They would continue to maintain their orientation to the conflicts within the Labour Party by a combination of "open" and "entry" work.

Moreover, the International Secretariat had kept them well informed about the difficulties which Trotsky and the French section had had in autumn 1935 in extracting their forces as a united body from the SFIO.

In general terms, therefore, they can be said to have conceived "entry", in the general conditions of the period, as a specific application of the United Front, and that they would continue to apply the same tactic in a new form after "entry" had ended.

However, the conditions in which they had to work during: the later 1930's, in which Stalinism and the threat of war contributed to paralysing the worker-militants, neither the "entrists" nor their opponents (whether inside or outside the Labour Party) could demonstrate their superiority by practical success. At the same time, sectarianism enjoyed something of a revival, fed by memories of the "Third Period". This is hardly surprising in the light of the prevalent opportunism of the Labour and Communist Parties. The possibility should not be excluded that, in more favourable conditions, the differences between the "Militant Group" and the other groups claiming to speak in Trotsky's name could not have been more deeply and successfully probed in the course of common work and discussion inside one organisation.

Today no one is likely to dispute that the central programmatic formula on which the "Militant Tendency" of later years, since 1965, has based itself has been that of "transforming the Labour Party", and that this came out of the head of Ted Grant. We should therefore consider how he came to play a leading role in the politics of Trotskyism in Britain and, to a certain extent, internationally. He arrived early in 1935 in Britain from South Africa. He had had some earlier political experience under the guidance of Ralph Lee, but had no previous knowledge or experience of the workers' movement in Britain. During his journey he had met Leon Sedov in Paris and soon joined "the Marxist Group in the ILP", in which the majority of the Trotskyists in Britain were grouped at the time. He contributed to drafting the "Marxist Group's" documents for struggle against the centrist leadership of the ILP at its National Conference at Easter 1935, at which the "Marxist Group" reached the top of its influence.

After Easter 1935 the "Marxist Group" could gain hardly any more ground in the ILP, which was falling to pieces. A long-drawn-out discussion in the "Marxist Group" followed, in the course of which Grant was to sign with a few others a letter appealing to the International Secretariat to intervene to resolve the differences about whether to leave the ILP or not and, if so, whether to turn to the Labour Party or to some kind of "open work", (It is hardly surprising that the International Secretariat took the view that the British comrades had themselves to go through the effort to resolve their problems, and that without that effort they would not develop politically. The International Secretariat did not hesitate to send Wolff to Britain at the end of 1936 to help the Labour Party "entrists" with advice about how to organise their work along the political line which they had decided for themselves.) But we missed the opportunities which the Socialist League offered in 1934/5.

By the autumn of 1936 the fraction work in the ILP had manifestly passed the end of its usefulness, and Grant joined the "Militant Group". In the spring on 1937 he was joined there by a second group of comrades from South Africa, led by Ralph Lee. Towards the end of 1937 Ralph Lee was to promote a "split" in the "Militant Group", which took out a minority of its members, including Grant and some recent recruits from the Communist Party such as Haston and Healy, to form a new group, the "Workers' International League". Early in 1938 the International Secretariat was to condemn the split as devoid of any political activation, while at the same time it censured the leaders of the "Militant Group" for their inept handling of the conflict. In retrospect, the writer, who supported the majority against Lee at the time, believes that the issues were by no means completely personal, but had to do with the difficulties of operating the "entry" tactic especially in the Labour Party League of Youth. Such differences do not appear from the surviving archives ever to have been clearly expressed, and in any case the conflict was embittered by impatience and frustration.

In the summer of 1938 the "Militant Group" fused with two smaller groups to form the Revolutionary Socialist League, which the Founding Conference of the Fourth International recognised as its British Section. The Workers' International League refused the invitation of James P. Cannon to join in the fusion. The documents in which it justified its separate existence and its refusal to participate are of political interest and will be considered later. The WIL was to join the Fourth International only in 1944.

This is not the place for the detailed study of the rich experiences of the Trotskyists in Britain during World War Two, which still awaits its historian. There was no significant difference between the political statements of the RSL and those of the WIL during the weeks immediately before World War Two was declared. However, soon afterwards, the WIL publicly attacked the RSL, interpreting its declarations in the "Militant" as being concessions to "pacifism" and as a retreat from a revolutionary attitude towards the war.

It is perfectly easy today to read in the archives what both parties actually wrote, but we cannot overlook that here we have an example of what has been a general feature of the experience of Trotskyists in Britain throughout over half a century of struggle. The same problems persistently recur in new guises in intergroup polemics, as, for instance, in connection with the Gulf War. Likewise the debates about the Labour Party become wearisomely repetitive. There is no continuous tradition of our history.

Lee went back to South Africa early in the war and a new leadership emerged in the WIL This was based on the former members of the Communist Party and of the YCL,. such as Haston and Healy and on a current of leftists and inexperienced worker-militants. None of these comrades had shared in the discussions in 1935-36 in which the leadership of the "Militant Group" had begun to work out its conception of "entry". In 1937 Lee and his supporters had found themselves "entering" the Labour Party as part of the "Militant Group" because at that time the "Militant Group" was the largest and best-functioning Trotskyist group in Britain. The documents which the WIL produced in summer 1938 expressed this background in an empirical acceptance of "entrism". Early in the war, in the changed conditions, they could quite easily write off the Labour Party as "moribund" and reject not merely its own "entry" but the Militant Group's orientation towards the Labour Party also.

The WIL seized the opportunity of directly participating in industrial struggle soon after the Reichswehr invaded Russia in June 1941. Grant, who had been invalided out of the army, soon became prominent in the role which he was later to play in the "Militant Tendency", writing political documents and doing the theoretical work for a predominantly activist group. The RSL and the WIL exchanged intensely polemical declarations between 1941 and 1943 about how best to assert the independence of the working class. While the Communist Party was collaborating with Churchill's government in its war-effort after the Nazi invasion brought the USSR into the war on the Allied side, the bold interventions of the WIL in defence of workers in struggle to defend trade union rights attracted a whole layer of militants and the WIL grew in numbers and influence. At the same time, the RSL lost a number of its political and industrial cadres who had been conscripted into the armed forces. Only a few of its members could play a prominent part in the industrial unrest, while at the same time it was divided into three internal factions on the theoretical questions which the war posed and the differences between it and the war of 1914-19, the nature of transitional demands, and the historic role of the LP.

Consequently in this period, the Workers' International League developed their presentation of their group as the future "alternative leadership", denouncing in their press the Labour leadership and especially the "lefts" in the Labour Party, appealing to workers to join them and to ignore the Labour Party and calling for Labour not merely to end the coalition but to take the power "on a socialist programme", which, partly copied directly from the Transitional Programme of 1938, was a propagandist expression of wholesale nationalisation such as could be read in the press of the "Militant Tendency". Grant was the author of its programmatic document, "Preparing for Power"; here he hedged his bets; he accepted that masses of workers in the course of their radicalisation would turn to their traditional organisations, while at the same time he forecast that large numbers would "by-pass" the Labour Party and come directly to the self-proclaimed "revolutionary" leadership.

Thanks to the enterprise of the American SWP, which ensured that a number of its members joined the mercantile marine rather than be conscripted into the army, the British groups had regular personal contact with New York through visiting comrades as well as through the press of the SWP. This is not the place to discuss the problems of the leadership of the SWP. (which included the jailing of their leading cadre) in the war, nor those of the International Secretariat, which had been moved from Paris to New York at the outbreak of the war. The authority of the SWP against the opposition of the majority of the leadership of the Workers' International League (which still harboured a grievance over Cannon's criticisms of its refusal to join the fusion of 1938), as well as the hesitation of the RSL, which rejected what it regarded as certain social-patriotic implications of the way in which the SWP advanced Trotsky's "Military Policy of the Proletariat", persuaded, in the optimistic atmosphere of rising class struggle and the imminent Nazi-led defeat of German imperialism that the groups should fuse. Healy, who had come into bitter opposition to the majority of the WIL and to Haston and Grant in 1942, led a "minority" in the WIL, which strongly supported the American view. The fusion was effected in spring 1944, on a basis of the WIL contributing 500 members and the RSL 100 (which may have exaggerated a little the actual strength of the RSL, many of whose people were in any case overseas in the British armed forces). The fusion conference voted down the documents of the three factions into which the RSL was divided and carried the positions of the WIL majority.

In the following month, the newly formed Revolutionary Communist Party came under a witch-hunt in Spring 1944 in which the Stalinists and the trade union bureaucracy associated with the tabloid press. The Government refused to ban the RCP, on the advice of the Home Secretary, Herbert Morrison, a Labour member of the Coalition Cabinet, who had been a conscientious objector in World War One and had seen the effect of making martyrs unnecessarily. But it did prosecute certain leading comrades on a charge under wartime "emergency" legislation of encouraging the movement of engineering apprentices to strike against being conscripted to work in coal mining. Their trial forced out of a reluctant witness, Ernest Bevin, the Minister of Labour (also a Labour member of the Cabinet) that he had received several requests from delegations representing the engineering apprentices and had refused to meet them. On appeal the defendants were set free. During the witch-hunt only two of its members quit. One of these had been a member of the RSL before the fusion and the other a member of the WIL.

The relations of the RCP with the working class changed decisively for the worse with the election victory of the Labour Party with a substantial majority in the summer of 1945. First the workers placed great confidence in the Labour Government and were in no mood to do anything which could be seen to embarrass it. Moreover, the Communist Party had marginalised itself during the elections by calling for a continuation of the coalition with Churchill. The membership of the RCP and the circulation of its press declined. Militants who had been impressed by its support for workers in struggle during the war now expressed the view that its purpose had been served, the coalition had been ended, and they had "their" government in power. The individual membership of the Labour Party soared.

At the same time, members of the pre-war RSL, now back from military service abroad, were refusing to join the RCP became they could not accept the "independent" line of the majority.

It is not generally realised that the RCP majority, despite its opposition to "entrism", and rejection of the view that "entry" was necessary to locate the party where it could grow, tolerated no less than two separate "entry" operations. One of these was the "minority" led by Healy. This tendency had the support of the international leadership, of Pablo and of Cannon. It shared their "catastrophic" economic and political perspectives. The other was a handful of former members of the RSL (the "Staines Group"), who supported the view of the "majority" that the conditions existed for an economic recovery. Some former members of the RSL in the North of England supported them.

A valuable opportunity offered itself in 1948 for the leaders (Gerry Healy and Denzil Harber) to collaborate in practical "entry" work when an important left current developed in the Labour Party and organised itself in the "Socialist Fellowship". This was far from being a revolutionary tendency, but it attacked the pressure of the right wing in the Labour Party to call a halt in the development of nationalisation and of social services, and called for "more socialist measures". On the one hand, it was full of reformist illusions, but on the other hand it was setting out on the road to testing by experience whether, and, if so, to what extent the Labour Party could be "transformed" into the instrument by which the working class could take power.

The "Socialist Fellowship" came into existence just at the time when the British Government, in alliance with the State Department, was decisively aligning itself in the "Cold War" against the government of the USSR. The "West;" now had the atomic bomb and it was not to unreasonable to speculate whether there was an immediate prospect of a Third World War. In Britain certain Stalinists who had managed to get elected as Labour Members of Parliament were being driven out of the Parliamentary Labour Party. In 1950 Healy's energy and enterprise mobilised the resources for a new journal entitled "Socialist Outlook", based on the Socialist Fellowship. It collaborated with certain fellow travellers of Stalinism in the Labour Party, in efforts to mobilise an opposition to the right wing.

In 1949 the RCP meanwhile was entering a terminal crisis. In 1950 the leaders of the "majority" decided that they could carry on no longer and wound it up. Ted Grant, the future ideological inspiration of the future "Militant Tendency", was one of those who supported their final statement, in which they declared their intention of entering the Labour Party. Since 1941 he had been among the most articulate critics of "entrism", and had played in the RCP the same role as in his later political life, of a theoretician and writer of documents for a group the orientation of which was towards activism.

In the early 1950's, the Socialist Fellowship broke up on the question of the Korean War. A number of its leading members supported the American attack on Korea in the name of the United Nations, while their opponents refused to associate themselves with what could prove to be threats to the Chinese Revolution and to the USSR.

However, Healy's operation, with "Socialist Outlook" as its axis, survived the break-up of the RCP and of the "Socialist Fellowship", and was making progress in the direction of becoming a stable "entrist" group: in this period the critics of the Labour right-wing (now led by Hugh Gaitskell) were developing towards what in a very few years was to be the "Bevan Movement" inside the Labour Party. At this time a number of former militants in the RSL joined Healy's group, which is known in history as "The Club" or "The Group", and widened its basis in the Labour Movement in the North of England,

At this time, the "state-capitalist" tendency led by Tony Cliff was attracting some of the militants who had been scattered by the termination of the RCP However, the former members of the RSL, who had no reasons to have any illusions about Healy, and who knew that his political conceptions and methods might present problems in the future, saw in the "Club", not so much a ready-made vehicle as the only positive means by which to go forward on the lines in which they had been trained before the war. In their eyes, the "Club" was at least a bulwark against the prevalent liquidationism and desertion to state capitalism was defending the Transitional Programme and could enable greater experience of the "entry" tactic to be got under Healy's vigorous leadership, with "Socialist Outlook" as the expression of the Labour Left.

In the early 1950's, Grant's political and organisational basis lay in ruins. When the RCP broke up he could not join Healy, who had been in bitter opposition to him and to Haston since 1942. He could not turn to Cannon and to Pablo, in the international leadership, because they had backed Healy, and he blamed the collapse of the RCP on their opposition to its "majority" leadership. Nor could he work with Sam Levy, Sam Bomstein and those who had the idea of "somehow" carrying on the RCP on its old basis (and who still were attacking "entry" in the late 1980's.) He can hardly have avoided feeling isolated for a time, and, to his credit, it must be remembered, that unlike many others, for instance Haston, he did not desert revolutionary politics to enter the service of the reformist bureaucracy, nor did he retire into private life,

In these conditions, it may well be that he first came to formulate the conception of an "entry" into the Labour Party based on the slogan of "transforming" the Labour Party. No one is likely today to challenge the claim that it was Grant from whom this conception first came.

Grant's writings during the war and later in the 1940s show that he was consistently arguing in favour of a somewhat rigid, formal, dogmatic position, "proclaiming" the "independence" of the party and opposing the entire "entry" perspective in bitter struggle against both the RSL and Healy's "minority". The mood of optimism which he owed to the rise of the WIL was based on the special circumstances of the war and was carried over beyond it into the immediate post-war years. He believed that there would at some unpredictable future date be a rise in the level of world revolution. This would undermine Stalinism and greatly reinforce the Fourth International. While in Britain more backward layers of the working class might still turn to the Labour Party in time of crisis, the more advanced workers must soon "inevitably" by-pass the Labour Party: the "open" Trotskyist party must therefore be prepared in advance, to put the revolutionary case to them and to receive them into an "independent" formation.

By 1950, however, events had by no means worked out in accordance with this formula. On the contrary, the Fourth International on the world scale had remained generally small and isolated, except in Bolivia and in Sri Lanka. Meanwhile, the Red Army had advanced to the frontiers of Western Europe. Communist Parties had won the leadership of millions of workers in France and Italy, while in China the Communist Party had destroyed the power of Chiang Kai Shek and formed a new government.

In Britain individual membership of the Labour Party had topped a million. It had five years of government behind it. In that time it had taken various measures directly aimed at benefiting the employers: these included its policy of limiting wage rises in a time of rising prices and full employment, with the help of the trade union leadership. It had continued British diplomatic support for US imperialism, on which the British economy depended, and had begun to manufacture nuclear weapons. But at the same time, such measures as nationalising coal-mining and the railways and as the National Health Service, which encroached on the freedom of action of the bourgeoisie but were of advantage to it, were also received by the working class with great satisfaction and the expectation of more.

This new situation cannot have failed to confront Grant with serious problems, for which his previous experience may be thought to have left him unprepared. Was there any role for the international which Trotsky had brought into being in 1938? How were the Marxist conceptions of the class struggle to be brought to the working class in Britain?

We have seen that there are grounds for questioning how far Grant ever grasped Trotsky's underlying strategy for building the Fourth International any better after the RCP collapsed than before. He seems simply never to have known that his formula, consistent as it is with his deep-seated formal method of thinking — had never occurred to anyone before the war and would have been ridiculed by Trotsky if it had!

It is possible that he was impelled, under the temporary pressure of the predominance of the Labour Party in the late forties and early fifties as well as the political collapse of his former allies such as Haston, to make empirically a new "turn" through misunderstanding an interesting passage in Trotsky's "Where Is Britain Going?" This is the passage which concludes:

"The Communist Party will occupy the place in the Labour Party that is at present occupied by the Independents (i.e. the Independent Labour Party)."

This was written more than twenty-five years earlier, in the winter of 1924-25, and first published in English in early 1925, before the General Strike (which it forecast) and, of course, many years before the world crisis of 1929-34 and World War Two. We discuss what Trotsky wrote in its context below.

But in any case the formula about "transforming the Labour Party" not only over-simplifies but seriously distorts the theoretical work of the pre-war "entrists".

Healy also shared with Grant the same ignorance of the pre-war experience. Neither had ever been in a position to contribute seriously to the discussions which led the founders of the "Militant Group" to lead their supporters out of the ILP. Nor was either long enough a member of the "Militant Group" in 1937 to absorb the ideas of Starkey Jackson and Denzil Harber. After Healy left it at the end of 1937 he spent several active years doing his best to destroy the "Militant Group" and the RSL, not without some success. Moreover, after 1950 the "Club" operated empirically in the Labour Party up to the early sixties, but never was there a serious discussion on perspective, if only because Healy's earlier role was being embellished with his highly imaginative re-telling of the history of Trotskyism in Britain! Thus the way was prepared for the Socialist Labour League to take the road towards "independence" which ended in the crisis of the WRP in 1985, under the dual pressures on Healy of Gaitskell's witch-hunt and of such ex-Stalinists as Cliff Slaughter, who had been brought in from the Communist Party in 1957 and had never been informed, let alone convinced by ideas of "entry" in any shape or form.

Early in the 1950s a movement arose among militant young workers in Merseyside, in struggle against the right wing of the Liverpool Labour Party and the "Braddock Mafia". These young workers were influenced by Jimmy Deane, an electrician who had been a member of the WIL during the war and a cadre of the "majority" of the RCP. (This can be no more than a broad outline. A more detailed study of the Trotskyist groups at this period would be welcomed.) It may be that this tendency found in Grant the source of theoretical argument and of ideas which seemed to them to be appropriate to their needs, Through many complications and difficulties, the "Revolutionary Socialist League", the second group with that title, was formed early in the 1960's, and followed in 1965 with the formation of the "Militant Tendency".

The "Militant Tendency" got its big chance in 1964, when the Socialist Labour League pulled its forces out of the Labour Party Young Socialists. Since 1958, elements of the "Club" and later of the SLL had been carefully studying how to approach young workers, with a good deal of success, and in building a substantial fraction in the LPYS round their journal, "Keep Left". They were opposed, not merely by the direct agencies of the right wing, but also by an alliance between supporters of the RSL and those of the "International Socialists", who for a time produced a joint paper, "Young Guard". When "Keep Left" appeared likely to win control of the LPYS at its national conference, the Labour Party apparatus, at the bidding of the NEC, abolished the National Conference of the LPYS and dissolved its National Committee. "Keep Left" then organised an "unofficial conference", which adopted "Keep Left" as its paper and elected a new leadership drawn entirely from "Healyites".

There followed a nationwide drive from the right to exclude supporters of "Keep Left" from local Labour Parties and the branches of the LPYS attached to them, to the number of several hundred.

We cannot overlook — otherwise the account would be unbalanced — that the "Club", the Socialist Labour League and "Keep Left" had been subjected to an un-relenting witch-hunt ever since 1958, when Gaitskell, who saw himself as the next Prime Minister, drove out of local Labour Parties various members of the "Club" who were long-standing and influential Labour Party members, such as Ratner in Salford, Lake in Leeds and Healy himself in Streatham. After Gaitskell's sudden death, Harold Wilson became Party Leader. He too had no desire to see Trotskyists influential in local Labour Parties and especially in CND, where they were working with some success to link the opponents of nuclear weapons to the opposition in the Labour Party and to mobilise those elements which saw the struggle against the bomb as a class question rather than a moral one, nor an active youth movement in the Labour Party when, as he confidently (and correctly) expected Labour won the next General Election.

Moreover, in 1963, Healy had got an account of the work of "Youth Militant" from 1935 to 1939 in the Labour Party League of Youth. This came from a comrade who had been deeply involved at the time, and highlighted the conditions of the second half of the 1930's, (Stay-in strikes in France and USA, civil war in Spain and impending world war), and helped to make up Healy's mind, that there was no future in more "entry" work in the LPYS and to withdraw as many of the forces round "Keep Left" as possible, in the hope of permanently smashing the LPYS. Healy therefore made a sudden, violent political "turn", announcing that the Labour Party and the LPYS were "dead". No serious fight, therefore, had to be put up against the witch-hunt, nor were such forces as could remain in the LPYS left there as a basis for future work.

At the same time, we had here a demonstration of two general characteristics of Healy's political work, first, that politically unstable empiricism which his repeated and sometimes inexplicable oscillations between opportunism and ultra-leftism revealed, and, secondly, that centralisation of control in his own hands which his empiricism made an indispensable condition for maintaining the organisation.

Shortly afterwards, the International Socialists also withdrew their forces from the LPYS and from the Labour Party. It may well be that Healy and Cliff alike were adapting their politics to the newly-radicalised forces outside the traditional centres of trade unionism, which were making their voices heard — teachers, students, white-collar workers, hospital workers, as well as women, gays and blacks. Nothing in the experience of these currents, which were to play a far from negligible role in building trade unions, in resisting the war in Vietnam etc., had prepared them for such a sophisticated perspective as relating politically to the opposition in the Labour Party under the Wilson Governments of 1964 to 1970. There was simply no one around in a position to revive on a national scale the "entrist" tradition of the pre-war "Militant Group" and RSL Tony Cliff knew nothing about it, while Healy had done his utmost to eradicate every memory of it, so much so that a long research into the archival record of pre-war Trotskyism in Britain was necessary to recover it, a research which was not possible until the archives themselves became available in the late 1960's.

Such was the success of the "Militant Tendency" in the early stages of the "Benn Movement" in the 1950's, thanks to the activism of its young comrades as well as the general radicalism raised by the disasters of Heath's Government, of the "Three Day Week" and the Miners' Strike, which they achieved in spite of their extraordinary "standoffish" (and political backward) attitude to everyone in the wide spectrum of political life around the Labour Party — written off as "all sects", regardless of what their ideas might in reality be — that in 1974 it could take the next step, following Grant's pamphlet of 1959 on "Entrism", which brought it into direct confrontation with the Labour Party apparatus and objectively posed the question of a split either in the Labour Party or in its own ranks.

This was the "British Perspectives and Tasks" document. Militant was organising its influence in local constituency Labour Parties to drive out particularly obnoxious or useless Labour MPs and to get selected in safe Labour seats people on whom the "Tendency" felt it could rely. (The "Tendency" was not, of course, the only Trotskyist group which defeated the choices of the apparatus). But this is the un-forgivable sin; it is precisely to ensure that Labour MPs are "safe, "reliable", "loyal" and generally acceptable to the Conservatives and to MI5 that the Labour Party apparatus exists as the "police" of the party, In September 1975, Underhill, already an experienced "smeller-out" of Trotskyists, got permission as National Agent to prepare a report on "entrism", producing a short nine-page document in November 1975. At that time his work made little impact on the Party leadership, though it was taken up enthusiastically by the bourgeois press.

*   *   *   *   *

The remainder of the document deals with the internal discussions in the Taaffe current and what Archer saw as their evolution towards a criticism of Grant's errors.

Meryl Fernando (1923-2007)

WITH the death of Meryl Fernando at the age of 84 we find ourselves almost at the end of that illustrious generation of revolutionaries whose great achievement it was to build the Lanka Sama Samaja Party (LSSP) from nothing, to defeat the Stalinist tendencies within the young party and to turn it into one of the most powerful and well-implanted Trotskyist parties in the history of our movement. It was the equally great tragedy of that generation that they were unable to prevent the deterioration of the LSSP which resulted in its entry into the Bandaranaike coalition government in 1964, and consequently a debilitating series of splits among the revolutionaries that left them marginal within a decade and a half.

The political formation of many of that generation of leaders in the London School of Economics will be a well known story to many of our readers thanks to the researches of Richardson and Bornstein, and of Bob Pitt as contributed to *Blows Against the Empire*, Vol 6 No 4 of this journal. Fernando however was not among them. Influenced by his older brother, Aloysius, he dropped out of university to undertake full time political work with the Bolshevik Leninist Party of India's "Ceylon Unit" in 1944, a grouping which was critical of many aspects of the LSSP's line until they merged in 1950. It was in the BLPI that he met Edmund Samarakkody, with whom he remained politically associated for most of his life.

He became the Secretary, and effective leader, of the workers at the Elephant Match Factory in Kelaniya, leading a successful strike. He also organised the workers in Moratuwa, his native town, against the Velona Garment Factory, and the Lanka Light Match Factory.

In 1950, following the merger, he was elected as LSSP member of the Moratuwa Urban Council for the Koralawella Ward. He held this position until defeated by the LSSP candidate Jayasumana Dharmabundu in1967, and chaired the Council for some years. He was arrested and imprisoned during the great Hartal of 1953. In 1956 he was elected to Parliament, again represented Moratuwa in the name of the LSSP. He held the seat until 1964. In 1958 he was one of twelve opposition MPs to be physically removed from Parliament while opposing the Government's extension of security powers in response to the communal tensions of the time. (His resolute insistence on the legal and social equality of the Sinhala and Tamil languages was one of the points for which he was praised at his funeral.)

In 1964, in opposition to the entry of the LSSP into the coalition, he worked with Samarakkody, Bala Tampoe, Karalasingham and others to found the LSSP(R). This party was plagued by interventions as the USFI and the International Committee descended to pick over the bones, both of them having their own candidates for leadership. In 1968 Fernando and Samarakkody split to form the Revolutionary Samasamaja Party, which soon changed its name to the Revolutionary Workers Party. He actively supported the JVP uprising in 1971, and took a distinguished part in the 1980 General Strike.

He was never a prolific writer. In 1997 he contributed an essay on the history of the LSSP to *Blows Against the Empire* which was translated and republished in the *Cahiers Léon Trotsky*. His article "Travelling the capitalist road" appeared in *What Next* No.5. His biographical article on Bernard Soysa has not yet been published outside Sri Lanka but can be found on the internet.

He had been born into a rich tea-growing family, but devoted most of his life, and all of his fortune, to the revolutionary cause. He was buried at the General Cemetery, Rawathawatta, Morutuwa, on 29 May. We extend our condolences to his family and comrades.

JJ Plant

Peter Fryer (1929-2006)

I AM in no position to write a full-scale obituary of Peter Fryer, since I lost touch with him a long time ago and had only fragmentary knowledge of his doings after that time. But for a brief while we were fairly close, and indeed he lived in my house during the traumatic months in which he broke his relations with Gerry Healy.

The background to this episode could be said to begin with the assignment given to Peter to cover what became the Hungarian Revolution in 1956 for the *Daily Worker*.

Peter had joined the Communist Party in Britain in 1942, and became a member of the staff of the *Daily Worker* in 1948. The following year he received his first assignment in Hungary, to report upon a show trial of the eminent Hungarian Communist, Laszlo Rajk. This was one of a series of purge trials which were calculated to put the impress of Soviet control over the so-called people's democracies in Eastern Europe. These both insisted upon Russian hegemony, and continued the frenzied vilification of President Tito and the Yugoslav Communists. In Hungary it was Rajk, in Czechoslovakia it was Slansky, in Bulgaria, Traicho Kostov. The similarities with the infamous trials in Moscow before the Second World War were all too evident to all but the true believers.

Peter dutifully wrote the official story for the *Daily Worker* and gathered plaudits for his loyalty, and the raw material for a tortured conscience, as the truth later dawned on him. Rajk was apparently promised his life and a secure retirement in Russia, provided only that he perjured himself in the Court in Budapest. Needless to say, the promise was broken, and he was apparently garrotted when the sentence was finally carried out. Huge posthumous ceremonies later celebrated his life.

Peter was sent off to Hungary again in July and August 1956, to write more articles about the events in Hungary. To his astonishment he found himself witnessing a full-scale revolution, and he wrote truthfully about what he saw. Far from being delighted with their scoop, the *Daily Worker* rushed to suppress it. The editor not only suppressed the contents of Peter's stories from his newspaper, but even withheld them from the other members of the paper's staff. On his return to London, Peter was shocked to find what had happened to his despatches, and felt that he had no alternative but to resign from the *Daily Worker*. Subsequently, he was expelled from the Communist Party.

Meantime, there were hundreds of other recently lapsed Communists who were agog to hear what he had to say. One of these was my friend, John Daniels, through whom, I am very sorry to say, he got in touch with Gerry Healy, the leader of the most strident of the several Trotskyist groups in Britain.

British Trotskyism was undergoing a very difficult passage. By 1956 there were three main groups, but none of them had more than fifty members. The largest group followed Gerry Healy, who had aligned himself with the French Lambertistes, whose most celebrated member was Lionel Jospin, later to become the Prime Minister of France, and with the American Socialist Workers' Party led J.P. Canon and Joseph Hansen. Two other groups counted something like a dozen supporters each. One was led by Tony Cliff and published the newspaper *Socialist Review*, while the other proclaimed its loyalty to the Fourth International based in Paris and Brussels, under the leadership of Michel Pablo and Ernest Germaine (Mandel). In Britain this group was led by Ted Grant, who had a handful of followers in Liverpool and East London.

Healy was quick to seek support from the melt down among British Communists, and recruited John Daniels as the first of a number of influential Communist intellectuals. This group was to include Tom Kemp, Cliff Slaughter, Peter Cadogan and Brian Pearce. Healy persuaded Daniels to become the editor of a journal called *Labour Review*. In the beginning Daniels was very useful, in that he could prevail upon a number of his friends in the Communist Party to contribute to the journal. When they began to contribute unorthodox thoughts, Daniels was first demoted, and then dismissed. But by then, Peter Fryer had moved into the orbit of *Labour Review*, and within a short time had been offered the editorship of the *Newsletter*, a weekly broadsheet, which rapidly gathered influence for Healy beyond the milieu of Communist intellectuals, and recruited Brian Behan, and a variety of active and capable trade unionists.

In the beginning Peter Fryer was in constant demand for his stories of the Hungarian Revolution. He must have spoken to dozens of public meetings, and to a very large audience of Communists and ex-Communists who hung on his every word. But as he became identified with the *Newsletter*, Peter found that this reportage was an insufficient basis for his new reputation. He edited a pretty dreadful book on the then predominant view of the Healy group, called *The Battle for Socialism* or some such title, in which he spelt out some sort of party line. In the beginning, the *Newsletter* had reflected the thinking of the new left in Britain, and reported on the movement of socialist forums in different cities. It carried sympathetic accounts of the visit of Claude Bourdet to England, for instance. But inexorably the line hardened, and dissident opinion was treated with greater and more rasping intolerance.

By now Peter was editing *Labour Review* as well as the *Newsletter*, but dependable old generation Trotskyists were carefully shadowing him. John Daniels was precipitated into outer darkness. The process by which this happened was quite tumultuous. Having greatly expanded its circle of acquaintances, the Healy group began to encounter more and more unorthodox opinions. True old timers would not have been surprised by this. But true old timers among the Healy circle were hard to find. Most had been fairly innocent recruits from the left wing of the Labour Party, and quite thoroughly insulated from the blasts of doctrine, heterodox or otherwise. A fairly basic party line was deemed to be sufficient for them.

Then, suddenly, there arrived a much larger core of supporters, whose curiosity had been stimulated by the traumas of the collapse of piety in the Communist Party. One such was Martin Grainger (Chris Pallis), who later helped to establish the broadsheet called Solidarity. He turned up at *Labour Review* meetings to make the perfectly sensible suggestion that the journal should seek an interview with C.L.R. James. James was by far the most distinguished independent Marxist within reach in London, and so his proposal aroused considerable curiosity, even among the less audacious of Healy's old guard. But the alarm bells which were set up by this proposal did not brook hesitation. Healy had no-one on call who could match James in argument, and his standard method of polemic in such circumstances required a facility for common abuse.

Developed though this was in his case, he now had a following which was more sophisticated. The time had come for the proclamation of a more ferocious orthodoxy.

There followed other earth-shattering polemics. Among them was the row about the Fourth International, which rumbled on over the years. The Fourth International sought to square the circle by developing a species of pluralism. The right of tendency, providing space for a variety of factions within a common political commitment was never easy to practise, and could be incredibly difficult in groups which were poor in human resources.

By the time that Peter Fryer was mastering the Healy orthodoxies on such matters, the Fourth International had nurtured a formidable faction around the Latin American Trotskyist, Posadas. This was convinced that the Third World War was inevitable, and drew a variety of unappetising conclusions from this premise. The largest mass movement in Britain at this time was the movement for nuclear disarmament, and young people who were coming in to some form of political activity were all touched by it. Gerry Healy's conspicuous attempt to translate the commitments of CND into orthodoxy was based on the classic syndicalism which is intricately embroiled in the history of British Communism, and therefore of British Trotskyism.

"Black the bomb, black the bases" was the Healy group's contribution to the anti-nuclear debate. More sophisticated arguments against nuclear weapons and nuclear warfare were available, so that the scope of this slogan to provide leadership to the anti-nuclear movement was severely restricted. But the pluralism of the Fourth International deprived it of the advantages which it could normally have anticipated in this discussion, because the thesis of the coming World War would inevitably be seen as a parody, and could not be taken seriously as a foundation for political organisation.

Much of this argument did not directly engage Peter Fryer in his editorial role in the *Newsletter* and *Labour Review*. I cannot remember the precise issues about which he fell out with Gerry Healy, and put into jeopardy his tenure of the editorial chairs. In any case, I was not privy to these arguments, which were internal to the then Socialist Labour League, which was the current embodiment assumed by Healy's group.

Undoubtedly Peter had become disillusioned with the frenetic pace of political life in that group which consisted of endless campaigning, and ceaseless selling of newspapers. He wanted to follow a more rationally ordered trajectory, with time to think, not to say study. But every dispute with Gerry Healy had a tendency to go nuclear. Very quickly, Peter found himself threatened, and surrounded by intimidatory cadres who would skilfully impugn his every motive. There began an intense phase of denunciation which unsurprisingly led directly to Peter's withdrawal from the field.

At this point began a nightmare of intimidatory threats. Gerry Healy proclaimed his determination to bring Fryer to book. He would not escape, Healy warned, "We shall search every rail terminal, and every airport". This heady mixture of paranoia and megalomania was quite adequately forbidding, and Peter duly got the message. He fled to Nottingham, and the counsel of John Daniels. That was how it came about that he stayed in my house for a few months, together with his companion of the time, Pat McGowan. During these months he wrote another book, describing these strange days. It was entitled *Twice Bitten*. I do not know whether the manuscript survives in Peter's papers, but I do remember it as being quite a hilarious text. Hand on heart, I could not be absolutely sure that it was intended to be as funny as it was. Healy had that kind of effect on people. More agnostic intellects would laugh, but many very decent citizens were quite liable to be scared out of their wits.

From that time on Peter was committed to earning his living from his writings. After staying with me, he went off with Pat McGowan to Portugal, where they produced a book which is still readable, and a good bit more than a travelogue. There followed a string of other works, about which others will write better than I can.

Ken Coates

Peter Fryer

PETER Fryer earned his place in history by his reporting of the Hungarian political revolution of 1956, which, despite the efforts of his Stalinist employers at the *Daily Worker*, played an immense role in crystallising the crisis in the CPGB which had been started by Kruschev's "Secret Speech". It need not now be a secret that when *Revolutionary History* first planned an issue on the events of 1956, a central idea, which Fryer had agreed to willingly, was to republish most if not all of *Hungarian Tragedy*. In the event, this job was undertaken and expanded upon by Index Books and our issue took a different form.

Obituaries have been published by comrades who were close to Fryer (Terry Brotherstone in the *Guardian* of 3 November 2006, Keith Flett in *Socialist Worker* of 11 November 2006, Charlie Pottins at http://randompottins.blogspot.com/2006/11/goodbye-to-good-comrade. html and http:// randompottins. blogspot. com/2006/11/more-tributes-to-peter-fryer. html) and he received a full radio obituary from BBC Radio 4's *Last Word*.

If his reporting of Hungary brought him first to light, it was no more than the beginning of a career in which he contributed valuably to the revolutionary movement and to historical studies. Following his parting from the Stalinists, he edited the press of the Trotskyist current led by Gerry Healy, and his presence was undoubtedly a major factor in the winning over to Trotskyism, at least for a time, of an important layer of intellectuals, among them John Daniels, Peter Cadogan, Cliff Slaughter and Brian Pearce. Several of his articles from *The Newsletter* were reprinted as pamphlets, including *Black the H-Bomb & the Rocket Bases!* (which argued for a trade union dimension to the struggle against nucler weapons) and *Defend the ETU against Fleet Street and King Street!*. From this period the pamphlet *Lenin as Philosopher* (1957) deserves to be reprinted (Fryer had agreed that *New Interventions* could reprint it provided we updated all the references, and it is still intended to do that.)

At this time he wrote *The Battle for Socialism* which is often unjustly described as a piece of Healyite hack work. Later in 1959 however, the internal life of Healy's Socialist Labour League, as it was then known, proved unbearable to Fryer as it was to do for many others. The parting of the ways was accompanied by an outburst of inner-party terrorisation at least the equal of Healy's later outrages. Fryer was a part of the "Stamford Faction" which opposed Healy's party regime, and in September 1959 he broke his silence with an open letter to SLL members. He was to have little to do with any aspect of Trotskyism until the spectacular disintegration of the SLL's succesor, the Workers Revolutionary Party, in 1985, after which he was able to contribute a regular column to the *Workers Press* with a number of his former comrades.

In the intervening period he distinguished himself through a passionate scholarship in three areas; sexual repression and censorship, the history of black people in Britain, and the history of black peoples' music. He also found time to translate two novels from the French. His first book after leaving the Trotskyists was *Oldest Ally. A Portrait of Salazar's Portugal* written jointly with his then partner Patricia McGowan Pinheiro.

In mocking and exposing hypocrisy about sexual matters he wrote some spirited and entertaining books, *Mrs Grundy. Studies in English Prudery* (1963) and *Private Case — Public Scandal* (1966). In the latter he brought to light the hidden existence of the British Museum Library's historical collection of erotica, which was subsequently opened to the public. Related to these studies was his book *The Birth Controllers*, a history of the struggles to make fertility control available to the masses in Britain. He also compiled two amusing and enlightening anthologies out of his researches ; *Venus unmasked, or, An inquiry into the nature and origin of the passion of love, interspersed with curious and entertaining accounts of several modern amours: an eighteenth-century anthology* (1967) and *The Man of pleasure's companion. A Nineteenth Century Anthology of Amorous Entertainment* (1968)

His 1984 *Staying Power. The History of Black People in Britain*, the result of extensive research, changed the general picture of Britain by establishing the long term presence of black people in the historical record. *Black people in the British Empire. An introduction.* (1988). He developed the theme with *Aspects of British Black History.*(1993) and a number of pamphlets, as well as becoming a much in demand public speaker.

Lucid, Vigorous and Brief. Advice to New Writers.(1993) remains a valuable guide. Fryer's lifelong love of black people's music (he had flowered as a jazz pianist in the last weeks of his life) was the spur to writing *Rhythms of Resistance. African Musical Heritage in Brazil* (2000), and he was working on a second book on the same subject when he died.

http:// www.sonic.net/~patk/Peter_Fryer. html presents what is probably the most complete bibliography of Fryer's work, up to 2004 at least.

To the very last days of his life he maintained friendly relationships with many of his former comrades, whom he would often meet around the British

Library where he did most of his work. He had suffered from severe heart problems and needed to ration his energies carefully. It was for this reason that he had declined the many requests for interviews on the 50th anniversary of the Hungarian events that first catapulted him into the public arena, and not from any sense that he wished to distance himself from his political past.

In January 1996 (in Workers Press) he obituarised his old friend Hubert Nicholson, and recalled:

> Nicholson urged me — after half a century the memory remains intensely vivid, more so than many a more recent conversation — to "be a live wire", to "make things hum around you" wherever I found myself whole-heartedly and passionately into whatever I undertook, to act always and everywhere as a piece of human yeast.
>
> Though my own energies were largely poured into political activity, rather than the poetry readings Nicholson loved to organise, I should like to think that this wise advice has borne some fruit along the way.

And we would agree that it did.

We proffer our condolences to his partner and family, and his many friends and comrades.

We are pleased to be able to present the following note from Ken Coates, a close comrade of Fryer's from the period of his first involvement with the Trotskyist movement.

JJ Plant

Mary Stanley Low (1912-2007)[2]

MARY Stanley Low died in Miami on 9 January 2007, aged 94 after a rich and distinguished life as a revolutionary, a creative writer and a teacher.

She was born in London to Australian parents, and educated in France and Switzerland. In Paris she joined left-wing political and artistic circles where she made the acquaintance and gained the friendship of leading surrealists. Surrealism was to remain one of the powerful creative drivers of her life. It was here, in 1933, that she met the Cuban born surrealist poet Juan Brea[3], who was to become her long-term partner and husband. After travelling through Europe and Cuba, Low and Brea, with many of their friends, among them Benjamin Péret, went to Barcelona to support the revolution in 1936.

The book they produced there together, the Red Spanish Notebook, remains the best known of all their work. It is one of the best accounts in English of the revolutionary transformation of the city, and Low's chapters capture it through sharp observation of the detail of life. George Orwell was to praise her skilled

---

2. This obituary draws heavily on the notes published by the Nin Foundation (http://www.fundanin.org) and especially those by Pepe Gutiérres-Alvarez.
3. For more on Brea, (and the history of the revolutionary movement in Cuba) see Revolutionary History Vol 7, No 3, pp 232-236.

writing as she described waiters refusing to accept tips, shoe-shine boys proudly displaying their union cards, and notices in brothels asking clients to respect the women working there as comrades. She found it hard to believe that even in this heated atmosphere the siesta was still almost universally practiced. Her description of the funeral of Durrutti is memorable; the tomb was too small for the hero's coffin and disorganisation reigned in front of the assembled mourning masses. Low joined the POUM, while Brea was a member of the "official" Trotskyist group. Low worked in the English language radio service of the POUM, financed and co-edited their English newsletter (which the British Trotskyists advertised and sold in solidarity despite the political differences between Trotsky's line and that of the POUM).

Low and Brea left Barcelona in December 1936 in an atmosphere increasingly dominated by Stalinist threats against the anarchists, POUM and Trotskyists. Brea had narrowly escaped death in an incident outside a POUM meeting which they did not believe was an accident.

Low translated Brea's chapters of the Red Spanish Notebook, which received its first publication in London in 1937 with a prologue by C.L.R. James. The couple were married in London shortly before the book appeared.

After further travels in France and Cuba they settled in Prague, where they resumed co-operation with surrealists, until leaving for Paris in the aftermath of the Nazi invasion in July 1939. A compilation of poetry by Low and Brea (Low's being written in French) was published in Paris in 1939, with the title *La Saison des flutes,* illustrated by the Cuban surrealist Wilfredo Lam.

In 1940 they left Europe and settled in Cuba, which was to be Low's home for the next 25 years. Brea was already seriously ill and lived there for only about a year. In 1943 a volume of essays by Low and Brea, *La verdad contemporánea* was published, based on their talks in 1936 at the Havana Institute of Marxist Culture, with an introduction by Péret. Low continued energetic support work for the Spanish Republican refugees and exiles; work which was recognised by the award of the National Medal of Excellence.

In 1944 she remarried, to Armando Machado, a Trotskyist trade union leader, and acquired Cuban citizenship. In 1946 she published a volume of poetry, *Alquimia del recuerdo* (Alchemy of memory), again with illustrations by Lam. During this period she developed a deep interest in the history of Rome, and especially the life of Julius Caesar.

In 1957 she produced a trilingual book of poetry, *Three Voices, Voces, Voix,* illustrated by José Mijares. In 1959 Low and Machado supported the Cuban revolution. Low took on senior teaching roles at the Instituto de El Vedado and the University of Havana, in English and Latin. Both were members of the re-formed Trotskyist organisation POR, which soon enough and predictably enough lost favour as the Castro government came to rely on Soviet support. Machado was arrested and only freed on the intervention of Che Guevara. In 1965 they left Cuba, and after a stay in Australia, settled in Miami. She worked closely with the Surrealist tendency associated with Franklin Rosemont.

Blacklisted from teaching in the state sector for her political history, Low made a living in the elite private schools, teaching Latin and classics. She produced further volumes of literature and poetry — *In Caesar's Shadow* (1975), *Alive in Spite Of* (1981), *A Voice in Three Mirrors* (1984), and *Where the Wolf Sings* (1994). (These two last were illustrated by her own collages and drawings, and are still in the list of AK Press.) Her writing appeared in a number of surrealist anthologies and her artwork was exhibited in surrealist group exhibitions.

After her retirement from teaching in 2000 she continued to travel extensively in Europe and maintained contact with the survivors of the revolutionary generation in Spain. In October 2002 she was one of the many signatories to the Surrealist-sponsored declaration *Poetry Matters: On the Media Persecution of Amiri Baraka*. Her final militant act was to sign a declaration of critical historians opposing the dominant historiography that depicts the Spanish revolution simply as a struggle between fascism and antifascism, (exemplified by Hobsbawm among UK academics) and seeks to erase the struggle between the classes from the historical record.

Mary Low's ashes were scattered in Cuba and in Paris.

JJ Plant

Sydney Wanasinghe 1932-2007

SYDNEY Wanasinghe died on 28 April 2007, at his Colombo (Sri Lanka) home. He was a long serving member of the LSSP (Lanka Sama Samaja Party), a member of its old guard, and remained a socialist until the end of his life.

Revolutionary History warmly appreciated the work he published, jointly with Wesley Muttiah, (to whom we are indebted for assistance with this notice) on the history of the LSSP and its struggles, which grew eventually to 6 volumes, "Britain, World War 2 and the Samasamajists" (1996), "The Bracegirdle Affair" (1998), "We Were Making History: The Hartal of 1953" (2002), "Socialist Women of Sri Lanka" (2006). "Two Languages, One Nation, One Nation, Two Languages" (2006) and the last being an anthology of the speeches and articles of Dr. Colvin. R. de Silva (to be reviewed in the next issue of *Revolutionary History*). In addition Wanasinghe and Muttiah edited "The Case for Socialism" (2004). Wanasinghe also republished in 2006, "Hundred Days in Ceylon under Martial Law" by Armand de Souza criticising the colonial government's response to the 1915 communal riots.

He graduated from the University of Ceylon, Peradeniya, where he first became an activist, selling party papers in villages around Peradeniya. After graduating he taught at Carey College, Colombo, later working for the State Distilleries Corporation and the National Savings Bank. He served on the LSSP's Central Committee and Political Committee, and at one time represented the district of Wellawatte North on the Colombo Council.

He organised the publication of an impressive sequence of pamphlets for the Young Socialists, including Luxemburg's "On the Spartacus Programme",

"Social Reform or Revolution", "What is Economics?", "The Mass Strike", "The Junius Pamphlet" and Trotsky's "My Flight From Siberia", "Marxism and Science", "The Problems of Life", "The Struggle for State Power" and "Whither Russia?". He was for a time the editor, publisher and principal writer of the *Young Socialist*.

His detailed knowledge of the history of the movement was often called upon by academic historians, and in 1999 he contributed an obituary for Mark Bracegirdle to the London *Independent*. He owned an enormous collection of books, documents, pamphlets and other material on the LSSP and ran the Suriya bookshop specialising in left-wing publications. As a scholar of the Sinhalese language he had translated and published pamphlets in that language, including material by Che Guevara.

Though often unwell recently he was planning further publications in Sinhalese. He was at work on his computer when taken ill on the 26th, two days before his death. He leaves a wife, daughter and two grandchildren, to whom we extend our condolences.

JJ Plant

Wesley Muttiah 1930-2007

AS we prepared this issue for the printers we learned of the death of our friend Wesley Muttiah. It seemed right to us to include a brief obituary, even if it could not be fully researched, in the same issue as that for his long-term collaborator Sydney Wanasinghe. It is poignant for us to prepare this notice, as Wesley had always been the source we turned to for information towards the obituaries of the Sri Lanka revolutionaries, and indeed he had provided valuable clarifications and corrections into the obituaries in this issue for Wansinghe and Meryl Fernando.

Wesley's work in preparing and publishing a central series of books on the history of the LSSP and the revolutionary movement in Sri Lanka has been described in the Wanasinghe obituary.

He was born in 1930, in Thellipallai, Jaffna. He joined the LSSP while a secondary school student in Kandy, before taking a Masters degree in Madras. On returning to Sri Lanka he devoted most of his professional career to working as an inspector in the Labour Department, enforcing the labour laws in the plantation sector. In 1952 he married Tency Fernando, and they had three children.

Following the death of their daughter, the family migrated to London, where Wesley took up teaching, until his retirement. He was an active trade unionist, and in addition was a key contributor to the London branch of the LSSP/NSSP, in which he held the posts of Secretary and Treasurer at different times. He also arranged the publication in England of the NSSP's election manifesto.

After his retirement he was able to travel regularly to Sri Lanka to research the history of the LSSP, and also to take part in the Democratic Left Front, to the Central Committee and the Executive Committee of which he was elected.

In addition he served as the General Secretary of the United Lanka Estate Workers Union.

At a commemorative meeting, Vasudeva Nanayakkara, the Opposition Leader on Colombo Municipal Council and former MP, spoke of Wesley's self-sacrifice and dedication, and of his great abilities as a mobiliser. Hector Abeywardene, a founding member of the LSSP described Wesley personally selling many copies of the books, travelling long distances around Sri Lanka to take copies to comrades and contacts.

He worked diligently for the unification of the forces of the left, and he saw the publication of the historical studies, especially of "What is Socialism?" as a key to promoting the discussions necessary for unification.

He was always generous with his knowledge and time towards Revolutionary History, and his family home in North London always offered a hospitable welcome. We extend our condolences to his widow and family.

JJ Plant

Yves Dechezelles (1912-2007)[4]

YVES Dechezelles was born in the Vendée, into a family with a strong socialist and trade union tradition. His grandfather had been deported to Algeria for his support of the Paris Commune. His father suffered the inevitable consequences of his early trades union work on the railways. At the age of eight Yves attended the Congress of Tours, with his aunt and uncle who were delegates. In this environment he acquired an admiration for socialism of Jean Juarès which he was to retain throughout his life. He joined the SFIO at the age of twelve.

After a prize-winning student career he began to teach philosophy. He became a friend of Albert Camus in Algiers, and there met his future wife Myriam Salama. After marrying he moved to Caen where he studied law. There he became increasingly politically active and came into contact with workers and unionists in the metallurgical industries.

In November 1936 he met and became a friend of Marceau Pivert with whom he corresponded and collaborated over the years. Determined to support the struggle of the Spanish republicans, and rejecting the policy on non-intervention he joined the Communist Party in 1937, immediately becoming the Caen district secretary. He set about organising practical solidarity and support.

---

4. Based on the obituary appended to the minutes of CERMTRI's annual general meeting on 3 February 2007, in the "Lettre d'Information" No 30, Feb 2007 and on the extended obituary notice in " La Commune".of January 2007 which was substantially the work of Dechezelle's family, as well as the Maitron entry. I am grateful to Ian Birchall for a copy of his article "Neither Washington nor Moscow? The rise and fall.of the Rassemblement Démocratique at Révolutionnaire". Interested readers may wish to consult Duncan Hallas's article "Fourth International in Decline: from Trotskyism to Pabloism, 1944-1953", available at http://www.marxists.de/trotism/hallas/fidecline for a view on the significance of the fusion discussions between Dechezelle's tendency and the PCI.

He was, wrongly, accused of Trotskyist deviations, but as he learned more about the Moscow trials and the Stalinist murders of anarchists and democrats in Spain he quickly separated himself from the PCF.

Conscription in 1938 interrupted work on his thesis on "Lenin and the Peasants". He saw no actual fighting, and after the Petain armistice was allowed to go to Algeria with his family, where he took up the practice of law. He took part in the daring action of the resistance organisation "Combat" against Admiral Darlan of 7 November 1942 which prevented the fleet from sailing. Dechezelles's part was to lead the taking of the telephone exchange. The Americans however, on occupying Algiers quickly reached a deal with Darlan. Dechezelles, with many of the resistance, was imprisoned for a time.

On the formation of De Gaulle's provisional government, he was awarded the Medal of the Resistance, and became private secretary to Tixier, the Minister for Social Affairs, and subsequently the Interior Minister. Declining offers of further advancement in the Government he devoted his energies to the SFIO and became the administrative secretary to its group in the National Assembly. It was here that he first established relationships with the Algerian, Senegalese and Malagasy deputies.

In 1946, he helped Guy Mollet's left wing to victory within the SFIO and became Assistant General Secretary. He was to become frustrated with the very limited support for the independence struggles within the SFIO, and this became acute following his meeting Ho Chi Minh, and his witnessing massive electoral fraud in Algeria. He resigned from the SFIO in 1947, taking with him a large section of the Socialist Youth.

He turned again to the law for his living, and was engaged in attempts to establish new political formations in the Action Socialiste at Révolutionnaire and the Rassemblement démocratique révolutionnaire (RDR). In 1948 he was one of a group of lawyers who, at considerable risk to themselves, went to Madagascar to attempt the legal defence of the leaders of the nationalist movement MDRM. Many of the accused were condemned to death and a number of the sentences were carried out.

He was to spend increasing amounts of time in defending such figures the North African nationalist leaders Habib Bourghiba and Ben Bella, Ferhat Hached the leading Tunisian trades unionist, and Allal El Fassi, leader of Al Istiqlal (Morocco). His life was again under threat, this time from the right wing extremists of the OAS, when he defended the Algerian nationalist leader Messali Hadj.

After the failure of the RDR initiative, Dechezelles was active in a series of regroupments, some of which involved Trotskyist and syndicalist groupings, as well as the followers of Pivert. There is evidence that Dechezelle's ASR actively collaborated with the Trotskyists of the PCI at this time. These regroupment efforts eventually created the PSU and for a time Dechezelles was one of its national secretaries. There he argued steadily for a broad movement of the democratic and progressive forces in French politics, but found himself unable to join the Socialist Party under Mitterand.

The focus of his activity shifted and he became a leading member of the League for the Rights of Man, and through its international affiliates he travelled to observe and oppose political repression in many parts of the world. He spoke regularly at public meetings in France, and was a founder member of the International Campaign Against Repression, inspired by the Lambert tendency of the Trotskyist movement. His legal case load continued to grow as his reputation as a defender continued to grow. Until the end of his life, as his children Jean-Jacques and Guy recalled at his funeral "Yves Dechezelles continued to hold public meetings to denounce acts of repression and infringements of basic rights."

He was a founding member of CERMTRI in 1977 and a member of its first board of directors, remaining a member until his death. As the CERMTRI obituarist put it; his whole life illustrated, in its highest sense, the meaning of the word "defence": defender of the rights of man, of the oppressed, of the truth, and of justice against the established powers.

For him this fight was inseparable from the fight for socialism. In 2000, in a interview with "Informations Ouvrières" (No 450, 2 August 2000) he explained "More than ever today we must fight for socialism i.e. the defence of the rights of man, but in the more general sense that encompasses not only human rights but also social rights. Only in that direction is there hope."As Dechezelles put it himself:

> I was not a Trotskyist, I was never a member of any organisation in the Fourth International, even if, over the years and in the course of shared battles, a bond in fact was established between me and the Trotskyist militants . . . any rebirth of a vast socialist movement must draw strength from Leon Trotsky's contribution. Trotsky's ideas are living still. I want proof of it in the form of organisations which nationally and internationally claim him. But I would say that the place occupied by Trotsky stands above those who claim him directly. Like other great figures, he belongs to the movement for the emancipation of the workers, and the whole of the people.

Thus Yves Dechezelles defined the importance that CERMTRI had for him and the contribution that he brought to it during his life.

Yves Dechezelles died on the 9 January 2007.

JJ Plant

Work in Progress

Reprints

ADMIRERS of the late Al Richardson and Sam Bornstein will be overjoyed to hear that Merlin have reprinted the now very rare and difficult to get hold of *Against the Stream* (£18.95) and *Two Steps Back* £12.95. In addition they have reprinted the special double issue of *Revolutionary History* Vol.4 Nos. 1/2 on the *Spanish Civil War; The View from the Left.*(£18.95). They will be available via Merlin or certainly at bookshops such as Bookmarks and Housmans.

Archives

Comrades and friends of Al Richardson and Jim Higgins will also be delighted to hear that the University of London Union have started to produce a much more detailed catalogue of the contents of the boxes, still only the published contents, the correspondence will have to wait, but this is an enormous step forward. Those wishing to consult the collection should ask me for a copy of the catalogue so far which I will send them as an email attachment. tcrawford@revhist.datanet.co.uk.

Internet Wars

The Marxist Internet Archive. www.Marxists.org has been in the wars and has suffered a massive denial of service attack from a whole number of servers under government control in the People's Republic of China. This burnt out our server and we have had to buy a new one with corresponding difficulties all of February and March it should be running more than adequately by the time this issue of *Revolutionary History* appears. Of course this **may** come from a couple of teenage boys who have not yet discovered girls and who have managed to take over the computers belonging to a whole number of government entities but despite bringing it to their attention via the Beijing Academy of Sciences the DOS have continued. We have as yet no evidence that it has been co-ordinated by a section of the PRC government machine but comrades may wish to come to their own conclusions. Farsi Language material on the MIA has also apparently been blocked in Iran.

New Material

New material has continued to appear on the MIA site and a further piece of indexing, in this case of the journal *Social Democrat* 1897-1911 then *British Socialist* 1912-1913 has appeared (it changed its name in 1912) the monthly theoretical paper of the SDF and later the BSP. There are a considerable number of articles which can be clicked on to. There are also complete indexes of *New International*, *Fourth International* and the British *Labour Review*.

Interesting Websites

A website which may be of interest to many comrades is that of *The International Newsletter of Communist Studies Online XIII* (2007), now at no 20, and found at http://www.mzes.uni-mannheim.de/projekte/incs.

Two French websites may be of interest to comrades: firstly, that devoted to Barta, the founder to the present LO tendency at http://unioncommuniste.free.fr, and secondly, one devoted to the history of the LCR at http://asmsfqi.org.

Ted Crawford

THE PCF & 1956

A colloquium on "The French Communist Party [PCF] and 1956" was held on 29 and 30 November at Bobigny in North-West Paris. It was a suitable location; to a visitor from outside, Bobigny seems like the last of the People's Democracies. One emerged from the *métro* into the avenue Maurice Thorez, and followed the route to the conference hall along the boulevard Lénine.

The colloquium was organised by the Seine-Saint-Denis departmental archives, and aimed to bring together veterans from 1956 and researchers from a new generation who are working on the copious archival material now available.

Yet the archives can only modify the picture so much. The fundamental facts are that in March 1956 the PCF voted for special powers to the French government to deal with the developing war in Algeria, and that in November it enthusiastically backed the Russian intervention in Hungary. There were doubtless hesitations, reservations, disagreements and moments of anguish. The pack distributed to those attending contained a summary of sound recordings of Central Committee meetings in 1956, which will make it possible to study some of the nuances of the Party's evolution. But given the PCF's traditions, strategy and organisational structure, it is hard to see how it could conceivably have acted otherwise.

There were some 28 speakers in the course of the two days, providing a substantial amount of information. With so many items a slippage of time-keeping could easily have led to chaos, but the organisers kept rigorously to the timetable. A wide range of viewpoints were presented in the papers and in the debate from the floor. Among the speakers was Michel Dreyfus, who has made many contributions to the history of Trotskyism; he argued that oppositional statements and publications by intellectuals in 1956 opened up a new period of the party's history. Yet as we moved from Algiers to Budapest, from lawyers to posters, it was often difficult to see the wood for the trees. Titles such as "1956: a boundary of operational periodisation for research" did not help to focus on the main political questions.

The central themes were Algeria and Hungary. To a British observer it was striking that Suez got only a few passing mentions; in the French context it was clear that Suez was very much a sideshow compared to the Algerian war. If Britain's traditional imperial role took a death blow in 1956, France fought on until 1962.

A recurring theme was the question of Popular Frontism. The PCF's main strategic aim, in the 1956 elections and the period thereafter, was to establish an alliance with the Socialist Party in order to reconstruct a Popular Front on the 1936 model. This was the justification for the line on Algeria. As PCF leader Thorez had put it in Spring 1956, the whole would not be sacrificed to the part. Opposition to Guy Mollet's murderous policy in Algeria must not be allowed to jeopardise the creation of a new Popular Front. It was claimed that if the PCF had not voted for the special powers, it would have been open to accusations of sabotaging Mollet's professed attempt to make peace in Algeria. Fifty years on, at the time of the colloquium, the PCF was still refusing to rule out the possibility of participation in a "left" government under Ségolène Royal — a striking instance of the continuity of Popular Frontism.

Yet loyalty to Moscow came before everything. The PCF's line on Hungary was a setback for its relations with the Socialist Party, but no concessions were made. A powerful reminder of the party's Stalinist past came in the vigorous contribution from Henri Martin, famously imprisoned in 1950 for activity against the Indochina war. Looking twenty years younger than his 80 years, he insisted that in 1956 American imperialism was preparing for world war against the Communist bloc, and that any criticisms of Stalin were a diversion. Other speakers justified the Thorez leadership's strategy by pointing out that there had not been mass defections from the PCF in 1956.

Another reminder of the mood in 1956 was a short film showing the assault by fascists and right-wingers on the headquarters of the PCF, which was defended by workers loyal to the party. The attacking mob seemed determined to burn, loot and destroy. The commentary, which drew parallels with Budapest, must have seemed all too plausible, making the case that the Hungarian insurgency was also a fascist rising against Communism. Far from weakening the PCF, the rightist attack aroused a powerful reflex of loyalty.

Much has changed since 1956, as was shown by Sandra Fayolle's paper on the debate on birth control. At a time when a commercial promotion meant that every newsstand in Paris was bristling with condoms, it must have been hard for the "young researchers" and those of their generation to imagine that until 1967 the sale of any contraceptive device was illegal in France — and that the PCF, ardent in its defence of "family values", did not challenge this. A speaker from the floor recalled that Khrushchev had compared birth control to cannibalism.

The papers from the colloquium are to be published. They will be a welcome contribution to out understanding of the period, but a sharper critical perspective will be required to appreciate just how so many militantly class-conscious workers fell prey to the monstrous lies and distortions propagated by the PCF in 1956.

Ian Birchall

Founding Conference

Ukrainian Labour History: From Everyday Life to Social Struggle

CHRIS Ford writes to us about the first conference of the Labour History Society held at Kyiv on March 24, 2007. This was an historic conference being the first Labour History Society founded in the former USSR and Eastern Europe. See below for the details. We hope to have a report on this in a future issue.

* * * * *

The conference will cover the study of history and contemporary state of working-class communities, culture, nationality, family life, gender, sexuality, migration, theory, politics and organization — that is labour history of Ukraine.

For six decades two historical orthodoxies have dominated the history of Ukraine: the official Soviet history which crystallized in the late 1920's, on the one hand; and diaspora's orthodoxy which made a significant impact on the orientation of contemporary Ukrainian history.

Both orthodoxies have their advantages as well as they share many commonalities which create obstacles for the development of Ukrainian history. Leading figures and movements in Ukrainian past were adopted by the Soviet orthodoxy and misrepresented to the meet the interests of the regime, which was afraid of any independent grassroots protest; whilst the National orthodoxy would adopted the same figures and movements diminishing their socialist ideas and emphasising only their advocacy of national ones.

These problems cannot be seen separately from the context of the historical climate in which they existed. Symmetrical ideological systems existed in the East and West, mutually antagonistic, elitist and conservative in their attitude towards grassroots movements for social transformation. Both ruled out the possibility of an alternative to the established facts of "actually existing socialism" or western capitalism, their assumptions were pervasive in intellectual life including history and social science. Following the collapse of the Soviet

Union many historians in Ukraine freely rejected the straightjacket of the old regime only to adopt orthodoxy of the neo-conservative historians in the West.

The conference «Ukrainian Labour History: From Everyday Life to Social Struggle» aims to attract attention and to give an impetus to deeper studies of issues that have been given no place of importance on the historical agenda of Ukraine. This debate is not simply of academic importance, it is also related to the current malaise in which Ukraine finds itself. To rediscover the past of Ukrainian labour is also to make use of that understanding to shape their future.

The conference includes but is not restricted to the following issues:
- The everyday life and culture of peasant and working-class communities in Ukraine;
- Working conditions and struggle for labour rights. Ukrainian trade-union and cooperatives movements;
- Peasant movements and rebellions: from Koliivshchyna to Makhnovshchyna;
- Transformation of social and class structure of Ukrainian society, from the end of the XIX to the beginning of the XX century;
- Radical intelligentsia and labour. Ukrainian contribution to revolutionary theories;
- History and activity of Ukrainian socialist movements and parties as well as of the branches of Russian and international socialist organisations in Ukraine;
- Waves of labour migration from Ukraine. Social struggle of Ukrainians in diespora.

The Historiography of German Trotskyism

THE year 1933, or to be more exact, its political consequences, marked a break in the continuity of the left in Germany. A small current like Trotskyism was particularly affected by it. In practice 1945 meant starting again from scratch. And in addition there were the consequences of the division of Germany between Stalinism in the East and anti-Communism — which was in fact directed against the whole left — in the West. In the West 1968 did bring a certain upturn. But the dominant tendencies in the newly emerging far left were Maoist — and by the end of the seventies the great majority of them had become supporters of the Green Party. Moreover in this prosperous country the charms of social democracy and Stalinism also did not remain powerless to integrate many other 1968 activists or to direct them towards some social niche. In general terms all this distinguished Germany from the other highly developed industrial countries of Europe. They had not experienced a comparable break, and over the decades despite the ups and downs a Trotskyist "milieu" with a certain tradition and continuity could be built up.

In addition the following specific feature of development in Germany should be taken into account. On the one hand the Communist Party in Germany after 1920, after the fusion with the Independent Socialist Party

(USPD), was the strongest in Western Europe and as a result the Bolsheviks put their hopes in it. But for a variety of reasons it also split very quickly into a number of factions, especially after the defeat of the "German October" in 1923. German Trotskyism, the German section of the International Left Opposition, developed out of the left and ultra-left currents which, in 1923-24, had initially supported Zinoviev against Trotsky. For the most part these were activists who in 1919-20 had still belonged to the USPD. On the other hand by far the greater part of the old nucleus of the Party, which during the First World War had belonged to the Spartakusbund of Rosa Luxemburg and Karl Liebknecht, formed the basis of the so-called "Right Opposition" round Heinrich Brandler and August Thalheimer. As longstanding opponents of Zinoviev they put themselves in opposition to Trotsky in 1926-27, and preferred to support Bukharin. They maintained their attitude after their expulsion in 1928.

In this situation a Trotskyist organisation came to be formed in 1928-29. Despite the domination of the Communist Party (KPD) it grew continuously, whereas the various other Communist opposition groups in the period before 1933 went through internal crises and tended to lose members. Certainly one of the main reasons for this was the great prestige enjoyed by Trotsky in the German labour movement. His writings had an enormous circulation far beyond the organisation. It was also helped by the violent opposition which he received from the Stalinists and the Social Democrats (SPD).

At the centre of the activity of the Left Opposition was the struggle for the united front. As a result after the defeat of 30 January 1933 it initially gained support. Many members of the KPD and the SPD or of smaller groups joined it. Its newspaper in exile *Unser Wort* (Our Word) had a broad circulation. But of course the Nazi regime did not fall apart. By its use of terror (and helped by the policy of appeasement) it was able to advance towards world war. This, in the context of preparation for war, made the working class passive. By around 1936 the organisation of the International Communists of Germany (IKD), as the German Trotskyists now called themselves, was practically destroyed within Germany, something which was largely true of the entire left.

In exile the surviving nucleus turned in on itself, and suffered a series of splits. Since, unlike comrades in France or Great Britain, they were cut off from class struggles in their own country, they began to orient themselves to "hibernation" for a whole historical period. Many fled to the USA, where there was now an actual break with the Fourth International which had been founded in the meantime. So the section was built afresh after 1945 by a few returning émigrés, who only succeeded over the years in very laboriously recruiting new forces.

In this situation, with no real continuities across several periods in the class struggles or in the political generations, the formation of a far left after 1968 did create a certain interest in the theoretical and historical heritage of the traditions linked in the broadest sense to the name of Trotsky. This however remained more limited than in other countries, with this being not so much an expression of the historical weakness of its object as a reflection of the marginal intellectual and political presence of "Trotskyism" in Germany in comparison with other Western European countries. Correspondingly, the number of publications was very limited, however interesting they might be. In particular here should be mentioned a presentation of German Trotskyism after 1930 by Wolfgang Alles: *On the Politics and History of the German Trotskyists from 1930*[1] (Frankfurt 1987 — originally written in 1978). The prehistory, the transition from the "ultra left" opposition in the KPD in the mid-twenties to the formation of the Left Opposition in 1929-30 was described by Rüdiger Zimmermann in *The Leninbund: Left Communists in the Weimar Republic*[2] (Düsseldorf 1978). Here we should also refer to the link between the two phases of the movement, which actually came from an Austrian historian: Hans Schafranek: *The Short Life of Kurt Landau. An Austrian Communist as Victim of the Stalinist Secret Police*[3] (Vienna, 1988). These were all academic works, which were complemented by two autobiographies of activists from the Left Opposition in the Weimar Republic and in exile: Karl Retzlaw: *The Rise and Fall of Spartakus: Memoirs of a Party Activist*[4] (Frankfurt 1971), and Oskar Hippe, *Und unsere Fahn' ist rot* (Hamburg 1979). This book is also available in English: *.. And Red is the Colour of our Flag : Memories of Sixty Years in the Workers' Movement* (London 1991). In addition reference should also be made to two important volumes containing collections of material about the two most important leaders of the Trotskyist group after 1945: Georg Jungclas, 1902-1975, *From the Young Proletarian Freethinkers in the First World War to the Left of the 1970s*[5] (Hamburg 1980), and Wolfgang Alles (editor), *Against the Stream: Texts by Willy Boepple(1911 — 1992)*[6] (Cologne 1997).

The extensive organisational fragmentation, corresponding to the numerous existing "Fourth Internationals", in the context of the decline of the political movement from the mid-seventies onwards, had the consequence that in the following years a succession of organisations disappeared and consequently the "periphery" which in some sense was politically or ideologically influenced by "Trotskyism" became even weaker. And as a result the interest in its history declined even further. Only in the course of the nineties was there a new upturn, connected to the formation of new organisations. This also awakened a new interest in the traditions of Trotskyism. A succession of works and initiatives, inspired by a variety of motives, were produced; these will be presented here.

One of the strong points was in regional and local studies, which extend from the last years of the Weimar Republic through the Nazi dictatorship to the post-war period. This reflects the development of the Trotskyist movement before 1933, whose organisational strength rested on a number of local groups,

---

1. Zur Politik und Geschichte der deutschen Trotzkisten ab 1930.
2. Der Leninbund. Linke Kommunisten in der Weimarer Republik.
3. Das kurze Leben des Kurt Landau. Ein österreichischer Kommunist als Opfer der stalinistischen Geheimpolizei.
4. Spartakus Aufstieg und Niedergang. Erinnerungen eines Parteiarbeiters.
5. Von der proletarischen Freidenkerjugend im Ersten Weltkrieg zur Linken der siebziger Jahre
6. Gegen den Strom: Texte von Willy Boepple (1911-1992).

which were firmly rooted in their local "proletarian milieu" and exercised a certain influence there. Of course such groups only existed in a few places, or even in particular areas of the larger cities. Hence the Left Opposition, with all its potential for local initiatives, did not go beyond the level of propaganda as a national force. In the last resort these groups frequently depended on a few local workers' leaders, who in the internal struggles of the KPD had followed the path of one of the various factions towards Trotskyism and had carried their local influence along with them. Thus already some years ago there appeared a local study by Stefan Goch in a journal of labour history about Gelsenkirchen, a town in the Ruhr region.[7] An interesting point is that the leading figure of the German Trotskyists in exile after 1933, Josef Weber, known in the movement under his pseudonym Johre, came from this group. Now there is also a noteworthy study of a Trotskyist group in Dresden: Barbara Weinhold, *A Group of Trotskyist Mountaineers from Dresden in the Resistance to Fascism*[8] (Cologne 2004).

Interestingly the group was formed at the end of the 1920s in a working-class suburb of the capital of Saxony in the framework of a labour movement leisure organisation, the "Friends of Nature", and specifically in the mountaineers' section. For to the south of Dresden lies the mountainous region on the Czech border known as the "Saxon Switzerland" with the neighbouring Sudeten. Disillusioned with the reformism of the SPD, they joined the KPD, but immediately came into conflict with its "ultra left" idea of "social fascism". They came into contact with the Trotskyist movement, which they joined in 1932. After 1933 they naturally found themselves in the sights of the new masters. While the members who had gone into illegality in good time developed a resistance activity, the "well-known faces" (Wenzel and Käthe Kozlecki) had to escape to neighbouring Czechoslovakia. There in Reichenberg (now Liberec) they cooperated closely with the Sudeten German Trotskyists. Under the pseudonym Julik, Wenzel became an important cadre of the organisation in exile and of the international movement. From Reichenberg the smuggling of material into the Third Reich was organised. As experienced mountaineers the Dresden comrades knew the frontier territory like the back of their hands and were able to evade the stringent border controls of the Nazi police. But in 1937 the Dresden group was broken up and its members sent to convict prisons or concentration camps. In the following year the Kozleckis had

---

7. Stefan Goch, „West German Trotskyists in the Resistance to National Socialism and in Exile" [Westdeutsche Trotzkisten im Widerstand gegen den Nationalsozialismus und im Exil] in: *Internationale wissenschaftliche Korrespondenz zur Geschichte der deutschen Arbeiterbewegung*, 1996, No. 2, pp143-171.

   One activist in this group was the designer and cartoonist Franz Meyer, who fled in 1934, played an important role for the exiled organisation in Antwerp, and eventually, after being interned in France at the beginning of the World War was able to escape to the United States. He depicted life in the internment camp in a series of drawings which were later published. Franz Meyer: *Escape from Germany: Pictures from Exile* [Flucht aus Deutschland. Bilder aus dem Exil](Frankfurt 1984).

8. Eine trotzkistische Bergsteigergruppe aus Dresden im Widerstand gegen den Faschismus.

to flee from the Nazis who were incorporating the Sudetenland into the Third Reich.

The paths of the pair now diverged. While Wenzel was able to get to Mexico through Trotsky's intervention, Käthe found exile in Great Britain, where she came into contact with the RCP and took part in forming a small German-speaking Trotskyist circle of émigrés, which after 1945 tried to exercise influence in Germany through a paper *Solidarität*. The other Dresden comrades, who had survived the concentration camp, participated from 1945 on in the reconstruction of Dresden and joined the KPD/SED(Socialist Unity Party). They abandoned any other political activities in a Trotskyist sense. Nonetheless they suffered in the late Stalinist purges. Even though it was not possible to attribute any activities to them, they were subject to reprisals which were only revoked after 1956. Wenzel Kozlecki had distanced himself from all political activity while he was still in exile in Mexico, and took no part in the exile circle of the former IKD, which had turned away from Trotskyism and had founded its own paper (*Dinge der Zeit*).[9] He later returned to West Germany, since he rightly supposed that he would not be welcome in the GDR. Käthe on the other hand concerned herself with the survival of the Trotskyist organisation in the Federal Republic, but then in the fifties, after giving up political activity, she returned to Dresden. The old group had completely disintegrated and survived only in the form of private contacts. They had had to pay a high price for their political activities — loss of freedom or of health, or "merely" of happiness in life. The political circumstances in the GDR did not permit them to draw up a broader balance-sheet. In all their personal contacts they had to avoid reference to their political convictions which had led them into anti-Nazi activities, and of course they had no other opportunity of explaining this in any way. On the contrary, in the Stalinist atmosphere of the GDR this had to remain a secret which could only be revealed after 1989. This was disclosed to the author, who was in fact the niece of Käthe Kozlecki and of another member of the group, only after the fall of the GDR, where she had worked as a scientist, when she went to examine the papers they had left after their deaths. With the assistance of interviews with the family and acquaintances she was finally able to reconstruct the fate of the group. In addition to this her work is based above all on documents of the Nazi state about the persecution and arrests after 1933 as well as material from the SED and the Stasi about various expulsions from the party and disciplinary proceedings; in addition this is complemented with material from the Trotsky archive and other collections from the Trotskyist movement. It is thus an exceptionally rich and detailed description which, despite its comparatively marginal subject-matter, made quite an impact. Not only was it discussed in both the left-wing daily papers in Germany, but it was

---

9. Its development has also found its historian: Marcel van der Linden, "The Prehistory of Post-Scarcity Anarchism: Josef Weber and the Movement for a Democracy of Content (1947-1964)", in: *Anarchist Studies*, 2001, No. 2, pp127-145.

also publicly presented several times, partly with the support of the Rosa Luxemburg Foundation of the PDS (Party of Democratic Socialism) in Saxony.

In the destinies presented here, in which the personal goes hand in hand with the political, the whole tragedy of the German workers' movement and its diverse defeats becomes clear. At the same time in the portraits drawn with empathy of all these male and female activists there is also a strong element of proletarian capacity for resistance, and hence the author has simply done justice to them, "to create a worthy memorial to the courageous men and women of a Dresden resistance group and to rescue their struggle from oblivion." (p10)

Other such studies, for example about Leipzig and the Rhine and Ruhr region, have been announced. Precisely in these places the KPD in the 1920s was strongly "ultra left" and in particular influenced by Karl Korsch. This Marxist theoretician had already come into conflict with the Comintern leadership around Zinoviev and was gradually isolated in the party. With his guiding participation there arose the oppositional grouping "Resolute Left", which for some time had a great influence in certain "proletarian strongholds" of the party, especially in the Rhineland. Until now this connection between the movement around Korsch, who himself had already withdrawn from organised politics after 1928, and the Trotskyist movement which evolved from 1929 onwards, has scarcely been noted. These works and those that will follow them will certainly make possible a more precise understanding of the various currents and tendencies in German communism.

Another at least equally important impulse for the reappropriation of history came from a quite different direction. It was produced by the opening of the archives in the former GDR. In particular this meant the archive of the former secret police, the State Security, better known by the abbreviation Stasi, with its extensive data about the persecution of the real or supposed opponents of "really existing socialism". Here the struggle against "Trotskyism" acquired a value for the apparatus of repression which, as in the Soviet Union, was out of all proportion to the actual influence of the Trotskyists. This was especially true in the time after the Second World War, when the organisational strength of the movement was greatly weakened by the various persecutions. And naturally it is this period of the years after 1945 which is central to these studies based on the Stasi archives.

Of course the Stalinist secret police was here connecting with a tradition which did not only go back to the struggle of the KPD party machine in the Weimar Republic. In particular the Spanish Civil War represents an important link to the Stasi in the GDR, not least in terms of personnel. Many of its central cadre had received their training in the various security organisations in Spain under the direct leadership of the NKVD.[10]

10. This has recently been investigated by Michael Uhl, *The Myth of Spain. The Legacy of the International Brigades in the GDR* [Mythos Spanien. Das Erbe der intentionalen Brigaden in der DDR](Bonn 2004). Important indications about the KPD security apparatus in Spain were already to be found in Peter Huber, *Stalin's Shadow in Switzerland. Swiss Communists in Moscow: Defenders and Prisoners of the Comintern* [Stalins Schatten in die Schweiz. Schweizer Kommunisten

One of the first extensive studies was only marginally concerned with "real" Trotskyism. It was a biography: Michael Kubina, *Utopia, Resistance and Cold War. The Untimely Life of the Berlin Council Communist Alfred Weiland (1906-1978)*[11] (Hamburg 2001). He of course came from the tradition of the KAPD and of "Council Communism" (as developed by such Dutch thinkers as Anton Pannekoek or Herman Gorter). After 1945 Weiland played the leading role from Berlin in gathering together the surviving members of this grouping and also sought close cooperation with all other tendencies of the anti-Stalinist opposition. The post-war situation demanded this, going beyond the old factional struggles of the time before 1933. If one tried to appear in public, even with strict precautionary measures, one came immediately into the sights of the NKVD, but Berlin did offer a certain room for manoeuvre as a result of the division of the city into four zones of occupation. Of course the region around the city, which contained many traditional industrial areas and hence strongholds of the working-class movement as far as Saxony and Thüringen, was under Soviet occupation and all activity to the left of Stalinist politics had to be carried on in a conspiratorial fashion.

Naturally the "council communist" tendency stands at the centre of this work. But for the history of Trotskyism it is interesting for the information it contains about cooperation with the Berlin Trotskyists, whose group was reconstructed after 1945 under the control of Oskar Hippe. This he has described himself briefly in his memoirs referred to above.

Here are to be found detailed indications from archival records. Mainly it is a question of SED reports about the activities of the Trotskyist groups. These also include numerous reports from informers. Hippe was arrested by the NKVD in 1948 when visiting political contacts in the Soviet zone and was released only in 1956. And Weiland was also arrested two years later. In fact he was kidnapped from West Berlin, which created quite a sensation. But after his release in 1958 participation in the political activities in West Berlin on the left fringe of the SPD was to be no longer possible. The erstwhile "ultra-left" Weiland had now turned to the American camp in the Cold War, and the differences in approach towards Stalinism had become irreconcilable.

Directly concerned with the actions of the Stasi against the German Trotskyists is an article by the East German historian Günter Wernicke with the eloquent title "Operative Procedure Scum".[12] For this was the official title which

in Moskau: Verteidiger und Gefangene der Komintern](Zurich 1994).
11. Von Utopie, Widerstand und kaltem Krieg. Das unzeitgemäße Leben des Berliner Rätekommunisten Alfred Weiland.
12. Günter Wernicke, "Operative Procedure 'Scum'. The Ministry of State Security (MfS) and the German trotskyists in the 1950s" [Operativer Vorgang 'Abschaum'. Das Ministerium für Staatssicherheit (MfS) und die deutschen Trotzkisten in den 1950er Jahren] in Andreas G. Graf (ed.) *Anarchists, Anarcho-Syndicalists and Council Communists in Resistance and Exile*, [Anarchisten gegen Hitler. Anarchisten, Anarcho-Syndikalisten, Rätekommunisten in Widerstand und Exil] Berlin, 2001, pp281-299.

the Stasi gave to their attempt to infiltrate the West German Trotskyists in the 1950s.

According to his account the Stasi succeeded in placing at least two agents in the Trotskyist movement, which enabled it to get an accurate picture during the 1950s. This was moreover of particular importance, since it also succeeded in exerting influence after the international split of 1953.

Thus a certain Helmut Schneeweiss was won over, who before 1933 had led the local KPD in Oranienburg, a suburb of Berlin, over to the Left Opposition, and had built a local united front. Trotsky himself drew attention to this several times in his writings on Germany. Schneeweiss had fled from the Nazis to the Netherlands, where he had come into contact with the Trotskyists there. In the 1950s he lived in Osnabrück and was active in the German section of the FI. There he worked closely with Pablo, and among other things was involved in the attempt to support the Algerian struggle by printing forged French francs, which was broken up by the West German police in 1960.[13] Through these and other actions the Stalinist apparatuses in the East had a far-reaching insight into important aspects of solidarity work with the FLN. And after his arrest Pablo himself came to suspect that Schneeweiss was a GDR agent.[14] The question which in any case follows from this, but which the author in his brief survey does not pursue, is how far was Stalinism able to manipulate the solidarity work, or what use it was able to make of this knowledge. This is also the case for the other informer who was attached to the German Trotskyists, and who from Berlin exerted himself to intervene in the discussions of the two international factions after 1953. The majority of the German section had declared itself in favour of the International Secretariat round Michel Pablo, Pierre Frank and Ernest Mandel, and had begun entry work in the SPD. At the same time the Swiss section, which belonged to the International Committee, was trying to build its own group from individual contacts in West Germany and West Berlin, which would also have an influence in the "socialist camp". All this took place very precisely under the eyes of the Stasi, as Wernicke makes clear. One marginal curiosity: Wernicke reveals a whole set of pseudonyms used by the Stasi for its informers which Kubina, apparently out of concern for the strict data protection laws in the federal republic, did not want to disclose.

His contribution is only a preliminary outline. Numerous questions remain. First of all certainly the question of the motives that led formerly oppositional communists to let themselves be recruited by the Stalinist apparatus as informers. And not least the question of the consequences for the development of the German Trotskyists. Additionally this short contribution makes clear what valuable information about the Trotskyist movement, also on an

---

13 This is also described in detail in a history of solidarity work with the Algerian liberation struggle: Claus Leggewie, *Carrying Suitcases: The Left's Algerian Project in Adenauer's Germany*, [Koffertträge. Das Algerien-Projekt der Linken im Adenauer-Deutschland]Berlin, 1984, pp129-144.
14 Ibid, p140.

international level, can be gained in the former East German archives by a critical examination.

This is very much true of the book which definitively uncovers the background to the murder of Wolf Salus. Salus was a leading member of the Czech Trotskyists from the 1920s on, who had had to flee in 1948, and who died in Munich in March 1953 in unexplained circumstances. Already in 1993 *Revolutionary History* reported that discoveries after the collapse of the Soviet Union confirmed the suspicion which had already emerged that he had been killed.[15] This is now corroborated by the researches of the author Hermann Bubke in the Stasi archive. (*The Action of the Stasi and KGB spy Otto Freitag in Post-war Munich*[16] Hamburg, 2004).

The "chief actor" in this book, Otto Freitag, was an officer in the German army from 1926 and also from 1938 a member of the Nazi party. He was wounded on the Eastern front in the Second World War, and a superior officer had him brought before a military court for alleged refusal to obey orders. This enabled him, immediately after the end of the war, to attribute to himself a sort of political persecution in connection with the 20 July plot to kill Hitler. Additionally he could assume that the Nazi party membership records were no longer accessible. Originally a native of Munich, he went to the Soviet zone of occupation, where his family had been evacuated. He knew who was in charge now, and already by 1 July 1945 he was a member of the KPD and began a rapid career on the regional level. He aroused the interest of the Soviet occupation authorities and was hired initially by the Soviet secret service for work in the West. After a simulated flight his first job consisted in joining the Independent Workers' Party (UAP), founded mainly by former KPD cadres after Tito's break with Stalin. Also numerous independent lefts joined, among others the small Trotskyist group. Freitag's task was not simply to deliver detailed information, but to inflame inner-party differences. The activities of the Trotskyists were of special interest. But the UAP was to break up in the course of 1951, because the Yugoslavs discontinued their financial support.

So he concentrated entirely on the Trotskyists, whose confidence he rapidly won. For example, Bubke quotes from the reports of his achievements which he sent to East Berlin, where he tells how he succeeded in searching through the briefcase of the unsuspecting Ernest Mandel and so managed to piece together important information about the condition of the Fourth International. But a particular target for him was Wolfgang Salus who had emigrated from Prague. From Munich, where he was also a member of the local Trotskyist group, Salus was apparently seeking contacts in Czechoslovakia, or at least arousing suspicions in the eyes of the Soviet secret service that he was doing so. At first Freitag made plans for his abduction, but in the winter of 1952-53 there was apparently a decision at the highest Soviet level that he should be killed with one of the undetectable "special poisons" developed by the Soviet secret service in

---

15. *Revolutionary History*, Vol 4 No 4, Spring 1993.
16. Der Einsatz des Stasi- und KGB-Spions Otto Freitag im München der Nachkriegszeit.

the thirties. About the reasons for this we can only put forward suppositions. This decision came at the same time as the Slánsky show trial in Czechoslovakia. Perhaps they had even intended to let him appear there, suitably prepared. Bubke himself suggests, without being able to find any proof in the documents, a connection with Stalin's last planned "purge" action in March 1953 in the Soviet Union, which, proceeding from a wave of anti-Semitism, also aimed at the elimination of prominent Stalinists like Beria and Molotov.

In any case he has documented thoroughly Freitag's observations and his detailed abduction plans. About the murder it is claimed on the basis of Stasi reports only that Freitag succeeded in "eliminating Salus". In fact there was no indication of a murder in 1953, although suspicion had arisen immediately. The secret was revealed for the first time in *Moscow News* (2 August 1992) — this is not mentioned here. But for the Trotskyist movement the murder of this important intellectual and activist was a bitter loss.

In the following year Freitag's main preoccupation remained the Trotskyists and the other leftists connected with them in one way or another. Above all he intervened in the 1953 split in the Fourth International, which he was to exacerbate. He put himself forward as the contact person for one of the two factions (the International Committee), whereas the great majority of the German group, as already mentioned, remained with the International Secretariat. The methods which he used to get himself to be trusted were the usual ones employed by police informers. He made himself indispensable by his permanent "unselfish" helpfulness in organisational tasks, while he was hardly noticed in political work. He even aroused thereby a certain distrust on the part of the leadership of the German Trotskyists, who however suspected careerism in the ordinary sense, as is shown by an internal circular documented in the appendix.

In the late fifties he worked closely in Munich with Theo Pirker, a well-known sociologist, who for a time played an important role in the independent left in West Germany. In a book of autobiographical interviews (Martin Jander (ed.), *Theo Pirker on Pirker*[17] Marburg, 1988, pp99-102) Pirker himself unfortunately only refers to Freitag very vaguely and even without naming him in connection with solidarity work for the Algerian liberation struggle. On this Freitag as a former officer could give good military advice.[18] But political projects directed at Germany also arose, for example a newspaper to be formed under the direction of Pirker. This was discussed at a session of the "International Committee of the Fourth International" in Munich in early 1959 with the two German representatives Freitag and Pirker, likewise documented in the appendix with a report by Freitag. Other participants included a representative of the Swiss section and Gerry Healy[19], who reported to the

17. Theo Pirker über Pirker.
18. But these activities were not noticed by Claus Leggewie in his book mentioned above.
19. In the book of interviews mentioned above Theo Pirker gave the following picture of Healy: "In Britain also I came into contact with representatives of the Fourth International. They inspired me with pure horror. He is still the leader. A beefy little Irishman, who always filled

meeting that his organisation did not want to leave the Labour Party under any circumstances. We are forced to consider the suspicion that Freitag (and hence the Stasi) imposed fraudulent projects for political work in Germany, in order to bury them all the quicker. Thus the project of a newspaper for Germany took as a model the *Newsletter*, with which Healy was preparing the foundation of the SLL, (without of course being able to count on a comparable circle of supporters). For undoubtedly the thing that was of the least interest to his employers in the SED was giving encouragement to the formation and promotion of an independent left in Adenauer's republic. And that is equally valid for the International. A note by Freitag, in which he sets down his task, states: "The split in the Fourth International must be pushed forward and we must strive to maintain it. Without unmasking ourselves in the process, we must always strive to reach an alliance with the forces that speak out against a reunification of the two main parts of Trotskyism." (p84) The irony (or rather the tragicomedy) of the story is that for factional reasons Gerry Healy hurled at leading figures in the world Trotskyist movement the accusation that they were agents of the Soviet secret service, but did not notice that for years he had been sitting down together with a real agent and had developed great political plans together with him.

In autumn 1961, in the context of various espionage affairs between East and West, Freitag was removed, possibly also as a delayed consequence of the discovery of the printing of forged money by Pablo with the assistance of Schneeweiss. He attempted to exert influence on the solidarity movement with Algeria from East Berlin (which was harmful to this solidarity work[20]) with a public declaration as "a refugee from the Federal Republic". Subsequently he was active as a senior official for the Stasi, among other things acting as an informer in GDR travel groups visiting other "socialist countries" until his excessive self-esteem got him entangled in the Stasi's net when he already was a pensioner. Out of revenge for restrictions imposed on his family and also from awareness of growing discontent among the population, he thought he could get his own back by passing information to the West German secret service. This did not go unnoticed, but he got off relatively lightly with two years in jail; he also lost all his material privileges, including his special pension obtained surreptitiously through his connections in the Central Committee as a "fighter against fascism". He died in the 1980s.

His action against the Trotskyists and what was at that time in the Federal Republic referred to as the "homeless left", is dealt with here in a relatively detailed fashion, because it was the core of his activity and therefore also forms the core of the book. But of course his activities were not limited to this. A list, prepared for the Stasi, of people he had got to know and on whom he had

---

me with terror. I though with dread of what would happen if he were to take power." (p100).
20   Unfortunately this episode also does not appear in Leggewie's account.

reported (pp124-125) shows, how widely stretched his activity as an informer was. Those from Britain listed were:

Healy, London, leader of the English Trotskyists.
Hunter, Liverpool, organising secretary of the English Trotskyists.
Slauther Leeds, Professor, Cannonite theoretician.
Fox, Professor, Sheffield, Trotskyist.
Murdoch, Iris, writer, Trotskyist.
Daniels, Professor, Nothingham, Trotskyist.
Castle, Barbara & Paul Ignatus — anti-nuclear movement.
Moffat, Abe, Trotskyist, miners' union.
Hamilton, Betty, Trotskyist.
Panter, Will, Trotskyist, miners union.
Arronsmith, PA. Member of the committe against nuclear war.
Pearce, Brian, Trotskyist functionary, editor of Labour Review.
Zilliacus, London, member of the House of Commions.
Dr. Horpen, Oxfort, Trotskyist.
Cliff, Glaskow, Trotskyist.
Fryer, Peter, Scotland, fomer CP of England, editor-in-chief "Daily Worker".
Jordan, Pat, leader of the English Pabloites.
Svan, J., Manchester, Trotskyist, miners' union official[21].

In addition he was put on to targets outside the left. A planned abduction of the head of the BND [the German MI6] Reinhard Gehlen, or actions against East European émigrés (such as the Ukrainian Borys Lewytzkyj, the author of numerous books on the Soviet Union in the 1950s and 1960s) show that he was permanently active. Thus the Stasi remunerated him "appropriately", although he was strictly camouflaged in Munich. Pirker said in his book of interviews (p102) that he lived "very frugally", so that although his many journeys were noticeable, in the end did not arouse suspicion. All these things are described by Bubke here in just as much detail.

Undoubtedly it is a gripping story, even if it could have been told in a more fluent manner. But in the last resort the book remains unsatisfactory because it only concentrates on cases reconstructed from the Stasi documents and simply enumerates them rather than placing them in a broader political context. So the author scarcely goes into the question of what Freitag's actions ultimately achieved or how much harm they caused. For that further research would be necessary which would bring in the context.

21. Spelling has been preserved as in the original. Both spelling and attributions reveal a limited knowledge of the subject-matter. Paynter and Moffat were Communists, certainly not Trotskyists, though they may have had some hesitations in 1956. Iris Murdoch had loose connections with the circle round *New Left Review*, but was never a Trotskyist. Tony Cliff never lived in Glasgow, but in the early 60s there was a strong International Socialist group in Glasgow, based in the Labour Party Young Socialists and Cliff visited Glasgow frequently. For a time *Labour Worker* (forerunner of *Socialist Worker*) was published from Glasgow. **[Translator's note.]**

Moreover Freitag himself remains pretty colourless. What drove this will o' the wisp figure on, what his personal environment was, we do not learn. Perhaps this cannot be reconstructed from the documents. But one thing is clear. In many ways it is very much a German career of someone who understood, uninterruptedly for at least most of the time, how to swim from right to left, how to attribute to himself the biography of an anti-Nazi resistance fighter, and then also betrayed without compunction the many people who trusted him politically. Exactly how people in Germany imagine an informer.

The local studies covering the last years of the Weimar Republic and the revelations from the Stasi archives — these are the two main themes which define the recent work on the history of German Trotskyism. Their appearance has also led to the circle of those working on the subject trying to form a network. Already there have been two meetings in Gelsenkirchen, in some sense inspired by the activities in this town before 1933, and in which family members from the activists' circle took part. The first meeting in February 2004 was reported only in a Trotskyist newspaper[22], but the second conference in February 2006 was described in a left-wing daily paper[23].

Here the provisional results of research still in progress were presented, for example about Bruchsal, also a place where a united front initiative was described as exemplary by Trotsky. A biography of Ruth Fischer will also portray her temporary connections with the Trotskyist movement during her exile in the 1930s. Even more important was the question of locating in broader context, in the history of all the opposition groups in the KPD in the 1920s and then of the left between the SPD and the Stalinist KPD as well as the relation of the IKD to the Spanish civil war, which because of the crisis of the German section in 1936/37 very soon became a de-facto non-relation.

Further meetings are being considered and also publishing projects such as a collected volume which would permit a broader comparative view. Thereby a forgotten tradition of the German working-class movement can be given its appropriate place. It is perhaps not by chance that this is happening just at the present time, and it is certainly not to be attributed to an academic conjuncture, even though most of the works originate in such a context. The real impulse comes from the political and ideological change produced by the search for a new left and hence also for the fresh evaluation of the traditions, which the hitherto influential currents of the German labour movement have extinguished. They are therefore above all part of the renovations following the collapse of Stalinism fifteen years ago, but also of the great breakdown which social democracy is now going through.

Reiner Tosstorff

---

22. BB "First conference on the History of the Left Opposition in the KPD and the IKD", in *Avanti*, No. 108, April 2004.
23. Reiner Tosstorff, "Not so Marginal. In Gelsenkirchen a Conference was Concerned with KPD Left Opposition groups", [Nicht so randständig. In Gelsenkirchen beschäftigte sich eine Tagung mit linken Oppositionsgruppen der KPD] in: *Junge Welt*, 3. 2. 2006.

Karim Landais

KARIM Landais joined the Parti des travailleurs (the French organisation often referred to as lambertiste after its leading militant Pierre Lambert) in 1999 and was active for two years. He then became an anarchist, but devoted much of his time to investigating the party which had raised his hopes and then disappointed him. In 2005, just before his twenty-fifth birthday, he committed suicide.

His copious writings have now been edited by Yves Coleman and published in two large volumes under the title Passions militantes et rigueur historienne (2006, no place or publisher given). [enquiries and orders to Guy Landais, La Bastide des capucins, 84 240 Cabrières d'Aigues, France.] The first volume (823 pages — 20 ?) deals with his researches on the PT and its antecedents, and contains some remarkable interviews with some of the veterans of French Trotskyism, notably Pierre Broué, Michel Lequenne, Boris Fraenkel, Alexandre Hébert, and Charles Berg.

Several of these interviews (in French) are also available at http://www.meltl.com/.

Ian Birchall

NOTES ON HUGH ESSON and THE GLASGOW LENINST LEAGUE[24]

HUGH'S father was of Norwegian or Swedish origin. Hugh was born in Aberdeen. Of his mother, we know only that she ran a café in Glasgow. According to Ernie Rogers, Hugh had a "Cockney half-brother".

Hugh joined the Communist Party at its very beginning in 1920 — whether he was an actual "foundation" member, as Rogers claimed, we cannot say. By the mid-1920s, he was living in London, a member of the Tottenham and Wood Green branch of the CPGB, where he became a friend of Henry Sara, who developed later as a notable Trotskyist.[25] During the 1926 General Strike, Hugh functioned as an officer of the Tottenham Trades Council. A building worker, he belonged to the Transport & General Workers' Union. Rogers recalled that Hugh worked on the Bank of England and also the Grosvenor House Hotel (or Grosvenor House Estate). But in what years? We have no idea.

Hugh was becoming progressively disillusioned with the Communist Party. Critical of the Comintern's disastrous policy in China, which led to the wiping out of most of its membership by the Kuomintang, Hugh was deeply involved with Henry Sara in the "Hands Off China" committee.

Living in Glasgow at the start of the 1930s, Hugh began to buy the American Trotskyist paper, the *Militant*, from the anarchist publisher, Guy Aldred. When the supply in Scotland ceased (it was assumed that Aldred wasn't

---

24. This little note was provoked by Hugh Esson's daughter-in-law contacting us while researching her husband's family history.
25. On Henry Sara see the article by John McIlroy in the *Dictionary of Labour Biography*, Vol XI.

paying the London distributor), Hugh began taking bulk orders direct from London: Scottish sales rose gradually from 30 to 200. Later, Hugh distributed the *Fourth International*. He distributed also the *Red Flag*, the British Trotskyist paper, but sales were poor in this case, it being perceived as a rather inadequate publication.

About 1932 the Glasgow Leninist League was formed, consisting of seven members, including Hugh and Ernie Rogers — a figure which remained static right to the end of the 1930s. It was a self-consciously elitist organisation, keen to take on only members of the requisite revolutionary calibre. And it affiliated with the American revolutionary organisation led by Hugo Oehler. Rogers always considered Hugh as politically the ablest member of the group, but not an efficient secretary. Finally, he gave up the League's secretaryship to Jimmy Allen. It should be noted that for a number of years Hugh operated under the alias of "Hugh Morrison" due — said Rogers — to "marital reasons".

In Glasgow, Hugh became secretary of a branch of the Transport & General Workers' Union, and through this connection the GLL were able to hold meetings on occasion at the T. & G. premises. Hugh remained an effective organizer within his trade union for many years. Ernest Bevin was keen to see the leading Communist Bert Papworth expelled at one stage. But an intervention by Hugh thwarted this move. Hugh broke at one point with the industrial line peddled by the Trotskyists. Ernest Bevin wrote a letter congratulating him on his independence in this respect. When the Trotskyist Jock Haston ran for an official post within the union, Hugh supported him, however.

Later, Hugh was involved with a shadowy organization known as "The Altogether Boys," of which we know nothing further apart from believing that Harry Constable, the docker, was a member. Rogers described them as "gin fixers". Hugh played some background role in getting the "Blue Union" of dockers to return to the T. & G., from which they had originally split. Hugh influenced a "Docherty" in Glasgow in this respect, we believe.

The policy of the Leninist League triggered a small disaster for Denis Levin and Rogers were on the run from the police, following agitational activity in London and Coventry. On 9 March 1941 the police raided Hugh's home at 6 Milton Avenue, Cambuslang. Denis Levin entered the premises bearing the identity card of Charlie Menzies whilst the police were actually there. Hugh vouched that he was Menzies. The police eventually charged Hugh with misleading them with false information. He was sentenced to 30 days in gaol plus a fine. This event probably influenced his decision to move to London.

The GLL was effectively defunct a year before the end of World War 2. We know next to nothing of Hugh's later political activities apart from the fact that he joined the Labour Party and attended Labour Party conferences as a member of the T. & G. delegation.

Anne Esson, Hugh's daughter-in-law, knew Hugh from 1957 onwards. He was then living in Walthamstow, running his own business fitting window frames. He was in bad health for many years, suffering from thrombosis. He died on 25 November 1985. Anne has commented on his extreme secretiveness about his past: she knew nothing about his political history.

There is one stray note by Rogers which mentions that Hugh was associated with someone called Jock Milligan, a painter. But there is no indication of what context this relates to.
Ron Heisler

Reviews

Charles Wesley Ervin, *Tomorrow is Ours: The Trotskyist Movement in India and Ceylon, 1935-48*, Social Scientists' Association, Colombo 2006. pp367, £10[1]

THIS book has grown from an article in "Revolutionary History" entitled "Trotskyism in India: Origins through World War II (1935-45)" (RH Vol. 1, no.4, Winter 1988-89, pp22-34). But it is more than just a history of Indian Trotskyism, however illuminating. As the author explains,

> The first chapter attempts to briefly summarize how the British conquered and transformed India, how the Indian nationalists responded, and how the Marxists analyzed and intervened in that long, complex and fascinating process. (p.iv).

As such it forms, with the rest of the book, an admirable introduction to the history of modern India. A lucid exposition of the actions and effects of British imperialism in India in the 19th Century C.E. is followed by a succinct summary of the rise of Indian nationalism and the responses of European socialists to the "colonial question". There is an excellent section (pp29-38) on the work of the neglected Indian Marxist M.N.Roy, who

> showed that the Indian bourgeoisie emerged not in *opposition* to the landed aristocracy, as in Europe, but *through* the system of landlordism that the British created (p33).

(This fact goes far to account for the subsequent political development of this class). Also included is a lot of useful material (plus extensive bibliographical references) on the question of the exact mode of production prevailing in India prior to its appropriation by the British Raj, i.e. the ongoing dispute between those who view this as a form of feudalism and those who see it as an example of the so-called "Asiatic Mode of Production". Various facts adduced by Charles Wesley Ervin would appear to support the latter contention.

The bulk of the book deals with the early leaders of the LSSP, its formation and subsequent history up to 1948, but in the context of the decision to found

---

1. Available from C. Chrysostom, 43 Harrold House, Finchley Road London NW3 6JX

the Bolshevik Leninist Party of India (BLPI) in 1941. Philip Gunawardena and his co-thinkers reasoned that an effective working class movement against the Raj needed to be organized on a sub-continental basis. The party was launched in time to intervene in the mass struggles which developed around Gandhi's call to the British to "quit India", which he issued following the dramatic victories won by the Japanese against Britain in 1942. The party urged support for any action against imperialism decided upon by Congress, but warned (correctly) that Gandhi might compromise. (Reading the descriptions of Gandhi's relations with the Indian masses throughout the period covered by the book, one is reminded of James Connolly's observations on Daniel O'Connell in "Labour in Irish History"). There was, on the part of certain comrades, however, a tendency towards an exaggerated optimism — see Ervin's comments on an article by Ajit Roy in 1943 (p130).

Some of the best reportage in the book can be found in Chapter Five, where visits to India by certain British Trotskyists in uniform in the Second World War are described, such as, e.g. the following encounter:

> Later that day Manickam took Scott to meet some of the party's sympathizers from the Perambur railway workshops. They met in a hut in the slums. None of the Tamil workers could speak English. Manickam translated. Scott saw what it meant to be a Trotskyist in India. Here, in a hovel, lit only by flickering candles, the BLPI was teaching Marxism to illiterate workers who had just come off a 12-hour shift. (p150).

However, the author rightly refuses to confine himself to mere description of events, but makes criticisms where he believes they are justified, such as, for example, in the run-up to independence in 1947, when quite clearly the danger threatened of a deal between Gandhi and Congress, on the one hand, and the British Labour Government on the other, over the heads of the masses. Ervin writes

> The Trotskyists wanted Congress to 'return to the road of struggle'. But Nehru cast his lot with Gandhi. The BLPI directed biting propaganda at the Congress Socialists, pointing out their contradictions. The Socialists wanted struggle, but refused to break with the 'bourgeois' Congress. But these barbs, fired from afar, carried little sting. If the Trotskyists had been working in the Congress Socialist Party, as Philip Gunawardena had urged all along, they might have been able to influence a chunk of the Congress left. (pp173-4).

I really do not wish to say much more about this wonderful book: read it yourself, and learn, and decide. The only other thing I would like to draw attention to is Appendix B, which contains the 1942 Programme of the BLPI. This, in my view, is an educational document of very great importance. An introductory section on early European capitalist penetration of India leads into a discussion of British imperialism and its effects in India, leading to the conclusion that

> The industrialization of India, on which her future depends, cannot be carried out without the overthrow of Imperialism and a sweeping transformation of agrarian relations. (p286).

This is followed by a survey of the various Indian social classes. The programme is then summarized in five points (p310) and set out in detail in the succeeding section ("The Programme of Transitional Demands"). The document concludes with a section devoted to international issues — the imperialist war, the Soviet Union and the various existing internationals.

Particularly useful is the section on trade unions, which surveys the whole range of institutions developed by the working class in this field up to and including sit-down strikes, factory committees and directly political soviets (see pp317-324).

Whatever one might think of the Fourth International's 1938 "Transitional Programme" and its demands, there is no doubt that the BLPI's 1942 Programme was a highly competent adaptation of such politics to the contemporary Indian situation, one which deserves serious study.

The author alludes to the possibility of a sequel to the work which would cover the period from the mid-1950s onwards. The appearance of such a volume would be very welcome.

Chris Gray

Jean-René Chauvin, *Un Trotskiste dans l'enfer nazi*, Editions Syllepse, Paris, 2006, pp245, 20 €

JEAN-René Chauvin became a Trotskyist in 1937. For seventy years he has remained true to his original commitment. In the 1940s he was a leading activist in Sartre and Rousset's Rassemblement Démocratique Révolutionnaire. During the Algerian war he was active in the Voie Communiste, and in the 1960s in the Parti socialiste unifié, after which he joined the Ligue communiste révolutionnaire. When I met him in Paris a few years ago he was, aged nearly eighty, visiting schools in Paris to tell of his experiences in the Nazi camps and to warn of the danger of the far right.

Now at the age of eighty-eight he has published an account of the most remarkable time of his life, his two years as a prisoner of the Nazis. He must be one of the few people alive who could write the staggering sentence about arriving in Buchenwald: "After being in Auschwitz and Mauthausen, the atmosphere there seemed to me to be much more relaxed." Chauvin evokes vividly the nature of everyday life in the camps — the squalor, the lice, the hunger, the backbreaking work. He recalls how prisoners were awakened at 5.00 a.m. to go to work by a guard banging a hammer on a piece of rail. He cites an account of a Chinese concentration camp where prisoners were awakened in the same fashion — but at 4.00 a.m.

Food rations were determined strictly by the work done by a particular prisoner. The Nazis had taken Marx's notion of the reproduction of labour power to its logical conclusion. At one point Chauvin was assigned to a more strenuous task without an increase in his ration. He had to confront a foreman and demand an increase.

As a true internationalist, he was able to establish relations of solidarity with fellow-prisoners of many nationalities, and even, on occasion, establish some sort of human relationships with those supervising him. But as a Trotskyist he also faced particular dangers. On one occasion he was attacked by two Stalinists, who screamed at him that he was a "Hitlero-Trotskyist" and began to beat him. Fortunately he was rescued when two other Communist Party members came to his rescue. The Stalinists in the camp were by no means a monolithic body — for some the Moscow line predominated, for others their sense of class solidarity. But as he notes, in other cases Trotskyists were put to death by Stalinists in the camps.

In January 1945 Auschwitz was evacuated and Chauvin took part in the notorious "march of death" when thousands of prisoners were moved out on foot. One prisoner cut off his finger with an axe in the hope of avoiding the evacuation, but he was forced to march with the others. Many did not survive the journey.

Later he was evacuated from Buchenwald by train. Chauvin's neighbour was leaning heavily on him, with his head on Chauvin's shoulder, so he tried to wake the man, but realised that "he would never wake again".

In retrospect it seems near miraculous that Chauvin should have lived to tell his story. He attributes his survival in some situations to the fact that he was fit and agile, having been a boxer and rugby player — a useful reminder to socialists who are disdainful of sport.

Chauvin has added one more to the set of Trotskyist autobiographies, of which a good number have appeared in France in recent years. [See my review of some of them in *Historical Materialism* Vol. 13, N° 4.] But the book is much more than just a personal memoir. Over the years Chauvin has found time to read and research widely on the question of concentration camps, and alongside his own story he gives a fascinating account of the history of this barbaric institution.

The earliest camps seem to have been set up by the Spanish general Weyler y Nicolau in Cuba, but much of the credit for developing them goes to the British (something not often recalled by those anxious to defend the "achievements" of the British Empire). He describes the use of the camps in the Boer War, and notes that Emily Hobhouse, who did so much to document the atrocious conditions in the camps where Boer prisoners were held, was not even allowed to visit the camps for black prisoners.

He gives an account of the Russian camps, from their origin in the late 1920s to the more brutal form they took under Stalin. He stresses the similarities between the Nazi and Stalinist camps and recalls the work done by such writers as Serge, Ciliga and Marcel Guiheneuf (Yvon) in publicising the camps when their very existence was denied by most of the left.

But as a revolutionary Chauvin knows the main enemy is at home, and he devotes some fascinating pages to the history of concentration camps in France. While the crimes of the Nazis on French soil are well documented, the camps set up in France *before* the German invasion have largely been written out of history. The first camps were those set up at the end of the Spanish civil war for the half million refugees who came over the Pyrenees, and who were less than welcome to the French government (still based on the Popular Front National Assembly elected with such hopes in 1936).They were initially simply herded onto the beaches, where some died of hunger and exhaustion; then they were redistributed to a number of camps in Southern France. At the outbreak of war, the government rounded up Germans, making the crude xenophobic assumption that all Germans (even German refugees who had fought against fascism in Spain) were on the side of Hitler. He notes in particular the internment of a group of nuns (obviously a serious threat to public order) on the grounds that they had been born in Alsace before 1919 when it was still ruled by Germany, and therefore were classified as German nationals! As he notes, there was much indignation in France when Pinochet used sporting stadiums for political prisoners, but France had done exactly the same in 1939.

Chauvin's account is both depressing and inspiring, but perhaps the saddest chapter is the concluding one. Quite unbroken by his suffering, Chauvin immediately rejoined his Trotskyist comrades. The Second World War had been Trotskyism's finest hour, when a small but courageous group of comrades had preserved the principles of proletarian internationalism.

Now there were new possibilities. Chauvin reproduces a document showing the precise membership figures for the Parti communiste internationaliste. In 1948 it had just 626 members, about one quarter of whom were industrial workers. Yet the press raised the spectre of "120,000 Trotskyists". There was a real chance of the PCI uniting with the Socialist Party youth, who had been expelled from the party, and the ASR [Action socialiste et révolutionnaire], another split from the Socialist Party; the fused organisation could have several thousand members and made a real impact on French political life. But the majority of the organisation turned its back on the opportunities; there were two debilitating splits, one in 1948 (when Chauvin was expelled), and another in 1952. At the start of the Algerian war French Trotskyism was reduced to a bunch of tiny squabbling sects.

Chauvin's concluding sentence is a melancholy one. But it is the fruit of tireless activism over eight decades, and may serve as a warning to the rest of us:

> In my humble opinion it [the failure to unite] was due to the difference between the weakness of our forces and the exaggerated picture that both sides had of the extent of our opportunities, as well as to the

passion for polemic, whereas all political decisions should be taken coolly.

Ian Birchall

Guy Debord, *Panegyric²*, Verso, 2004, pp181

DEBORD remains known to the English reader, if at all, as one of the leaders of the tiny Situationist International (SI), a body that produced some almost completely incomprehensible texts and exerted a temporary influence over a group of students during the May 1968 uprising in France. Having presided over the inner life of an "international" that consisted to a large degree of expelling its members for minuscule political deviations and thereafter producing supremely obscure texts denouncing them, Debord went on to dissolve the rump of the SI in a self-conscious parody of Marx's winding up of the First International. The dissolution more closely paralleled the break-up of the Beatles, with the main lyricists' parts being taken by Debord and his long time collaborator Raoul Vaneigem. Out of this career of wreckage and refusal, through processes that are difficult to understand, Debord became a kind of image of a certain kind of revolutionary attitude. In fact he became everything he must have hated to become — a projection not a person, projected by those who hated what they thought he wrote while failing to understand it, projected onto those who sought a cipher of revolution without wishing to make the effort to understand it.

The volume in review here consists of Books 1 and 2 of a projected larger work. Book 3 was said to be completed, and material in progress existed for other sections. This remaining material however was destroyed at or around the time Debord killed himself, at the end of November 1994, either by Debord or according to his expressed wishes. Book 2 is a collection of photographs and images that bear a relation to the text of Book 1, with some additional captions and quotations. Standing alone, it would carry no value. Discounting the pages of Book 2, we have about 65 pages of text that are to represent Debord's account of himself, his times, his actions and refusals to act.

Debord and the other situationists are best read in the most banal of circumstances: the re-reading that led to this review was begun on the westbound platform of the Central Line at Liverpool Street, at 10:48 am on 28/12/05. I was on the way to the Tate Modern to see the Rousseau exhibition — imaginary predators in imaginary jungles circling compassless in the Saatchi shark tanks. Part of the situationists' legacy is an acute awareness of the contrast between the worthless everyday and the full human potential of life — its intensity and variety, contrast and brightness. Part of their failure lies in their inability to relate to this contrast with anything more political than (richly merited) contempt.

2. Translated by James Brook and John McHale.

Debord took the trouble to provide the reader with a clarification of the term "panegyric"; it goes beyond "eulogy" in so far as it "entails neither blame nor criticism". My Collins English Dictionary goes, if anything, a little further, in defining panegyric as a "formal public commendation". Debord certainly succeeds in the aim of excluding "criticism" from his text; there is no attempt to evaluate or assess his own actions or refusals to act. (This may be more valuable than it seems on the surface — the refusal to act and to explain refusal may be a way through the pro-situ mind-game, in which experienced players challenged newcomers to set down their positions, and then queried their follow up action on the basis of individualistic judgement. Is your critique radical enough to bring down the universe? Then why have you not launched upon it? Is it not? Then why have you not thought far enough?) He intended, as he describes it in the early parts of Book 1, to say what he did, what he wanted, what he loved, and he expected that all else would follow. With only the stump of his work we cannot take a view on whether he might have succeeded in such an enormous task. And if it is unfair to judge the failure of the whole by the survival of the part, the writer (and destroyer) not the reader must accept the blame and criticism.

Over twenty years ago I made a series of photographs, in Epping and Hainault Forests, and in Greenwich Park, of old trees pollarded and coppiced. My idea was to try to show the thwarted rhythmical power of the parental parts of the tree in contrast with the scarred, sedimented (but ecologically enriched) survivor. In some cases these old trees had lived through nearly four centuries of "management". Debord himself was responsible for the destruction of his own text and his stump promises much that later sections were intended to deliver.

It would be a Borgesian exercise to attempt to reconstruct a memoir from the surviving introduction and the often disputed biographical information, but we can point to certain significant absences as well as presences. Debord states very early "My method will be very simple. I will tell what I have loved, and, in this light, everything else will become evident and make itself well enough understood."

He loved to drink, and his most lyrical section is devoted to the pleasures of drinking and of drunkenness (an important distinction). In a passage that deserves to be remembered, he writes "Although I have read a lot, I have drunk even more. I have written much less than many people who write, but I have drunk much more than most people who drink." Some of the judgements arrived at after a lifetime of dedicated drinking seem to me to be open to dispute. To raise up Pilsen as the greatest of beers, above the monastery beers of the lowlands and the white beers of Germany creates a difference with him as severe as any that his politics might. But in concluding his chapter on drink he mourns the destruction of splendid local beers, spirits and wines by the expansion of industry, and their replacement by undistinguished multinational products. "The bottles, so that they can still be sold, have faithfully retained their labels; this attention to detail gives the assurance that one can photograph them as they used to be — but not to drink them." (The small group that used to foregather with me in the Bulldog in Oxford, following WSL national aggregates, to quaff the now extinct Courage Reading bitter will endorse vigorously.) Here is the theory of the spectacle, presented more concisely, concretely and movingly than in all the pages of his 1967 "The Society of the Spectacle" and his 1988 commentary thereon.

Alcohol seems to have been the only intoxicant from which he benefited. Hashish and opium, well known to the bohemian heroes of his youth, seem not to have appealed to him, and he writes nothing of the psychedelics, either synthetic or natural. At one point his mask slips and he describes some of his critics as "a group of English drug addicts".

Larger absences from the collection of what Debord loved present themselves — the proletariat never engaged his emotion, nor yet did Marx, nor any of his collaborators in the SI or earlier in his career, among the Lettrists. Cinema, to which he contributed some characteristically difficult works, did not receive his love.

Debord expends a short chapter on the interests to be enjoyed in the study of war. He had invented a board game "Kriegspiel" that he considered to have enshrined the lessons of this study. Compared to the computer war games on the market, his invention seems simple to the point of superficiality. Having attempted a few times to play it, I can confirm that it presents one of the key aspects of war — surprise — more ruthlessly than any army of programmers have achieved. If R.C.Bell were able to update his classic "Board and Table Games", then Kriegspiel would certainly receive a honourable description. To those jaded chess and go-moku players whose hearts have leapt with pleasure at encountering the Mancala or Owari games, I commend Debord's invention. In the labyrinth of delights that men have invented to stroke their brains to glow, to parody the soul in a soulless world, it is a wondrous conurbation of blind alleys.

Book 1 then, promises much — it promises facts and precise details, none of which are delivered. The claims made for its "classical" style are not without merit — the language and style are dignified, spare and precise (also formal as befits the definition of panegyric) even when considering the author's own mortality. The translator allows the jarring Americanism "every which way" into the text at one point, but otherwise does an excellent job. Debord remarks on page 8, "the ability to make oneself understood is always a virtue in a writer". True enough. It was not always a virtue that Debord possessed.

In summary, much more of a memorial than a memoir. To have lost so much of the history in Debord's final potlatch is very regrettable, and not to have had his definitive assessment of the central aspects of the whole situationist project is sad indeed. Towards the end of his text, Debord writes "no-one has twice roused Paris to revolt" — an historical insight from which Trotsky might have learned, if not gained. For his contribution to having once roused it, Debord should be remembered.

JJ Plant

Sobhanlal Datta Gupta, *Comintern and the Destiny of Communism in India 1919-1943*, Seribaan, Kolkata, 2006, pp329

THE author is a professor of political science at Calcutta University, a historian of Marxist ideas, as well as of the movement inspired by them. His sympathies lie, however, not with officialdom and its interpretation of the movement's history, but with the critical evaluations produced since the archives became more accessible, and the dissenting, even oppositional, figures who advanced alternative strategies and programmes. In this spirit the author set to work examining Indian communism during the life of the Comintern. In the course of a decade's research he used, among many other sources, the archives of the Comintern (Moscow), the CPGB (Manchester), and valuable collections of a noted GDR scholar and an anonymous Indian communist leader. In the preface Sobhanlal Datta Gupta (henceforth SDG) describes his task as having been "challenging", due to the left in India being "still heavily dominated by the spirit of Stalinism", but hopes that, by attempting "to understand the moments of crisis which communism in India has encountered and examining the possible alternatives", the book will "encourage critical thinking and thus assist the left in finding a way forward," (p xx).

The first chapter sets out key issues for investigation vis-à-vis Comintern and the new historiography, and SDG points out that prior to the opening of the archives to Soviet scholars in 1987, and internationally in 1991, it was not possible to make an objective evaluation of the Comintern, one had the official view on one hand, or ones tending to subjective judgements, as evidence was lacking. Initially critical scholars attempting to reassess Comintern were met with resistance both in Russia and the GDR. The Stalin-Hitler Pact, the sectarian line towards social democracy, the repression meted out to political emigrants in the USSR, for example, investigated by the likes of F. Firsov and A. Vatlin, threatened to undermine the SED's fundamentals. While party historians tried to shore-up the Stalinist view, it was Kurt Hager of all people, the SED's chief ideologue, who came out for a reassessment. This encouraged Erwin Lewin to reassess the Comintern and the Pact, which "had led to severe downplaying of anti-fascist propaganda... seriously hamper(ing) the resistance of the KPD...since not fascism, but British imperialism and its accomplice, namely, the leadership of Social Democracy, came to be targeted as the main forces responsible for the war" (p 11).

Assorted opinions on how to periodise the Comintern's history are examined, the question of how much autonomy the parties enjoyed, the role of the Cadre Department, which was "an organ of surveillance...act(ing) in close coordination with the ECCI and the NKVD" (p 21), the Russification process that meant decisions being first taken in the WKP(b) Politbureau. The process was possible, SDG informs us, resting upon a Russian source, "because no democratically conceived procedure for elections to the posts of Chairman, Secretary, General Secretary, members of the ECCI and the Presidium of the ECCI existed and their functions also were not clearly defined in the rules" (p

22). In discussing the repression in the Comintern, in which the ECCI was complicit, SDG refers to the resistance to it, which in my opinion was too little too late, and alternatives. The Pact, the Comintern's dissolution, Stalin's letter on Bolshevism's history, are all brought in to the discussion prior to SDG going on to Indian communism vis-à-vis the new historiography.

Besides the Comintern archives, those of the CPGB provide a vital source for elaborating a reliable history of communism in India, as from the late 1920s it was through the CPGB that the Comintern related to the CPI, and from the mid-30s, India was represented in the Comintern officially by Ben Bradley, the other leading personality...in this connection being R. Palme Dutt (pp 35/6).

Apart from the Asiatic Society in Calcutta, which has begun an ambitious publishing project on Indo-Russian relations, in collaboration with the Institute of Oriental Studies in Moscow, SDG regards the response to the possibilities opened up by the access to these priceless archives as "dismal, if not puzzling", characterised by "a strange apathy, if not resistance, towards exploration of this area" (p 36). In fact, "after the opening or the archives, the Communist Party of India (Marxist), the leading party of the mainstream Left in India today, has published several volumes and commentaries containing documents on the history of Indian communism in the Comintern period (without reference to the archives or new research), resulting in a simple repeat of the official version of Party history..." (p 37).

MN Roy was the dominant figure vis-à-vis Comintern and Indian communism until the late 1920s, and helped shape policy on the National Question, but in his research SDG has been able to flesh out the views of other Indian currents that were not so dismissive of mainstream nationalism in India, namely, the Indian Revolutionary association located in Tashkent, and the grouping in Berlin. The former insisted that a proletarian revolution under CP leadership was not just around the corner in India, and that one had to take into account not just of nationalism(s) but religion, caste and community. Neither could one gain influence by pure hostility to Gandhi. The Berlin group favoured an anti-imperialist front perspective uniting communists and non-communist revolutionaries.

SDG was also able to find materials relating to the political and military training of Indian revolutionaries in Soviet Russia and the key role played by the Soviet Embassy in Kabul in transporting them back to India. Amir Amanullah of Afghanistan was friendly disposed towards Soviet Russia, and his relations with Britain were strained. The break-up of empires, emergence of new states; wars in the Caucasus, the Bolshevik appeal to Muslim and oriental peoples, all helped create fear regarding India. This led to literature from' or about Soviet Russia or Lenin being seized at special checkposts set up all over India. Indian communists residing in Russia during the purges suffered from the terror, and SDG found out what had happened to prominent figures.

With the exit of MN Roy from Comintern in 1929, the CPGB became de-facto guardian of the CPI, and SDG examines the reason why no Indian was entrusted with Indian affairs there. This was problematic from the start, he discovered, as the CPGB, was, as were European parties in general, "Eurocentric", and seemed to be indifferent to the colonial question, and moreover, tended to "boss" Indian communists. Documents were found from the 20s to the 40s in which CP leaders express exasperation at an "empire consciousness" present within the ranks of the party, whereby the plight of India was absent from their minds. One can imagine the existence of such a consciousness within the working class in general, perhaps among some party members, but I doubt that it was a common feature. Surely communists would have faced great difficulties advancing policies opposed to British imperialism, perhaps they chose to prioritise other matters and put India on the back-burner, The private papers of both Palme Dutt and Bradley confirm their vehement hostility towards Gandhi, continuing a line set out by Roy, which harmed the CPI. It turns out that the CPGB maintained a close link with Jawaharlal Nehru during the late 30s and 40s.

The ultra-left line imposed by the Comintern following the adoption of the programme in 1928, and its consequences for India, is also examined. The orientation for the colonies set out in his time by Lenin, and elaborated at the 4th Congress into the anti-imperialist united front, was junked and all nationalist forces were denounced as henchmen of imperialism, particularly those on the left. Not only Gandhi but Nehru and Subhas Chandra Bose were labelled "agents of British imperialism", Crazy instructions were sent to the CPI which, at that time, barely existed as a party.

Comintern directives, SDG discovered, were not as hitherto believed, accepted uncritically by the CPI, and if the ultra-left line created problems, the shift following the 7th Congress of Comintern in 1935, proved difficult to gain acceptance, as the previous line, it was insisted, was not an error. With the Nazi-German attack on the Soviet Union in June 1941, WW2 underwent a change of character, the CPI had to be convinced to stop opposing British imperialism, which had ceased to be the most malign force on the planet, but to support this ally of the Soviet Union. This would have enormous repercussions for the CPI. These bizarre zig-zags of the Comintern seem to be all the more grotesque when imposed on the CP of a colony struggling for independence.

The book is divided into six chapters, the last of which discusses oppositional currents within the Comintern and what could have been, based on SDG's analysis of the new research. For what it is worth I would agree with his general conclusions. The book has all the necessary scholarly attributes, including a bibliography and an index, and for ease the notes follow each chapter. There is an enormous amount of material packed into this study, of which I have only been able to give a flavour. It broadens our knowledge of the Comintern, Indian communism and the CPGB, as well as the relationship between them. One can only hope that the book gets a wider readership in India, where the communist movement is still an important political force, which could benefit from the knowledge contained within if discussed in an open fashion.

Mike Jones

Julien Papp, *La Hongrie libérée; Etat, pouvoir et société après la défaite du nazisme (Septembre 1944 — Septembre 1947)*, Presses Universitaires de Rennes, 2006, pp363

READING this book gave me many intense pleasures. And so too does the opportunity to present it to a wider readership. For one thing, the author is a friend, a former optical technician and Hungarian exile who by sheer courage and determination completed a long and difficult course of university study as an external student to become a French secondary school history teacher and a talented historian. For another, he has taken on the not inconsiderable difficulties and complexities of the immediate post-war period in a country previously dominated by an archaic social system, Hitler's last satellite.

My personal satisfaction is all the greater in that I myself lived through those times. Young as I was, I participated actively in the struggles described in this book. My knowledge of them is intimate, however circumscribed its scope. Moreover, I read this book with the feelings and fervour of a committed contemporary.

The book's first and most obvious merit is that it exists at all. It has immediately assumed an important place among the wealth of Hungarian historiography devoted to the problems of the birth and early years of the new regime and of democracy. It is one of those rare works which attempts to summarise and synthesise the overall history of that period in a monograph. But it is also distinguished — advantageously in my view — by its concentration on a few short but decisive years in the formation of the new regime. The very few other monographic works that exist cover a much longer period of several decades, within which the short period which concerns us is necessarily proportionately reduced. Our author, on the other hand, considers the period concerned to be essential. By concentrating on a few brief years, Papp's study is able not only to focus on a number of different topics in minute detail but also systematically to study historical development in its various components.

It is this very globality of investigations, embracing the wide variety of different subjects that go to make up the structure of historical development, which marks Papp's book out from the majority of other Hungarian historical studies. Most, if not all, of the great wealth of historical writing devoted to the period in question tackles a number of different topics, events or developments taken in isolation.

The monograpic character of Papp's study of the whole range of historical development as well as its concentration and focus on two or three essential years give this book an intrinsic value which marks it out favourably from almost everything that has been produced in the way of Hungarian history. These qualities place the work in the front rank amongst them.

What makes it particularly valuable is that it was published, not in Hungarian, an isolated language and one not easily accessible to non-speakers, i.e. to the vast majority of historians and political activists interested in history, but in French. It thus fills a significant gap in our knowledge (or rather quasi-ignorance) of the history of that part of Europe.

And there is much more. Most, if not all, the Hungarian historians who have tackled this subject in one way or another have been subjected to considerable influences, first and foremost those of the Stalinists in power, at least in the modified form of Janos Kadar. Others — very often the same people — have been ensnared by the mirage of the various kinds of historical writing guided by newer political modes and imperatives. Consequently the independent role of the popular masses and their organs, however present and visible they were, has been unceremoniously downplayed, not to say entirely suppressed. To say the least it has been obscured and distorted. In this, Stalinist state power under Rakosi and then Kadar as well as the democratic regime which followed have inspired exactly the same attitude amongst a range of different authors.

As far as I know, apart from one or two notable but very isolated exceptions, only Papp's work has restored them their rightful pre-eminent role and function in the country's quasi-revolutionary transformation from fascist dictatorship to democracy. Moreover, he is the only one to have clearly and unequivocally pointed out how prominent they were in these decisive developments. Workers, peasants, the popular masses as a whole in their spontaneously-formed committees, occupy a primordial place here in the whole historical development.

The author not only presents their birth, their composition and their activity in detail — he devotes more than a third of the book to this! — but also considers them to be the principal actors, the axis and pivot of democratic transformation. As he says in the Introduction:

> My approach aims to restore the workers, peasants and other 'little people' of Hungary to their true place as protagonists, which dominant memories have never ceased to distort and efface since the Stalinist turn of September 1947. (p10).

As he sums up in his "Conclusions": "It was the minorities most interested in social transformation" (actually the great majority — B.N.) "who were led to take in hand the cause of bourgeois democracy..." (p305). And Papp has no hesitation in seeing in this "in a sense the delayed action of the Russian revolution, its social 'momentum'!" (p304).

Here lies the book's fundamental interest and its main merit. The author provides a detailed account of the struggles of workers and peasants who gathered together spontaneously. They organised committees which arose as the the whole socio-political system of the old regime and its state collapsed. More than that: he puts the whole activity of these committees at the centre of his book and his analyses, without, however, betraying his commitment as a historian or, indeed, forgetting other aspects of the country's life and the unfolding of its history.

Precisely because they set out to establish and organise a new democratic regime. Papp explains, the people in action and their spontaneous organs collided with the installation and re-inforcement of the new state power: not only with reactionary forces from the past — strong remnants of the fascist administration as well as exponents and defenders of bourgeois social relations, mixed with living relics of feudalism — but also no less violently with the organisations and representatives of the new rulers, above all the Stalinists.

The author shows and fully documents how the latter did everything they could to maintain the old social relations and keep bourgeois political forces — however modified — in a coalition of parties representing the new democracy and its state. In doing so, the coalition of parties faithfully reflected the wartime allied powers. Apart from drawing spheres of influence, none of these powers — including and above all the Soviet Union — had any plan prepared for the social order in Hungary or, indeed, the general shape of the new democracy born of the outcome of the war. The author demonstrates that, by common agreement, these powers tried to preserve the preceding bourgeois order in broad outline, including its state administration, virtually intact.

In their role of occupiers, the allied powers forcibly imposed this policy, the USSR well to the fore and playing a particular role. The author lays bare their arrogance and their insistence on making the country pay not only excessive war reparations but also the daily costs of the occupation and its various bodies. One reads with amazement how the politico-military and diplomatic bodies (and not just those of the USSR) made a Hungary bled white by war pay not only onerous reparations but also for their occupiers' personal luxuriess, such as flowers! Presenting the enormous financial burden imposed on the country in detail, the author makes no bones about saying that " … the cost of the upkeep of the ACC (Allied Control Commission) and the (Soviet) army of occupation took Hungary to the very limit of what she could manage". (p73).

But the author affirms that the main grievance against the the allied occupation forces was political. And he presents in minute detail their continual and daily interference in political life in order to shore up the coalition against the concrete and permanent threat presented by the committees. In particular Papp shows the Soviet Commission's systematic efforts as the main occupation force led by Marshal Voroshilov to channel the country in that direction — both as the main occupying army but also through its local agents, the Hungarian Communist Party.

The non-communist parties in the coalition constantly appealed to the Allied Control Commission — and especially it main Soviet component — to intervene in order to "regularise" the situation by restraining the committees' revolutionary zeal.

The committees did indeed show impressive power and energy. The author presents the three different forms which they took: factory committees, land committees and finally national committees. The first took direct charge of the factories at the end of the war, when the majority of the owners fled or were scared. These spontaneous workers' organs took complete control of the factories. In fact what they wanted was not ownership of the plant but a share in the way they were managed. Papp shows that in this way they achieved genuine workers' control. The Hungarian Communist Party worked up a hysterical campaign and a constant struggle against them, resolutely siding with the bourgeois owners and their organisations which, although still weak, grew ever stronger bolder thanks to that support. This was despite the fact that the great majority of committees were communist or social democrat, and that "all" they wanted was workers' control. Even so, they represented an enormous threat to class collaboration. Not for nothing was the Communist Party's main and permanent propaganda and political campaign — how vividly I still remember it to this day — directed against the "men of 1919", referring to the short-lived Hungarian soviet republic of 1919! The workers really did not understand the class-collaboration with the borgeoisie forced on the masses by those in power. And the author describes those years as a period of "latent civil war". (p58).

In parallel with this development and immediately after the cessation of hostilities, there began the occupation and expropriation of the land on quite a large scale and the appearance of committees of — landless — peasants. Although it was a less important phenomenon than the factory committees, it was nevertheless very widespread and general. In any case the serious pressure they exerted forced a radical distribution of the land, a quasi-revolutionary act which quickly and officially did away with the great agricultural estates. Despite any difficulties it may have caused them, all the coalition partners quickly agreed the radical terms of the land reform in order to avoid a major social upheaval.

As for the national committees, they arose to replace the state administration, which had completely collapsed and fragmented and a large part of whose members had fled abroad. A network of these committees covered the entire country and took over local government. They replaced the missing state administration and like the other committees, with the participation of rank-and-file members of various parties, particularly workers' parties, they took control locally, just as the soviets did in their day.

This veritable network of committees, which in reality was council rule in embryo, also very quickly collided with attempts by the coalition government to reorganise a central state power. The Communist Party appeared to defend these committees, but only as organs of the coalition of parties. At the same time it stated openly that they "could not constitute a second organ of power side by side with the government authorities." (p190). The author quotes Rakosi's own memoirs to show how frequent the conflicts were between the Budapest committee and the government: "… from the simple fact that the government was far to the right of the national committee which was under the influence of the (Buda) Pest workers." (p188).

One way to neutralise the committees as a whole (factory committees, land committees and the local committees) was quickly and artificially to centralise them under the almost total domination of the Communist Party. Papp writes: "… the party only embraced the movement in order all the better to strangle it". (p177). Thus centralising them on a national level was only a prelude to their early death, since it was essentially designed and carried out by the Communist Party.

To convey the character of the permanent conflict between the coalition's emerging central power and the committees, the author quotes a speech made decades later by Ferenc Donáth (under secretary to the minister of agriculture, Imre Nagy's assistant in 1945). He said: "Nothing demonstrates better the strength and social significance of the popular desire to exercise public authority than the attitude of the new central power, which opposed it in practice from the very first moment of its existence and which did everything it could to stifle it ... In this respect, there was no difference between left and right in the coalition ... the strength of the popular movement shattered against the massive and unyielding wall of the coalition." (p194). This same Donáth wrote, of the factory councils: "All of us who participated in the leadership at the time ... did what we could to limit and, as soon as we could, suppress democracy in the factories, the institution of factory councils." (p195).

How clear and eloquent. I must say that, alongside Imre Nagy, Donáth became one of the leaders of the communist opposition and then of the revolution of 1956. But he was not the only one. In his book Papp also quotes the opinion of István Bibó who, as a prominent member of (as it happens) the peasant party in 1944 — 1947 stated his fervent support for the committees. Or one could mention István Márkus, a young sociologist who wrote important studies devoted to the committees.

In fact — although the author doesn't say a word about this — I can personally state that between 1944 and 1947 Hungary saw the unfolding and then the rapid stifling of the permanent revolution as worked out by Trotsky. In his view, the bourgeois democratic revolution in a backward country can, in our epoch, only be brought about under the leadership of the proletariat. And so in Hungary — as the author actually tells us — all the demands of bourgeois democracy were achieved under constant pressure from the working class and the peasantry, including the radical and revolutionary land distribution. All the Communist Party itself could do was at best to follow a movement which went far beyond what it wanted. In doing so, it took great care to strangle the autonomous organs of that revolution.

"Prospects for and limitations upon the Political and Social Revolution" is the title the author gives to one section of the book — the longest one, and the backbone of the whole work. His great merit is to show us this permanent revolution in progress, channelled and finally strangled by the USSR and the Stalinist Communist Party. Although the author never uses the adjective "permanent" in relation to the revolution then underway, and does not use Trotsky's name, his book talks constantly about the direct democracy of the masses and does involuntary hommage to the theoretician of permanent revolution.

Papp's main thesis, which he develops and documents very well, is that although the revolution was stifled, channelled and deformed, it largely, not to say decisively, dictated the polical path the international protagonists finally followed. The USSR and the Hungarian Communist Party were obliged to go much further than they wanted to in bringing about and establishing a "socialism" which, it is true, was in their image and shaped in their very largely deformed and falsified way. But they had to do it despite their initial intentions. After all, the bourgeois western Allies, in line with their agreements with the USSR at Yalta and Potsdam, had given Moscow a free hand to sort out the threatening revolution — while of course maintaining the appearance of being "defenders of democracy".

Papp uses the tools of historical science to prove that, in the course of this process, the USSR and the Hungarian Communist Party were obliged to change their initial programme. Instead of participating in the peaceful formation of a bourgeois democracy, as they planned in advance, they were confronted with the birth and superabundant activity of the popular masses' direct democracy. Even though they were able to withstand them and ultimately suppress their organs, they nevertheless had, while establishing their own anti-popular dictatorship, to expropriate the bourgeoisie and introduce essential reforms, all, of course, in their own repulsive and fundamentally anti-democratic image. Of course the author says nothing about this poisoned fruit of the conflict between the committees and the authorities in those years. But his book enables us to understand how the path to it was traced by the struggle the Hungarian Communist Party and the USSR waged against the committees.

The author also says nothing about the revolution of 1956. However, reading his book, one inevitably thinks of the rapid and widespread formation of workers' councils and other popular committees in which the revolutionary people spontaneously and very quickly found the logical and obvious successors to its post-war committees. The Hungarian workers were inspired not only by their fathers' struggle for the Hungarian soviet republic in 1919, not only by the Russian Revolution, but also and to a great extent by their own struggles in 1944-1947. In the speed with which their councils appeared and the vigour which they displayed, should we not see the living inspiration provided by these post-war committees? I certainly think so. It is no accident that all the prominent politicians whom Papp quotes as acknowledging the fundamental role the committees played in those years themselves participated actively in events and later played an leading and important role in 1956; men like Donáth, Bibó and Márkus.

I must mention that this author is a historian and not an ideologue. He examines all the components and aspects of historical development in detail, from the profound devastation of the war, through the persecution and massive and atrocious extermination of the Jews and the role of abject anti-Semitism, the inhuman population transfers and the establishment and role of military and diplomatic occupation, to the re-constitution of a central power, the state and its organs. It is a vast overall picture that Papp presents which even a reader familiar with the subject can study with interest and also pleasure. The very occasional omissions or mistakes easily recede in the face of this book's many merits and virtues.

Not the least among them is the impressive apparatus at the end supporting the book. The footnotes and references on each page alone provide a rich and varied documentation to accompany the text. The author enumerates in an extensive summary the archives and materials consulted and the many books and articles referred to. They are presented in an impressive way and moreover introduce the reader to a mass of original sources and a rich and varied literature on the subject. A short biographical resumé of the main actors and events and an index of names and places usefully completes the book.

To summarise: a significant and precious contribution which enriches the historiography of contemporary Europe. A translation into English would fill a significant gap in the historical material available to the English reader.
Balazs Nagy[3]

Rick Kuhn, *Henryk Grossman and the Recovery of Marxism*, University of Illinois Press, Chicago 2006, pp333

IN a Smithian world of abstract trade, it would be easy to imagine that a bag of apples might be taken to a market and sold there at a profit. This simple process of production and market exchange should be capable of infinite reproduction. But add contemporary capitalism, and the apple will be grown from copyrighted seeds, sprayed with insecticide manufactured by one of two or three giant producers, grown to tasteless colours and anodyne proportions, waxed, bagged, and probably binned uneaten at the end in a dump where (due to inadequate airing), the apple itself might be preserved for a hundred years without rotting. Capital is accumulated, wages are made, but finite resources (oil, land, time) are wasted indefinitely.

The widespread environmental consciousness that capitalism is an economic order barely compatible with human sustainability reminds us of an earlier set of economic arguments, which also portrayed capitalism as breakdown system. In his sixties, living in America far from the Austria into which he had been born, the Marxist economist Henryk Grossman explained to his friend the novelist Christian Stead why he had become a Marxist: 'I feel as if I saw a dangerous badly made deadly machine running down the street, when it gets to that corner it is going to explode and kill everyone and I must stop it. Once you feel this it gives you great strength, you have no idea, there is no limit to the strength it gives you.' The publication of Rick Kuhn's biography is a timely opportunity to show that such insights were not accidental to Grossman's life but in fact intrinsic to his whole way of thinking.

Born to a prosperous, assimilated Jewish family, Grossman became a socialist in his teens. His campaigning life reached an early peak in May 1905, just weeks after Grossman's 24th birthday, when a Jewish Social Democratic Party of Galicia was launched. Grossman authored the group's first pamphlet, on the Jewish Question. For the next three years, he was the party's unofficial

---
3. Translated by Bob Archer

leader. Although Galicia was then part of the Austro-Hungarian empire, the majority language in the region was Polish. The JSDP was strongly influenced by the main trends of Russian socialism, including both Bundism and Bolshevism. The mass strikes seen in Russia and Poland in 1905 spread, and Grossman was soon addressing marches of up to 50,000 people. The JSDP grew, reaching its highest membership of around 3,000. For the next two years, he threw himself into party activity. Only slowly did the upturn subside. Grossman left for Vienna in 1908, but was re-elected to the party's executive, in absentia, for several years following his departure.

From a period as a revolutionary agitator, Grossman settled into the very different life of a university academic. He spent the 1914-18 war working for the Austrian government as a statistician. Travelling to Poland in 1919, he was appointed to a professorship on economic policy and joined the Communist Party. Later Grossman settled in Germany, where he became the Frankfurt School's leading economist. It was from this post in 1929 that he published his best-known book *The Law of Accumulation and the Collapse of the Capitalist System*. For most readers today, Grossman is known if at all through the Pluto 1992 edition of this study: an incomplete text which misses out the entire last chapter of Grossman's work.

The Law of Accumulation was a polemic with at least three targets in mind. The first was Edward Bernstein's claim, from thirty years' previously, that capitalism was an economic system marked by increasing order and stability. Grossman disagreed. A second target was Rosa Luxemburg, the woman seen by most of Grossman's contemporaries as the heroine of their generation. Luxemburg's considered response to Bernstein was to argue that capitalist reproduction depended on the expansion of market relationships to the countries of the non-capitalist world. At some point, this task would be finished, and capitalism would be incapable of further expansion. Grossman argued that such a method had in essence little in common with Marx, who located the key contradictions of capitalism not in circulation but in production. A third target was the parliamentary socialist Otto Bauer, who had used a simplified version of the calculations set out in the second volume of Marx's *Capital*, to show that so long as the state regularly intervened to stabilise capitalism (by maintaining the correct ratio of outputs between means of production and means of consumption), the system could go on forever without crisis.

Grossman disagreed. His basic premise was as follows: in a system of competitive exchange, producers will invest in new machinery in an attempt to achieve an advantage over their rivals. For a single producer, investment will enable the same or a rising quantity of goods to be produced with a falling labour cost. Investment enables the sole manufacturer to produce more cheaply. The same processes, however, multiplied across the system as a whole, result in a general process whereby total output grows, but so does the proportion of total spending taken up by new machinery. The ratio of constant capital (machinery) to variable capital (wages) tends to rise in favour of the former. In a passage in the third volume of *Capital*, whose prominence in Marxist discussions since 1929 is largely Grossman's doing, Marx describes this process as the tendency for the organic composition of capital to rise. Bauer acknowledged that the rate of profit might decline, but argued that this process was not fatal to the system, so long as some profit was made. Decline could be offset by state investment. Grossman took the same equations, ran them for a longer period, and used them to show that where the rate of profit declines inexorably, the result is inevitably a crisis to the system. By year 35 of Bauer's model, there was no longer any surplus either for investment or even for private consumption. The system could run no further.

There is all the difference in the world, of course, between showing that a model of private economic exchange must lead to crisis, and showing that the same dynamics are manifest not in a intellectual model, but in the real economy. In the concluding chapters of his book, Grossman listed the countervailing tendencies that might result in sustained expansion. Among these he mentioned decreases in world commodity prices, decreases in the unit cost of labour power, more efficient transport, the emergence of new commodities, even war, one of whose consequences was the destruction of capital value on a giant scale. Conversely, he identified the struggle for reforms as a major impediment to indefinite expansion: where workers could increase the unit price of labour, inevitably this placed greater costs on the system, and brought closer the possibility of social transformation.

How relevant is this model to contemporary Green thinking? While the detail of each model is different, the outline is similar. A system familiar to us as one of dynamic reproduction contains beneath its surface elements of both movement and inertia. Over time, the static becomes increasingly significant, with the result that the machine comes eventually to a halt. This breakdown is not a peaceful, natural process. It is accompanied either (to Grossman's mind) by bitter strikes and labour tumults or (in contemporary ecological thought) by drowned cities, plains lost to the desert, the inexorable expansion of wasteland, by migration, hunger and poverty. The successful avoidance of this catastrophe will require a pooling of great collective effort, and an extraordinary redistribution of human ingenuity. In that long process, Grossman's politics will surely seem more relevant than ever.

David Renton

Alter Litvin and John Keep, *Stalinism: Russian and Western Views at the Turn of the Millenium*, Routledge, London, 2005, pp48.

THIS is an odd review to write. It is a review of a review, or rather of an extended review of recent Russian and Western (defined as British, American, French and German) writings on Stalinism. The authors aim to illustrate 'what has been achieved of late by professional historians', 'to take stock of this literature, to offer encouragement or constructive criticism where it seems to be called for, and to indicate how the gaps in our knowledge might best be filled by future researchers' (p.vii). The book is divided into two parts, the first a survey of Russian writings by a Russian (Alter Litvin of Kazan) and the second a survey of Western writings by a Westerner (John Keep of Bern). The surveys are of necessity confined to certain key works related to 'political, economic, social and cultural matters, and even so have had to be selective' (p.ix). The division of labour is all too obvious. Might it perhaps have been better to treat 'knowledge' as complete whatever its point of origin and had a genuinely co-authored book; or why not have had Litvin comment on the West and Keep on the East? As it stands the book is a reflection of current world politics in that Russia is included but marginalised, with Keep writing the bulk of the material plus the conclusion. Nevertheless the authors do provide what they promise, especially when all of the relevant qualifications have been put in place. The book can therefore be consulted for a flavour of what has been said by professional historians with comments from our authors. There also emerges a picture of what trends have dominated recent writings from those on offer.

First the status of the archives and archival research. Litvin begins the first chapter on sources thus: 'The quest for truth about the Stalin era must begin with a look at the situation in Russian archives' (p3), and by 'situation' he means issues of access, bemoaning the fact that 'it used to be much easier to gain access to sensitive material under Boris Yeltsin than it is today' (p3). This no doubt tells us something about the changing political situation from Yeltsin to Putin but even with complete and open access to the archives we should be clear that 'truth' would not leap out at us. This is partly because the archives were not kept with the intention that one day they would reveal the truth to curious historians. It is important to understand how archives were established, at what time and by whom. How was material stored and has it undergone any reorganisations? This comment relates in particular to local archives targeted by some historians in the expectation that they provide a 'view from the periphery' but often ignoring the fact that local archives were modelled on or affected by the central archivists. It is also because documents are only ever a partial reflection of individuals, groups, movements, institutions, and historical and social processes. One may thus read every document in the Trotsky archive at Harvard and still not know 'the full Trotsky'. Keep's comment that even after the opening of the archives 'the inner recesses of Stalin's mind (and it was he who took the decisions) still invite speculation' (p192) can come as a surprise only to anyone who thought that the archives would reveal the inner recesses of Stalin's mind. Of course they will not!

Second, there is the issue of no matter how many materials one reads what counts is what sort of questions one asks of documents, i.e., one's methodology is key. Here attention focuses on the use of 'revisionism and post-modernism' and the 'totalitarian controversy'. Keep acknowledges that there are nuances within these 'schools' and that there can be a fair amount of overlap between different methodologies. The conclusion however that 'all approaches are valid and there is something to learn from each' (p99) is just bland and all too typical of the type of 'critical analysis' engaged in throughout the text. The authorial judgements are brief and passed on very brief summaries. I wonder, for example, of the use to anybody to know that Keep wonders whether 'the subtitle of her study (Melanie Ilic's *Women Workers in the Soviet InterWar Economy: From 'Protection' to 'Equality')* is appropriately worded' (p141). The only way to reach one's own view is to read the work itself, but then This is true of every work mentioned.

Third, the issue of morality and moral stances is clearly of import for both authors. For Litvin, 'state socialism turned out to be rotten at the core and eventually collapsed. This means that there can be no excuse for the Terror either: it is in fact unpardonable from every point of view. In the Soviet era, its only defenders were the people responsible for it; the rest just went along with them out of fear.' (p69) For Keep, 'licensed and arbitrary violence was the principal characteristic of Stalinist rule...'Stalinist civilization' is a phenomenon of our own age and has to be judged by contemporary criteria of right and wrong' (pp214-215). For Keep the lesson that Russians must draw is how wrong the USSR was to take Russia from the path of capitalist, liberal democracy. A study of Stalinism should help Russians 'to promote the development of a mature civic society, democracy and the rule of law, and to make industrial enterprises more efficient and internationally competitive, for in today's globalized world market increased trade (preferably not just in raw materials) and foreign investment are the surest means of improving popular living standards' (p216).

Such 'liberal morality' is no doubt shared by most authors considered in this book for ultimately one is struck by how little an understanding of Stalinism is promoted by modern scholarship. Stalin did not operate in this moral universe. Rather his rule was the outcome of battles won and lost within the revolutionary movement. It is this movement that seems to be completely forgotten by modern scholars — a reason no doubt that Keep did not consider any of the volumes of *Revolutionary History* in his survey of recent Western literature on Stalinism. Rather than trouble oneself with the modern academe, readers are better advised to go back to the classics of contemporary Marxism, particularly Trotsky and even the Menshevik observers around *The Socialist Herald*. My failure to connect with revolutionary politics is a flaw of my Trotsky biography and reading this book has helped me to understand that better if nothing else.

Ian D Thatcher

Jean-François Fayet, *Karl Radek (1885-1939)*, Biographie politique, Bern, Peter Lang, 2004, pp813

KARL Radek has fascinated historians again and again, With his linguistic ability to move in the different cultural spaces and just as nimbly on the political terrain between Russia and Germany, or the level of the established state power as of the Communist International, the Jewish intellectual from Galicia was made into the prototype of the professional communist revolutionary This was particularly valid for Germany, the country that surely stood most strongly at the centre of his interest. Although the first comprehensive biography came from the USA[4], it was soon followed by a series of studies devoted to his activities concerning Germany.[5] The occupation with his biography then finally took a turn into fiction.[6]

Without doubt he embodied in a graphic way the rise, and equally the decline of the communist movement, as early as the thirties, expressed in the mass terror. His reputation as an intriguer and a not very trustworthy person too, belonged to the picture of him presented already by his contemporaries. As the Swiss social-democrat Robert Grimm; who collaborated with him in the Zimmerwald movement, discretely put it, "Radek a very experienced journalist in colonial questions, but not an outstanding character".[7]

What united the various works about him, owing to the requirement to know one's way about in the appropriate countries and languages, and above all due to the inaccessibility of the Soviet archives, was the obligation for a long time to limit them to investigating only a part of his life, mostly the years connected to Germany. The (partial) opening of the Moscow archives has at least removed the greatest hindrance. It has then, however, taken still more years until one found in the Genevan Jean-Francois Fayet someone who also possessed the linguistic preconditions. As a result of his many years of research; not only but mainly in Moscow, there now exists an extensive biography, of which one can say in advance that it has everything in order to become the standard work on Radek.

Introduced with short explanations about the fate of Radek's personal archive — what can be found where again today in Moscow, and what could possibly be in archives still inaccessible today — the author develops his presentation in a fairly chronological way. Although Fayet has his own quite particular interests, he considers in a suitable manner; which constitutes the great value of this biography, all Radek's biographical periods, in which the latter, as is known, was active in very different political contexts and places,.

He begins with a detailed portrayal of Radek's — or more precisely Karl Sobelsohn's — youth in an "enlightened" Jewish parental home. Born in Lemberg in 1885, following the early death of his father, his mother brought him up alone in Tarnow. Versed in the traditions of the Polish struggle for freedom from his earliest youth, his "political socialisation" then followed at Krakau university. Though German was the language of the empire and thus represented an offer of assimilation for a developed Jewish middle-class, it also influenced Radek from his childhood. The road to social democracy was thus, in

---

4. See Warren Lamer, *Radek: The Last Internationalist*, Stanford, 1970.
5. Eg Marie-Luise Goldbach, *Karl Radek und die deutsch-sowjetischen Beziehungen 1918-1923*, Bonn-Bad Godesberg, 1973; Dietrich Möller, *Revolutionär, Intrigante, Diplomat: Karl Radek in Deutschland*, Köln, 1976.
6. Jochen Steffen & Adalbert Wiemers, *Auf zum letzten Verhör. Erkenntnisse des verantwortlichen Hofnarren der Revolution Karl Radek*, München, 1995.
7. Cited in Jules Humbert-Droz, *Der Krieg und die Internationale. Die Konferenzen von Zimmerwald und Kienthal*, Wien, 1964, p131.

a sense, sketched out, and led him into the revolutionary grouping around Rosa Luxemburg, the SDKPiL, which gave the national struggle no great importance — rather saw it as a distraction from the class struggle. This first chapter about his "apprenticeship years" comprises a tenth of the volume and ends with the Russian revolution, his relatively short participation and firm establishment in the SDKPiL, then the next comprises almost double the length.

It is almost entirely devoted to the "Radek Affair" which lasted until the outbreak of war and would influence his image just as his journalistic brilliance which he very quickly demonstrated in the SPD press. Radek was not only the discerning analyst of imperialism; who was so to speak "at home" in every world conflict. He entangled himself in trench-warfare with his closest comrades in arms in the SDKPiL, above all with Rosa Luxemburg. This rebounded into the SPD, when the right-wing enthusiastically seized upon it, and reverberated into the Russian social-democracy, due to the numerous double and cross-memberships of the different protagonists. That this was really politically based is also put in doubt by Fayet's detailed presentation. Though here he follows, in part, terrain already explored long ago in the various works of the SPD or the SDKPiL about Rosa Luxemburg. It is a shame that the author does not examine so intensively Radek's analysis of imperialism, also in relation to the whole discussion in the party and the International.

Out of this "affair" however; an initial contact with the Bolsheviks resulted, that after the outbreak of war then led to Radek's adherence while in his Swiss sanctuary, which soon made him into the leading Bolshevik propagandist on the international stage. Firstly in the Zimmerwald movement, but then above all, as during 1917 they first became a mass party and then a state party. Here the rational discussion by Fayet of the rumour, which has circulated for decades; about their financing by the German government, the accusation of being agents, is particularly worth stressing (pp 210-219). He analyses the various versions and traces back the alleged signs to their real significance. Everything else remains hypothetical in his view.[8]

It was then the October revolution that brought Radek back to Germany as its envoy, and which now, in the correlation between Russia and Germany allowed him to pursue what one could somewhat solemnly describe as his "true destiny". That included his involvement in the creation of a mass communist party, as well as his appearances in the salons of the new republic, in order to promote an "Eastern Alliance" between the states. For him however, this was undoubtedly only a stage towards the world revolution; it would have transferred its centre from Moscow to Berlin. Here too the terrain is not entirely unknown; his role in these first years of the KPD and also simultaneously in the leadership of the Communist International, above all in the dispute with the

---

8. In comparison e.g. the very latest Gerd Koener, *Der Russland-Komplex. Die Deutschen und der Osten 1900-1945*, München, 2005, by chance pp92-97 and 119-126, wheresoever it, *faute de mieux*, says "would seem'", "appears . . .". In this work Radek not for the last time with a glance at the time to come, is one of the central figures.

KPD leader Paul Levi and over the development of the United Front policy, is already thoroughly evaluated in the existing literature. Fayet however once more succeeds in adding new facets to the portrayal from his abundant source studies. One can though make critical comments on two points. Radek's aversion to collaborating with the syndicalists which the Bolsheviks had striven for, a key to the creation of mass communist parties in southern Europe, brought him into conflict which here is only touched on in relation to the "ultra-left" split from the KPD, the Communist Workers Party (KAP) (pp 351-353). Yet due to his leading position in the Comintern in 1920, he was occupied quite generally with the "trade union question", on which he reported at the second Comintern congress, and offended the syndicalist representatives as well, wholly in the style of the pre-war social democracy, for whom (even including most of the left) syndicalism was the greatest possible conceivable "deviation".[9]

In addition there is also an alternative interpretation of his dismissal as Comintern secretary in August 1920 (although that would in fact turn out to be meaningless). Fayet attributes it to the dispute over the KAP, whereas Branko Lazitch and Milorad Drachkovitch suspected that this "punishment" was due to his critical position towards the Red Army advance on Poland in the summer of 1920.[10] The high point of Radek's "German mission" was the year 1923 with the crisis caused by the Ruhr occupation. Here Radek's name will above all be linked to his "Schlageter speech" at the session of the Comintern Executive Committee in June, that has to suffer again and again for the attempt "to push the KPD into an alliance with radical rightists groups in the course of the Ruhr struggle" as one of the best experts on the KPD's history, Hermann Weber, writes. This problem is also fully dissected by Fayet (pp 445-467). He comes to a substantially more refined picture of an attempt at recruiting and influencing a milieu that, however, yielded little but instead harmed the party's image, though without the party having abandoned its fundamental hostility towards the radical rightist milieu. Radek's role as the chief Soviet delegate during the attempted KPD uprising, the "German October", was much less precisely known. There were hardly any documents on it, mainly just memoirs and similar material. Since the opening of the archives in 1993 successive single documents were made public and at last a documentation as well as a recent monograph, though it arrived too late for Fayet.[11] He has thought himself seen a good part of the material in the archives, and his presentation also leaves no doubt about it, that Radek had good grounds to prevent the KPD from launching an isolated attack that October.

9. According to the representative of the revolutionary syndicalist anti-war opposition from France, Alfred Rosmer, *Moskau zu Lenin*, Zeiten, Frankfurt 1989, p78: "He tackled this difficult question with the mentality of a German social-democrat, for whom the subordinate role of the trade unions was obvious, and discussing it not worth while."
10. Branko Lazitch & Milorad Drachkovitch, *Lenin and the Comintern*, Vol. 1, Stanford 1972, p274.
11. See n. 8 for the documentation; Harald Jentsch, *Die KPD und der "Deutsche Oktober" 1923*, Rostock, 2005.

With that Radek was of course also made responsible for the "defeat". The more so as already for some months the struggle had broken out in the Soviet party between — briefly described — the Troika Stalin, Zinoviev and Kamenev on one side, and Trotsky on the other, and Radek had clearly placed himself behind the latter. The years now following until his death during the Stalinist terror represent the most interesting part of the book. As the relevant details were the least known prior to the opening of the archives, more than 150 pages are devoted to his activity in the opposition, and a further hundred to the years after his capitulation to Stalin in 1929, whom he then served until the latter got rid of him.

In the ranks of the opposition, he was especially prominent in the debate over the second Chinese revolution, which was underway between 1925 and 1927. Since he had been branded as the one "most guilty" for the disaster in Germany in early 1924, he had been shunted off to the leadership of the Sun Yat Sen University, which had been set up in Moscow. What had been regarded as marginal suddenly, wholly unforeseen by the party leadership, owing to world history took on significance and Radek, with his own intellectual energy and enthusiasm for world affairs, threw himself into this problem. By means of Radek's internal correspondence with key leaders of the opposition, above all Trotsky, never previously made full use of, Fayet can describe in detail numerous new aspects of the opposition's struggle, and particularly its internal arguments, in which Radek occupied a leading — and vacillating — role. After he had first pressed for a sharp demarcation, as far as a break in an "ultra-left" manner, particularly after the expulsion from the party and banishment in early 1928; in 1929 he executed a turn, as Stalin broke with Bukharin and the "right" and using "left" rhetoric introduced the course towards forced collectivisation and hurried industrialisation.

Radek was the most prominent of the "capitulators"; and with this step almost caused the collapse of the opposition; which was by then essentially reduced to a few thousand in banishment or prison. What many passed off as a type of arrangement (or perhaps better: as self-justification), in order to save the revolution in view of internal and external threats, whereby one chose to only show the Stalinist party leadership a verbal reverence, was though in Radek's case a deeply rooted change of mind, a "reconversion" (p 594). He knew what was now demanded of him, was Stalin's hagiographer (after he had years previously sung hymns of praise to "Trotsky as the organiser of the victory"), adhered to Stalin's notorious verdict against the left around Rosa Luxemburg, was a propagandist of "socialist realism" and from 1933 won Stalin's trust as a foreign policy advisor. A special body was created for him, that was formally attached to the CC, so that it was directly subordinate to Stalin, and by which the latter, besides the official foreign policy of the Foreign Commissariat under Litvinov, could conduct an informal additional foreign policy, in order if possible to have two cards in play. So in 1933, Radek explored the possibility of a deepening of Polish-Soviet relations; or during the visit to Moscow of the then Königsberg professor (and later minister under Adenauer) Theodor Uberländer, met with him hoping by this, surely in an error of judgement, to establish a "back channel" to the nazi leadership. Radek wrote numerous memoranda of which one must however suspect, that they are still not all accessible and many still lie among Stalin's papers in the Kremlin archives. Radek also gave his name to the so-called Stalin constitution of 1936, on the eve of the great terror. Pseudo-democratically veiled; his authorship however, due to its waiving of world revolutionary goals, was essentially a signal abroad, where Radek -similarly Bukharin — was still the Soviet representative of choice. Interestingly though, Fayet found no evidence at all among the papers of the constitutional commission of any real participation by Radek.

Actually Radek may already have been aware for some time that there was little chance of escape. He dealt with the strain under which he stood — according to eye-witness reports — in his own way. Whereas he previously seldom touched alcohol; he became a heavy drinker. Even his public support for the first show trial in the August (against Zinoviev and Kamenev, the "Trotskyist Centre"), no longer helped him. A month later he was arrested. Yet it is a waste of time seeking out a direct cause, as Fayet does. Stalin wanted to root out the whole old generation of Bolsheviks, and Radek occupied one of the most prominent places among them. After a relatively short time he had been softened up in order to appear in the second show trial of January 1937 (against the "parallel Trotskyist Centre"). There are many rumours, which have not all been able to be verified, that he wrote much of the script himself. Actually he gave the cue not only for further trials (against the "right", and the military leadership around Marshal Tukhachevsky) but also, which for the most part is not recognised, for the hunt for "Trotskyists" in Spain that ensued in the following months. He strove at his trial, like Bukharin in 1938, in Aesopian language, to give clues as to the real context, obviously with a view to his place in history, but also in relation to his family, who were eventually not spared the persecution too. Though his collaboration saved him from immediate execution, he vanished in the Gulag where, in May 1938, surely not without instruction from above, he was killed by criminal fellow prisoners. Despite this, for a long time a rumour existed, that he had somehow been spared and secretly worked for the Soviet government.

Fayet has produced a comprehensively documented biography, not without sympathy for its "hero", at least until the time where, with his submission to Stalin, he ceased to be "un homme defendable" (p 721). He has extensively contextualised the biography, so that the development of the Soviet state also, from its roots in the left of the social democracy prior to the first world war up to Stalin's bloody settling of accounts with the Bolshevik old guard is distinct. If in his last messages to his family, Radek apparently believed the revolution would be able — in later generations — to supercede its results, then he was, as is known, mistaken. For the first years of the revolution hardly anyone else could have been a better representative on the international stage, "As a Galician Jew raised in the socialist movements of Galicia, Poland, Germany and Russia together, hardly anyone else could better represent their internationalist pretensions. Though all in all he proved to be more an improviser (than) a theoretician". He has argued so much with the historiography concerning Radek, though the interest is aimed at his contemporary deeds and not least on his political journalism as the interpretation of the juncture. He inspired no sort of "Marxist school" at all. With the present work of Jean-Francois Fayet, Radek has undoubtedly found his historian.

It is to be regretted — in these times of turbo-matriculation standards and short studies with correspondingly receding knowledge of foreign languages — that this work only exists in French though undoubtedly it is no longer possible to take a position on questions of central and eastern European history in which Radek was involved without referring to it. Perhaps an institution or publisher does exist that is not put off by the high cost of translation for a German or English version and thus makes it available for the first time for a wider audience of interested readers.
Reiner Tosstorff

Eros Francescangeli, *L'incudine e il Martello. Aspetti pubblici e privati del trockismo italiano tra antifascismo e antistalinismo* (1929-1939), Morlacchi Editore, Perugia, 2005

THIS is a book about a small number of Italian men and women who stood against the tide, placing themselves between the anvil of fascist secret agents who probably wanted to kill them, and the hammer of Stalinists who often wanted to do the same. (The title translates as: 'The Hammer and the Anvil. Public and private aspects of Italian Trotskyism between anti-fascism and anti-Stalinism').

So it is a book about a tiny number of Italian Trotskyists living in exile in France seventy years ago. What can it offer to readers of *Revolutionary History*? Not that much I fear — this is not to criticise the analysis and research of the author, merely the subject matter he has chosen to deal with.

If they had become bigger a force following the main events described, then the book would carry more weight. Having said that, the Italian historiographical tradition needs to redress the balance: Trotskyism has been much maligned on the left due to the previous dominance of Stalinism and the strength of autonomism today — where Trotskyism came from certainly needs to be explained.

As with his previous book on the *Arditi del popolo* [see review in previous issue of *Revolutionary History*], this book is the result of intensive work in left-wing and state archives.

Although Francescangeli's story really begins with the Stalinist turn to 'social fascism' of 1929-30, the Italian Communist Party had intrinsic qualities that led it towards sectarian isolation. At the Fifth congress of the International in July 1924 party leader Amadeo Bordiga declared, in typical fashion: 'we cannot wait that the two methods of bourgeois offensive to create a synthesis, and that together social democrats and fascists lead a violent offensive against the revolutionary movement'. (p24).

The Italian delegation concurred, which is not particularly surprising. The PCI leadership was Bordighist, by and large, or had been until recently. So the sectarian ultra-left rejection of socialists and others therefore went unchallenged. This feeling was very much part of the party's DNA for many years.

However this ultra-left lunacy would take on a more systematic form four years later, with the notions of 'class against class' and 'social-fascism' launched at the Sixth Congress of the International in July 1928, a meeting that heralded the move into its 'third period'.

Apparently there was a 'radicalisation of the masses' — but above all social democracy had become the main enemy. In many ways, the closer a political force was ideologically, the more it had to be mistrusted and fought.

This virulent denunciation of any perceived political heresy meant ideological purging within individual communist parties. The first bomb was dropped at a meeting of the Third International executive committee in December 1928, when Stalin attacked the PCI representative, Angelo Tasca, and Jules Humbert-Droz for 'opportunism'. Tasca in particular, Stalin said, was like 'those lawyers in the provinces who try to prove that black is white and white is black'. (p42)

The problem for Italian communists was now this: what position to take in the face of Stalin's attack? They criticised Tasca.

But Tasca wasn't for backing down. The following month he wrote to Palmiro Togliatti, who was emerging as party leader: 'The entire situation rotates around Stalin. The International doesn't exist; the USSR CP doesn't exist; Stalin is the "lord and master" who moves everything. [...] With this policy and methods Stalin is advance guard of the counter-revolution; he is the liquidator of the spirit of October.' (p43)

This was very much Trotsky's view, for a while, but Tasca was still the Italians' man in Moscow, and was on the International's executive committee. For other Italian communist leaders, agreeing with Tasca meant attacking Stalin and Moscow — and by implication agreeing with Trotsky. But if they didn't agree with him that had to take their first major Stalinist step — expel him. The leadership first agreed to remove Tasca from the CC, and to demand a public retraction of his views.

In a parallel with what had happened earlier in Russia with many of Stalin's allies in the mid-1920s, in many respects it was Pietro Tresso who led the charge against Tasca — a man who would later pay the ultimate price.

Tasca was deemed guilty of denying the 'fascistisation of social democracy'. In the leadership meeting which decided his expulsion, which Tasca attended, Togliatti chillingly argued: 'The working class can only move forward by passing over the body of social democracy. [...] Just as we must pass over the body of social democracy, in the same way we must pass over the body of opportunists'. (p63) The political bureau (a smaller organ, higher than the CC) voted to expel Tasca because he refused to 'recant'.

The vote was unanimous. Once again, in the near future there were to be echoes of the fate suffered by Stalin's allies. Three of the political bureau who voted for expulsion (Leonetti, Ravazzoli and Tresso), created the precedent for their own expulsion as 'the Three' in little more than a year.

Indeed at the core of the book is the huge bloodletting within the party's political bureau — during 1929-31 five of its eight members would be expelled: Alfonso Leonetti, Paolo Ravazzoli, Ignazio Silone, Angelo Tasca and Pietro Tresso. (Although Francescangeli does debate the case of Ignazio Silone, due to both his own political evolution and his torment at being a police informer, his expulsion was quite a different political event).

The next crisis came with a meeting of the Italian leadership in September 1929, in which it was proposed to set up an 'internal headquarters' by sending leaders back into Italy — given that a revolution was apparently more or less imminent. Perhaps it was also justifiable self-interest which led Paolo Ravazzoli to counter: 'I'm more than willing to accept this if it can be shown that the results which could derive from it would make it worthwhile. Yet you can't obtain many results when you'd just be speaking to three or four comrades.' (p60)

The Stalinist machine was now in full flight: two months later another report argued, given that the revolutionary situation was apparently so ripe, for the removal of the entire organisation and leadership from France to Italy in a matter of weeks.

The reality was that over a thousand communist party members were in Italian jails, including Antonio Gramsci. Pietro Tresso wrote a counter-proposal, which also included spelling out reality: 'In these three years of special laws our Federations and branches have been swept away three, four or five times.' (pp70-1) In a further twist, he added that the real party leadership — which had been formed in years of struggle — was now in jail.

After Ravazzoli and Tresso came Alfonso Leonetti, the last in the group which became known as 'the Three': 'where is the mass movement today?' (p75) Not only were the Three guilty of pessimism — their worst heresy was expressing outright dissent.

In the leadership meeting called to expel them, Tresso voiced an excellent put-down of the wily Togliatti, also present at the meeting: 'I believe that he has always been absolutely determined in his oscillating.' (p86)

Yet the weakness in the tale recounted by Franscescangeli is what happened next. When 'the Three' were expelled their perspective was one of 'reforming' the PCI: this made it difficult to attract activists to their cause, also because they didn't even have a newspaper for nearly a year after their expulsion, and when it did start it had a print run of just 300. They claimed the PCI had 2,500 members, but also admitted that it was in a terrible state, given the nature of fascism. All their contacts were with Italians living in France. Furthermore they also had an image problem, having voted for both Bordiga's and Tasca's expulsion, and had signed up to criticise Silone.

One very stark factor was the practical meaning for Italian communists to be expelled from the Italian Communist Party in France during the 1930s. It meant that the party you had previously built now violently attacked you. It was common for the Stalinist press in France to name Trotskyists publicly, thus leaving illegal Italian immigrants liable to arrest and even deportation back to Italy. The false documents activists carried were provided by the PCI, who would no longer help them on their expulsion.

And if you became a Trotskyist in fascist Italy the party would automatically attack you, accuse you of being in league with fascists — in essence you ran even greater risk of being picked up by the police because of all the fuss that was made about you. And if you ended up in jail, Stalinists would often physically attack you.

A different horizon opened up after 1933, to some degree. The failure of the German left to seriously oppose Hitler's rise to power had shown Trotsky that the Third International could not be saved — a notion that caused huge instability among small groups.

The move towards 'entryism' into mass organisations which followed soon after was also a wasted opportunity. The activities recounted by Francescangeli list meeting after meeting, definition after definition, denunciation after denunciation — there is very little discussion about changing events in the real world. When all Italian Trotskyists joined the French Socialist Party, Angelo Tasca haughtily wrote of them: 'Their spirit is sectarian and loud-mouthed. All they deal in is high politics, with composite motions, extracts from resolutions, etc.' (p199) The first General Council of the French SFIO proved him right: Tresso and another Italian presented their own separate motions, which gained one vote each — their own.

When Italy invaded Ethiopia Tresso's group wrote a document demanding 'strikes, street demonstrations, armed attacks on town halls, fascist offices and bosses' clubs'. (p204) It was just wishful thinking: not only did none of this happen, Italian Trotskyists in exile had no hope of influencing events. These individuals were subject to the same desperation which had led Trotksy to proclaim the Fourth International — the experience of living through epoch-making events without being able to influence them.

One of the more positive discoveries of Francescangeli's research is the discovery of close relations between these Trotskyists and *Justice and Liberty* — a radical left grouping led by Carlo Rosselli. Up until now, most Trotskyists had denied these links because *Justice and Liberty* was considered too moderate. Similarly it had been denied by many scholars of *Justice and Liberty*, anxious to present it in as moderate as light as possible — yet the links were so close in some cases that joint membership of both organisations was not uncommon.

Although the organisation's politics were perhaps too idealistic, the practical nature of their collaboration was again found wanting. In three years of intense discussions, just one edition of a newspaper was the result. Yet the attraction was real — Paolo Ravazzoli ended up joining the organisation.

Francescangeli refreshingly criticises Trotsky, and points out his sectarian attitude towards *Justice and Liberty* leader Carlo Rosselli, who was told by Trotsky when they met in spring 1934: 'I know you... We got rid of all you counter-revolutionaries like you in Russia'. (p13)

Yet both men would be murdered by counter-revolutionaries — Trotsky by a Stalinist agent in 1940, and Rosselli by French fascists in 1937.

Stalinists behaved appallingly towards these small band of Trotskyists — for example Alfonso Leonetti was severely beaten up in 1933, and in all probability the people who murdered Pietro Tresso in 1943 were Stalinist agents. The historical facts show that more Italian communists died at Stalinist hands than through fascist acts during the 1930s. Other attacks were more personal — 'the Three' were also accused of 'socialising' the personal relationships between their partners.

For all these reasons, Italian Trotskyism was very weak at its birth, suffering all the bad habits of exile politics. And by 1945 the communist party's activity in the anti-fascist Resistance had created a mass party which would soon have a million and a half members. Such was the weakness of Italian Trotskyism compared to other European countries that the first edition of *The Transitional Program* was only published in Italian in 1972.

Francescangeli illustrates this forgotten page of the Italian left well. The problem is that these brave individuals left very little behind them.

Tom Behan

Speak One More Time
Jim Higgins — Selected Writings

Jim Higgins was one of the most remarkable figures in the British revolutionary socialist movement, a self-taught working-class militant, union activist and leading member of a revolutionary organisation. This book brings together a selection of his extensive writings, some learned, all witty, from the publications of the International Socialists, from the internal documents of the faction fight that split that group in the mid-1970s, from the pages of the *Spectator*, and from his later writings in the pages of *New Interventions*, *What Next?* and *Revolutionary History*.

Order your copy now, £9.50 plus p+p (UK £0.94, Europe £2.01, rest of the world air £3.59, surface £1.69), to order e-mail Barry Buitekant at Barry.Buitekant@tesco.net, or write to Socialist Platform Ltd, London WC1N 3XX.

Printed in the United States
128163LV00001B/148-273/P